D1564789

The Organic Development of the Liturgy

Alcuin Reid OSB

The Organic Development of the Liturgy

The Principles of Liturgical Reform and their Relation to the Twentieth Century Liturgical Movement Prior to the Second Vatican Council

Saint Michael's Abbey Press
MMIV

SAINT MICHAEL'S ABBEY PRESS
Saint Michael's Abbey
Farnborough
Hants. GU14 7NQ

Telephone +44 (0) 1252 546 105
Facsimile +44 (0) 1252 372 822

www.farnboroughabbey.org
prior@farnboroughabbey.org
www.theabbeyshop.com

ISBN 0 907077 43 9

Cum permissu superiorum

A catalogue record for this book is available from the British Library.

Printed by Newton Printing Ltd., London, UK. www.newtonprinting.com

Table of Contents

Introduction

THE liturgical reforms enacted following the Second Vatican Council occasioned some disquiet, even controversy.[1] To this day the unity of the Roman rite of the Catholic Church suffers from the breakaway of various so-called 'traditionalist' groups, and from the absence of those, whose number is unknown, who simply stay away from the Liturgy as it is currently celebrated. In the words of Archbishop Rembert Weakland, "there is discontent among our faithful with regard to liturgical renewal,"[2] and "few dispute that the liturgical reforms of the Second Vatican Council have been implemented with mixed results."[3]

Over thirty years after the promulgation of the missal of Paul VI in 1970, calls for a re-evaluation of the work of the post-conciliar reformers, or for a "reform of the reform," as well as for a revival of the Liturgical Movement of the twentieth century are increasing. These voices are by no means unanimous as to the path to be taken. Yet most agree that the present liturgical state of the Roman rite is not all it should be, nor what it was intended to be by the Liturgical Movement or even by the Fathers of the Second Vatican Council.[4]

At the same time, those exclusively committed to the Pauline reform energetically dispute that a re-evaluation or a reform of the reform is desirable or even legitimate. A re-evaluation of the Council, they assert, necessarily involves its repudiation, as would any

---

1 Cf. S.M.P. Reid, *A Bitter Trial*; A. Cekada, *The Ottaviani Intervention*; M. Davies, *Pope Paul's New Mass*; Society of Saint Pius X, *The Problem of the Liturgical Reform.*

2 "The Song of the Church" in: *Origins* vol. 23, p. 12.

3 "The right road for the Liturgy" in: *The Tablet* 2 February 2002 p. 10.

4 Cf. K. Flanagan: "The liturgical renewal movement as it came to fruition after Vatican II has made many unfortunate detours from its original purposes;" *Sociology and Liturgy,* p. 326; J. Ratzinger, *The Spirit of the Liturgy*; J. Ratzinger, "Klaus Gamber: L'intrépidité d'un vrai témoin" in: Gamber, *La Réforme Liturgique en Question* pp. 6-8; B.W. Harrison OS, "The Postconciliar Eucharistic Liturgy: Planning a 'Reform of the Reform'" in: T.M. Kocik, *The Reform of the Reform?*, pp. 151-193; J.P. Parsons, "A Reform of the Reform?" in: T.M. Kocik, *The Reform of the Reform?*, pp. 211-256; S. Caldecott, *Beyond the Prosaic*; A. Nichols OP, *Looking at the Liturgy*; B. Spurr, *The Word in the Desert* (Spurr also examines similar Anglican phenomena); A. Reid OSB, *Looking Again at the Question of the Liturgy with Cardinal Ratzinger: Proceedings of the July 2001 Fontgombault Liturgical Conference.* C. Pickstock's *After Writing* critiques the reform's philosophical naïveté. Cf. also her "Medieval Liturgy and Modern Reform" in: *Antiphon* vol. VI no. 1 pp. 19-25.

assumption that the Liturgical Movement has not enjoyed anything other than its springtime since the Council.[5]

They also vehemently argue that permitting the use and perpetuation of former liturgical rites (a solution to the liturgical malaise adopted by significant numbers),[6] is a betrayal of the Council, and an inappropriate response to belligerent traditionalists whom they stigmatise as refusing to accept the 'renewed' Liturgy. To allow such would be, for them, tantamount to blasphemy against the Holy Spirit.[7]

In some circles the demarcation is absolute, with the result that, on the one hand, anything "pre-conciliar" is regarded as utterly disloyal and reprehensible, and on the other, the slightest suggestion of development or reform beyond a given point (1962, 1955, etc.), is anathema. Such uncritical stances are understandable, but unhelpful. This study seeks to begin a critical examination of the factors involved in the complex process that is liturgical development.

As the Council's liturgical reforms are claimed as the consummation of the work of the twentieth century Liturgical Movement,[8] any assessment of these reforms must clearly understand the nature of this Movement. In determining whether the rites promulgated by Paul VI herald the apotheosis of liturgical history, or its nadir, we must know the mind of Guéranger, St Pius X, Beauduin, Guardini, Parsch, Casel, and others.

We must also grasp the principles of liturgical reform operative in the history of the Roman rite, and the relationship of the Liturgical Movement to them. As these principles are one of the pillars upon which the legitimacy of the Council's mandate rests, if they are not indeed its *a*

---

[5] J.D. Crichton "Review Article" in: *Liturgy* vol. 20 pp. 249-258, 263; N. Mitchell, "Reform the Reform?" in: *Worship* vol. LXXI pp. 555-563; R. Weakland OSB, "The right road for the Liturgy" in: *The Tablet* 2 February 2002 pp. 10-13.

[6] Cf. the American journal *The Latin Mass: Chronicle of a Catholic Reform*, published since 1992.

[7] Cf. C. Geffré, "Traditionalism without Lefebvre" in: *Concilium* no. 202 pp. xi-xvi; R. Weakland OSB, "Liturgical Renewal: Two Latin Rites?" in: *America* vol. 176 pp. 12-15; D. Crouan, *The Liturgy Betrayed* & *The Liturgy After Vatican II.*

[8] Referring to the Constitution on the Sacred Liturgy, Council Father Archbishop Paul Hallinan told the 1964 American Liturgical Week: "The Liturgical Movement reached its maturity last December by a vote of 2,147 to four;" "The Church's Liturgy: Growth and Development," p. 95. Lancelot Sheppard wrote in 1964 "It seems that what has come to be known as the Liturgical Movement has achieved at one stroke all that it has been working for for some fifty years;" Priests of St Séverin and St Joseph, *What is the Liturgical Movement?* p. 136. Of late, K. Hughes RSCJ, *How Firm a Foundation: Voices of the Liturgical Movement*, p. 12; J.D. Crichton, *Lights in the Darkness*.

priori foundation,[9] an assessment of the Council's mandate or of its implementation must be clear as to what they are. It must also ask whether the Council and those who implemented it were faithful to them. Only then can discussion of the legitimacy of any "reform of the reform," or of its possible shape, be sufficiently informed.

This study seeks to contribute to the first part of such a discussion. The first chapter provides a (necessarily brief) review of liturgical reform in the history of the Roman rite. Significant reforms and the principles operative therein are considered.

The second chapter details the origins of the Liturgical Movement and demonstrates its nature as primarily a movement seeking to return liturgical piety to its rightfully central place in the life of the Church. The Movement's consequent consideration of the desirability of liturgical reform, and the stance taken by the Holy See with regard to the Liturgical Movement and to liturgical reform are examined.

The third chapter details the work of liturgical reform commenced by the Pian Commission for Liturgical Reform in 1948 and carried through to the eve of the Second Vatican Council. The reforms enacted by the Holy See throughout this period are studied, as are the parallel activities and writings of the Liturgical Movement in relation to liturgical reform.

Whilst the history of the Roman rite and the origins, writings and activities of the Liturgical Movement witness to the existence of fundamental principles of liturgical reform, it will be demonstrated that, at times, liturgical reforms have been enacted—even authoritatively—which, when critiqued in accordance with such principles, may be said to be flawed. In delineating principles, and in drawing attention to instances of reprobate liturgical reform in the history of the Roman rite, this study seeks to furnish some of the apparatus necessary for a critique of the controversial work of the post-conciliar *Consilium Ad Exsequendam Constitutionem De Sacra Liturgia*, the body entrusted with the implementation of the mandate for liturgical reform given by the Second Vatican Council.

Herein pertinent authors have been quoted at length, not only to illustrate the narrative and to ground analysis, but in order to collect a substantial amount of primary material. Illustrative material has been selected from English-language sources where possible, though not exclusively. Where unpublished or obscure material has been translated, or a passage is of particular importance, the original language has been provided in a footnote. Full bibliographical information is provided in the bibliography.

---

[9] The other being the authority of the College of Bishops assembled in Ecumenical Council, acting in union with its head, the Bishop of Rome.

I am indebted to: the Most Rev'd Thomas Francis Little, DD, KBE, Emeritus Archbishop of Melbourne, without whom the circumstances in which this book was written would not have arisen; the Conventual Prior and Community of Saint Michael's Abbey, Farnborough, for enabling me to complete it; Dr Judith Champ, Dr Graham Gould and Dr Brian Horne for their academic supervision of my research; the Alcuin Library, Collegeville, Marco Balestrieri, Lee Bradshaw, The Rev'd Carlo Braga CM, The Rev'd Gabriel Burke, Cambridge University Library, Cardinal Hinsley High School London, Monsieur Guillaume Carteau, Paul Cavendish, CNPL Paris, Daniel P.J. Coughlan, The Rev'd Msgr J.D. Crichton (RIP), Madame François Demon-Dupuy, The Rev'd Dr Gerard Diamond, The Rev'd Ian Dickie, Murray Dovey, The Andrew Duncan Historical Trust, The Rev'd Msgr Peter J. Elliott, The Rev'd Joseph Fessio SJ, Dr Raphael Foshay, Ian Foster, Scott Gibson, Dr Sheridan Gilley, The Rev'd Dr Nicholas Glisson, Carl Green, Monsieur Philippe Guy, The Rev'd Pierre-Marie Gy OP, Shaun Harper, The Rev'd Brian Harrison OS, Dom David Hayes OSB, Heythrop College Library, London, Professor James Hitchcock, The Rt Rev'd Cuthbert Johnson OSB, The Rev'd Dr Peter Joseph, The Rev'd Paul Keane, King's College London Historical Trust, Frau I. Krasny, Monsieur Gilles Lacombe, Victor Lombardi, The Rev'd A.G. Martimort (RIP), H.E. Paul Augustin Cardinal Mayer OSB, The Rev'd Msgr Frederick R. McManus, The Rev'd Dom G. Michiels OSB, The Very Rev'd Aidan Nichols OP, The Rev'd Dom Alban Nunn OSB, The Rev'd Dr Drago Ocvirk CM, Mrs Christine Parkin, Ashley Paver, Michael Pearce, Stuart Rowland, Dr Tracey Rowland, Mrs Elizabeth Stephens, H.E. Alfons Maria Cardinal Stickler SDB, The Rev'd Turek Boguslaw CSMA, and The Rt. Rev'd Gordon Wheeler (RIP), for their assistance.

Dom Alcuin Reid OSB
26th January 2004

Chapter 1

Liturgical Reform in History

Introduction

THE Roman rite, the ritual of the local church at Rome and of most Western Churches in communion with her,[1] may broadly be said to have undergone a gradual development throughout the first Christian millennium, being enriched by the introduction of some customs and suffering the loss of others, over time.

The central rôle of the Church of Rome in the Christian West meant that particular attention was given by other local Churches to its liturgical forms. The early Carolingian monarchs showed it particular reverence. Franciscan mendicants of the thirteenth century would spread the Roman *missale* throughout the West. The post-reformation papacy would impose it upon all Western Catholics where no venerable local rite existed.

Early Liturgical Development

The last two centuries have benefited from the work of scholars on the historical development of the Roman rite.[2] Perhaps the most widely and popularly accepted of these, Theodor Klauser, divides the development of the Western Liturgy in the first Christian millennium in two. He summarises the first period, up to the year 590:

> The fundamental acts of worship of the early Church—the celebration of the eucharist, the rites of the sacraments, prayer in common, and the liturgical sermon—all go back to the express command of Jesus, or

---

[1] Some local churches had their own ancient and distinctive rites, those of Milan (the Ambrosian rite), Toledo (the Mozarabic rite), and Lyons being the most famous.

[2] Cf. E. Bishop, *Liturgica Historica: Papers on the Liturgy and Religious Life of the Western Church*; A. Fortescue, *The Mass: A Study of the Roman Liturgy*; J.A. Jungmann SJ, *The Mass of the Roman Rite: Its Origins and Development (Missarium Solemnia)*; A.A. King, *Liturgy of the Roman Church*; T. Klauser, *A Short History of the Western Liturgy*; G.G. Willis, *A History of Roman Liturgy to the Death of Gregory the Great*; J. Harper, *The Forms and Orders of Western Liturgy from the Tenth to the Eighteenth Century*; Y. Hen, *The Royal Patronage of Liturgy in Frankish Gaul*; C. Vogel, *Medieval Liturgy*.

> are at least based on his example and commendation. Jesus, however, did not originate these liturgical acts, but took them over from the practice of late Judaism. The primitive Church continued this policy; to a limited extent it created of its own accord forms of worship which had not already been laid down by Jesus; but to a much greater extent it fashioned its worship according to the liturgical customs of Judaism. In Gentile congregations, borrowings were made increasingly from the religious practices of the Graeco-Roman world.[3]

In the words of Klaus Gamber, "in their origins, the forms of Christian worship, so far as their relation to Judaism is concerned were nothing fundamentally new."[4]

This is the period of the initial formation of the Liturgy. As Christianity spread, its forms of worship develop and diversified. The language, gestures, prayers, vesture and music used were influenced, but not exclusively produced, by the local Church. In the West, according to Joseph Jungmann SJ, "by the turn of the fifth century" we find the "framework of the Roman Mass" established.[5]

The Venerable Bede witnesses to the formation of the Liturgy in England. Late in the sixth century St Augustine of Canterbury writes to Pope St Gregory the Great asking about liturgical customs. Gregory replies:

> My brother, you are familiar with the usage of the Roman Church, in which you were brought up. But if you have found customs, whether in the Church of Rome or of Gaul or any other that may be more acceptable to God, I wish you to make a careful selection of them, and teach the Church of the English, which is still young in the Faith, whatever you have been able to learn with profit from the various Churches...select from each of the Churches whatever things are devout, religious, and right; and when you have bound them, as it were, into a Sheaf, let the minds of the English grow accustomed to it.[6]

It is difficult to identify principles of liturgical *re*form in the period of the very formation of the Liturgy. We can, however, observe that the Liturgy is a developing entity. There was no one time in the first six centuries where its development halted. The Liturgy was a living reality, an organism, and was capable of further growth. This cannot but be a fundamental component of any principles of liturgical reform.

Similarly, we can observe in St Gregory's reply to St Augustine that there is a clear sense in which the Liturgy is received and was not simply constructed anew according to the tastes of the people amongst

---

[3] *A Short History of the Western Liturgy,* p. 5.

[4] *The Modern Rite,* p. 77.

[5] Cf. *The Mass of the Roman Rite,* vol. I p. 58.

[6] Bede, *A History of the English Church and People,* p. 73.

whom he found himself, and that innovation must be for good reason and carefully integrated with the tradition. We can also see that the pope and the bishop exercise authority over the liturgical forms to be used. St Gregory recognises the possibility of diversity in local forms, and indeed—within the principles outlined above—he allows considerable freedom to St Augustine in the formation of rites for the English.

The Liturgy contained elements handed on that were regarded as untouchable. Clearly the words and actions of our Lord with bread and wine fall into this category. However later, non-Dominical, products of Tradition were also accorded such reverence, the prime example being the Roman canon. Whilst this certainly underwent further development in the seventh and eighth centuries,[7] Klauser reports that by the sixth century it was "looked upon as part of the most sacred apostolic Tradition."[8] Thus, at the close of the sixth century we find developed liturgical rites that are themselves sacred, yet capable of further development: a living, but nevertheless objective, Tradition.

The Sixth to Eleventh Centuries & the Carolingian Reform

Klauser's second period spans 590-1073:

> The Liturgy of the Roman Church had, in its new Latin form, been gradually developed by the labours of the popes in writing prayers, in particular by St Leo the Great and Gelasius I [492-496]. Under Gregory the Great and his immediate successors, it received its final form, which found its concrete embodiment in the so-called Gregorian Sacramentary, the so-called Gregorian Antiphonary, the *Capitulare evangelorium*, and the *Ordines*. The Gregorian Sacramentary contains the prayers to be recited by the celebrant at mass throughout the liturgical year, and those to be said at the administration of the sacraments...the *Ordines* give directions to the clergy containing the ritual procedure to be observed at each liturgical function.[9]

Klauser also notes that "there is no trace of any real advance in the development of the Roman Liturgy during this period," with the minor exceptions of the introduction to the Mass of the Lord's prayer by Gregory the Great, and of the *Agnus Dei* by Pope Sergius I (687-701).[10]

Nevertheless, this period sees the so-called "Carolingian reform." Yitzhak Hen has recently argued that this period suffers from a scholarly "illusion"[11] that Pippin III effected an "official Romanisation of the

---

[7] Cf. Willis, *A History of Roman Liturgy to the Death of Gregory the Great*, pp. 19-53.
[8] *A Short History of the Western Liturgy*, p. 44.
[9] Ibid., p. 45.
[10] Cf. ibid., pp. 46-7.
[11] Certainly present in Klauser's account.

Frankish rite,"[12] and, Hen argues, that under Charlemagne, whilst "Roman books and liturgical practices were undoubtedly introduced...both voluntarily and by legislation," contrary to received opinion "the traditional non-Roman rites were neither deliberately suppressed nor lost. Continuity in liturgical celebration is apparent, even when it seems that new practices and prayers were introduced..." and that it is "highly improbable that liturgical uniformity was aimed at by the Carolingian court."[13] Thus, "diversity on top of an underlying unity" Hen argues, "is a more accurate way of describing the Frankish situation...an eloquent witness to the richness of religious life and culture in the period."[14]

It is nevertheless true that towards the end of the eighth century, Charlemagne sent for Roman liturgical books to copy. What arrived was a book designed for papal use (the *Hadrianum*), which omitted the texts necessary for liturgies not celebrated by the pope, but that were ordinarily used by priests. This was clearly inadequate.[15]

Scholars have widely assumed that Charlemagne authorised the travelled and scholarly Alcuin of York, himself familiar with the Roman usages from England, to compensate for the *lacunæ*. Hen questions his rôle, and ascribes it to St Benedict of Aniane. Whoever in fact was the Carolingian editor,[16] his work is of importance.

---

[12] *The Royal Patronage of Liturgy in Frankish Gaul*, p. 64.

[13] Ibid., pp. 94-95. Bishop's summary of the Carolingian editor's significance in the development of the Roman rite illustrates the view Hen opposes: "After Alcuin, all is changed; a levelling hand has passed over the particularism that before prevailed; liturgical texts assume a more uniform tenor, their colour is less varied and local. The older liturgies have almost everywhere been put out of use, and the copies of the missal become uniform: under reserve, of course, of very numerous variations of detail and continual minor alterations. But at least this result was achieved: since Alcuin the only missal in use is the Gelasiano-Gregoriano compilation. The older liturgies, the pure Roman, the Gallican, and at length the Mozarabic disappear, to give place to a common and universally accepted rite based, as its main factor, on Roman observance. And that is what Charlemagne had willed should be. In a word, it is the Englishman Alcuin who has been the instrument to settle the structure and tenor henceforth of the Liturgy of the Western Church;" "The Earliest Roman Mass Book" in: *Liturgica Historica*, p. 55.

[14] *The Royal Patronage of Liturgy in Frankish Gaul*, p. 153. Archbishop Weakland's recent repetition of the "Carolingian uniformity" theory fails to account for Hen's scholarship; cf. "The right road for the Liturgy" in: *The Tablet* 2 February 2002 p. 11.

[15] Cf. ibid., pp. 75ff.

[16] Cf. p. 77. A decision on this lies beyond our scope. A letter from Alcuin to Eanbald, Archbishop of York, in 801 demonstrates his attitude towards liturgical innovation. The Archbishop wanted a newly arranged missal from his former teacher. Alcuin's reply: "I don't know why you asked about the order and

Eleanor Shipley Duckett asserts that:

> [He] found this charge neither easy nor simple. In the first place, the copy of the book which had been sent...had been hastily made, held many errors, and...was extremely incomplete. [He] had to begin his work with a thorough revision and correction of its text by the aid of Gregorian manuscripts already current among the Franks.[17]

Nevertheless, the editor undertook the task carefully, completing the work shortly after 800. He did not, however, integrate his 'new' texts with the extant Roman ones, but appended them as a supplement. The preface to this supplement reveals both his profound respect for the sacramentary sent by Rome as well as what Dom Cabrol calls the editor's "scruple"[18] in making a clear distinction between his compositions and those of the existing Sacramentary:

> The aforesaid Sacramentary [the *Hadrianum*], although marred by many a copyist's error, could not be reckoned to be in the condition in which it had left its author's hands, [so] it was our task to correct and restore it, to the best of our bent, for the benefit of all. Let a careful reader examine it, and he will promptly agree with this judgement, unless the work again be corrupted by scribes.
>
> But since there are other materials which Holy Church necessarily uses, and which the aforesaid Father [Gregory], seeing that they had been already put forth by others, left aside, we have thought it worth while to gather them like spring flowers of the meadows, collect them together, and place them in this book apart, but corrected and amended and headed with their [own] titles, so that the reader may find in this work all things which we have thought necessary for our times, although we had found a great many also embodied in other sacramentaries.
>
> But for the purpose of separation we have placed this little preface in the middle, so that it may form the close of one book and the

---

arrangement of the missal. Surely you have plenty of missals following the Roman rite? You have also enough of the larger missals of the old rite. What need is there for new when old are adequate?" cf. S. Allott, *Alcuin of York*, pp. 27-28. Bishop's translation: "Have you not an abundance of *libelli sacratorii* arranged in the Roman fashion? You have also enough larger sacramentaries of the older use. What need is there to draw up new when the old suffice?" "The Earliest Roman Mass Book" in: *Liturgia Historica* p. 55, note 1. Hen (p. 79) sees in this Alcuin's repudiation of the result of the Carolingian editor's reform. Alternatively, it could be read as an expression of the scrupulosity with which the editor (if indeed Alcuin) regarded his work.

17 *Alcuin, Friend of Charlemagne*, p. 194.

18 "scrupule;" F. Cabrol OSB, "Alcuin" in: *Dictionnaire d'Archéologie Chrétienne et de Liturgie*, col. 1086.

> beginning of the other; to the intent that, one book being before the preface and the other after it, everyone may know what was put forth by Blessed Gregory and what by other Fathers.
>
> And as we thought it was not at all decent or possible to pay no regard to the wishes of those who look to find these so excellent and varied holy observances, we would at any rate satisfy the most worthy desires of all these persons by the present abundant collection.
>
> If it please anyone to accept what, without any desire of imposing ourselves on others, we have collected with pious affection and the greatest care, we beg him not to be of [a] mind ungrateful for our toil, but with us to render thanks to the Giver of all good things.
>
> But if he consider our collection a superfluity and not necessary for himself, let him use the work of the aforesaid Father alone, which in not a tittle may he reject without peril to himself; and let him also tolerate those who demand [our supplement] and wish piously to use it.[19]

This is an editor who, out of necessity, compensates for the inadequacy of the Roman book by drawing from existing traditional sources. He is not a creator of Liturgy or an innovator.

His insistence that what is new in his Sacramentary is not of obligation is significant, demonstrating a respect for the Liturgy as traditional, as something that is received. This is not a false humility. The editor has scholarly confidence in his work which, authorised by royal mandate, stands alongside the traditional forms as putative forms drawn from traditional sources. Yet he states that, precisely because they are newly posited, they are not of the same obligation: they have not (yet) become part of the liturgical Tradition of the Church. His preface accepts that they may be legitimately regarded as "a superfluity and not necessary."[20]

Later generations integrated the supplement with the Gregorian texts, with the result that the Carolingian editorial work spread widely. Gerald Ellard SJ observes:

> His Little Preface, standing like a sentinel between what was obligatory and what was optional, was thrown away, and soon Supplement had quite fused with that strange half-book Pope Hadrian

---

19 Text: G. Ellard SJ, *Master Alcuin, Liturgist,* pp. 112-114. Ellard's translation reproduces Bishop's version (cf. *Liturgica Historica* pp. 51-53) with critical emendations in the light of the work of the Lyonese scholar Robert Amiet: "Le prologue *Hucusque* et la table des *Capitula* du Supplément d'Alcuin au Sacramentaire Grégorien," in: *Scriptorium* vol. 7 pp. 177-209. Ellard reproduces Amiet's Latin text. Cf. also: C. Vogel, *Medieval Liturgy,* pp. 86ff.

20 "Si vero superflua vel non necessaria sibi illa judicaverit..." ibid., p. 113.

> had sent. [The editor] here supplied about half of the Roman missal, but since he drew his additions mostly from old Roman sources, these were *in place* – and have stayed there ever since.[21]

According to Bishop, the Carolingian reform does not see "'the abolition of the ancient and national Liturgy of France' and the substitution for it of an 'innovating Roman rite' by the mere fiat of 'imperial authority.'" Rather:

> It is only a final consummation of a process of attraction and change – of an approximation to Roman fashion in Liturgy, to the Roman style in prayer and worship – that had been maturing in Frankish lands for nearly two centuries. It was an essentially native movement indeed.[22]

Although authority is intricately part of Carolingian liturgical development, its exercise is in harmony with the organic development of the Liturgy. To regard the Carolingian reform as a liturgical "earthquake," which could be taken as a precedent for reforms imposed by authority which are not organic developments – as does J.D. Crichton[23] – does not take sufficient account of this.

The Carolingian editor was at pains to respect the traditional Liturgy whilst, out of necessity, compiling what was required to complete the Sacramentary. This he did in so far as possible from "old Roman sources." The editor's work was eventually integrated, to give us the missal of which Bishop speaks above. In this the following principles are discernible:

(i) a necessity for the development (the sacramentary supplied was inadequate; further texts were required);

(ii) a profound respect for liturgical Tradition (in so far as possible the compilation of required texts using elements already belonging to the Tradition, in this case Roman);

(iii) little pure innovation (the editor collects rather than composes);

(iv) the tentative positing of newer liturgical forms alongside the old (his preface accepts that they may be considered a "superfluity");

(v) the integration of the newer forms following their acceptance over time.

This is the principle of the organic development of the Liturgy in operation. It combines profound respect for the received liturgical Tradition with the openness to necessary development. Continuity and

---

21 Ibid., p. 225.

22 "The Liturgical Reforms of Charlemagne: their meaning and value" in: *The Downside Review* vol. XXXVII no 4. Cf. Dom A. WilmartOSB's note prefacing the French translation: "La Réforme Liturgique de Charlemagne" in: *Ephemerides Liturgicæ* vol. XLV pp. 186-207.

23 Cf. interview by the author of J.D. Crichton, 24th August 1994, Pershore, England.

harmony with Tradition are primary concerns. Liturgical orthopraxy and orthodoxy are thus ensured, without precluding necessary and natural development.

In the Carolingian period development is demonstrably organic. Respect for this principle is further underlined by Hen's observation that "there is no evidence that Charlemagne and his advisers made any effort to attain...liturgical uniformity" by imposing their revision of the *Hadrianum*.[24]

Subsequently, Klauser points out, the eighth and ninth centuries also witness the embellishment of the Roman Liturgy, due largely to the desire of bishops to imitate more elaborate liturgical customs, particularly those pertaining to Holy Week, which they had experienced whilst on pilgrimage.[25] Crichton also observes that the somewhat ceremonially austere Carolingian Liturgy was itself embellished in the ninth century.[26] Bishop states that:

> By the close of the ninth century and the early years of the tenth all delicacy in regard to the preservation of the official mass-book of Charles the Great had disappeared...not merely were the elements of the *Gregorianum* of Charles' own *Supplement,* and the *private selections* of votive masses and of benedictions, fused into one indistinguishable whole, but in addition rites or orders found in the *Gelasianum of the Eighth Century* were brought back bodily once more and took their place amongst the rest.[27]

It is the Roman rite as developed in the Carolingian period, with these embellishments, which include the resurgence of elements discarded in the Carolingian reform, that returns from the Franco-Germanic lands to a liturgically weakened Rome in the tenth century, and conquers it. The result, according to J.A. Jungmann SJ, was that: "in the West, liturgical unity was achieved...it was not the members that yielded to the head, but rather the head accommodated itself more and more to members grown meanwhile strong and wilful."[28]

We must be careful to distinguish "unity" from "uniformity" here. In no sense can it be maintained that the authentic diversity of liturgical practice that pertained to local Churches was compromised, or indeed that centralised authority supervised their liturgical practices. Here, liturgical unity refers to that fundamental kinship of rites within the Roman ritual family. Yet, of this period Cyrille Vogel states:

---

[24] *The Royal Patronage of Liturgy in Frankish Gaul,* p. 81.
[25] Cf. *A Short History of the Western Liturgy,* pp. 81-84.
[26] Cf. interview by the author of J.D. Crichton, 24th August 1994.
[27] "The Liturgical Reforms of Charlemagne: their meaning and value" in: *The Downside Review* vol. XXXVII p. 16.
[28] *The Mass of the Roman Rite,* vol. I p. 97.

> The entire process was one of osmosis, amalgamation, and hybridisation; liturgies were never simply substituted for one another; they influenced and modified one another, and even the dominant Roman liturgy issued from the process changed and enhanced.[29]

The Later Middle Ages

Klauser delineates 1073-1545 as the next epoch in Western liturgical history. He summarises:

> From Gregory VII (1073-85) onwards, the popes took firmly into their own hands once more the task of leadership in the realm of the Roman Liturgy which for almost three hundred years they had left to rulers and bishops on the northern side of the Alps. Gregory himself attacked the preceding period in which 'the government of the Roman Church had been handed over to the Teutons' and criticised the Teutons for having shortened the liturgical day hours out of a consideration for the lazy and the negligent. Hence he himself felt obliged to rediscover and restore once more the original Roman *Ordo*. Such a plan of campaign however, seems to have endangered the entire shape of the Romano-Frankish Liturgy now firmly established at Rome...It was now already impossible to 'wind back' the Roman Liturgy to ancient Roman usage (*ordinem romanum et antiquum morem*). Nevertheless, the Pope now demanded that the episcopal sees of the Western Church should follow exclusively the liturgical customs of the Roman see and rigidly obey all liturgical prescriptions from this source.[30]

There is little evidence of major liturgical reform at this time. Yet the development of the Liturgy, and the impossibility of winding back this development in order to return to earlier practices, are not without interest. Klauser speaks of this period as a one of "dissolution, elaboration, reinterpretation and misinterpretation,"[31] lamenting amongst other things the multiplication of private masses and the allegorical methods of piety adopted by laity who could not directly participate (in the late twentieth century meaning of participation) in an increasingly clerical liturgy.

J.A. Jungmann SJ describes this as a time where:

> The individual and subjective, seeing and feeling on one's own personal activity and personal capability—these came to the fore, and led to a stressing of the concrete and realistic, and consequently to a multiplicity of forms which could be kept together and coherent only

---

[29] *Medieval Liturgy*, p. 3.

[30] *A Short History of the Western Liturgy*, pp. 94-95.

[31] Cf. ibid., pp. 94-116.

> by a renewed desire for organisation. This new spirit did not call a halt even with regard to divine service; the arrangement of Mass felt its influence in a most profound manner. Already there was talk of that multiplicity of forms which had developed after the year 1000, but an effort was also made to codify the new forms; we can see in this a parallel to an attempt at mastering the heaped-up resources of knowledge by means of the *summas* which have been ranged side by side with the daring architecture of the gothic cathedrals.[32]

The centrality of the rite of the Church of Rome in the Western Church was further facilitated by the advent of some mendicant orders, who adopted the liturgical books of the Roman Curia, in part because of their convenient size, and spread them widely. Klauser concludes:

> Through the agency of the Franciscan itinerant preachers, these serviceable editions, principally the *Missale* and the *Breviarium* of the Roman Curia became well known, were received with respect, and as is only natural, were copied everywhere in the world of that time. Thanks to the disciples of St Francis, therefore, the Western Liturgy received a measure of unification which was not merely a theoretical or legislative unification, but one which was carried out in practice. To a great extent it was thanks to the Franciscan Order that the Western world was prepared in the age of printing for a short codified form of the Roman Liturgy which was to be binding on all, a Liturgy moreover which on the whole was readily accepted.[33]

The appearance of printed missals in the fifteenth century thus accelerated the spread of the Roman rite. One of the earliest, if not the first, was published in 1474 and is thought to be precisely that following the use of the Roman Curia.[34]

That liturgical development in this period tended towards a unity if not uniformity of rite is true. But we ought not to fall into the revisionist error of imagining a complete centralist 'Roman whitewash' of the Western Liturgy: diversity continued within the embrace of this unity. Another mendicant order, the Dominicans, carried with them their

---

[32] *The Mass of the Roman Rite*, vol. I pp. 103-104.

[33] *A Short History of the Western Liturgy*, p. 95. Cf. Van Dijk & Walker, *The Origins of the Modern Roman Liturgy*.

[34] An edition of this was published in 1899 by the Henry Bradshaw Society (R. Lippe, *Missale Romanum Mediolani 1474*). The introductory note asserts that it "appears to follow" a later edition of which the colophon is "*Missale completum secundum consuetudinem romanæ curiæ...*" (p. x). In 1996 Ward & Johnson published *Missalis Romani Editio Princeps: Mediolani anno 1474 prelis mandata*. Both supply fragments missing from the other.

own Liturgy.[35] Other orders also maintained distinctive rites.[36] Local churches (Milan, Lyons, Braga, Toledo etc., as well as the major English medieval centres: Salisbury, Hereford, York, Bangor and Lincoln),[37] cherished their own liturgies, and even those dioceses that adopted the Roman rite freely incorporated their own particular feasts and customs. In this the local bishop demonstrated his legitimate "independence in liturgical matters" which stretched "right back to the early Church."[38] Yet each belonged to the Roman liturgical family.

The desire for liturgical uniformity that arose in this period must, then, be understood as one that simultaneously respected authentic local diversity. Where a venerable local rite flourished, it continued to do so. Where there was a need or a desire for reform, the rite of the Roman church, now conveniently to hand, was frequently adopted. The operative principle was: the Western Church follows the rite of Rome unless venerable local liturgies are in place.

St Thomas Aquinas

We can learn something of the medieval attitude to liturgical development from the *Summa Theologica* of St Thomas Aquinas. Whilst he devotes no question or article specifically to "liturgical reform" or "liturgical development," itself suggesting that liturgical reform was not an issue in his time, his discussion "Of Change in Laws" is applicable.

The philologist Geoffrey Hull underlines the connection between liturgical custom and law in the teaching of Aquinas:

> The ancient Jews viewed their *masoreth* as a law, and it is no coincidence that the Latin *traditio* was originally a legal term. Accordingly, St Thomas Aquinas taught that the disciplinary and liturgical traditions of the Church are actually canonisations of *custom*, and custom "has the force of law, abolishes law, and is the interpreter of law" (ST I-II, Q. 97 art. 3).[39]

Aquinas himself draws upon Augustine's teaching:

> The customs of God's people and the institutions of our ancestors are to be considered as laws. And those who throw contempt on the

---

35 Cf. W. Bonniwell OP, *A History of the Dominican Liturgy*. For a description of the twentieth century Dominican rite cf. W. Bonniwell OP, *The Dominican Ceremonial for Mass and Benediction*.

36 Cf. A.A. King, *Liturgies of the Religious Orders*.

37 Cf. A.A. King, *Liturgies of the Primatial Sees*, and *Liturgies of the Past*.

38 Klauser, *A Short History of the Western Liturgy*, p. 118.

39 *The Banished Heart*, p. 204.

> customs of the Church ought to be punished as those who disobey the law of God.[40]

In the light of this interrelation we can appreciate the implications for liturgical reform of Aquinas' teaching that:

> Human law is rightly changed, in so far as such change is conducive to the common weal. But, to a certain extent, the mere change of law is of itself prejudicial to the common good: because custom avails much for the observance of laws, seeing that what is done contrary to general custom, even in slight matters, is looked upon as grave. Consequently, when a law is changed, the binding power of the law is diminished, in so far as custom is abolished. Wherefore human law should never be changed unless, in some way or other, the common weal be compensated according to the extent of the harm done in this respect. Such compensation may arise either from some very great and very evident benefit conferred by the new enactment; or from the extreme urgency of the case, due to the fact that either the existing law is clearly unjust, or its observance extremely harmful.[41]

Aquinas' later discussion "Of the Rite of This Sacrament" (i.e. the Eucharist), is also of interest.[42] He treats, approvingly, of such details of liturgical practice as the use of sacred buildings and vessels, the words and actions of the priest at Mass, and of problems ("defects") encountered in the celebration of Mass. One could dismiss these as scrupulous concerns, peculiar to the medieval mind and of little importance in liturgical history. Alternatively, one can recognise in the attention given them by the pre-eminent medieval theologian the intimate connection between Liturgy, custom and law outlined above.[43]

The importance of liturgical ceremonies in St Thomas has recenlty been underlined by the German Thomist scholar, David Berger:

> Whoever begins to grasp with St Thomas what mysteries, torn from transitoriness, are articulated in the ceremonies of the Liturgy in such a reality-saturated way, and how their importance is emphasised through their repetition, will also be able to fill the rite wholly with prayer and loving contemplation. He will in turn find it hardly

[40] Augustine, Ep. ad Casulan, cited in: ST I-II, 97-3.

[41] ST I-II, 97-2. Note the connection between this and article 23 of *Sacrosanctum Concilium:* "Innovationes, demum, ne fiant nisi vera et certa utilitas Ecclesiæ id exigat;" (there must be no innovations unless the good of the Church truly and certainly requires them).

[42] Cf. ST III, 83.

[43] Kieran Flanagan's *Sociology and Liturgy* explores this relationship in current liturgical practice.

> possible to tear from the Liturgy's integral structure whatever has no direct correlation with the current spirit of the age.[44]

St Thomas Aquinas certainly recognised the legitimacy of the development of liturgical forms. However his counsels about the inherent dangers of change in custom and law are clear, and reflect the caution inherent in the principle of organic development.

Contemporary Views of Medieval and Renaissance Liturgy

Writers in the second half of the twentieth century often used pejorative tones when speaking of the liturgical life of these periods.[45] The prevalent assumption was that, certainly by the early sixteenth century, the Liturgy was rife with:

> Abuses which in part typified liturgical life…Raging objectivism (the exaggerated emphasis on the *ex opere operato* effects of the sacraments), a one-sided concern not for sacramental sign and meaning but for efficacy; liturgical formulas need not be meaningful or understood, merely said (God understands Latin even though the people do not); the cultivation of false ultimates (the dislocation of the true eucharistic moment by the isolation of the consecration; the concentration on showing and seeing the body of Christ); ritualism...every word of the form must be carefully pronounced lest God be hindered from acting); the quantification of the Liturgy (Masses, festal and votive, were multiplied so that 'altarists,' priests whose function was simply to say Mass, were numerous...the proliferation of private Masses and of feasts); liturgical clericalism (the appropriation of worship by...the clergy, while the people watched in reverent passivity from afar...); the fixity of all liturgical forms (what is not commanded is forbidden; society and culture change but liturgical forms do not); and...the neglect of preaching.[46]

There certainly were abuses that warranted reform. However, in the light of the work of Professor Eamon Duffy[47] we cannot accept uncritically the assertion that all liturgical forms or developments in this period were illegitimate, acultural, historically corrupt or of no spiritual or pastoral benefit in their day.[48]

---

[44] *Thomas Aquinas and the Liturgy*, p. 40.

[45] And also today: cf. K.F. Pecklers SJ, *Worship*, pp. 56-66.

[46] K. McDonnell, "Calvin's Concept of the Liturgy and the Future of the Roman Catholic Liturgy," p. 43; cf. also A. Chupungco, OSB, "History of the Roman Liturgy until the Fifteenth Century" in: A. Chupungco, *Handbook for Liturgical Studies*, vol. I pp. 150-151.

[47] *Stripping of the Altars* and *The Voices of Morebath*.

[48] In *The Forms and Orders of Western Liturgy from the Tenth to the Eighteenth Century* pp. 40-41, J. Harper recognises the "liveliness of lay spirituality" of the

Yet, no less influential a liturgical scholar than Jungmann views this period as having "liturgical life…in a wholesale and declining form" which was "no longer a Liturgy of the faithful."[49] But Jungmann does admit that:

> We can speak of a flowering of liturgical life on the eve of the Reformation, even in respect to the people's share in it. But they were autumn flowers, late products of an ancient Tradition, like the late scholastic philosophy whose conclusions were often meaningless play. It was a rich, empty facade.[50]

The assumption of overall medieval and renaissance liturgical decadence, or corruption, is the essential foundation for his conclusion, one widely accepted by mid-late twentieth century liturgists, and one that enables the marginalisation of the principle of organic development of the Liturgy in favour of reform based on the findings of historical research and archaeologism:

> The task that confronts us now is that of analysing the core of our faith and liturgical life, of discerning the essence of our faith from the periphery. By doing so we will not only be returning to a more evangelical Christianity in the true meaning of that term, but we will find at the same time that the Christian people will be far better disposed for hearing the "Good News" of Christ our Lord.[51]

Thus the developed Liturgy and the significance of its integrated rôle within the fabric of the society in which it flourished are dismissed.

In terms of the Liturgy itself, we must note that there was reform which sought to correct abuses prior to the Council of Trent, most notably the 1513 *Libellus ad Leonem X,* a plea by the two Camaldolese monks Blessed Paul Justiniani and Peter Quirini for widespread reform in the Church and in its devotional practices—including a call for the use of the vernacular readings from Sacred Scripture in the Liturgy and the correction of questionable pious practices.[52]

At a local level Dom Jean-Marie Pommarès lists the Diet of Spire (1526), provincial synods in Bourges and Sens-Paris (1528), Cologne

---

period, but criticises the physical distance of the priest and people, and the lack of aural and visual participation, as well as the lack of "active involvement" of the laity in the Liturgy. One may question the application of such late twentieth century criteria to a period of history operating from quite different assumptions.

[49] "Liturgy on the Eve of the Reformation" in: *Worship* vol. XXXIII pp. 507, 508.

[50] Ibid., pp. 513-514.

[51] Ibid., p. 515. That this was published in 1959 is significant.

[52] Cf. G. Bianchini, *Lettera al Papa: Libellus ad Leonem X*. For their call for the use of vernacular readings from Sacred Scripture see pp. 203ff.

(1536), and Trèves (1546), as well as various reformed editions of local missals,[53] as examples of pre-tridentine reform.

Pommarès also observes the emergence of episcopal law with regard to the promulgation of missals, and suggests that this is a development, in reaction to contemporary abuses, from the prevalence of customary law in such matters.[54] The bishop's exercise of his traditional liturgical authority (to ratify and to correct) is thus augmented and somewhat personalised. For the first time bishops issue decrees about what may or may not be in liturgical books.

This development in episcopal liturgical authority, although salutary in its origins, would itself prove open to abuse, as implicit in such personal liturgical authority is the personal power to order or authorise liturgical innovation; something hitherto quite foreign to liturgical Tradition. The medieval and renaissance world did not witness its widespread exercise. However the ground was laid for this possibility—as we shall see in the reform of Cardinal Quignonez, something from which even the Bishop of Rome was not immune.

We have followed Klauser's delineation of periods in liturgical history. However Archdale King makes further distinctions which are perhaps more subtle and helpful in our study of liturgical development. King describes the first three centuries as those of the primitive Liturgy. The fourth to the eighth century see the formation of the Liturgy; the eighth to the fourteenth century, the enrichment of the Liturgy. He regards the fourteenth and the fifteenth centuries as those of the decline of the Liturgy and the sixteenth century onwards those of the reform of the Liturgy.[55] It is significant that, in King's view, the development and enrichment of the Liturgy continues as far as the fourteenth century before experiencing decline. As we shall see, this is the stance taken by the reform following the Council of Trent, but not that of most twentieth century writers or reformers.

The Liturgical Reform of Cardinal Quignonez

At the beginning of the sixteenth century, the humanist Pope Leo X (1513-1521) engaged Bishop Zacharia Ferreri of Guarda to produce a new breviary, "made much shorter and more convenient, and purged from all errors."[56] Ferreri produced a new edition of the liturgical hymns ("laboured poetry, redolent of classical reminiscences and full of clever tricks of versification"),[57] which received the approbation of Pope

---

[53] Cf. J.M. Pommarès OSB, *Trente et le Missel*, pp. 49-50.
[54] Cf. ibid., p. 49.
[55] Cf. *Liturgy of the Roman Church,* pp. 3-45.
[56] P. Batiffol, *History of the Roman Breviary* (1912 edition), p. 178.
[57] Ibid., p. 179.

Clement VII (1523-1534) in 1523. The historian of the breviary, Pierre Batiffol, observes:

> What was deplorable in this experiment of Ferreri's was the whole state of mind which produced it, the ignorance of all liturgical Tradition, and utter aversion to the study of it.[58]

Ferreri's death and the prevailing political and ecclesiastical climate brought an end to his work.

Yet, in 1529, at the request of Pope Clement, the Franciscan Francis Cardinal Quignonez took up anew the task of a reform of the Roman breviary. This reform is noteworthy due to its origin and because of its guiding principles, its reception and its eventual authoritative reversal.[59]

Quignonez understood that his task was:

> So to arrange the canonical hours as to bring them back as far as possible to their ancient form, to remove from the office prolixities and difficult details: it was to be faithful to the institutions of the ancient Fathers, and the clergy were to have no longer any reason for revolting against the duty of reciting the canonical prayers.[60]

Batiffol explains:

> It is no longer a question of praying according to the rules of "true latinity," but in accordance with "the institutions of the ancient Fathers"—not to flatter the Ciceronianism of the clergy, but to enjoin on them an office against which they should have no ground for objection.[61]

The operative principles were: antiquarianism—a desire to return to the liturgical practices of antiquity, ignoring subsequent developments—in keeping with renaissance humanism of the age, and a measure of

---

58 Ibid., p. 181.

59 Also because Annibale Bugnini CM would write in 1963: "I am convinced that the experiment of Cardinal Quignonez answered a real and specific need. It was a silent but justified reaction, meaning: 'Give us a breviary which satisfies priestly piety and which at the same time allows effective performance of the apostolic ministry.' The same situation obtains today...Today Quignonez' plan would be counted as one of the more moderate;" "Breviary Reform" *Worship* vol. XXXVII p. 224. Bugnini's stance casts doubt upon the assertion of S. Campbell FSC that whilst "the post-Vatican II structure of the Roman Office is, in fact, remarkably similar to that of the Quignonez Office," "there was apparently no conscious effort on the part of the postconciliar reformers to imitate it;" *From Breviary to Liturgy of the Hours*, pp. 13-14.

60 Cited in: P. Batiffol, *History of the Roman Breviary* (1912), p. 182.

61 Ibid.

pastoral expediency, as it would appear that the clergy found the office as it stood too much of a burden.

Such principles, Batiffol states, were:

> A dangerous novelty...reforms to be carried out by a return to antiquity, while what antiquity is meant is not expressed, nor is the method to be followed in returning to it! Was not this just such a way of speaking as had been employed by the Protestant Reformers?[62]

And, Batiffol asks, was not the traditional office:

> Conceived on a certain plan, a plan harmonious in itself? And had not the details of this ancient edifice their own beauty of form, to which historical associations had added interest? But Quignonez sweeps all away, and proceeds to build up a new edifice on a new plan…
>
> [Responsories] are suppressed without mercy, and therewith disappears at one stroke all that beautiful literature of the responsorial, the most original portion of the Roman Office! The Roman distribution of the psalms disappears equally; the psalms are rearranged on a new plan, in an order which is no doubt practical, easy, attractive, but unknown to the ancient Church.[63]

Quignonez' breviary was published in 1535 under Paul III as a consultation, from which he welcomed critical comments.[64] Comments were received, taken into account, and Paul III promulgated a new edition in 1536. This was intended for private recitation, not public celebration. Quignonez intended that the choir office be left untouched.

His so-called "breviary of busy people," was not well received, except by the Jesuits.[65] The judgement of the Sorbonne was that:

> The author of the new breviary has preferred his private judgement to the decrees of the ancient Fathers, and to the time-honoured customs of the Church.[66]

---

62 Ibid.

63 Ibid. (1898 edition), p. 241. The 1912 edition omits these remarks, perhaps in the light of St Pius X's own 'practical rearrangement' of the psalter in 1911, and perhaps because of the caution practised by many scholars during the modernist period: Batiffol's book *L'Eucharistie, la présence réelle et la transsubstantiation* had been placed on the Index in 1907.

64 Reprinted in 1888 by J.W. Legg, *Breviarium Romanum a Fr. Card. Quignonio editum et recognitum, juxta editionen Venitiis A.D. 1535 impressam.*

65 "Breviarium in occupatorum hominum levamen editum;" cf. Batiffol, *History of the Roman Breviary* (1898), p. 244. Sheppard points out that "before he set out on his mission to the Indies, St Francis Xavier was offered permission to use Cardinal Quignonez' shorter rescension of the office, but he would have none of it;" "Reform of the Liturgy: Another View" in: *Orate Fratres* [hereafter *OF*] vol. XII p. 536.

66 Ibid. (1912), p. 186.

Or, as Dom Baudot reports, the Sorbonne:

> Convicted as audacious an author who had suppressed ancient and universal customs, and broke away altogether from Tradition in order to welcome all sorts of liturgical novelties.[67]

In spite of Quignonez' intentions,[68] his breviary did find its way into public use. The people of Saragossa reacted violently to it at *Tenebræ* one Maundy Thursday. Suspecting that their canons had become Huguenots, Batiffol reports that there was "uproar" in the cathedral which "went near to making an *auto da fé* of the canons and their new breviary."[69] Batiffol concludes: "Thus these good folk defended in their own fashion the just rights of liturgical Tradition."[70]

Quignonez' breviary suffered a severe blow from a Spanish theologian, John of Arze, who in 1551 submitted a memorandum to the Fathers of the Council of Trent in which he:

> Enters his protest on behalf of the rights of the traditional *Ordo psallendi* of the Roman Church, the traditional distribution of the psalms among the various canonical hours, the traditional allotment of the lessons from different parts of Holy Scripture to different seasons of the Christian year, the traditional number of nocturns—in fact on behalf of the whole of that liturgical order, based on deep mystical reasons (*haud obscura vestigia*) [sic] of the most venerable antiquity.[71]

He also warns the Fathers of Trent, in the words of Batiffol, "to be on their guard against that innovating spirit which despises antiquity and takes up with novelties."[72]

John of Arze's criticisms are passionate, yet the principles upon which they stand are clear: Quignonez' reform did not respect objective liturgical Tradition. It was an innovation, not an organic development, and as such, however well intentioned or authorised, was illegitimate.[73]

It is significant that Quignonez' breviary, produced at the request of and duly promulgated by the Apostolic See, was itself nevertheless not

---

67 J. Baudot OSB, *The Roman Breviary*, p. 129.

68 Batiffol emphasises that his work was "full of originality and courage," and concludes that we may "pronounce a full and free acquittal of the *intentions* of the pious Cardinal;" *History of the Roman Breviary* (1912), p. 186.

69 Ibid.

70 Ibid. (1898), p. 244. 1912 omits this sentence.

71 Ibid., p. 246.

72 Ibid., p. 191.

73 Jungmann deprecates Arze's arguments, and the repudiation of Quignonez' breviary: "...it is apparent that all of these arguments carried weight only because of the state of things at the time and because of lack of knowledge of history;" *Pastoral Liturgy*, p. 209. Jungmann's attribution of great importance to the "knowledge of history" is itself significant.

regarded as beyond criticism. The repudiation of this breviary by rescript of Paul IV in 1558,[74] and its subsequent proscription by St Pius V in 1568,[75] is the pre-eminent demonstration in liturgical history of the priority organic development of the Liturgy enjoys over approbation by competent authority. The prudential judgement of Paul III promulgating this reform in 1536 was an error, finally corrected some five popes and thirty-two years later, in the light of the evident dissatisfaction of the faithful and at the prompting of scholars.

Paul IV (1555-1559) did not simply repudiate the breviary of Quignonez. He saw the need for some reform. Yet, according to Batiffol:

> Paul IV understood better than Clement VII or Paul III the conditions of a good reformation of the breviary, which he, equally with them, felt to be needed: viz. that such a reform ought be a return, not to an ideal antiquity such as Quignonez dreamt of, but to the ancient Tradition represented by the existing Liturgy; that there was no need of change in the traditional arrangement of the Divine Office as it stood in the old breviary of the Roman Curia: all that was necessary was to purge the breviary from errors of history, from literary defects, and from the wearisome prolixities which discouraged the clergy from using it with devotion.[76]

His efforts were consummated in the breviary reform of the Council of Trent, considered below. Paul IV's stance, one of healthy respect for received, developed liturgical Tradition, and one which demonstrates a salutary desire to purify it from errors, is an example of becoming behaviour by a pope in the supervision and respectful reform of objective liturgical Tradition.

In the nineteenth century, Dom Prosper Guéranger's examination of Quignonez' reform articulated the following principles which he regarded as essential to all liturgical reform. Although *a posteriori*,[77] they are pertinent:

> 1. A liturgical form drawn up to satisfy the requirements of literary pretensions can never last.
> 2. The reform of the Liturgy, if it is to last, must be brought about, not by the learned, but must be done with due reverence, and by those invested by competent authority.

---

74 Dated 8th August 1558, stating that there was no reason to allow its reprinting; cf. Batiffol , *History of the Roman Breviary* (1912), p. 191.

75 In the Bull *Quod a nobis* promulgating the breviary reformed by the post-Tridentine commission.

76 P. Batiffol, *History of the Roman Breviary* (1912), p. 194.

77 Given that Quignonez' reform occurred before the Council of Trent's reform of the training of the secular clergy, one may question whether Guéranger's seventh principle is fair. However in Guéranger's day, and subsequently, it can be seen as valid.

3. In the reform of the Liturgy one needs to guard against the spirit of novelty, restoring ancient forms that have become defective to their original purity, and not abolishing them.
4. Abbreviation is not liturgical reform: the length of the Liturgy is not a defect in the eyes of those who should devote their lives to prayer.
5. To read large quantities of Sacred Scripture in the office does not satisfy the whole obligation of priestly prayer, because to read is not to pray.
6. There is no foundation to the distinction between public office and private office because there are not two official Prayers of the Church...
7. It is not an evil that the rules of divine worship are numerous and complicated because the cleric is trained with such diligence that he is perfectly able to accomplish the *opus Dei*...[78]

The Council of Trent

Protestant reformers not only rejected what they perceived to be abuses in the Church, they rejected the medieval Liturgy. The protestant reformation has been described as "essentially an anti-liturgical revolution."[79] Its typical desire was for a "service" newly "made out of the scriptures and other authentic doctors."[80] Protestant rites thus "broke away utterly from all historic liturgical evolution."[81] The legitimacy of the organic development of the Liturgy throughout history was rejected,

[78] "1. Ce n'est point une forme liturgique durable que celle qui a été improvisée pour satisfaire à de prétendues exigences littéraires. 2. La réforme de la Liturgie, pour durer, a besoin d'être exécutée non par des mains doctes, mais par des mains pieuses et investies d'une autorité franchement compétente. 3. Dans la réforme de la Liturgie on doit se garder de l'esprit de nouveauté, restaurer ce qui se serait glissé de défectueux dans les anciennes formes. et non les abolir. 4. Ce n'est point réformer la Liturgie que de l'abréger; sa longuer n'est point un défaut aux yeux de ceaux qui doivent vivre de la prière. 5. Lire beaucoup d'Écriture sainte dans l'office n'est pas remplir toute l'obligation de la prière sacerdotale; car lire n'est pas prier. 6. Il n'y a pas de fondement à la distinction de l'office public et de l'office privé: car il n'y a pas deux prières qui soient à la fois la prière officielle de l'Église... 7. Ce n'est pas un mal que les règles du service divin soient nombreuses et compliquées, afin que le clerc aprenne avec quelle diligence il faut accomplir l'oeuvre du Seigneur..." *Institutions Liturgiques* (second edition, 1878) vol. I pp. 378-379. Translation adapted from Baudot, *The Roman Breviary*, pp. 135-136.

[79] D. Tucker, "The Council of Trent, Guéranger and Pius X," in: *OF* vol. X p. 538. Cf. P. Guéranger OSB, *Institutions Liturgiques* (1840) vol. I pp. 405-425; M. Davies, *Cranmer's Godly Order*.

[80] Thomas Cranmer, quoted in: E. Duffy, *Stripping of the Altars*, p. 432.

[81] A. Fortescue, *The Mass*, p. 206.

freeing the reformers to construct heteroprax liturgies according to their heterodox ideologies.

The decree of the twenty-second session of the Council of Trent on the Sacrifice of the Mass (17th September 1562), rejects this stance. Its supplementary *Decree Concerning the Things to be Observed, and to be Avoided, in the Celebration of the Mass* reasserts the legitimacy of rites, ceremonies and prayers "which have been approved of by the Church and have been received by a frequent and praiseworthy usage."[82]

Trent did not stop at condemning such departures from the living Tradition of the Church. It called for new editions of the missal and breviary, the completion of which the twenty-fifth session entrusted to the pope in 1563. Pius IV appointed a commission to carry out this work, which was augmented by his successor St Pius V. The commission yielded the 1568 *Breviarium Romanum* and the 1570 *Missale Romanum*.

The reform effected by the Tridentine commission is of singular importance. What principles did these individuals, working at the behest of papal authority, employ to meet the request of an ecumenical council of the Church?

The proceedings of the commission on the new edition of the missal are practically unknown,[83] though we do have the result of their work.[84] It is clear that their task:

> Was not to make a new missal, but to restore the existing one "according to the custom and rite of the holy fathers," using for that purpose the best manuscripts and other documents.[85]

By twentieth century standards the quantity of research into the origins and history of liturgical development available to this commission was minuscule. We know, however, that the commission had access to ancient manuscripts from which they could, arguably, have distilled a purer, more ancient rite, or from which they could have drawn ancient forms to replace ones of later origin.

---

[82] *Dogmatic Canons and Decrees*, p. 148: "ab ecclesia probatæ ac frequenti et laudabili usu receptæ fuerint;" *Canones et Decreta Concilii Tridentini*, p. 128.

[83] Apart from the Bull of St Pius V *Quo Primum* of 14 July 1570, there are two extant documents in the Vatican Library: One containing twelve questions treated by the commission [cod. Vat. lat. 6171, f. 67r-v] and another containing information on the correction of the missal [cod. Vat. lat. 12607, ff. 8r-11v]; cf. Anthony Chadwick's unpublished research, "The Tridentine Mass and Liturgical Reform," p. 78; also H. Jedin, "Das Konzil von Trient und die Reform der Liturgischen Bücher," pp. 34-38.

[84] Cf. M. Sodi & A.M. Triacca, *Missale Romanum Editio Princeps 1570*. The British Library contains a 1571 Venetian copy [1486.b.22] and a 1572 Parisian copy [1475.bb.15].

[85] A. Fortescue, *The Mass*, p. 206.

We have seen, though, that the same popes responsible for the liturgical reform of Trent rejected the liturgical antiquarianism of Cardinal Quignonez. The Tridentine reformers did not feel free to go down this path.[86] Rather, organically developed liturgical forms of later origin were respected as legitimate.

The fundamental principle of this reform was indeed one of restoration. But it was not a restoration based on protestant, iconoclast or antiquarian principles, nor was it a reform that sought to innovate. It was a restoration that sought to recover the beauty of the Roman Liturgy. The organism was pruned that it might flower again. Certainly, "the standard of the commission was antiquity,"[87] but by antiquity the commission understood the developed Roman Liturgy of the eleventh century: the missal of the Roman Curia spread by the mendicants.[88]

Thus, the phrase used by St Pius V's bull *Quo Primum* to describe the fundamental principle of the reform of Trent, "ad pristinam Missale ipsum sanctorum Patrum normam ac ritum restituerunt" (restored the missal itself to the pristine rite and form of the holy fathers),[89] does not, when read in its context, mean a return to some supposedly 'pure' form of the Liturgy found in antiquity such as the early liturgical forms, say of the first four or six centuries, as is assumed today.[90] Rather, they referred to developed liturgical forms with a living Tradition of over two hundred years. St Pius V's provision in *Quo Primum* for the continuance of local rites that have a custom of this length illustrates precisely where the bounds of antiquity lay in his mind. He forbids:

> Henceforth and forever throughout the Christian world to sing or to read Masses according to any formula other than that of this missal...saving only those [churches] in which the practice of saying Mass differently was granted over 200 years ago...*and those in which there has prevailed a similar custom followed continuously for a period of not less than 200 years: in which cases We in no wise rescind their prerogatives or customs aforesaid.*[91]

---

[86] Jungmann appears to lament that they did not: cf. *The Mass of the Roman Rite,* vol. I pp. 136-137.

[87] A. Fortescue, *The Mass,* p. 208.

[88] Cf. J. Jungmann SJ, *The Mass of the Roman Rite,* vol. I p. 135.

[89] M. Sodi & A.M. Triacca, *Missale Romanum Editio Princeps 1570,* p. 3; translation: M. Davies, *Pope Paul's New Mass,* p. 531.

[90] In an address "Fidelity to Tradition in Liturgical Renewal: A Case of Back to the Future?" delivered at Heythrop College, London, on 6th December 2003, Dr Paul Bradshaw, a renowned scholar of early liturgical forms, questioned the desirability of returning to any supposed golden age of the Liturgy.

[91] Emphasis added; "...ipsa institutio super duocentos annos Missarum celebrandarum in eisdem Ecclesiis assidue observata sit: a quibus, ut præfatam celebrandi constitutionem, vel consuetudinem nequaquam auferimus;" Sodi &

Antiquity, then, as recognised and respected by the liturgical reform of St Pius V, included what twentieth century liturgists deprecate as relatively late, and therefore corrupt, liturgical forms.

Thus Trent:

> Abolished later ornate features[92] and made for simplicity, yet without destroying all those picturesque elements that add poetic beauty to the severe Roman Mass. They expelled the host of long sequences that crowded Mass continually...they reduced processions and elaborate ceremonial, yet kept the really pregnant ceremonies, candles, ashes, palms and the beautiful Holy Week rites.[93]

The commission made prudential decisions about which one can argue. Their failure to incorporate an offertory procession, a possibility, given that it featured in Burchard's 1502 *Ordo Missæ* which was one of the commission's sources;[94] their elevation of the importance of the prayers at the foot of the altar by insisting that they be said at the altar rather than on the way to it, etc. Yet taken as a whole their work restored the Roman Mass of antiquity, where by antiquity we understand developed liturgical forms from early in the second millennium.

The same principle was operative in the reform of the breviary. Dom Baudot says of the commission charged with this work:

> Their object was not to create a new breviary, but to restore that already in existence to its primitive condition, having regard at the same time to altered circumstances.[95]

Of this principle he observes:

> Thus alone can the continuity of the liturgical Tradition of Christianity be preserved free from essential alteration, while allowing for the development and progress necessary in every living body.[96]

Batiffol asserts that in the reform of the breviary promulgated by St Pius V, "liturgical Tradition (*pristinus mos*) found the highest authority of all able to comprehend and willing to protect it."[97]

Triacca, *Missale Romanum Editio Princeps 1570,* p. 3; translation: M. Davies, *Pope Paul's New Mass,* p. 532.

92 For example tropes overlaid on the Kyrie and Gloria (cf. Jungmann, *The Mass of the Roman Rite,* vol. I p. 123), and private *apologiæ* of the priest (cf. Sodi & Triacca, *Missale Romanum Editio Princeps 1570,* p. xviii). The calendar was pruned of an excess of local saints.

93 A. Fortescue, *The Mass,* p. 208.

94 Cf. A. Chadwick, "The Tridentine Mass and Liturgical Reform," p. 87; also Jungmann, *The Mass of the Roman Rite,* vol. II p. 17.

95 *The Roman Breviary,* p. 147.

96 Ibid.

97 P. Batiffol, *History of the Roman Breviary* (1912) p. 194.

Anthony Chadwick argues that the principles guiding the work of the same commission on the breviary (published in 1568) apply to their work on the missal.[98] In the case of the breviary, the working documentation survives. He points out that the president of the commission protested that their work was not a compilation (it is described as "compilatum" in the bull promulgating it), but a correction and a restoration.[99] That similar principles should have guided their work on the missal appears reasonable.

The result of the Tridentine reform was a thoroughly traditional missal: its structure and content were not radically rearranged or abridged, nor disproportionately supplanted by innovations. Early in the twentieth century Fortescue poetically expressed his appreciation of the centuries of development evidenced in it:

> Our missal is still that of Pius V. We may be very thankful that his Commission was so scrupulous to keep or restore the old Roman tradition. Essentially the missal of Pius V is the Gregorian Sacramentary; that again is formed from the Gelasian book, which depends upon the Leonine collection. We find the prayers of our Canon in the treatise *de Sacramentis* and allusions to it in the IVth century. So our Mass goes back, without essential change, to the age when it first developed out of the oldest Liturgy of all. It is still redolent of that Liturgy, of the days when Caesar ruled the world and thought he could stamp out the faith of Christ, when our Fathers met together before dawn and sang a hymn to Christ as to a God...there is not in Christendom another rite so venerable as ours.[100]

Dom David Knowles expressed a similar opinion in 1971:

> The missal of 1570 was indeed the result of instructions given at Trent, but it was, in fact, as regards the Ordinary, Canon, Proper of the time and much else a replica of the Roman missal of 1474, which in its turn repeated in all essentials the practice of the Roman Church of the epoch of Innocent III, which itself derived from the usage of Gregory the Great and his successors in the seventh century. In short the missal of 1570 was in essentials the usage of the mainstream of medieval European Liturgy which included England and its rites...The missal of 1570 was essentially traditional...[101]

I.H. Dalmais OP stated:

---

[98] "The Tridentine Mass and Liturgical Reform," p. 83.

[99] Cf. Cod. Vat. 6171, fol. 15: "Fu riformato co'li Brevarii antichi quanto alle cose essentiali e importanti;" quoted in: ibid. Cf. M. Sodi & A.M. Triacca, *Breviarium Romanum Editio Princeps 1568,* pp. 3-6.

[100] Fortescue, *The Mass,* p. 213.

[101] Knowles continues "far more so than the New Missal of today;" letter to the editor, *The Tablet,* 24 July 1971, p. 724.

> The reformers' first concern was to return to the true Roman Tradition, in so far as it could then be known and as the legitimate development of the devotion of the Church allowed. For with every true liturgical reform it has always been the rule that it should avoid both archaeologism and untimely novelty. Changes were reduced to a minimum and great care was taken to preserve the old prayer forms even when their latinity was not that of the humanists.[102]

The Tridentine liturgical reform, initiated in order to correct abuse and ensure doctrinal orthodoxy, was thoroughly traditional. It produced nothing radically new. It promulgated and—facilitated by the development of the printing press—published a missal that could be used uniformly throughout the Roman rite, without prejudice to venerable local uses, which it respected.[103] Neither clergy nor laymen were astounded by this reform, and there is no evidence of disparity between the mandate of the Council and the work of its liturgical commission. It was another growth of the living organism that is the Roman rite, involving little substantial change.[104]

The Legacy of the Council of Trent

The period following Trent has been described as one of "rigid unification in the Liturgy and of rubricism."[105] Historians concur that centralism, rigidity and legalism were the overriding hallmarks of the Roman rite,[106] and to some extent of Catholic theology,[107] following the Council of Trent. Jungmann called it "the Age of Rubricism."[108]

---

102 *Introduction to the Liturgy*, p. 168.

103 N. Mitchell's revisionist assertion that Trent created "a single, standard, invariably 'uniform' Liturgy for the entire Latin West," or that its work was "a 'wholesale replacement' of cherished local liturgies by a strange 'new' rite concocted by 'specialists' and promulgated by persons with 'juridical competence,'" is without foundation; "Rereading Reform" in: *Worship* vol. LXXI pp. 464-465.

104 We concur with Bouyer that Trent safeguarded the "true idea of [liturgical] Tradition...The Council of Trent was far from allowing any individual the freedom to make up a Liturgy or para-liturgy of his own, which would usurp the place of the Church's one whole Liturgy. But it was far from any desire to impose any prefabricated and immovable Liturgy on the Church. The authority of the Council and its appeal to the authority of the Holy See itself was to be understood as the safeguard at once of the genuine authenticity and of the continual adaptability of Tradition;" *Life and Liturgy*, p. 71.

105 T. Klauser, *A Short History of the Western Liturgy*, p. 117.

106 Cf. A. Fortescue, pp. 208-213; P. Jounel, "From the Council of Trent to Vatican II," in: A. Martimort, *The Church at Prayer: Introduction to the Liturgy*, pp. 41-48; A. Chupungco, *Cultural Adaptation of the Liturgy*, pp. 33-34; J.D. Crichton, "An Historical Sketch of the Roman Liturgy," in: L. Sheppard, *True Worship*, pp. 72-76;

Edmund Bishop declared that:

> With the missal and breviary of St Pius V, the pontifical of Gregory XIII, the ritual of Paul V, and, finally, the *Cæremoniale Episcoporum* of Urban VIII, the history of the Roman Liturgy may be said to be closed.[109]

These liturgical books were guarded by the Sacred Congregation of Rites, established by Sixtus V in 1588 with the explicit purpose of overseeing their exact implementation and of providing official interpretations and new texts as the need arose.[110] The supervision of this Congregation gave rise to a strong emphasis on liturgical law. Bishop explains:

> By the action of St Pius V and his successors in stamping the Roman books put forth by them with a definitive character, and by the institution of a Congregation of Rites designed to keep observances on the lines laid down in those books, such manipulation[111] of the public service books of the Church as was common in the middle ages in every country in Europe was destined to be finally put an end to. But the spirit then active has never ceased to be active still, and it still finds a field for its operations. Unable to act inside and on the Liturgy itself, it acts with yet greater freedom without. One path shut up, it seeks its ends by another. And this is the explanation of the rapid growth, the wonderful variety, and great development in the last two or three centuries of what we call, to distinguish them from the fixed official services, 'devotions'...[112]

Pommarès regards Rome's arrogation of authority with regard to the publication of missals following Trent as a "revolution," brought to completion by the establishment of the Congregation of Rites.[113] Thus, papal authority, exercised by the Curia, was paramount. It is by no means clear that the fathers of Trent envisaged such liturgical centralism.

K. Pecklers SJ, "History of the Roman Liturgy from the Sixteenth until the Twentieth Centuries" in: A. Chupungco, *Handbook for Liturgical Studies*, vol. I pp. 160ff.

107 Cf. O. Chadwick, *From Bossuet to Newman*, ch. 1.

108 *Liturgical Renewal in Retrospect and Prospect*, p. 11.

109 "The Genius of the Roman Rite," in: *Liturgica Historica*, p. 17.

110 Cf. *Decreta Authentica: Sacrorum Congregationis Rituum*, vols. I-V. This collection, published at the end of the nineteenth century, contains 4,051 responses given since 1588.

111 Sic. Bishop means that the Liturgy was used as the ground for medieval devotion, not that the liturgical books were manipulated in a pejorative sense. On the link between the Liturgy and medieval devotion see Duffy, *The Stripping of the Altars*, chapters 1-5.

112 "The Genius of the Roman Rite" p. 18.

113 Cf. *Trente et le Missel*, pp. 54-55.

Klauser states that part of the legacy of the Council of Trent was to eclipse "episcopal independence in liturgical matters" which stretched "right back to the early Church."[114] Earlier episcopal independence was not, however, autonomy. Bishops had recognised organic developments, but they had not initiated or carried out root and branch reforms on their own authority. They acted as the proper custodians of Tradition, as did the popes of Trent, save in the Quignonez debâcle.

Further reforms followed Trent. The principles from which they operated are significant.

The Breviary Reform of Pope Clement VIII

Clement VIII's (1592-1605) 1602 edition of the breviary, whilst simply correcting some of the manifest errors found in that of the 1568 edition,[115] according to Batiffol:

> Established a point of great importance (implicitly recognised by Clement VIII by his not reproducing, in his bull prefixed to the new edition of the breviary, the strictly prohibitive terms of the bull *Quod a nobis* of Pius V), *that is to say, that the text of the Roman breviary is something susceptible of amendment.*[116]

Here the nature of the Liturgy as a living organism is underlined, giving the lie to those who would close liturgical history or development with the Council of Trent.

The Breviary Reform of Pope Urban VIII

The breviary reform of Urban VIII (1623-1644), can be described as mainly a "typographical revision,"[117] and it could be described as a minor development in the liturgical organism, but for the personal interest (interference?) of the pope, with the help of a commission of four Jesuits, in reforming the text of the hymns of the breviary "to give satisfaction to the taste of his time."[118]

The judgement of liturgical historians is clear. Batiffol:

> That these Jesuits outran their commission, and, under pretext of restoring the language of the hymns in accordance with the rules of metre and good grammar, deformed the works of Christian antiquity, is a thing now universally acknowledged.[119]

---

114 *A Short History of the Western Liturgy*, p. 118.
115 Cf. P. Batiffol, *History of the Roman Breviary* (1912) pp. 211-217.
116 Ibid., p. 217.
117 Ibid., p. 221.
118 Ibid.
119 Ibid.

Ulysse Chevalier:

> The Jesuits have spoiled the work of Christian antiquity, under pretext of restoring the hymns in accordance with the laws of metre and elegant language.[120]

Pimont: "Christian sentiment and true piety have lost by the change, without any advantage to poetry."[121] Clemens Blume SJ: "Hymnody…received its death blow as…the medieval rhythmical hymns were forced into more classical forms by means of so-called corrections."[122] And Fortescue:

> No one who knows anything about the subject now doubts that the revision of Urban VIII was a ghastly mistake, for which there is not one single word of any kind to be said.[123]

So too is the judgement of history itself. This error in the pope's judgement was partially redressed following St Pius X's reform of the breviary in 1911, and eventually reversed in the breviary produced following the Second Vatican Council.[124]

Significantly, Dom Baudot observed that "it is well to state that it [Urban's reform] has always been looked upon as a disciplinary act."[125] Dom Matthew Britt agrees: "The act of Urban VIII was a purely disciplinary act, one which the Church may recall at any time."[126] In other words, Urban VIII's reform of the hymns of the Roman breviary was an exercise of his prudential judgement (and not of his teaching authority). Thus they were seen by scholars as mandated for liturgical use whilst being at the same time quite repugnant to liturgical Tradition.

This instance serves to warn against accepting the personal enthusiasms, tastes or even the judgements of popes as all-sufficient justification for liturgical reforms. Whilst Urban VIII was right to correct the breviary, fulfilling his responsibility toward its organic development as had his predecessors (and indeed, as should his successors), his presumption to undertake a root and branch reform of the hymns of the Roman Liturgy based on the tastes of his age can be seen as a radical and unjustified departure from what is seen as the "authentic"[127] Tradition.

---

120 Cited in: J. Baudot OSB, *The Roman Breviary*, p. 187.

121 Ibid.

122 Cited in: M. Britt, OSB, *The Hymns of the Breviary and Missal*, p. 24.

123 "Concerning Hymns," xxxvii. See also J. Connelly, *Hymns of the Roman Liturgy*, p. xvii.

124 Cf. A. Bugnini CM, *The Reform of the Liturgy* [hereafter *TRL*], p. 550.

125 *The Roman Breviary*, p. 186.

126 *The Hymns of the Breviary and Missal*, pp. 24-25.

127 A. Fortescue, "Concerning Hymns" p. xxxviii.

The Proposed Reform of Cardinal Tommasi

St Giuseppe Tommasi (1649-1713) submitted a personal proposal for a reformed breviary to the Sacred Congregation of Rites in 1706. He suggested a breviary for private recitation and for limited public use. Unlike Quignonez, Cardinal Tommasi largely respected the traditional distribution of the psalms. However in many other respects his proposal was an even more radical departure from liturgical Tradition than Quignonez' breviary.

His overriding principle was that the breviary should be purged of everything not from Sacred Scripture. Thus antiphons, responsories, hymns and collects were removed in an attempt to produce a "new, or rather...[a] restored ancient breviary," "brought back to its original form,"[128] in order to promote "greater knowledge of the holy scriptures" amongst "indolent priests and clerks," and to provide for "the oratories of lay brotherhoods and for country churches, so that these, though poor and lacking in clerks able to sing the anthems and responds, might yet by this means still have the divine service at least on festivals."[129]

Tommasi was motivated by pastoral concerns. But he shows scant regard for developments in the Liturgy beyond a particular point, which he fixes around the beginning of the fourth century, after which all developments are regarded as accretions. This is antiquarianism: denying the legitimacy of the organic development of the Liturgy, regarding only the form of Liturgy in antiquity as venerable. It is the same principle as that of the protestant reformers, which may account for the enthusiastic introduction given the 1904 edition of Tommasi's breviary by its Anglican editor, J. Wickham Legg.[130]

Tommasi's proposal was never promulgated. There appears to be little research into the reasons behind this.[131] In the light of the earlier proscription of Quignonez' breviary by St Pius V and of his deliberate restoration of the traditional breviary, however, we may suggest that the rejection of Tommasi's proposal was another instance of the rejection of

---

[128] "novo, imo veteri renovati Brevario;" and "ad pristinam normam;" cited in: J.W. Legg, *The Reformed Breviary of Cardinal Tommasi*, p. 25. Similar language is found in *Sacrosanctum Concilium* n. 50: "...restituantur vero ad pristinam Sanctorum Patrum normam..." J.D. Crichton notes a similarity between Tommasi's wishes for reform and those of the Second Vatican Council; cf. *Lights in the Darkness*, p. 12.

[129] *The Reformed Breviary of Cardinal Tommasi*, p. 27.

[130] Cf. ibid., pp. 5-19.

[131] P. Batiffol, *History of the Roman Breviary* (1912) pp. 238-239, devotes a footnote to Tommasi. Neither S. Campbell FSC's *From Breviary to Liturgy of the Hours* or R. Taft SJ's *The Liturgy of the Hours in East and West* mentions him.

antiquarianism as a valid principle of liturgical reform. In this instance even the "prince of liturgists,"[132] and a saint, was in error.

Enlightenment and Gallican Liturgical Reforms

We have noted that, following Trent, the right of local churches to retain their venerable liturgies having a tradition of at least two hundred years was respected, and that twentieth century writers emphasise the liturgical uniformity consequent upon the publication of St Pius V's reformed missal and breviary. The latter was certainly not the case in France. The French recoiled from the prospect of Roman liturgical uniformity in varying degrees for a further three centuries. The arguments advanced and the reforms carried out throughout this period are of significance.

In 1583 the Sorbonne reacted to the prospect of adopting the Tridentine reform:

> The adoption of the Roman breviary would diminish the authority of bishops and of dioceses...The bishops have regulatory and police powers in their dioceses, just as the Bishop of Rome in his; this great good would be lost by the change in question. This enterprise would be against the liberty of the Gallican church, which, if she submitted on so capital a point, would remain subject to her in all the rest.[133]

Two principles are articulated here. The first, that ordinary episcopal jurisdiction includes authority over liturgical reform, is itself not remarkable. This had been the case more or less from antiquity. In France some bishops exercised that very authority by freely adopting the Tridentine liturgical books; others chose to reform their own liturgical books in the light of Trent.[134]

The second principle, that the Church of France must (at all costs) retain her liberty, is fundamental to what is termed Gallicanism; something that was to plague the popes of the following centuries. Gallicanism's liturgical progeny are of particular interest.

Jansenism is also a factor at this time. It:

> Started with the desire to restore the purity of primitive Christian doctrine and practice; almost immediately it became involved in the argument over grace and human freedom; then it manifested itself as a self-conscious asceticism that became increasingly puritanical; and finally it enclosed itself in total separation from the world and from

---

132 E. Bishop, *Liturgica Historica,* p. 117.

133 Cited in: D. Tucker, "The Council of Trent, Guéranger and Pius X," p. 540.

134 Cf. C. Johnson OSB, *Prosper Guéranger (1805-1875): A Liturgical Theologian,* pp. 150-153.

> the rest of Christianity by a futile attempt to restore the eremitical life, as if to set up a little church within the Church.[135]

Thus placing scripture and the fathers, particularly Augustine, above and against living Tradition, Jansenism produced a type of severe antiquarianism, which infected the French Church and beyond from the seventeenth century.

Dom Cuthbert Johnson explains the connection between Jansenism and Gallicanism:

> Whereas Gallicanism represented a form of anti-Roman spirit on the institutional plane, Jansenism was a form of anti-Romanism on the spiritual level. The Jansenists were able to use the Gallican movement of independence to promulgate their teaching.[136]

This ideological alliance motivated a series of liturgical reforms by people often called "the enlightenment liturgists." Theirs was "an anthropocentric concept of the Liturgy" wherein "the purpose of the Liturgy…was to make people better."[137] The two salient examples from the eighteenth century are the French Abbé Jacques Jubé d'Asnières, and the reforms of the Jansenist Synod of Pistoia, called by the Italian Bishop Scipio Ricci in 1786.

Jubé, who resigned his parish in 1717 to go to Russia on an ecumenical mission, and who died in exile in Holland in 1720:

> Wanted no more than one altar in his church. "The words *Sunday Altar* were inscribed upon it for no one was to celebrate Mass there except on Sundays and feast days. Once Mass was over this altar was promptly and completely stripped, just like all the altars in the Latin Church on Holy Thursday after the morning office. At the actual time of celebration the altar was covered with a cloth, but even then there were neither candles nor a cross. It was only in going to the altar that the priest was preceded by a large cross, the same which was carried in processions and the only one in the church. Arriving at the foot of the altar he said the opening prayers, and the people answered in a loud voice. He next went to a chair at the epistle side of the sanctuary. Here he intoned the Gloria and the Credo, without, however, reciting either of them through; nor did he say the Epistle or Gospel. He only said the collect. He did not usually recite anything that the choir chanted. The bread, the wine and water, were offered to the celebrant in a ceremonious way, in which there was nothing blameworthy; for this was a long-standing custom in many of the churches of France. But to these offerings of the sacrificial elements was joined that of the

---

135 J. Aumann OP, *Christian Spirituality in the Catholic Tradition,* p. 232.

136 C. Johnson, *Prosper Guéranger (1805-1875): A Liturgical Theologian,* p. 173.

137 T. Filthaut, *Learning to Worship,* p. 29. For other examples of Enlightenment reforms: cf. pp. 23-27.

season's fruits. In spite of inconveniences these fruits were placed upon the altar. After they had been offered, the chalice, without veil, was brought from the sacristy. Both deacon and priest held it aloft, reciting the Offertory prayer together, according to the custom of both Rome and France; but they recited the formula aloud to show that their offering was being made in the name of the people. The entire Canon, as might be expected, was likewise recited aloud. The celebrant let the choir say the Sanctus and Agnus Dei. The blessings which accompanied the words: *Per quem hæc omnia*...were made over the fruits and vegetables on the altar, and not over the bread and wine."[138]

Ricci, Florentine bishop of Pistoia and Prato, decreed similarly that there should be no more than one altar in a church; and as well as forbidding numerous devotional and pious practices, including the rosary, he ordered a simplification of the Liturgy and its translation into the vernacular. The people rose up and rejected the imposed reforms.[139]

These reforms, the significance of which is debated,[140] were enshrined in the decrees of the Synod of Pistoia.[141] The 1794 bull of Pius VI, *Auctorem Fidei,* condemned eighty-five of its propositions.[142]

---

138 This summary of the account given by Guéranger in *Institutions Liturgiques,* vol. II pp. 250-251, is from O. Rousseau OSB, *The Progress of the Liturgy,* pp. 28-29. Also cf. E. Koenker, *The Liturgical Renaissance in the Roman Catholic Church,* p. 24.

139 For an incisive treatment of the theological and historical background, and of the reactions of the faithful, see J. Parsons, "The History of the Synod of Pistoia."

140 Some look upon them favourably: L. Bouyer Cong. Orat., "We of today can see in most of them intelligent and healthy improvements, had they been introduced with the proper authority;" *Life and Liturgy,* p. 54. The Priests of St Séverin and St Joseph in: *What is the Liturgical Movement?* p. 101, go further, calling Jubé a "hero." L. Sheppard claims that many of the reforms "were in fact excellent in themselves, as we are now beginning to see;" *The Mass in the West,* p. 98. Others expressed concern: pre-eminently W. Trapp in: *Vorgeschicte und Ursprung der liturgischen Bewegung, vorwiegend in Hinsicht auf das deutsche Sprachgebiet* (Regensburg, 1940, Münster, 1979), and L. Beauduin OSB, who in 1945 describes Jubé's reforms as "audacieuses et indisciplinées;" "Normes pratiques pour les réformes liturgiques" pp. 12-13. J. Jungmann SJ, relying heavily on Trapp, speaks of Enlightenment liturgists who "absolutely misjudged the essence of the Liturgy and wanted to make of divine service a human service designed for instruction and moral admonition." Nevertheless, he identifies an underlying recurring theme: "the participation of the faithful had reached a certain critical stage;" *The Mass of the Roman Rite,* vol. I pp. 153, 154. Also H.A. Reinhold; "it is not only the vernacular that makes us uncomfortable neighbours to some schismatics and heretics. Just read the condemnation of the Synod of Pistoia by Pius VI and you will be amazed at certain resemblances;" "Jubé d'Asnières" in: *OF* vol. XXI p. 513; and in a note to "The Liturgical Movement to Date" p. 9: "nobody can any longer pretend to see a resemblance between Pistoia or Abbé Jubé [and pioneers of the Liturgical Movement]." In 1960 Reinhold again alluded to the similarity of

The reasons given for their condemnation are illustrative. Restoring the custom of only one altar was decreed to be "rash, injurious

---

twentieth century trends, and their underlying attitudes, cf. *Bringing the Mass to the People*, p. 35, n. 8. In *Mediator Dei* Pius XII saw a need to warn the Liturgical Movement against "the exaggerated and senseless antiquarianism to which the illegal Council of Pistoia gave rise;" cf. A. Reid OSB, *A Pope and a Council on the Sacred Liturgy*, p. 55 no. 64. Recent writers have commented upon the relationship of these reforms to those following the Second Vatican Council: T. Filthaut (writing in the *early* 1960's) finds "only an external agreement" between "the reforming attempts of the Enlightenment with those of our own time;" *Learning to Worship*, p. 29. J. White speaks of the "seeds planted in the eighteenth century, even if trampled on at the time, that have grown and blossomed into many twentieth century liturgical reforms." He regards Ricci's reforms as "curiously modern;" *Roman Catholic Worship: Trent to Today*, pp. 47, 54. A. Chupungco OSB, comments that "the similarity between Pistoia and Vatican II is not due to any borrowing on the part of Vatican II, but to the historical and traditional sources that were common to both," *Cultural Adaptation of the Liturgy*, p. 36. G. Hull has called these events "the prototype of the Pauline reform;" cf. *The Banished Heart*, pp. 44-53. C. Bolton in *Church Reform of 18th Century Italy* finds that a good deal of the concerns of Pistoia have "been accepted in the work of Vatican Council II," p. ix. J.D. Crichton regards de Ricci as an extremist; cf. *Lights in the Darkness*, p. 38. K. Pecklers SJ, speaks of Pistoia as "a very significant attempt at liturgical renewal" which was "far ahead of its time." He continues: "the liturgical reforms bear a remarkable resemblance to liturgical concerns of Vatican II because both relied upon the same sources for their reforms: the liturgical tradition of the Church that ancient texts began to propagate. Unlike...Pistoia, however, Vatican II enjoyed a fifty-year preparation in the work of the Liturgical Movement;" "History of the Roman Liturgy from the Sixteenth until the Twentieth Centuries" in: A. Chupungco, *Handbook for Liturgical Studies*, vol. I p. 165. A. Nichols OP, drawing upon Trapp, argues in *Looking at the Liturgy* that the "reform measures" of the second half of the twentieth century, with their similarities to those of the eighteenth, may well have become a tool for "the recreation of the imperfect attitudes of the European Enlightenment;" p. 29. B. Luykx OPraem responded to Nichols' thesis in: "The Liturgical Movement and the Enlightenment" arguing that "If ever there was a movement in the Church the radical opposite of the Enlightenment, it was the Liturgical Movement;" p. 23. In the opinion of the present writer, the similarity in both form and in motivation between the work of the enlightenment liturgists and of those who implemented the mandate of the Second Vatican Council is clear.

[141] "Poichè l'ordine de' Divini Ufizi, e l'antica consuetudine della Chiesa persuadono esser cosa conveniente, che in ciascun Tempio sia un solo Altare, piace però al Sinodo di ristabilire questo uso;" "Persuaso di questi principi desiderebbe il santo Sinodo, che si togliessero quei motivi, per i quali essi sono stati in parte posti in oblio, col richiamere la Liturgia an una maggiore semplicità di riti, coll esporla in lingua volgare, e con proferila con voce elevata;" *Atti e Decreti Del Concilio Diocesano Di Pistoia Dell'Anno MDCCLXXXVI*, pp. 130-131.

[142] Cf. Denzinger & Schönmetzer, *Enchiridion Symbolorum*, nos. 2600 ff., especially propositions 31-33.

to the very ancient pious custom flourishing and approved for these many centuries in the Church, especially in the Latin Church."[143] Forbidding relics and flowers on the altar was condemned as "rash, injurious to the pious and approved custom of the Church."[144] Simplifying rites, reciting all prayers aloud, and using the vernacular were decreed to be "rash, offensive to pious ears, insulting to the Church, favourable to the charges of heretics against her."[145]

Ricci certainly exercised episcopal independence over the Liturgy, but this was a radical autonomy that had never been enjoyed by bishops, not even bishops of Rome. As the condemnations in *Auctorem Fidei* illustrate, his reforms failed to respect the principle of organic development, a constituent element of which is continuity with Tradition: his reforms were "injurious to the very ancient pious custom flourishing and approved for these many centuries in the Church."

In Ricci's condemnation for being "rash," we see another facet of the principle of organic development: its respect for continuity with Tradition, which guards against sudden or spectacular changes which cause scandal. Authentic liturgical reform, we may say, involves the pastoral prudence which is inherent in gradual, organic development.

Similarly, we may see as excluded here liturgical reform based upon ideological convictions, in this case those of Jansenism, Gallicanism and of the so-called 'enlightenment.' The ideologues required that the traditional Liturgy be expunged of anything that was foreign to their convictions and reconstructed it accordingly: nothing short of renovation was acceptable. There was no question of an organic development of the objective liturgical Tradition.

The exclusion of these reforms is not based on their lack of due authorisation: had they been imposed by the Supreme Authority they would have been equally defective. Rather, the ground for their exclusion is that the reforms themselves are repugnant to living liturgical Tradition, either because of their ideological origin or content, or because of the radical discontinuity with Tradition their introduction would involve. In this instance, the Bishop of Rome exercised his juridical authority in a salutary manner to protect liturgical Tradition.

---

143 Proposition 31: "temeria, perantiquo, pio, multis abhinc sæculis in Ecclesia, prasertim Latina, vigenti et probato mori iniuriosa;" ibid., no. 2631.

144 Proposition 32: "temeria, pio ac probato Ecclesiæ mori iniuriosa;" ibid., no. 2632.

145 Proposition 33: "temeria, piarum aurium offensiva, in Ecclesiam contumeliosa, favens hæreticorum in eam conviciis;" ibid., no. 2633. The heretics whose convictions are seen as directly favoured by this proposition are the Jansenists and Gallicans. Whilst *Auctorem Fidei* was not occasioned by protestantism, its stance may be seen as applicable to it also.

Ricci and Jubé were by no means alone. Many French bishops reformed their liturgical books along similar lines, or adopted books thus reformed. Jubé's reforms influenced the Gallican missal of the diocese of Troyes published in 1736.[146] The Archbishops of Paris led the way, publishing their own editions of the breviary and missal beginning in the second half of the seventeenth century. As Johnson points out:

> There is no doubt that the Archbishop of Paris had within the terms of the Bulls of Pius V, the right to revise his diocesan liturgical books. Rome had given an example in amending the Pian liturgical books. The problem does not centre upon the right of a diocesan bishop to revise his liturgical books but in the present instance, to determine whether after 1670 the works produced were revisions or new compositions.[147]

The principles of reform behind Gallican books were:

> i. To remove as far as possible all non-scriptural texts, especially antiphons and responses and to replace them with scriptural texts.
> ii. The diminution of the rank and number of celebrations in honour of the Saints; this included a reduction of Marian Feasts.
> iii. A revision of the lectionary and the hymns and a redistribution of the Psalter.[148]

These principles were later expanded to include: giving Sunday primacy over all feasts except those of our Lord; suppressing all feasts during Lent to give it primacy; shortening the length of the ferial Office to lighten the burden on priests; simplifying the gradation of feasts to five; and using only verifiable historical texts in the readings of the Office for feasts.[149] Even Lyons, with its own ancient Liturgy, succumbed, in 1771 adopting a missal that "servilely followed the text of the neo-Gallican missal of Paris, with a calendar of the saints proper to the Church of Lyons."[150]

Dom Baudot provides an apposite evaluation of the Jansenist and Gallican reformers. Their attempt, he asserts:

> Was to lower the Liturgy, hitherto regarded as a monument of Tradition, to the level of a merely human document which everyone was free to criticise and alter according to his taste.[151]

---

[146] Cf. J.D. Crichton, *Lights in the Darkness,* p. 48; C. Johnson, OSB, *Prosper Guéranger (1805-1875): A Liturgical Theologian* pp. 158-159.
[147] Ibid (Johnson) p. 181.
[148] Ibid.
[149] Cf. ibid. Johnson notes the acceptability of these principles today, but cautions that they "must be studied within their historical context and in relation to the *discipline* of the Church then in force;" emphasis added.
[150] A.A. King, *Liturgies of the Primatial Sees,* p. 47; also C. Johnson OSB, *Prosper Guéranger (1805-1875): A Liturgical Theologian,* p. 160.
[151] *The Roman Breviary,* p. 197.

Dom Guéranger's Response to Gallicanism

It was only in the nineteenth century that the Gallican reforms were successfully displaced, largely due to the energetic work of Prosper Guéranger, a secular priest who re-founded the Benedictine order in France in 1833 at Solesmes.[152] Guéranger's principal theoretical work, the *Institutions Liturgiques,* is sometimes derided,[153] but in spite of its defects it did draw attention to and prompt debate on his two principal themes: the centrality of liturgical piety (or spirituality) in the Christian life, and the importance of liturgical unity (if not uniformity) with Rome.

Guéranger objected strongly to the fact that the local French liturgies were produced without appropriate papal authorisation.[154] An overriding feature of his liturgical theology is his ultramontanism, a clear and understandable reaction to the Gallicanism he so detested. Johnson cites the example of his dealings with one bishop:

> In the course of his discussion with the Bishop of Orleans, Guéranger suggested...that he should send his liturgical books to Rome for approval. If the Holy See approved the Liturgy of Orleans then it would be able to take its place as an authoritative witness to Tradition alongside all the other approved liturgies. The fact that the Liturgy of Orleans was of recent composition was of little importance since Guéranger declared that it was the authority that approved a Liturgy that gave it a value ("la valeur d'une Liturgie procède de l'autorité qui la confirme.")[155]

And in his account of the reform of Quignonez, rather than admit that it was possible for a pope to err in his prudential judgement in matters of liturgical reform, Guéranger obfuscates, saying that the prevailing

---

[152] Dom Guéranger and his abbey became a centre of liturgical piety, prompting some to call him the "Father of the Liturgical Movement." Cf. J. Fenwick & B. Spinks, *Worship in Transition,* p. 17; J. White, *Roman Catholic Worship: Trent to Today,* p. 76. Some give this title to St Pius X (cf. G. Ellard SJ, "Pius Tenth and the New Liturgy" in: *OF* vol. I p. 243), and to Dom Beauduin. Given that the Liturgical Movement is properly a twentieth century phenomenon, it is probably more accurate to call Dom Guéranger its "grandfather."

[153] O. Rousseau OSB, "The exaggerations of the author of the Institutions...are plentiful, and his historical conclusions are sometimes baffling," *The Progress of the Liturgy,* p. 23. For critiques of the work of Dom Guéranger see: J. Jungmann, SJ, *The Mass of the Roman Rite,* vol. I pp. 158-159; L. Bouyer Cong. Orat., *Life and Liturgy,* chapters 1-2, 4-5; E. Koenker, *The Liturgical Renaissance in the Roman Catholic Church,* pp. 10-11; J. Fenwick & B. Spinks, *Worship and Tradition,* pp. 19-20.

[154] Cf. C. Johnson OSB, *Prosper Guéranger (1805-1875): A Liturgical Theologian,* p. 188.

[155] Ibid., pp. 330-331.

circumstances were exceptional and that, in any case, the Holy See only gave Quignonez' breviary a "domestic approbation."[156] Guéranger does, however, admit the possibility of papal error in matters of (liturgical) governance.[157]

As a principle of liturgical reform, ultramontanism is foreign to liturgical Tradition. Whilst the Bishop of Rome certainly has authority to authorise and confirm liturgical reform, we must ask: is his rôle to confirm authentic liturgical Tradition, and developments in conformity with it, or does confirmation by the Bishop of Rome *of itself* grant authenticity, without regard to liturgical Tradition? Guéranger appears to tend towards the latter.

Given the possibility of a pope approving a liturgical reform that was repugnant to liturgical Tradition, and given the primacy in history of organic development, we need look no further than the errors of popes made in this regard in the sixteenth century reform of Cardinal Quignonez, or the errors of Urban VIII in the seventeenth century for pertinent examples that necessitate rejecting approbation by authority as a principle of liturgical reform that can stand alone, without regard for, and indeed being subject to, objective liturgical Tradition. The latter, we submit, even popes must respect.

Paradoxically, Guéranger also objected that the local French liturgies were unfaithful to Tradition.[158] He was acutely aware of the fundamental dogmatic rôle of the Liturgy in the living Tradition of the Church so often recalled in the theological principle *lex orandi, lex credendi*. This, combined with his conviction that many of the Gallican liturgies were inspired by Jansenism, led him to formulate a condemnation of what he called "the anti-liturgical heresy."

---

[156] "approbation domestique" *Institutions Liturgiques* (1840) vol. I p. 377.

[157] Cf. his critique of John VIII's concession of the liturgical use of the Slavonic language to Saints Cyril and Methodius; *Institutions Liturgiques* (1883) vol. III pp. 103ff. Guéranger writes: "These examples of human weakness are rare on the chair of St Peter; but history records them, and the Church's children have no reason to cover them up, since they know that He who has assured the Roman Pontiffs of infallibility in teaching of the faith, has not at all protected them from every defect in the exercise of the supreme government;" translation: P.M. Joseph ed., M. Sheehan, *Apologetics and Catholic Doctrine*, p. 198; "Ces exemples de l'infirmité humaine sont rares sur la Chaire de Saint-Pierre; mais l'histoire les enregistre, et les enfants de l'Église n'ont aucun intérêt à les dissimuler, parce qu'ils savent que celui qui a assuré aux pontifes romains l'infaillibilité de la foi dans l'enseignement, ne les a point garantis de toute faute dans l'exercice du gouvernement suprême;" *Institutions Liturgiques* (1883) vol. III p. 107.

[158] Cf. C. Johnson OSB, *Prosper Guéranger (1805-1875): A Liturgical Theologian*, p. 189. Johnson appears unsure: "The general principles followed by the revisers were in general quite sound and conducive to a recovery of traditional liturgical values, and yet at the same time there are untraditional elements in these works."

Guéranger traces the origins of this heresy from the controversy between Vigilatius and Jerome over the use of candles at the close of the fourth century, through the iconoclast heresy of the eighth century, and the eleventh century eucharistic theology of Berengar of Tours, to the doctrines of Wycliffe, Calvin, Luther and Zwingli. He finds in it echoes of the Gnostic and Manichean heresies and regards it as the logical outcome of quietism. Upon these foundations, the Gallican spirit imbued with enlightenment rationalism, in Guéranger's view, rejects Catholic Liturgy as foreign to true religion.[159]

Guéranger delineates twelve characteristics. The first is the hatred of Tradition in the formulas of divine worship.[160] The second is to replace formulas composed by the Church by writings from Sacred Scripture.[161] The fabrication and introduction of new liturgical formulas is the third.[162] Fourth is the contradictory principle that operates from an affectation for antiquity which seeks to "reproduce divine worship in its original purity" whilst spurning development later in liturgical Tradition and yet introducing new elements of "incontestably human" origin.[163] Fifthly, noting that similar attitudes are to be seen in protestant liturgical reform, Guéranger proscribes the rationalistic removal of ceremonies and formulas that leads to a loss of the supernatural or mystical element of the Liturgy without regard for its tangible and poetic nature.[164] The sixth characteristic is the total extinction of the spirit of prayer or unction from the Liturgy. Guéranger speaks here of pharisaical coldness, and cites the protestant insistence on the vernacular by way of example.[165] The protestant exclusion of the cult of the Blessed Virgin Mary and of the saints, on the grounds that one should ask for one's needs from God alone, is the seventh characteristic.[166] The use of the vernacular itself is the eighth. Here Guéranger warns of the transience of the vernacular and

---

159 Cf. *Institutions Liturgiques* (1840) vol. I pp. 408-414.

160 "la haine de la Tradition dans les formules du culte divin;" ibid., p. 414.

161 "remplacer les formules de style ecclésiastique par des lectures de l'Ecriture Sainte;" ibid., p. 415.

162 "fabriquer et d'introduire des formules nouvelles;" ibid. p. 417.

163 "une habituelle contradiction avec leurs propres principes;" "repraître dans sa première pureté le culte divin;" "formules nouvelles...qui sont incontestablement humaines;" ibid., pp. 417-8.

164 "à retrancher dans le culte toutes les cérémonies, toutes les formules qui expriment des mystères." Examples include regarding the altar as a mere table and emphasising 'meal' at the expense of 'sacrifice.' Cf. ibid. pp. 418-9.

165 "l'extinction totale de cet esprit de prière qu'on appelle Onction dans le Catholicisme." Cf. ibid. p. 419.

166 "Elle exclut toute cette idolâtrie papiste qui demande à la créature ce qu'on ne doit demander qu'à Dieu seul;" ibid.

of the dangers of using mundane language in worship.[167] An overriding desire to lessen the burden of the Liturgy (by shortening it), is the ninth characteristic.[168] Rejection of all things papal or Roman is the tenth.[169] A consequent presbyterianism that downplays the ministerial priesthood forms the eleventh characteristic.[170] Finally, Guéranger deprecates secular or lay persons assuming authority in liturgical reform lest the Liturgy, and consequently dogma, become an entity limited by the boundaries of a nation or region.[171]

We have seen that Guéranger's critical efforts are not beyond reproach, and it may be observed that his foundations for the anti-liturgical heresy are very broad indeed. Nevertheless, they are grounded to some extent in both the historical antecedents upon which he draws, and in the liturgical activity of the Gallicans to whom he is reacting.

We may deduce positive principles of liturgical reform from Guéranger's outline, principles as applicable today as at the time of the Gallican liturgical controversy,[172] namely to: protect the place of non-scriptural texts in the organic whole of the Liturgy; innovate rarely and only where necessary; reject antiquarianism out of respect for the living, developed Liturgy; protect all that speaks of the supernatural and of mystery in the Liturgy; similarly, protect the nature of Liturgy as prayer and worship lest it be reduced to a didactic exercise; treasure the rôle of the Blessed Virgin and of the Saints in the Liturgy; reject vernacularism; resist the temptation to sacrifice the Liturgy for the sake of speed; rejoice in liturgical unity with the Church of Rome; and, to respect the particular liturgical rôles and authority of the ordained.

In other words, Guéranger would urge respect for the organic nature of the Liturgy. His adherence to this principle is evident when he

---

167 "revendiquer l'usage de la langue vulgaire dans le service divin." Cf. ibid. pp. 419-421.

168 "l'affranchisement de la fatigue de la gêne qu'imposent aux corps les pratiques de la Liturgie Papiste;" ibid. p. 421.

169 "Haine à Rome et à ses lois;" ibid. p. 422.

170 "un vaste Presbyterianisme, qui n'est que la conséquence immédiate de la suppression du Pontificat souverain;" ibid. p. 423.

171 Cf. ibid. pp. 423-424.

172 Johnson takes the stance that the anti-liturgical heresy is inapplicable to the changes following the Second Vatican Council: "In no way can the writings of Prosper Guéranger be interpreted as a criticism of the Church of today;" *Prosper Guéranger (1805-1875): A Liturgical Theologian,* p. 289 n. 34; also pp. 288-9. Whilst logically correct, Johnson is too eager to dismiss what may well furnish much for a critique of these changes. Cf. also: W. Waldstein, "Le mouvement liturgique de Dom Guéranger à la veille du concile de Vatican II," pp. 165-168.

writes: "progress in Liturgy must be an enrichment by the acquisition of new forms rather than by the violent loss of the ancient ones."[173]

The plethora of persons and projects that comprise the Gallican liturgical reforms provide much by way of negative example from which we can learn. We cannot but agree with Batiffol that:

> We must reject the French liturgical Utopia of the eighteenth century even as we rejected the Roman Utopia of the sixteenth. The Liturgy of De Vintimille and that of Quignonez, of Coffin or of Ferreri, have...no claim to take the place of the existing traditional Liturgy.[174]

The Proposals for Reform of Pope Benedict XIV

Pope Benedict XIV (1740-1758) was a prolific writer on liturgical matters. The edition of papal teachings on the Liturgy compiled by Solesmes cites no fewer than sixteen documents,[175] concerned with the reform of sacred music, the reception of Holy Communion from hosts consecrated at the same Mass,[176] and the general "decency and cleanliness" of churches and of everything associated with worship.[177] Yet he rejected the possibility of inculturating the Roman Liturgy to incorporate Chinese traditions: seen by some as "curiously untypical,"[178] for an otherwise forward-thinking pope. His projected reform of the breviary is of interest.

Prompted to some extent by the Gallican reforms, he appointed a commission in 1741 which, at its outset, considered two requests made to him. One was to give the breviary a new form, the other was to purge the existing breviary of errors, particularly historical ones, and otherwise to reform it. The latter emphasised that the "existing breviary comprised certain essential elements, which could not be modified without destroying the Roman rite itself."[179] The commission accepted this. Their

---

[173] "Le progrès pour la Liturgie doit consister bien plutôt à s'enricher par l'accession de nouvelles formes qu'à perdre violemment les anciennes;" Johnson, 333. Johnson's translation: "progress in the development of the Liturgy has always been by degrees, by a process of enrichment and renewal," misses an essential element of the French original ("qu'à perdre violemment les anciennes"), which does not read: "Le développement de la Liturgie a toujours été un processus progressif d'enrichissement et de renouvellement."

[174] *History of the Roman Breviary (*1898) p. 352. Coffin was an 18th century Gallican reformer.

[175] *Papal Teachings: The Liturgy,* pp. 19-84.

[176] Cf. ibid., p. 22.

[177] Cf. ibid., p. 47.

[178] M. Walsh, *An Illustrated History of the Popes,* p. 181.

[179] P. Batiffol, *History of the Roman Breviary* (1912) p. 249.

first task was reform of the calendar, once again overgrown to the detriment of the seasons.

Benedict XIV's personal wish, however, was not for a reform of the existing breviary, but for a newly constructed breviary. In a private letter written in 1743 he looks forward to a breviary "in which everything should be drawn from Holy Scripture," and "the most universally accepted writings of the most ancient Fathers." Saints other than those in these categories would merely be commemorated.[180] In effect, the pope expressed a desire for a radical departure from Roman liturgical tradition that would canonise the principles behind the Gallican reforms.

By September 1744 the pope had changed his mind and publicly accepted the commission's principle to work on "the reform and not the recasting of the breviary."[181] Two months later he and the commission's secretary, Valenti, are on record as expressing the same view.[182]

One proposal made to the commission in 1745, equitable in Batiffol's opinion, was rejected on the grounds of the operative principle of reform. Valenti states: "that which is from antiquity is retained, and that which is new is reprobated, that is, it is best to change nothing."[183] This principle was not, however, seen as preventing the commission from expunging historically false documents in the lessons of matins,[184] or as preventing a new reform of the calendar, as had been done by St Pius V.

By Eastertide of 1747, Benedict XIV had the finished project on his desk: clearly the traditional Roman breviary, with a radically reformed calendar. Yet he died eleven years later without promulgating any reform: he judged the finished work of the commission inopportune. Batiffol suggests that the radically reformed calendar was itself not beyond question,[185] and that the attendant difficulties of such a reform caused Benedict XIV to hold back. The quasi-Gallican views expressed by the pope in 1743 may also have been a factor. In the last eleven years of his life Benedict XIV expressed the hope to conclude the revision of the breviary personally.[186] This hope was never realised, and the projected reform was not revived by his successors.

---

180 Cf. ibid., pp. 260-261.

181 Ibid., pp. 265-266.

182 "propterea quod Breviarii reformatio sibi esset in votis, non innovatio," ibid., p. 276.

183 "retenta est antiquitas et reprobata novitas, hoc est, nihil placuit immutari," ibid., p. 267.

184 Batiffol points out that "along with the chaff, not a little good grain was thrown out," indicating perhaps an excessive influence of Gallican principles in this aspect of the reform; ibid., p. 278.

185 Cf. ibid., pp. 277.

186 Cf. ibid., pp. 281-283.

Liturgical Piety

From the seventeenth to the nineteenth centuries several individuals promoted liturgical piety: drawing one's spiritual nourishment from active and conscious contemplation of the faith of the Church as it is celebrated and expressed in the liturgical rites and prayers throughout the annual round of seasons and feasts of the liturgical year; as distinct from the practice of an unrelated, however worthy, devotional exercise.

J.D. Crichton lists St Giuseppe Tommasi (1649-1713) first amongst such proponents. At Tommasi's 1986 canonisation Pope John Paul II extolled his "promotion of the liturgical life...[which] ranged from the publication of research and scholarship to the work which he performed for the liturgical education of the people and of the simple faithful."[187] Others include the French Nicholas Le Tourneaux (1640-1686), whose writings reflected his abiding concern "that the celebration of the Liturgy should be an exercise of the mind and heart;"[188] the Italian Ludovico Antonio Muratori (1672-1750), who also combined liturgical scholarship with promotion of liturgical piety; and his later compatriot Antonio Rosmini (1797-1855), who promoted active and conscious participation in the Liturgy whilst *rejecting* the use of the vernacular.[189]

In the same period a significant range of books was published for the laity, encouraging them to follow the rites and prayers of the Mass[190] rather than other devotional manuals, fostering liturgical piety. They were well established by 1815.[191] Throughout the nineteenth century

---

187 "New saint gives special witness to scholars and pastors," *L'Osservatore Romano,* 20 October 1986, p. 8.

188 J.D. Crichton, *Lights in the Darkness,* p. 57. Crichton's assumption is that the Second Vatican Council and the ensuing liturgical changes are the apotheosis of these "lights in darkness:" cf. pp. 7, 9, 10, 24, 26, 32, 67, 92, 94, 104, 109, 123, 128, 137, 138.

189 Cf. ibid.

190 It was forbidden by the Sacred Congregation of Rites to translate the Ordinary of the Mass. This legislation was renewed as late as 1857, though, as will be shown below, was widely ignored; cf. J. Jungmann SJ, *The Mass of the Roman Rite,* vol. I p. 161. Nevertheless in 1882 Cardinal Dechamps of Malines would scruple at the translation of the Canon for *Le Missel des Fidèles;* cf. A. Haquin, *Dom Lambert Beauduin et le Renouveau Liturgique,* pp. 9-11.

191 *The Roman Missal for the Use of the Laity,* Keating, Brown & Keating 1815: a daily missal with epistles and gospels in English and the introit in Latin and English in parallel columns on Sundays and feasts. On other days the introit is in English only, as are the other parts of the proper. The Order of Mass is in Latin and English in parallel columns. The book contains no devotional texts other than a page of "Resolutions" for use before and after Mass.

publishing houses continued to produce editions of the missal,[192] the breviary[193] and even the pontifical[194] for the use of the laity. The very availability of these volumes, and in some cases their prefaces, invited people to that "actual participation"[195] in the Liturgy about which the Liturgical Movement would say a great deal. Traces of this can be found as early as the seventeenth century.[196]

---

[192] In 1822 Bishop John England of Charleston, USA, published *The Roman Missal Translated into English for the Use of the Laity;* cf. John K. Ryan "Bishop England and the Missal in English" in: *American Ecclesiastical Review* vol. XCV pp. 28-36, cited in: O. Rousseau OSB, *The Progress of the Liturgy*, pp. 198-208. In England, the people's missal was popular: cf. F.C. Husenbath, *The Missal for the Use of the Laity with the Masses for All Days Throughout the Year According to the Roman Missal,* 1845. The numerous French people's missals (particularly given the many local usages prevalent until the latter part of the nineteenth century), are ample evidence that this was not solely an English-speaking phenomenon: cf. *Le Grand Paroissien Complet Contenant L'Office des Dimanches et Fêtes en Latin et Français Selon L'Usage de Paris,* 1839; *Nouveau Paroissien Romain Très-Complet A L'Usage Du Diocèse De Carcassonne Contenant en Français et en Latin Les Offices De Tous Les Dimanches et De Toutes Les Fêtes De L'Année Qui Peuvent Se Célébrer Le Dimanche,* 1874. The dates of these missals belie the 1989 claim: "About 100 years ago there appeared a 'People's Missal' created by the pioneers of the Liturgical Movement;" J. Lang, *Dictionary of the Liturgy,* p. 433. B. Spurr, *Word in the Desert,* pp. 17-18, also appears unaware of the early genesis of the bilingual people's missal.

[193] John, Marquess of Bute, *The Roman Breviary.*

[194] *The Roman Pontifical for the Use of the Laity: Part II The Ordination Service,* 1848. This volume, in the author's collection, carries an advertisement envisaging the publication of eight further volumes from the pontifical, and is bound with *The Service for the Consecration of a Church in English and Latin* (no date). The British Library catalogue includes some such volumes, though they are missing due to war damage sustained in 1941.

[195] The Second Vatican Council's *Constitution on the Sacred Liturgy: Sacrosanctum Concilium,* n. 14; *Acta, vol. II Pars. VI,* p. 414, used *actuosa participatio,* which when translated "actual participation," is less misleading than the usual English rendering "active participation." This underlines that the participation in the liturgical rites and prayers is primarily through mind and heart and secondarily through external action. Cf. J. Ratzinger, *The Feast of Faith: Approaches to a Theology of the Liturgy,* pp. 68ff; G. Shirilla, *The Principle of Active Participation of the Faithful in Sacrosanctum Concilium,* pp. 356-357.

[196] Apart from the practices condemned at the Synod of Pistoia, in England, the order of Mass printed in *A Collection of Prayers Containing the Mass in Latin and English,* 1688, besides including the text in both Latin and English, instructs the people to answer the priest at the prayers at the foot of the altar and at the *suscipiat* in the offertory. Crichton mentions a similar example printed in 1676; cf. *Lights in Darkness,* pp. 65-67. These practices appear to have avoided censure.

In England Nicholas Cardinal Wiseman worked to promote liturgical piety as a seminary rector,[197] and as a bishop from 1840 onwards. Of the missal he went as far as to say:

> Catholics, in general, learn far too little of it; and we do not hesitate to say, that he who knows it not, cannot have any idea of half the grandeur of his religion. Why there is not a place, or a thing, used in the worship which he attends upon which there has not been lavished, so to speak, more rich poetry and more solemn prayers, than all our modern books put together can furnish.[198]

And of the use of parts of the breviary by the laity he believed:

> Such are the...prayers which the Church has drawn up for her children; and, for our part, we can wish for nothing better. We know not where an improvement could be suggested; and, therefore, we see not why anything should have been substituted for them.[199]

Wiseman uses the language of a campaigner when he says that:

> The family united in prayer should speak the very language of the Church; should observe the forms of devotion which she has herself drawn up and approved; and, as in good discipline, in spiritual affection, in communion of good works, in mutual encouragement to virtue, so likewise in the regularity and in the order of prayer, assimilate itself to those religious communities which, in every part of the Christian world, praise God in her name, and under her especial sanction. We strongly suspect, that many who will join the Church, will hail with joy every such return, however imperfect, to the discipline and practice of the ancient Church; they will warm to us the more in proportion to our zeal for the restoration of its discipline.[200]

We have noted the centrality of liturgical piety to Guéranger. The general preface to *L'Année Liturgique* is a treatise of abiding value:

> The Prayer of the Church is...the most pleasing to the ear and heart of God, and therefore the most efficacious of all prayers. Happy, then, is he who prays with the Church, and unites his own petitions with those of this Bride...

---

197 Cf. N. Wiseman, *Four Lectures on the Offices and Ceremonies of Holy Week*.

198 "On Prayer and Prayer Books," from *The Dublin Review*, Nov. 1842, in: N. Wiseman, *Essays on Various Subjects*, vol. I p. 404.

199 Ibid., p. 395.

200 Ibid., p. 396. Cf. pp. 386-389 & 420-421. A postscript (p. 430) remarks "When this article was written, it was impossible to foresee how many of the desires expressed in it would be granted by a merciful Providence," no doubt rejoicing in the type of the publications noted above. A less precise presentation of Wiseman's views, suffering from the effects of translation into French and back again, is in: O. Rousseau OSB, *The Progress of the Liturgy*, pp. 95-96.

> Prayer said in union with the Church is the light of the understanding, it is the fire of the divine love for the heart. The Christian soul neither needs nor wishes to avoid the company of the Church when she would converse with God...
>
> Liturgical prayer would soon become powerless were the faithful not to take a real share in it, or, at least not to associate themselves to it in heart. It can heal and save the world, but only on the condition that it be understood.[201]

He continued with words that Johnson enthusiastically regards as "the signal which marks the beginning of the modern Liturgical Movement:"

> Open your hearts, children of the Catholic Church, and come and pray the prayer of your Mother.[202]

This sentiment was the kernel not only of the life of Solesmes, but of the activity of the twentieth century Liturgical Movement, many of the leaders of which imbibed liturgical piety either personally at Solesmes, or in monasteries whose founders had. These included: the Benedictine monastery of Beuron, Germany, founded in 1863 by the two brothers, Maurus and Placidus Wolter; Beuron's German daughter house Maria Laach,[203] re-founded in 1893; Beuron's Belgian daughter, the abbey of

---

[201] P. Guéranger, *The Liturgical Year: Advent*, pp. 2, 3, 6-7. A careful reading of this preface, and the popular success of *The Liturgical Year,* suggests that the conclusion of E. Koenker in *The Liturgical Renaissance in the Catholic Church*, that Dom Guéranger's work "did not involve bringing the Liturgy to the masses as does the work of the modern movement," and that "it did not aim at general participation" is overly harsh; cf. p. 11. K. Pecklers' assertion that "Guéranger failed to promote the fundamental liturgical principle of 'full and active liturgical participation by the whole assembly;'" must also be contested; "History of the Roman Liturgy from the Sixteenth until the Twentieth Centuries" p. 166. Recently D. Torevell, whose sources on Dom Guéranger are decidedly secondary, and who misnames him "Pierre" throughout his work, argues that the preoccupation of the later twentieth century Liturgical Movement that the Liturgy had "to be intelligible" and "participation established through understanding" is to be found in Dom Guéranger's liturgical theology; cf. *Losing the Sacred* pp. 119-122. In the light of the principles of liturgical reform present in Dom Guéranger's exposition of the anti-liturgical heresy, we must reject any interpretation that suggests that Guéranger sought that the Liturgy be rendered intelligible as this term was frequently understood following the Second Vatican Council (vernacularism, radical ritual recasting and simplification, etc.).

[202] C. Johnson OSB's translation, *Prosper Guéranger (1805-1875): A Liturgical Theologian,* p. 350; French: "Dilatez donc vos coeurs, enfants de l'Eglise catholique, et venez prier de la prière de votre Mère."

[203] Cf. G. Ellard SJ, "'A Spiritual Citadel of the Rhineland,' Maria Laach and the Liturgical Movement" in: *OF* vol. III pp. 384-388.

Maredsous, founded in 1872; Farnborough established by Solesmes monks in 1895, and Maredsous' daughter house, Mont-César, in 1899.[204]

Amongst the contributions of these abbeys, Dom Gérard van Caloen of Maredsous' publication in 1882 of the *Missel des Fidèles,* a Latin-French people's missal was significant. An attempt to facilitate liturgical piety by making the Mass intelligible to the laity, its introductions and explanations rendered it more than simply a missal. Haquin points out that whilst "*L'Année Liturgique* of Dom Guéranger was a small liturgical encyclopaedia, the *Missel des Fidèles* is a book on the Mass."[205] Its popularity[206] assisted the widespread promotion of liturgical piety.

In the 1860s an Italian curate in Tombolo (Trentino), began to teach his choir Gregorian chant and to encourage the congregation to sing.[207] In his first parish, Salzano, he started a school for Latin and ecclesiastical music.[208] From 1875 as a cathedral canon and seminary professor, eventually as rector, teaching Liturgy was one of his many duties.[209] As Bishop of Mantua (1884-1893) he included ecclesiastical music and Gregorian chant amongst the topics for his 1888 diocesan synod.[210] Two years after Giuseppe Sarto's arrival in Venice as Cardinal Patriarch in 1895 he issued a pastoral letter on ecclesiastical music, promoting Gregorian chant, polyphonic music appropriate to liturgical worship (e.g. Palestrina rather than baroque and operatic compositions), and again, congregational singing. The future St Pius X's conviction was that music in the Liturgy must serve the general purpose of the Liturgy ("the worship of God and the edification of the people"), and conform to the "specific purpose of chant and sacred music which is to stir up a greater devotion in the faithful by way of these melodies and to dispose the faithful to receive the fruits of grace with greater alacrity, which is only appropriate to the solemn celebration of the holy mysteries."[211]

---

[204] O. Rousseau OSB relates the central rôle of Solesmes in forming monks and other persons in liturgical piety. See *The Progress of the Liturgy,* pp. 14-15, 69-72, 98. Also: K. Pecklers SJ, *The Unread Vision,* pp. 1-4; A. Haquin, *Dom Lambert Beauduin et le Renouveau Liturgique,* pp. 1-27.

[205] "*L'Année Liturgique* de Dom Guéranger était une petite encyclopédie liturgique, le *Missel des Fidèles* est un livre de Messe;" *Dom Lambert Beauduin et le Renouveau Liturgique,* p. 11. Also O. Rousseau OSB, *The Progress of the Liturgy,* pp. 99-100.

[206] Cf. A. Haquin, *Dom Lambert Beauduin et le Renouveau Liturgique,* p. 13.

[207] Cf. K. Burton, *The Great Mantle,* p. 41.

[208] Cf. L. von Matt & N. Vian, *St Pius X,* p. 25.

[209] Cf. K. Burton, *The Great Mantle,* p. 61.

[210] Ibid., p. 80.

[211] "...al *fine generale* della stessa liturgia, che è l'onore di Dio e l'edificazione dei fedeli, sia al *fine speciale* del canto e della musica sacra, che è di eccitare per mezzo della melodia i fedeli alla devozione, e disporli ad accogliere con maggore alacrità in sè medesimi i frutti della grazia, che sono proprii dei santi misteri

This is but another example of the emergence, by the end of the nineteenth century, of a principle of liturgical reform, which we may call the principle of liturgical piety. It seeks not to reform the liturgical rites and prayers, but the spiritual dispositions and practices of the Catholic faithful. A correct understanding of this principle, and of its origins, is essential for any evaluation of twentieth century liturgical reform.

John Henry Cardinal Newman

Preaching on January 1st 1831 "On Ceremonies of the Church," John Henry Newman enunciated the importance of continuity in liturgical forms:

> Granting that the forms are not immediately from God, still long use has made them divine *to us*; for the spirit of religion has so penetrated and quickened them, that to destroy them is, in respect to the multitude of men, to unsettle and dislodge the religious principle itself. In most minds usage has so identified them with the notion of religion, that the one cannot be extirpated without the other. Their faith will not bear transplanting...
>
> The services and ordinances of the Church are the outward form in which religion has been for ages represented to the world, and has ever been known to us. Places consecrated to God's honour, clergy carefully set apart for His service, the Lord's-day piously observed, the public forms of prayer, the decencies of worship, these things viewed as a whole, are *sacred* relatively to us, even if they were not, as they are, divinely sanctioned. Rites which the Church has appointed...being long used cannot be disused without harm to our souls.[212]

Whilst this is Anglican High Church apologetic, it is also an accurate articulation of the Catholic principle of respect for developed liturgical Tradition, displaying the Catholic tendencies of this member of the Oxford movement.

In 1845 Newman sent his *Essay on the Development of Christian Doctrine* to the printer (shortly afterwards he was received into the Catholic Church). Its principles, already present early in theological

---

solennemente celebrati;" A. Nero, *Quaderni della Fondazione Giuseppe Sarto,* p. 66. Sarto's promotion of liturgical piety from the poor of Tombolo to the gondoliers of Venice was inspired by liturgical and musical ideals of Guéranger: "Musicien, professeur de chant depuis son séminaire, Pie X était très au courant de la question grégorienne et des travaux de Solesmes;" M. Sablayrolles, "Le Chant Grégorien" in: R. Aigrain, *Liturgia*, p. 452.

212 Sermon on the Feast of the Circumcision of the Lord, *Parochial and Plain Sermons,* vol. II pp. 75, 77-78.

tradition,[213] are applicable to the development of the Liturgy. Newman states that:

> An eclectic, conservative, assimilating, healing, moulding process, a unitive power, is of the essence...of a faithful development...
>
> A doctrine, then...is likely to be a true development, not a corruption, in proportion as it seems to be the *logical issue* of its original teaching.[214]

The consonance with the principle of the organic development of the Liturgy is clear.[215]

Anglican Orders

Following Leo XIII's[216] 1896 Apostolic Letter *Apostolicæ Curæ* on Anglican orders, the Archbishops of Canterbury and York addressed a response to the Cardinal Archbishop and the bishops of the Province of Westminster. In 1898 the Catholic bishops replied. Their letter considers the legitimacy of the various Anglican reforms to the ordinal by re-stating Catholic principles of liturgical reform. To the charge that Sacred Scripture left no precise instructions for what is essential for ordination, and with an obvious concern to ensure the validity of the ordination rite, they reply:

---

213 St Vincent of Lérins (d. c. 450) speaks eloquently of dogmatic development and continuity: "Is there to be no development of doctrine in Christ's Church? Certainly there should be great development.
Who could be so grudging towards his fellow-men and so hostile to God as to try to prevent it? But care should be taken to ensure that it really is development of the faith and not alteration. Development implies that each point of doctrine is expanded within itself, while alteration suggests that a thing has been changed from what it was into something different.
It is desirable then that development should take place, and that there should be a great and vigorous growth in the understanding, knowledge and wisdom of every individual as well as of all the people, on the part of each member as well as of the whole Church, gradually over the generations and ages. But it must be growth within the limits of its own nature, that is to say within the framework of the same dogma and of the same meaning.
Let religion, which is of the spirit, imitate the processes of the body. For, although bodies develop over the years and their individual parts evolve, they do not change into something different..." *Commonitories*, chapter 23; cited in: *The Divine Office*, vol. III pp. 626-627.

214 *An Essay on the Development of Christian Doctrine*, pp. 186, 195.

215 For a further treatment of Newman on the development of doctrine, cf. I. Ker, *Newman on Being a Christian*, pp. 31-38.

216 Leo XIII had revised the missal by simplifying the calendar slightly in 1884.

> But if it were true that our only sources of guidance have left us in ignorance of the essentials of a valid Ordinal, surely the inference would be, not that National Churches (or, as we should prefer to call them, Local Churches) are at liberty to cut themselves loose from a constant Tradition, and unfettered by any other restrictions to devise Ordinals according to the requirements of their own local conceptions, but rather that they must not omit or reform anything in those forms which immemorial Tradition has bequeathed to us. For such an immemorial usage, whether or not it has in the course of ages incorporated superfluous accretions, must, in the estimation of those who believe in a divinely guarded, visible Church, at least have retained whatever is necessary; so that in adhering rigidly to the rite handed down to us we can always feel secure; whereas, if we omit or change anything, we may perhaps be abandoning just that element which is essential.[217]

They continue, witnessing to the organic development of the Liturgy throughout history, and enunciating the respect that must be shown to the Liturgy as an organic whole:

> That in earlier times local Churches were permitted to *add* new prayers and ceremonies is acknowledged...But that they were also permitted to *subtract* prayers and ceremonies in previous use, and even to remodel the existing rites in the most drastic manner, is a proposition for which we know of no historical foundation, and which appears to us absolutely incredible.[218]

Historical Research

The continued growth of historical liturgical research, linked with the renaissance of patristic studies, another nineteenth century phenomenon (by no means solely English), raised the academic profile of liturgical studies, yielding more and more historical material. The development of the Roman rite throughout the exigencies of history could be studied in ever-greater detail, and we have drawn upon their labours above. The work of Bishop and the foundation of the Henry Bradshaw Society in 1890 with the aim of editing and publishing rare liturgical texts are leading English examples.[219]

---

217 Cardinal Archbishop and Bishops of the Province of Westminster, *A Vindication of the Bull 'Apostolicæ Curæ,'* p. 42.

218 Ibid., pp. 43-44.

219 Bishop was invited to be involved in the foundation of the Henry Bradshaw Society by J. Wickham Legg; cf. N. Abercrombie, *The Life and Work of Edmund Bishop,* pp. 161-162. The Society, predominantly Anglican, was a scholarly tributary which fed into the Liturgical Movement, and gives evidence of early ecumenical collaboration. The Society's publications, themselves of wide interest,

Conclusion

At the close of the nineteenth century a healthy respect for the Roman rite as a developed organic reality exists. Batiffol wrote:

> The Roman breviary is, in its main lines, the old edifice which was completed in the eighth century. And if, from the ninth century to the thirteenth, from the thirteenth to the fifteenth, too many hands have been busy in decorating, modifying and encumbering it, at all events in the sixteenth century it was saved by the prudence of Paul IV, Pius V and Clement VIII from the plans of arbitrary restoration or disastrous reconstruction proposed by Leo X and Clement VII, even though it did not afterwards escape the embellishments of Urban VIII. In this living work, still the rule and canon of our prayers, the edifice of the eighth century is standing yet.[220]

Dom Baudot, quoting the work of Dom Bäumer, wrote similarly:

> The unity of liturgical Tradition...has not suffered from those lawful changes through which the office has passed in the course of centuries. "The official prayer-book of the Church has remained in its main features the same as prescribed by St Pius V. Essentially his breviary was the same as that of Innocent III and the pontifical chapel of the thirteenth century, which, in its turn, was only an abridgement of the public office recited during the eighth, ninth, tenth and eleventh centuries in the Roman basilicas, and the cathedrals of France, Germany and England...Leo III and Charlemagne never dreamed they were reciting any other office, a few additions apart, than that prescribed by St Gregory the Great or his disciples. The work of Gregory was nothing else than a codification and abridgement of the canonical hours recited during the fourth, fifth, and sixth centuries in Rome, throughout Italy, and even in other countries. Thus the canonical hours are a magnificent growth of divine service, the germ of which had been planted in apostolic times: it is the living development of ritual devotions which have their root in the needs of the human heart and in the relations of the man and of the Christian with his Creator and Redeemer."[221]

Fortescue wrote similarly about the missal.[222]

The Roman rite arrived at this point in history much developed indeed, but still that living organism that was the Roman Liturgy of the

---

often involved cross-confessional collaboration; cf. the 1899 publication: *Missale Romanum 1474,* involving the Ambrosian Library in Milan.

220 *History of the Roman Breviary* (1898), p. 354.

221 *The Roman Breviary,* pp. 237-238.

222 Cf. supra, p. 34.

first Christian millennium. The developments had been prompted in part by necessity, and in part by the vicissitudes of history. Care had been taken to respect objective liturgical Tradition and to develop it organically. Reforms that were not organic were eventually proscribed.[223]

---

223 Though the reversal of Urban VIII's reform of the breviary hymns had to wait until the twentieth century.

Chapter 2

The Liturgical Movement and Liturgical Reform up to 1948

Introduction

GIUSEPPE Alberigo and Joseph Komonchak's recent and comprehensive five-volume *History of Vatican II* presents the Liturgical Movement thus:

> The period just before the first world war saw the birth, in Belgium, of a Liturgical Movement. Originating with the Benedictines, it experienced considerable growth first in Germany and then in France, before moving more or less easily into other areas of the Catholic world. Like its biblical counterpart, with which it cultivated close relations, this Movement aimed at transcending what it called the rubricism of the preceding century with its fussiness and rigidity and its demand for uniformity. This Movement, too, turned back to the early Church with a view to restoring venerable ways and putting an end to the countless later additions, a work of learned dust removal that occupied many monasteries. The Movement also attempted to derive from all this work a theology of prayer...Finally, this Movement made an effort to change passive believers into active participants, both by emphasising the principal rites at the expense of the others and by explaining them and even celebrating them in the language of the people.[1]

This account says more about the revisionism pervading post-conciliar liturgical thinking than it does about the Liturgical Movement, the origins of which do not lie in a reaction to rubricism. Nor was the Movement fundamentally antiquarian or vernacularist. It was (but certainly not "finally") a movement that sought to return liturgical piety to its rightful place in the life of the Church. Only later, and secondarily, would questions of appropriate reform arise.

---

[1] É. Fouilloux "The Antepreparatory Phase" in: vol. I pp. 86-87.

Pope St Pius X

On November 22nd 1903 St Pius X issued the *Motu Proprio, Tra le sollecitudini* on the restoration of ecclesiastical music.[2] Its fundamental principle became the cornerstone of the Liturgical Movement:

> It being our ardent desire to see the true Christian spirit restored in every respect and preserved by all the faithful, we deem it necessary to provide before everything else for the sanctity and dignity of the temple, in which the faithful assemble for the object of acquiring this spirit from its indispensable fount, which is *the active participation in the holy mysteries and in the public and solemn prayer of the Church.*[3]

Various acts of his pontificate applied this principle beyond the field of sacred music. In 1905 *Sacra Tridentina Synodus* declared that "frequent and daily communion...should be open to all the faithful."[4] *Quam singulari* of 1910 allowed children from the age of reason (approximately seven) to receive Holy Communion.[5]

The principle of active participation in the Liturgy promoted by St Pius X necessitated the reform of the quality of the celebration of the traditional Liturgy (purification in the case of decadent music,[6] improvement in quality in the case of slovenliness, etc.), and the reform of the people's attitude and practices to it. It did not directly encompass a reform of liturgical rites.

However, St Pius X shared the concerns of:

---

[2] His restoration was not *ex nihilo*: attempts at reform were made under Pius IX and Leo XIII. Cf. *Decreta Authentica Sacrorum Congregationis Rituum,* vol. III n. 3830, pp. 264-272. The exiled Benedictine community of Solesmes, resident at Appuldurcombe House, Isle of Wight, played a key rôle in its implementation; cf. L. Regnault, *Dom Paul Delatte: Lettres,* pp. 113ff.

[3] K. Seasoltz OSB, *The New Liturgy,* p. 4. Emphasis added. The original document is Italian: "Essendo infatti Nostro vivissimo desiderio che il vero spirito cristiano rifiorisca per ogni modo e si mantegna nei fedeli tutti, è necessario provvedere prima di ogni altra cosa alla santità e dignità del tempio, dove appunto i fedeli si radunano per attingere tale spirito dalla sua prima ed indispensabile fonte, che è la partecipazione attiva ai sacrosanti misteri e alla preghiera pubblica e solenne della Chiesa;" *Acta Sanctæ Sedis,* vol. XXXVI p. 331. The official Latin: "Etenim cum nihil Nobis potius sit et vehementer optemus ut virtus christianæ religionis floreat et in omnibus Christifidelibus firmior sit, templi decori provideatur oportet, ubi Christicolæ congregantur ut hoc virtutis spiritu ex priore fonte fruantur, quæ est participatio divinorum mysteriorum atque Ecclesiæ communium et solemnium precum;" *Acta Sanctæ Sedis,* vol. XXXVI p. 388.

[4] K. Seasoltz OSB, *The New Liturgy,* p. 13.

[5] Cf. ibid., pp. 17-22.

[6] Though some would criticise the uniformity of the chant imposed by St Pius X in a somewhat ultramontane manner, to the detriment of diverse interpretations practised hitherto; cf. M. Pérès, "The Choirmaster and His Liturgical Role" p. 176.

> A great number of bishops in various parts of the world [who] have sent expressions of their opinions...to the Apostolic See, and especially in the Vatican Council when they asked...that the ancient custom of reciting the whole psaltery [sic] within the week might be restored as far as possible, but in such a way that the burden should not be made any heavier for the clergy...[7]

Accordingly, *Divino afflatu* of 1911 promulgated a reform of the breviary and calendar.[8] It prudently tidied the breviary, restoring the integral weekly psalter, reasserting the priority of the temporal cycle over the sanctoral, as well as removing the daily obligation to various supplementary offices. It was a pastoral reform in that it sought not to overburden the parochial clergy.[9]

But it was also, according to Batiffol, "a root and branch reform," which radically rearranged the ancient arrangement of the Roman psalter for the breviary, which had affinities that "would seem to be Gallican of the late seventeenth and of the eighteenth centuries."[10] Batiffol regrets this indebtedness.[11] He similarly regrets the summary abolition of the ancient and universal tradition of the daily recitation of the *Laudate* psalms (148-150) at Lauds, and of the same psalms daily at Compline.[12]

In respect of the abolition of the *Laudate* psalms, Anton Baumstark is scathing in his critique:

> Down to the year 1911 there was nothing in the Christian Liturgy of such absolute universality as this practice in the morning office, and no doubt its universality was inherited from the worship of the Synagogue...Hence to the reformers of the *Psalterium Romanum* belongs the distinction of having brought to an end the universal observance of a liturgical practice which was followed, one can say, by the Divine Redeemer Himself during His life on earth.[13]

In respect of discarding the traditional psalms for Compline in 1915 Dom Cabrol regretted that:

---

[7] K. Seasoltz OSB, *The New Liturgy*, p. 24.

[8] Cf. ibid., pp. 22-26. The effect on the missal was minor, mainly due to the reform of the calendar.

[9] Cf. A. Hetherington, *Notes on the New Rubrics*, pp. 4-18; E. Burton, & E. Myers, *The New Psalter And Its Use;* S. Campbell FSC, *From Breviary to Liturgy of the Hours*, pp. 16-18. Dom Cabrol's *La Réforme du Bréviaire et du Calendrier* provides tables detailing the structure of the Roman breviary before and after the reform, as well as the Benedictine office.

[10] E. Bishop, *Liturgica Historica*, pp. 17-18. Bishop opines: "It is a great advance."

[11] Cf. *History of the Roman Breviary* (1912), p. 329.

[12] Cf. ibid., p. 327.

[13] *Comparative Liturgy*, p. 38.

> The hymns, psalms, antiphons and versicles of Lauds all proclaim the mystery of Christ's Resurrection, and the light which enlightens our souls. The reform of the Psalter in 1911 has not always preserved this liturgical idea.[14]

Later, Pius Parsch commented:

> It is rather amazing that despite the extremely conservative character of the Church, Pius X should have resolved upon this vast change which went counter to a practice of fifteen hundred years' standing.[15]

The Jesuit Robert Taft agrees: "For anyone with a sense of the history of the office, this was a shocking departure from almost universal Christian Tradition,"[16] whilst the Dominican liturgical historian, William Bonniwell, states bluntly: "in the revision of Pius X the venerable office of the Roman Church was gravely mutilated."[17] Crichton observes: "The boldness of the pope's step has not always been appreciated."[18]

The principles involved are important. St Pius X's overriding principle was to reform the breviary so that it might meet the needs of the clergy of the time. He judged that both a radical recasting of the psalter and the adoption of some of the Gallican proposals were appropriate in the light of this. As pope, whose supreme juridical authority had but recently been vigorously underlined at Vatican I, he held that he had the authority so to do. One may suggest that in an ultramontane age the personal wish of the pope, in itself laudable, may have contributed to the promulgation of a reform that did not take sufficient account of historical or liturgical principles.

Did this reform respect the fundamental principle of organic development? Or, did the pope exercise this authority without sufficient regard for liturgical Tradition? Contemporary commentaries do not raise this question, perhaps because anti-modernist measures stifled critical discussion of papal acts. In 1912 Batiffol hints at displeasure:

> The projects of Benedict XIV made us tremble...we applauded in its principles the criticism by Dom Guéranger of the Gallican modernism which gave us the Parisian breviary of 1736. And from all this it is evident that our aversion to change would tend to exclude from our view many practical considerations which belong to the present time.[19]

---

[14] "Introduction" to *The Day Hours of the Church,* pp. xxiv & xviii. For a more detailed commentary, and also his opinion on the reform of the compline psalms, see his *La Réforme du Bréviaire et du Calendrier*, pp. 54-55.
[15] "The Weekly Psalter of the Roman Breviary," in: *OF* vol. XIII p. 270.
[16] *The Liturgy of the Hours in East and West*, p. 312.
[17] *A History of the Dominican Liturgy*, p. 354. Bonniwell details the effect of this reform on the subsequent reform of the Dominican office; cf. pp. 347-358.
[18] *The Once and the Future Liturgy*, p. 11.
[19] *History of the Roman Breviary* (1912) p. 322; also pp. 325, 327, 329.

But Batiffol himself had a book placed on the *Index of Prohibited Books* in 1907.[20] This may account for his expressions of "joy."[21] Perhaps the most critical contemporary study was Dom Cabrol's 1912 *La Réforme du Bréviaire et du Calendrier*, but even with its regrets, this small work predicts that the reform's "immediate effect" will be "renewal of the Christian spirit."[22]

The reform of St Pius X is a practical one in the light of contemporary pastoral needs. Such needs can certainly be a valid component of organic development. If pastoral considerations were excluded, the living organism that is the Liturgy would be reduced to an archaism rambling throughout history. However, were pastoral needs to be the sole or overriding principle of reform, the objective traditional organism that is the Liturgy would be subjected to the mercy of each passing age. We have seen the effects of the efforts of Quignonez, of Urban VIII, and of the Gallicans, in whose reforms we find a disproportionate weight being given to one principle or set of principles above and beyond others.

For this reform, we cannot but conclude, with Batiffol, Parsch, Taft, et al., that St Pius X's abolition of ancient elements of the received Tradition was to the detriment of the Roman breviary and was unprecedented in liturgical history. This break with Tradition was not so great as to be complete: the structure of the breviary remained the same, the texts of the offices themselves were not completely recast, and the redistribution of the psalter followed traditional and not purely Gallican lines.[23]

Nevertheless, it was a singular moment in liturgical history. That a pope could discard ancient liturgical Tradition by sole virtue of his own authority is found nowhere in liturgical history before St Pius X. Lamentably, in a period where the prevalent ultramontanism led to the assumption that even prudential judgements of popes were unquestionably correct, St Pius X contravened that part of the principle of liturgical reform that obliges even popes to respect objective liturgical Tradition and to develop it organically.

St Pius X also foresaw that, in order to foster greater liturgical participation, some *emendation* of the Liturgy would be necessary. *Divino afflatu* includes the explicit statement that:

> It will be clear to everybody that by what we have here decreed we have taken the first step to the emendation of the Roman breviary and

---

[20] Cf. 1930 edition, pp. 42-43.
[21] Cf. *History of the Roman Breviary* (1912) p. 330.
[22] "L'effet immediat, nous ne craignons pas de le prédire, sera un renouveau de l'esprit chrétien;" p. 74.
[23] Cf. *History of the Roman Breviary* (1912) p. 327.

> the missal, but for this we shall appoint shortly a special council or commission.[24]

The commission did not get beyond a new edition of the breviary and the integration of the reform of the calendar into the missal,[25] hindered by both the death of St Pius X and the outbreak of war in 1914.[26]

St Pius X's call to restore liturgical piety to its rightful place in the life of the Church was a firm and particularly authoritative foundation on which others would build.[27] It must also be observed that his use of papal authority in the rearrangement of the breviary was also capable of providing an authoritative precedent for others.

Dom Lambert Beauduin & the Foundations of the Liturgical Movement

If St Pius X underlined the centrality of liturgical piety, the Liturgical Movement, of which Dom Lambert Beauduin was effectively the founder, strove to restore it to its rightful place.

A spiritual grandson of Guéranger, Beauduin was a thirty three-year-old priest from Liège who entered Mont-César in 1906. Dom Bernard Botte, a monk of Mont-César until 1980, met Beauduin in 1912. He recounts that Beauduin "discovered the Liturgy...only during his novitiate: in the celebration of the divine office and the Mass with this young, small community."[28]

The combination of this discovery and of his pastoral experience was articulated in a report "De Promovenda Sacra Liturgia" submitted to the General Chapter of the Beuron Benedictine Congregation in July 1909.[29] In September 1909 he presented the same insight in a

---

24 K. Seasoltz OSB, *The New Liturgy*, p. 25. "...nemo non vidit, per ea, qui hic a Nobis decreta sunt, primum Nos fecisse gradum ad Romani Breviarii et Missali emendationem: sed super tali causa proprium mox Consilium seu Commissionem, ut aiunt, eruditionem constituemus;" *Acta Apostolicæ Sedis*, vol. III 1911 p. 636. In *La Réforme du Bréviaire et du Calendrier* pp. 61-69, Dom Cabrol called for the augmentation of the weekday texts of the missal and a facultative expansion of the lectionary drawing upon ancient texts, as well as for the correction of Urban VIII's reform of the breviary hymns.

25 Cf. Pius X "Abhinc duos annos" 1913.

26 It was envisaged that it would be at least thirty years before the reform of the breviary would be completed; cf. *Sacra Rituum Congregatio*, Circular letter, 15 May 1912: "...putamus enim spatium ad minus triginta annorum necessarium, ut Breviarii reformatio feliciter absolvatur." S. Campbell FSC's *From Breviary to Liturgy of the Hours* does not mention this.

27 His initiatives and their effects are summarised in: G. Ellard SJ, *The Mass in Transition*, pp. 331-337.

28 *From Silence to Participation*, p. 15.

29 Cf. A. Haquin, *Dom Lambert Beauduin et le Renouveau Liturgique*, pp. 234-237.

communication to the Catholic Conference at Malines.[30] "This extraordinary man appealed courageously for a renewal of the liturgical life of the Church."[31] His paper "La vraie prière de l'Église"[32] earned the patronage of Cardinal Mercier, and the support of the historian Godefroid Kurth. Kurth had advocated liturgical piety at the Brussels Eucharistic Congress in 1898.[33] In response to Beauduin's appeal and Kurth's endorsement, the conference passed the following resolutions:

> 1. To emphasise the use of the vernacular missal as a book of piety and to popularise the complete text of at least Sunday Mass and Vespers by translating it into the vernacular;
>
> 2. To give a more liturgical character to popular piety, especially by the recitation of Complin [sic] as an evening prayer, by assistance at the parish High Mass and Vespers, by using the Mass prayers as a preparation for, and thanksgiving after, Holy Communion, by the restoration of ancient liturgical traditions in homes;
>
> 3. To work for a wider and more perfect use of Gregorian chant as desired by Pius X;
>
> 4. To promote annual retreats for parish choirs at some centre of liturgical life, as, for example, at the Abbey of Mont-César or at Maredsous.[34]

The ideas presented in his 1909 paper were developed and published by Beauduin in 1914 as *La Piété de L'Église*. Their kernel is Guéranger's liturgical theology, and they apply the fundamental principle of St Pius X to the whole life of the Church:

> It is impossible, therefore, to overemphasise the fact that souls seeking God must associate themselves as intimately and as frequently as possible with all the manifestations of the hierarchical priestly life which has just been described [the Liturgy], and which places them directly under the influence of the priesthood of Jesus Christ Himself.
>
> That is the primary law of the sanctity of souls. For all alike, wise and ignorant, infants and adults, lay and religious, Christians of the first and Christians of the twentieth century, leaders of an active or of a contemplative life, for *all the faithful of the Church without exception*, the greatest possible active and frequent participation in the priestly life of the visible hierarchy, according to the manner prescribed in the liturgical canons, is the *normal and infallible path* to a solid piety that is

---

30 B. Spurr, *The Word in the Desert*, p. 14, inaccurately describes it as a "liturgical conference."

31 T. Klauser, *A Short History of the Western Liturgy*, p. 122.

32 Cf. A. Haquin, *Dom Lambert Beauduin et le Renouveau Liturgique*, pp. 238-241.

33 Cf. S. Quitslund, *A Prophet Vindicated*, p. 19.

34 O. Rousseau OSB, *The Progress of the Liturgy*, 165.

sane, abundant, and truly Catholic, that makes them children of their holy mother the Church in the fullest sense of this ancient and Christian phrase.[35]

Beauduin clearly accepts that the Liturgy is an objective tradition capable of organic development:

> Above all the Liturgy is: 1. *One.* Unity of belief, of discipline, of common fellowship, must necessarily show itself in worship; and despite certain divergences the Liturgy is fundamentally, profoundly *one.* 2. *Traditional.* This unity must be realised also in point of time. The Church of today is the Church of all times and of all peoples; hence her Liturgy is traditional. This characteristic is so important that it receives precedence over that of uniformity, as is seen in the preservation of the Oriental rites. 3. *Living.* The former characteristic does not make of the Liturgy a fossilised antique, a museum curiosity. The Liturgy *lives* and unfolds itself also today and, because universal, is of the twentieth century as well as of the first. It lives and follows the dogmatic and organic developments of the Church herself.[36]

Bouyer argues that Beauduin thus "augmented" the inheritance of Guéranger "by the discovery of a most important principle:"

> That we must not try to provide an artificial congregation to take part in an antiquarian Liturgy, but rather to prepare the actual congregations of the Church today to take part in the truly traditional Liturgy rightly understood.[37]

Thus, the Liturgical Movement was not founded in order to create oases of medieval liturgical splendour or archaeological delight, but to nourish everyday Christian life by *participation in the Liturgy*

---

[35] L. Beauduin OSB, *Liturgy the Life of the Church* (2002 edition) pp. 15-16; "On ne saurait donc trop inculquer aux âmes qui cherchent Dieu de s'associer aussi intimement et aussi fréquemment que possible à toutes les manifestations de cette vie sacerdotale hiérarchique que nous venons décrire et qui nous met directement sous l'influence de sacerdoce de Jésus-Christ. Telle est la loi primordiale de la santeté des âmes. Pour tous, savants et ignorants, enfants et hommes faits, séculiers et religieux, chrétiens des premiers siècles et chrétiens de XXe, actifs et contemplatifs, pour *tous les fidèles de l'Eglise catholique sans exception,* la participation la plus active et la plus fréquente possible à la vie sacerdotale de la hiérarchie visible, selon les modalités fixées par celle-ci dans son canon liturgique, constitue *le régime normal et infallible* qui assurera, dans l'Église du Christ, une piété solide, saine, abondante et vraiment catholique; qui fera de nous, dans toute la force de l'ancienne et si chrétienne expression, les enfants de notre Mère la sainte Église;" *La Piété de L'Église,* p. 8. Its 1926 publication by Dom Virgil Michel as the first volume of his *Popular Liturgical Library,* underlines its importance as the Movement's foundational charter.

[36] Ibid., p. 34.

[37] *Life and Liturgy,* pp. 14-15.

celebrated in local churches and chapels. In its origins it sought to awaken people's consciousness, including, and primarily, that of the clergy, to the Church's traditional spiritual treasury that was widely ignored. As one of its American pioneers declaimed in 1929:

> Why do we speak of a liturgical revival? Has the Church perhaps lost her Liturgy? Surely not. Because without it the Church could not live, no more than a body can live without its soul, for the Liturgy is the very soul and life of the Church. We speak of a Liturgical Movement because for centuries we have been too far removed from this divine furnace and its all penetrating sacred fire. We have always felt some of its heat, but not enough to get warm. We were chilled by a degenerated humanism and rationalism and frost-bitten by materialism and religious indifference. We lost a goodly portion of the *sentire cum Ecclesia*—the mind of the Church; and, by and by, quite a bit of our living the liturgical life of the Church.[38]

Significantly, Dom Bernard Botte states:

> We should note that the Liturgical Movement, at its beginning, was not a reformist movement. Dom Beauduin knew very well that there were some cobwebs on that venerable monument called Liturgy. One day or another these would have to be dusted away. But he did not consider this as essential and, at any rate, it was not his business...He regarded the Liturgy as a traditional given which we first of all had to try to understand.[39]

This stands in sharp contrast to the (revisionist) view of Crichton who asserts that Beauduin's 1909 paper was:

> The beginning of the *pastoral* Liturgical Movement…Beauduin himself had been a priest in a parish…like many others he realised the defects of the Liturgy and the impoverishment of the people because they couldn't latch on to it.[40]

Crichton distinguishes "pastoral" from what he calls the "monastic" Liturgical Movement, and asserts that henceforth the Movement sought to change the Liturgy to accommodate pastoral needs. As the literature of the period makes clear, the former distinction was not made, and the latter intention was not present.[41] This clarification is fundamental. As we shall see, the Movement considered ritual reform, but such was not its primary aim.

---

[38] M. Hellriegel, "A survey of the Liturgical Movement," in: *OF* vol. III p. 334.
[39] Ibid., pp. 22-23.
[40] Interview by the author of J.D. Crichton, 24th August 1994.
[41] The term "pastoral Liturgical Movement" is more properly a post world war II phenomenon.

The essence of the Movement is articulated in the detailed "plan of action" published in *La Piété de L'Église*. It expands on the Malines resolutions, and puts flesh on the principles outlined previously:

> The central idea to be realised by the Liturgical Movement is the following: "To have the Christian people all live the same spiritual life, to have them all nourished by the official worship of holy mother Church."
>
> The means to be employed towards this end are of two kinds. The first have reference to the acts of worship itself; the others to the liturgical activity exercised outside these acts.
>
> *The Acts of Worship.* In this field, the members of the Liturgical Movement desire to contribute with all their strength to the attainment of the following aims:
> 1. The active participation of the Christian people in the Holy Sacrifice of the Mass by means of understanding and following the liturgical rites and texts.[42]
> 2. Emphasis of the importance of high Mass and of Sunday parish services, and assistance at the restoration of collective liturgical singing in the official gatherings of the faithful.
> 3. Seconding of all efforts to preserve or to re-establish the Vespers and Compline of the Sunday, and to give those services a place second only to that of the Holy Sacrifice of the Mass.
> 4. Acquaintance, and active association, with the rites and sacraments received or assisted at, and the spread of this knowledge among others.
> 5. Fostering a great respect for, and confidence in, the blessings of our Mother Church.
> 6. Restoration of the Liturgy of the Dead to a place of honour, observance of the custom of Vigils and Lauds, giving greater solemnity to the funeral services, and getting the faithful to assist thereat, thus efficaciously combating the dechristianising of the rite of the dead.
>
> *Liturgical Activity outside of cultural[43] acts.* In this field there are four ways in which the members can assist at the furtherance of the Liturgical Movement:
>
> A. *Piety.*
> 1. Restoration to a place of honour among Christians of the traditional liturgical seasons: Advent, Christmas Time, Lent, Easter Time, octaves

[42] "Faire participer activement le peuple chrétien au Saint Sacrifice de la Messe en comprenant et en suivant les rites et les textes liturgiques;" *La Piété de L'Église*, p. 50.

[43] "...en dehors des actes cultuels;" ibid., p. 51. Better translated "outside acts of worship."

of feasts, feasts of the Blessed Virgin, the Apostles, and the great missionary saints of our religion.
2. The basing of our daily private devotions, meditation, reading, etc., on the daily instructions of the Liturgy, the Psalms, the other liturgical books, and the fundamental dogmas of Catholic worship.
3. Reanimation and sublimation of the devotions dear to the people by nourishing them at the source of the Liturgy.

B. *Study.*
1. Promotion of the scientific study of the Catholic Liturgy.
2. Popularisation of the scientific knowledge in special reviews and publications.
3. Promotion of the study and, above all, the practice of liturgical prayers in educational institutions.
4. Aiming to give regular liturgical education to circles, associations, etc., and to employ all the customary methods of popularisation to this end.

C. *Arts*
1. Promoting the application of all the instructions of Pius X in his *Motu proprio* on Church music.
2. Aiming to have the artists that are called to exercise a sacred art, architecture, painting, sculpture, etc., receive an education that will give them an understanding of the spirit and the rules of the Church's Liturgy.
3. Making known to artists and writers the fruitful inspiration to art that the Church offers in her Liturgy.

D. *Propaganda*
1. Using all means to spread popular liturgical publications that show the import of the principal part of the Liturgy: Sunday Mass, Vespers, Sacraments, Liturgy of the Dead, etc.
2. Reawakening the old liturgical traditions in the home, that link domestic joys with the calendar of the Church, and using for this end especially the musical works composed for such purposes.

To all Catholics we address a burning appeal in favour of the activities that aim to realise as far as possible the program of liturgical restoration we have here outlined.[44]

To this end the Liturgical Movement promoted the dialogue Mass,[45] people's editions of the missal[46] and other liturgical books,[47] and

---

[44] *Liturgy the Life of the Church* (2002) pp. 52-53.

[45] Cf. G. Ellard SJ, "'Tiptoe on a Misty Mountain Top:' Thoughts on the Dialog Mass" in: *OF* vol. IV pp. 394-399, and *The Dialog Mass*. Emphasis on the oral participation of the congregation, which became one of its distinguishing features, probably contributed to a distortion in understanding the active

participation called for by St Pius X and promoted by Beauduin et al. as primarily external participation.

[46] In 1921 Benedict XV congratulated Marietti, the Italian publishers: "There are two reasons why the devotion of the people does not progress as it should from the hearing of Mass, namely, the ignorance of Latin and ignorance of the Liturgy; to both of these evils you apply the remedy by this volume, and it is well indeed that you do so in favour of the Italians, who up to now have been quite without such an aid;" cited in: G. Ellard SJ, *The Mass in Transition*, p. 340. "Cum igitur duæ sint fere causæ cur pietas popularis non adeo quod potest, Missam freqentando proficiat, ignoratio scilicet linguæ latinæ et liturgiæ, utrique rei te videmus, occurrere hoc volumine; quod quidem optimo consilio est a te confectum in gratiam Italorum, utpote qui huius generis subsidio prorsus indigerent." A. Bugnini CM, *Documenta,* p. 54. The most famous was the *Saint Andrew Daily Missal* produced during the first world war by Dom Gaspar Lefebvre of the Belgian abbey of St André and widely translated; cf. B. Botte OSB, *From Silence to Participation,* p. 34. For an early account of this abbey's involvement in the Liturgical Movement see: G. Ellard SJ, "From a Pilgrim's Notebook: St André by Bruges" in: *OF* vol. IV pp. 301-305. Archbishop Hinsley's 1937 preface to its 1940 English edition captures the importance of the missal: "A re-issue of the Daily Missal is a welcome sign of the renewal of liturgical piety among Catholics. The Church is calling all her children to a deeper understanding of her Sacred Liturgy. It is her wish that all the Catholic people should take an active part in the sublime sacrifice of the Mass, joining together with heart, mind and voice in the corporate prayer of the Church. May the unity of Catholics in offering the Mass, the central act of our religion, inspire us to a holier life, and to a restoration in human affairs of the rule of Christian charity and social justice. The Daily Missal, which besides the Ordinary and the Proper of the Mass throughout the year includes the liturgical offices of Prime, Vespers and Compline, should be of assistance to those who wish to pray with the Church. It is my earnest desire that those who use this missal may find in the Liturgy the road to sanctification and the love of Christ;" *Saint Andrew Daily Missal,* p. v. An edition was prepared for military personnel during the second world war. The preface speaks of the plea of St Pius X for "active participation," and of how this missal "will help in the field to understand and take part in the Liturgy at the Altar;" cf. J. Steedman, *My Military Missal,* p. 5. Steedman was the editor of *My Sunday Missal,* popular in the USA from its first edition in 1932. The *Denver Register* of September 26, 1943, reported that "more than 1,000,000 copies of *My Military Missal*...are now being used;" cf. Coppersmith, "Liturgy and the Armed Forces," in: The Liturgical Conference, *National Liturgical Week (USA) 1943,* p. 144. The people's missal may be said to have reached its apotheosis with the publication in 1957 of *Mass and Vespers with Gregorian Chant for Sundays and Holy Days: Latin and English text* edited by Benedictines of the Solesmes Congregation. In 1956 G. Ellard SJ, declared: "...missals for the laity have become so commonplace it is hard to think of anything else;" *The Mass in Transition*, p. 153.

[47] Cf. The Benedictine Monks of Farnborough, *The Layfolk's Ritual* (The introduction to this splendid volume states that "the present volume will be followed by *The Layfolk's Pontifical;*" p. viii. This does not appear to have been published.); *The Holy Week Book,* The Benedictine Nuns of Stanbrook, *The Day*

liturgical periodicals.[48] It held liturgical weeks,[49] established schools of liturgical music[50] and eventually institutes of academic liturgical study.[51]

Hours of the Church; The Benedictine Nuns of Stanbrook & C. F. Brown, *The Roman Breviary*, parts I-IV.

48 *Questions liturgiques et paroissiales* began at Mont-César in 1911, aimed at parish clergy; *Rivista Liturgica* commenced in 1914 "dedicated to enlisting the interest of lay people in the Liturgy;" G. Ellard SJ, *The Mass in Transition*, p. 338; cf. F. Brovelli, *Ritorno alla liturgia*, pp. 236-241. In 1916 *Ons Liturgisch Tidschrift*, was published by the Priest's Interdiocesan Liturgical League of Holland. In 1918 the series *Ecclesia Orans* was launched by Maria Laach. Later that year the same abbey inaugurated a series of volumes dedicated to liturgical research: *Liturgiegeschichtliche Quellen*; cf. G. Ellard SJ, *The Mass in Transition* pp. 338-339. In 1923 the Italian *Bollettino Liturgico* was launched; In 1926 the major English-language journal *Orate Fratres*, was launched at St John's Abbey, Collegeville, USA. Michel wrote: "Our general aim is to develop a better understanding of the spiritual import of the Liturgy...We are not aiming at a cold scholastic interest in the Liturgy of the Church, but at an interest that is more thoroughly intimate, that seizes upon the entire person, ...affect[s] both the individual spiritual life of the Catholic and the corporate life of the natural social units of the Church, the parishes..." P. Marx OSB, *Virgil Michel and the Liturgical Movement*, p. 124. 1926 saw the publication of the Portuguese *Opus Dei* and of Parsch's *Bibel und Liturgie* at Klosterneuberg; in 1927 *L'Artisan Liturgique* was published in Belgium; 1929 brought forth *Liturgische Zeitschrift* in Berlin and *Mysterium Christi* in Poland, and saw *Liturgy* launched by the newly formed English Society of Saint Gregory; the Turin-based *Liturgia* commenced in 1933; Germany added *Liturgisches Leben* in 1934; the USA added *Living Parish* in 1941; Spain offered *Liturgia* from 1944; in 1945 the French *La Maison-Dieu* [hereafter *LMD*] appeared; Portugal contributed *Ora et Labora* in 1953. The periodicals and the increasing number of scholarly works devoted to liturgical piety, served to inform and support the endeavours of the Movement, particularly those isolated from the monastic or other liturgical centres, and to recruit others to its ideals.

49 Liturgical Weeks were organised at Mont-César from 1910, and at Maredsous, in French, from 1912. cf. *Cours et Conférences de la Semaine Liturgique de Maredsous 19-24 Août 1912; Des Semaines Liturgiques: Louvain du 10 au 14 Août 1913.* They resumed following the war, and provided opportunities for the exchange of ideas and formed newcomers: the Belgian weeks recommenced in 1924; cf. *Cours et Conférences des Semaines Liturgiques: Tome III – Congrès Liturgique Malines du 4 au 7 Août 1924; Cours et Conférences des Semaines Liturgiques: Tome IV – La Paroisse: Louvain du 10 au 13 Août 1925; Cours et Conférences des Semaines Liturgiques: Tome V – La Sainte Messe: Huy 1926; Cours et Conférences des Semaines Liturgiques: Tome VI – La Préparation de l'Eucharistie: Louvain du 1 au 4 Août 1927; Cours et Conférences des Semaines Liturgiques: Tome VII – Le Canon de la Messe: Tournai du 25 au 29 Juillet 1928; Cours et Conférences des Semaines Liturgiques: Tome VIII – Tables (1912-1928).* V. Michel OSB organised a liturgical day in Collegeville in 1929; Canada held its first Liturgical Week in 1931; cf. "The Apostolate" in: *OF* vol. V pp. 343-344. In 1940 the first USA Liturgical Week was held in Chicago, continuing annually until 1967; in 1944 a congress to study pastoral Liturgy was held at Vanves; 1945 saw both the first national liturgical conference in France and Canada's first

The literature generated by the activity of the Liturgical Movement is vast. We focus on its discussion of liturgical reform and the principles articulated therein.

Joseph Göttler

In 1916, Göttler, a university professor at Munich, at that time a chaplain to the German forces, delivered a paper "Pia Desideria Liturgica."[52] He called for the abolition of "accretions" (popular German practices not strictly part of the liturgical rite), and for an end to "unnecessary duplication" (readings read once in Latin and again in the vernacular). He argued for the possibility of the vernacular in the first part of the rite of Mass asking: "would it really be *uncatholic* to say the Fore-Mass only once—in German?"[53]

Writing in 1957, H.E. Winstone commented:

> It is impossible to read this paper and not to marvel at the courage, the almost prophetic foresight and...the thoroughness and clarity of vision of the author. He covered every department of the Liturgy...the sacramental ritual, the Mass and the breviary.[54]

---

maritime Liturgical Week; in 1946 a liturgical congress was held in Maastricht; Canada's second maritime Liturgical Week took place in 1948; the first Italian Liturgical Week occurred in 1949; 1950 saw both the first German national liturgical congress and the first Luxembourg liturgical conference; the first Irish liturgical meeting was held in Glenstal Abbey in 1953; in 1955 an Australian Liturgical Week was held. England is conspicuously absent from this list.

50 For example in 1916 the USA "Pius X School of Liturgical Music" commenced (cf. G. Ellard SJ, *The Mass in Transition,* p. 339).

51 In 1931 Abbot Herwegen founded the Institute of Liturgical and Monastic Studies at Maria Laach. 1943 saw the foundation in Paris of the *Centre de Pastorale Liturgique* by the Dominicans A.M. Roguet and Pie Duployé, with the assistance of a young professor from Toulouse, A.G. Martimort. A Chair of Liturgy was founded at the faculty of theology in Trier in 1947, held by Balthasar Fischer. The same year saw the formation in Trier of a Liturgical Institute directed by Johannes Wagner. After the war Maria Laach recommenced this work through the foundation of the Herwegen Institute for the Promotion of Liturgical Studies in 1948. One of the most influential faculties was established as part of the *Institut Catholique* of Paris in 1956, the *Institut Supérieur de Liturgie,* bringing together personnel from Mont-César and the *Centre de Pastorale Liturgique.* Cf. G. Ellard SJ, *The Mass in Transition,* p. 345; L.G.M. Alting von Gesau, *Liturgy in Development,* pp. 48, 51-52; B. Botte OSB, *From Silence to Participation,* pp. 93-106.

52 Originally published in *Theologie und Glaube* in 1916 and reprinted in *Liturgisches Jahrbuch* VII (1957) 39-64. Reported in: H.E. Winstone, "Pia Desideria: A Chapter in Liturgical Reform" in: *Liturgy* vol. XXVII pp. 97-99.

53 Ibid., p. 99.

54 Ibid.

In Göttler we find an early espousal of liturgical reform, but one that is primarily motivated by a desire to remove *from* the Liturgy those practices which smother it. Göttler certainly discusses minor simplifications of the rite of Mass (asking whether psalm 42 and the prayer *munda cor meum* were not superfluous?),[55] however a substantial ritual restructuring is not proposed. Rather, his aim is to allow the Liturgy the freedom to nourish piety.

Adrian Fortescue

Fortescue, rector of St Hugh, Letchworth, from 1907-1923,[56] was an early English pioneer of liturgical piety.[57] Most of his writings were historical, though his most famous work is his ceremonial manual *The Ceremonies of the Roman Rite Described*.[58]

In the 1917 preface to the first edition of that manual, Fortescue mentions a desire for liturgical reform. He objected to some of the more elaborate ritual gestures, for example "the constant kissing" of hands and objects when passed, and suggested:

> It may perhaps be admitted that some measure of simplification is desirable. Now that liturgical reform is so much in the air, we may hope for reform in this direction too. The chief note in the Roman rite has always been its austere simplicity. That is still its essential note, compared with the florid Eastern rites. It is surely worth while to

[55] Cf. ibid., pp. 98-99.

[56] The author has examined unpublished material from his liturgical activity that has not hitherto been studied academically. References to Fortescue in Crichton, *English Catholic Worship* are cursory. J.D. Crichton numbers him amongst "three forgotten liturgists;" *Lights in Darkness*, pp. 111-116, using only published source material, adding: "One could have wished that someone before now would have written a full scale biography" (p. 116). O'Connell's essay "The Liturgical Movement in Great Britain and Ireland" in: J. Jungmann SJ, *Liturgical Renewal*, only mention's Fortescue as editor of the people's missal. M. Richards affords Fortescue a paragraph in: *The Liturgy in England*, p. 35. J. Fenwick and B. Spinks' *Worship in Transition* ignored him.

[57] A letter about his annual retreat is illustrative: "Each day we sang the office in choir. That is glorious too. Of course the office is all made to be sung in common. Now, except at retreats, a secular priest never has a chance of singing it properly. One gabbles it all to oneself in a hurried whisper in trains and on a bicycle. It is enormously finer when we sang the verses of the psalms...across the stalls of the choir and heard the reader chant the lessons from the ambo." Manuscript letter to M. Crickmer, 2nd December 1909.

[58] Fourteen editions of which have been published, the most recent being in 2003.

> preserve this note externally also, to repress any Byzantine tendencies in our ceremonies.[59]

He suggests "some measure of simplification." The proposed reform is relatively minor, a slight pruning of the organic whole. His justification is the nature of the Roman rite.

But ought not this reform to be rejected, as were the antiquarian projects surveyed above? Not if we distinguish the removal of something foreign to the Roman rite ("some measure" of pruning), from reforms that would replace substantial parts of the rite with something else entirely, as envisaged in the antiquarian projects of Quignonez and Tommasi. The history of the Roman rite knows many such minor ritual reforms: they are a part of its organic development. Root and branch reforms, however, are another matter.

Indeed, in a letter to the noted typographer, Stanley Morison, Fortescue displays his disdain for the fabrication of liturgies as well as his appreciation of the organic development of the Liturgy in history:

> I think the habit of making up new liturgies could easily grow on a man, like dram drinking. It must be quite fun to spread out before one translations of all the best liturgies, and then to pick out and string together the prettiest snippets from each. Orchard[60] has not the ghost of a sense of liturgical style; he understands nothing about the historic development or the inherent build of the rites he plunders. He just takes the pretty bits and strings them together anyhow. Lots of people have done this sort of thing. The Irvingite Liturgy is another famous example; so are all the High Anglican combinations of their Prayer book with the juiciest morsels from the Roman Mass. To me all this is silly and ugly. It is like a man with no sense of construction or style who tries to make a new architecture by jamming together all the pretty details of all the buildings he has seen. I admire the dome of St Peter's and the windows of Chartres and the Propylaia at Athens and the columns of Karnack; but I should not like to see them all jammed together.[61]

In 1930, some years after Fortescue's untimely death, Henri Leclercq underlined Fortescue's contribution to the promotion of

[59] Ibid., p. xix. An alternative position is argued by P. Tanner "Why omit the liturgical kisses?" in: *OF* vol. VII pp. 130-132.

[60] Fortescue is responding to Morison's gift of a prayer book compiled by Orchard. William Edwin Orchard (1877-1955) was a Congregationalist minister at the time and President of a society of "Free Catholics." He became a Catholic in 1932 and was ordained priest in 1935; for information on W.E. Orchard I am indebted to the Rev'd John R. McCarthy.

[61] Typewritten letter, 26th April 1920.

liturgical piety in an otherwise not uncritical notice in his *Dictionnaire d'Archéologie Chrétienne et de Liturgie*:

> Adrian Fortescue had that originality among few others to be able to realise in his priestly, artistic and intellectual life his ideal of the beauty of Christian worship in all its fullness, and to make the Liturgy a living reality.[62]

The Benedictines of Farnborough

In 1895 monks of Solesmes accepted the invitation of the exiled French Empress Eugénie to establish a priory at the Imperial mausoleum in Farnborough. Its first Abbot, Fernand Cabrol, is reported to have complained that "the average English Catholic show[s] little interest in the Liturgy."[63] Yet the foundation, another of the heirs to the liturgical spirit of Guéranger, would go some way to bridge the gulf between England and the predominantly continental Liturgical Movement.[64] Farnborough was certainly informed by its founder: Beauduin preached the community retreat in 1915, and visited again in 1917 and 1918.[65]

Farnborough became a community whose liturgical publications earned the abbey the appellation "the book factory,"[66] the outstanding product of which was the thirty-volume *Dictionnaire d'Archéologie Chrétienne et de Liturgie*, published from 1924 onward. Doms Cabrol,

---

[62] "Adrien Fortescue a eu cette originalité parmi quelques autres, de vouloir réaliser dans sa vie sacerdotale, artistique et intellectuelle, son rêve de beauté du culte chrétien sous toutes ses formes, et de faire de la liturgie une vivante réalité;" "Liturgistes" in: *Dictionnaire d'Archéologie Chrétienne et de Liturgie*, col. 1739.

[63] O. Rousseau OSB, *The Progress of the Liturgy*, p. 94.

[64] On the Movement and England, J.D. Crichton: "In all this, as in other matters, the English Channel proved to be an all-too-effective Water Curtain;" *English Catholic Worship*, p. 73. However, the English writer Donald Attwater was involved with the development of the Movement in the USA from 1926 onward, and through him Eric Gill (cf. R.W. Franklin & L. Spaeth, *Virgil Michel: American Catholic*, p. 74). The English Dominican Conrad Pepler brought the Movement's ideals from the continent in the 1930s (cf. A. Nichols OP, *Dominican Gallery*, pp. 348, 386-392; also C. Pepler OP, *Sacramental Prayer*). Cf. further: W. Busch, "Travel notes on the Liturgical Movement," in: *OF* vol. I pp. 53-54; D. Attwater, "The Liturgical Movement in England," in: *OF* vol. I pp. 343-345; G. Ellard SJ, "Blossoms of the second spring: the Liturgical Movement in England," in: *OF* vol. II pp. 310-314; D. Attwater, "The Liturgical Revival in England" in: The Liturgical Conference, *Sanctification of Sunday: National Liturgical Week (USA) 1949*, pp. 150-156.

[65] Cf. C. Brogan OSB, "Chapters in the History of Saint Michael's Abbey" in: *Laudetur* December 2001, pp. 16-17.

[66] Cf. C. Brogan OSB, "Chapters in the History of Saint Michael's Abbey" in: *Laudetur* August 2001, p. 16.

Férotin, Wilmart (a protégé of Edmund Bishop),[67] Baudot, Gâtard, Gougaud, Villecourt, Leclercq and Wesseling all published works, some the result of scholarly research, others intended for popular consumption, contributing to the spread of the ideals of the Movement in the French and English-speaking worlds.[68]

The introduction to the 1921 edition of the Cabrol missal gives eloquent testimony to his abbey's grasp of the nature of the Liturgy and of the aims of the Liturgical Movement:

> The missal should not be looked upon as intended for the priest alone. The Mass is not a 'devotion' reserved to the clergy—it is the Common Sacrifice of all the faithful. The laity have their own part to play in this Holy Sacrifice, and they should be able to follow the prayers and ceremonies and to understand their meaning.
>
> No method of assisting at Mass can compare with what we may call the Church's own method.
>
> The missal, too, as we shall see, is a summary of the authentic teaching of the Church and an important witness to the famous axiom, *lex orandi, lex credendi*...
>
> The missal is a monument of Christian antiquity, reaching back, as it does, to the very beginnings of the Church...
>
> But in all this there is no mere question of archaeology. The antiquities of the missal are a practical reminder to us of the venerable antiquity of the Church herself—of her continued existence in all ages. We Catholics live by Tradition: but the Western Church has never, like the Eastern Church, confused fidelity to Tradition with mere antiquarianism. While she never denies her past, while she clings to the relics of earlier times, the Catholic Church ever adapts herself to changing circumstances—she lives and grows—and yet, like her Divine Master, she remains 'the same, yesterday, today, and for ever.'
>
> This wonderful adaptability—the power to make herself 'all things to all people'—is admitted even by her enemies. Here we have, too, the explanation of that 'liturgical renaissance' which we see to-day—the Liturgy wins credit because it is a witness, at once to the past and to the present, of the Christian faith. What we may call the 'archaisms' of

---

[67] N. Abercrombie, *The Life and Work of Edmund Bishop*, p. 408. Bishop recalls receiving from Farnborough "a benevolence which I had done nothing to deserve, and a degree and measure of appreciation of my small bits of work in print that overwhelmed me;" p. 407.

[68] The 1926 Latin-French missal, vesperal and ritual *L'Office Liturgique de Chaque Jour*, compiled by Doms Cabrol and Baudot, exemplifies the contribution made to the Liturgical Movement at a popular level, providing simple introductions to the Mass and office of each day, and the rites of the sacraments.

> the missal are the expression of the faith of our fathers which it is our duty to watch over and to hand on to posterity…
>
> What is meant by the liturgical spirit? By the liturgical spirit is meant that disposition of mind which leads the faithful to follow, even in their private devotions, the way marked out by the Church in her Liturgy, and to take an intelligent and loving interest in her feasts, her rites and her ceremonies…
>
> We should accept from her hands, as from the hands of a wise and prudent mother, the prayers and ceremonies which she has instituted as the means to lead us to God, we should ever treat them with the greatest respect, and make them the inspiration of our personal spiritual life…
>
> The prayers of the Mass are not a kind of magic formula reserved to the priest alone, and 'not understood of the people.' The Church desires that all should understand...This is the reason for the present translation of the missal: to put at the disposition of the faithful the best and simplest means of understanding the Mass and taking part in its rites and prayers…[69]

A publisher's advertisement in a 1926 Cabrol missal claimed:

> When the history of the present-day Liturgical Revival is written, one of the names to be placed right in the forefront of the Movement will be that of…Cabrol…
>
> Cabrol's work…has been of a two-fold nature. On the one hand his learned treatises on the subject command the respect of Liturgiologists the world over. On the other, he has worked unceasingly to develop the Liturgical Spirit among the ranks of the laity by means of popular editions of the missal, etc.[70]

In fact, Cabrol and his community are barely considered in writings on the period.[71] When in 1947 Farnborough ceased to be a house of the Solesmes Congregation its liturgical specialisation was somewhat dissipated, although amongst others, Dom Benedict Steuart (a monk of Farnborough from 1911-1926 who had played a key rôle in Cabrol's publications), continued the abbey's tradition of liturgical scholarship and of promoting the Liturgical Movement.

---

[69] F. Cabrol OSB, *The Roman Missal*, pp. vii-xxiii. Similar ideals were expressed as early as 1915 in Dom Cabrol's introduction to *The Day Hours of the Church.*

[70] F. Cabrol OSB, *My Missal*, p. 353.

[71] M. Richards accords seven words: "the work at Farnborough of Dom Cabrol;" *The Liturgy in England*, p. 39. J.D. Crichton says that "the scholarship of the French monks of Farnborough cannot be claimed by English Catholics, though they were the beneficiaries of it;" *English Catholic Worship*, p. 38.

Romano Guardini

Romano Guardini's memoirs reveal that he discovered the Liturgy assisting at the liturgical offices at the abbey of Beuron.[72] Whilst still a student Guardini authored *Vom Geist der Liturgie* (The Spirit of the Liturgy). Published in 1918 as the first volume in the *Ecclesia Orans* series, it quickly went through several editions, and was translated.[73] The importance of this work cannot be underestimated: its principles underpinned much of the activity of the Liturgical Movement. Its definition of Catholic Liturgy is of abiding value:

> The Catholic Liturgy is the supreme example of an objectively established rule of spiritual life. It has been able to develop κατὰ τὸν ὅλον, that is to say, in every direction, and in accordance with all places, times and types of human culture. Therefore it will be the best teacher of the *via ordinaria* – the regulation of religious life in common, with, at the same time, a view to actual needs and requirements...
>
> The Liturgy is the Church's public and lawful act of worship, and it is performed and conducted by the officials whom the Church herself has designated for the post...In the Liturgy God is to be honoured by the body of the faithful, and the latter is in its turn to derive sanctification from this act of worship. It is important that this objective nature of the Liturgy should be fully understood. Here the Catholic conception of worship in common sharply differs from the Protestant, which is predominatingly individualistic.[74]

Guardini established a community of young people at Burg Rothenfels[75] who lived according to these principles up until the Nazis evicted them in 1939. He celebrated the Liturgy according to his principles. The description of the chapel and the style of liturgical celebration sounds familiar to the contemporary reader:

> The walls were white; daylight, or candlelight in the evening, provided the main decorative element. The altar was not placed against the back wall...but forward toward the people who sat on small black cubes arranged around it on three sides. The presider was

---

[72] Cf. J. Ratzinger, "Assessment and Future Prospects" in: A. Reid OSB, *Looking Again at the Question of the Liturgy with Cardinal Ratzinger*, pp. 145-146.

[73] The translation *The Spirit of the Liturgy* appeared in 1930, five years earlier than R. Tuzik allows: cf. *How Firm a Foundation: Leaders of the Liturgical Movement*, p. 8. His reference is to the American edition *The Church and the Catholic* and *The Spirit of the Liturgy*.

[74] R. Guardini, *The Spirit of the Liturgy*, pp. 4, 6.

[75] Guardini was part of a wider movement; cf. J. Lord, "Neu-Deutschland and German Catholic Youth" in: *OF* vol. V pp. 303-308.

seated behind the altar and so closed the circle. With this arrangement Guardini reintroduced and applied the very old concept of the *circumstantes* of the early church's eucharistic celebration. The *missa recitata* was the most frequent style of celebration; because many of those attending knew Latin, a most lively exchange was possible.[76]

There is no evidence that Guardini altered the text of the rite:[77] his reforms were to the style of celebration. However, did such reforms of style themselves fail to respect the organic whole of the rite, which includes style and gesture as well as text? Certainly Conrad Pepler's reservations make a valid point: he "took issue with...*The Spirit of the Liturgy*, in which it sometimes seems that the universal, hieratic and restrained ethos of the Roman rite is to be adapted to 'modern man,' rather than modern man, for his welfare, to it."[78] Man "should be more ready to learn the language of the Liturgy, rather than expect the Liturgy to learn his language," Pepler states.[79]

This highlights a key assumption underlying the study of the principles of liturgical reform: the Liturgy in which the Liturgical Movement sought to bring about greater participation assumed a Christian culture. One writer clearly articulated the problem that this assumption posited:

> The most significant mark of a Christian culture is an appreciation not only of the unity of Christendom, but also of the Christian orientation of every human activity; when the Church is regarded as that divine being in which redeemed mankind can realise its position in the hierarchy of creation, then the Christian approach to any problem is naturally adopted. Whether that problem be the making of a building, of a picture, or of a prayer, is of no account; in its execution the work will be signed with the mark of Christianity, for this is of the very life of the workman. In such circumstances the art of the Liturgy is most properly and reasonably cultivated. It is natural to the people, nor is there any self-consciousness in the 'participation in the public and solemn prayer of the Church.' The manner in which it is carried out is the effect and not the cause of a manner of living.

---

[76] R. Kuehn, "Romano Guardini: The Teacher of Teachers," in: R. Tuzik, *How Firm a Foundation: Leaders of the Liturgical Movement*, p. 44.

[77] J. Jungmann SJ, notes that in 1942 Guardini called for a two or three year cycle of readings as a "very pressing desideratum;" cf. *The Mass of the Roman Rite*, vol. I p. 403 note 54.

[78] Cited in: A. Nichols OP, *Dominican Gallery*, p. 390. In 1946 Pepler wrote of "the perilous condition of a great deal of what is classed as the Liturgical Movement," asserting that in order to fruitfully participate in the Liturgy "the modern Christian must be prepared in mind and sense;" *Lent*, p. 127.

[79] C. Pepler OP, *Sacramental Prayer*, p. 24.

> With the disappearance of the mentality that produced that mode of life, the Liturgy is found to be no longer a part of the life of the people. In its place have arisen those expressions of devotion which are to the Liturgy what every modern corruption is to the reality for which it is substituted. There is need for reform—but at which end shall the reformers start? They have apparently attempted to cure the disease by removing those symptoms only which appear on the surface. There can be no doubt—any parish priest can verify this—that even to this day the prayer which is offered up publicly is of a nature which is consonant with and produced by the culture of the congregation. You may cut down their 'devotions' and drive them to Vespers in the evening, but their attendance, as a general rule, at these services is unnatural and incompatible with the principles upon which their daily life is built. It is these which must first be changed.[80]

Liturgical reform had, then, to bridge this divide. The Movement faced two options: change the world, or change the Liturgy.

Guardini, whilst respecting the textual integrity of the traditional Liturgy had nevertheless begun to go down the path of changing the Liturgy to suit the modern world. In this context we note that Karl Rahner SJ underlined his influence in 1965 saying: "It is a widely known fact that the Rothenfels experience was the immediate model for the liturgical reforms of Vatican II."[81]

We observe a similar principle of conforming the Liturgy to the prevailing age operative in the enlightenment liturgists' reforms. And we have seen how this principle when used as the sole basis for liturgical reform leads to the violation of the organic whole that is objective liturgical Tradition. No doubt Guardini's profound appreciation of the Liturgy prevented his taking the path of Jubé or Ricci. Nevertheless, on his own authority, he had begun to head in that direction.

In contrast to what we may call "specialised" liturgical centres such as Rothenfels, the Liturgical Movement continued to work for its fundamental liturgical reform: participation in the traditional Liturgy at the local level. The following complaint in 1930 about the slowness of many to embrace reform in the USA is illustrative:

> Until all having the care of souls are inspired by a love of the Liturgy, springing from a love of God and a desire to advance his glory; with also an intelligent appreciation of the beauty, majesty, and artistic

---

[80] From a letter published in no. 3 of an English journal *Order* (c. 1930), quoted in: D. Attwater, "Two Years Later—and a Query" in: *OF* vol. IV p. 152. Attwater does not cite the author's name.

[81] Quoted in: R. Kuehn, "Romano Guardini: The Teacher of Teachers," in: R. Tuzik, *How Firm a Foundation: Leaders of the Liturgical Movement*, pp. 47-48. In 1965 the phrase "the liturgical reforms of Vatican II" did not include the (1970) missal of Paul VI.

> perfection of our public worship, there is every reason to fear that the progress of liturgical reform in our country will be slow.[82]

Here it is attitudes, minds and hearts that are to be reformed, not the given liturgical rites or ceremonial.

Dom Theodore Wesseling OSB

This fundamental thrust of the Liturgical Movement was underlined by the 1938 work of Wesseling, *Liturgy and Life,* a more philosophical articulation of the nature of the Liturgy, in which he pointedly states that:

> The great inherent weakness of the Liturgical Movement of today is precisely the lack of 'philosophy' both in the individuals and in the Movement as a whole. Many have remarked on the appalling sterility of so much hard labour in the way of propaganda and Catholic action, the irritating irrelevancy of so many discussions, such as those on the introduction of the vernacular, and on other such off-hand suggestions for 'Liturgy-Reform' (of all things!)...[83]

> Before 'doing something,' before 'acting,' we should concern ourselves about *being;* before you think of Catholic action, *be* a Catholic; before you think of the Liturgical Movement, *be* fully liturgical yourself...Having done this you will see much more clearly than anyone can tell you which are the lines on which the Liturgical Movement must develop...You will soon realise that the problem is very different from a question of the use or not of the vernacular...[84]

> In order to cope with [the] difficulties of the present moment the vernacular is urged, reforms are demanded, in short, a plain mutilation of the Liturgy is required so that those people, that is, the passing generation, may profit more than they do. This seems the very limit of short-sightedness, is a cruelty to the generation which we are supposed to build up, and incidentally greatly hampers the progress of mankind's evolution. Nor is it very intelligent, for, first of all those partial measures will not more than any other measures bring about that fundamental change we desire, and secondly, it is psychologically certain that to see the Liturgy in reality worked out by their own children, by the rising generation with their still supple and enthusiastic minds, and by the young clergy who will soon transform parish life from a formula into an organic expression of the Church,

---

[82] J. McMahon, "The Green Wood Reproaches the Dry" in: *OF* vol. IV p. 528.
[83] *Liturgy and Life,* p. 4.
[84] Ibid., p. 119.

> that all this, we say, will have a far deeper influence on the men and women of our generation than any artificial exterior devices.[85]

Wesseling, like Pepler, gives the traditional Liturgy priority: it is man and his attitudes that must first be reformed, not the Liturgy.

Yet in a 1939 article Wesseling develops his ideas on possible liturgical reforms. He agrees that the liturgical texts "should be purged from all those spurious elements which allowed Cardinal Gasquet famously to say that someone 'lied like a second nocturn.'"[86] However he sharply criticises the view which:

> Takes the present situation of society as an absolute norm...and starts from the principle that instead of educating this society and of aiding mankind to strive after the completion of the Christian synthesis, we should bring down the exigencies of the Liturgical ideal to the coarseness and platitudes of a degenerate civilisation...This attitude is nothing less than a "practical" heresy for it emasculates the meaning of Christianity, it "evacuates the cross," in the words of Saint Paul. If Christianity is not fundamentally an obligation and a power of always higher perfection, it has no right to have a cross, still less to impose one. These reformers would like to upset the structure of the liturgical synthesis, even to suppress wholly or partly such feasts as the Ascension of Our Lord, in order to "adapt" the Liturgy to the mentality of a passing generation.[87]

Nevertheless, Wesseling accepts liturgical reform that:

> Would leave the Liturgical structure intact, yet purify the manifestations of the Liturgical synthesis on such points as breviary, Church Year and other points, but not in order to change the dynamism of the Liturgy. Therefore [it] would start with deepening the notion of the Liturgy and then proceed to distinguish in the evolution of the manifestations of the Liturgy the elements that are but signs of a certain period from those that are destined to be lasting contributions to the growth of Liturgical life in space and time.[88]

Wesseling's principles are clear. First one should have, and live, a profound understanding of the essence of the Liturgy. Then, any reform should purify and perfect the organic growth of objective liturgical Tradition. The desires or tastes of a particular age, place or group are not decisive criteria; indeed allowing such things to influence liturgical reform leads to a subjectivisation of the Liturgy in a manner which empties it of its very content.

---

[85] Ibid., p. 123.

[86] "Liturgy and Liturgy Reform" in: *The Tablet*, 28 January 1939, p. 126.

[87] Ibid.

[88] Ibid.

Dom Virgil Michel OSB

Michel, who had studied under Beauduin in Rome, founded the Liturgical Press and the periodical *Orate Fratres* at Saint John's Abbey, Collegeville, USA, in 1926. Both profoundly influenced the Liturgical Movement in the English-speaking world.

Michel's work faithfully promoted the liturgical piety enunciated by St Pius X and Beauduin. In one of the earliest publications, a collection of Michel's sermons on the Liturgy, he decried the situation whereby:

> Those who flock to the Sunday Masses recite one, two, or three rosaries while attending Mass, read litanies and other prayers from their books, recite the Angelus and the morning prayers, or even follow the devotional prayers set down in their books for recitation during Mass.[89]

And he asked:

> Should not every devoted Catholic try to the utmost of his power to participate actively in the Holy Sacrifice of the Mass, to follow the priest in mind and heart, to pray with him and act with him?[90]

This was the fundamental liturgical reform to which his endeavours were oriented. However, before his death in 1938 he came to speak of reform of the Liturgy itself. His *The Liturgy of the Church* locates the possibility of liturgical reform within the history of the organic development of objective liturgical Tradition:

> In the earlier days there was much liberty left to bishops and priests in the detailed development of the liturgical services. But as the Church grew in numbers and spread over distant places, this liberty ran the danger of destroying all unity and uniformity of worship in the one Church. Hence, after centuries of tradition, the liturgical texts, forms, rites, seasons and the like, were definitely fixed by laws and regulations. They are no longer subject to arbitrary change by individuals. Yet new customs still arise even now that in the long run affect the liturgical worship itself. After all, the latter is something living, and not the least of the hopes among many modern liturgical apostles is for various changes in the present liturgical forms or customs. As real liturgical changes, of course, they must be official, that is, sanctioned and set down by the Church herself.[91]

That authority is seen as the test of "real" reform is noteworthy.

---

[89] *My Sacrifice and Yours,* pp. 5-6.
[90] Ibid., p. 10.
[91] *The Liturgy of the Church According to the Roman Rite,* p. 7.

Paul Marx OSB's 1957 study, *Virgil Michel and the Liturgical Movement,* which draws upon Michel's unpublished manuscript *Liturgy and Catholic Life,*[92] demonstrates the development in Michel's thinking:

> Virgil Michel was first and last the practical apostle with his feet on the ground, and both eyes wide open. This practical sense showed itself...in his whole attitude to liturgical reform. Here his spirit was: Let us first understand what we have, and above all live it—then, we will be in a position to begin to think of and possibly suggest changes...That certain reforms were desirable was a plain fact to Michel, but there was no point in urging them as long as "Liturgy" meant "sanctuary etiquette." Besides, changes in the Liturgy, precisely because the Liturgy "is grounded mainly on the eternal bonds that unite the human to the divine and on the eternal needs of man as man," would always be slight and gradual even though the Liturgy had developed considerably through the centuries and would continue to develop provided it became once again the Catholic's daily bread. In 1936 he wrote: "One of the effects of a wide liturgical revival in the Church will undoubtedly be that of considerable changes in her Liturgy made in terms of the new conditions and needs of our day."[93]

Here, we have an understanding of the organic development of the objective liturgical Tradition open to the "new conditions and needs of our day." Nevertheless, we may observe Michel's strong emphasis on contemporary needs, and that he is prepared to speak of "considerable changes" in order to meet them.

What were these "considerable changes"? Under Michel's editorship *Orate Fratres* advocated the restoration of the offertory procession.[94] He also argued for an increased use of the vernacular in the Liturgy:

> 'Vernacular in the Liturgy' permits of many degrees in practical interpretation, such as the use of the vernacular in all instructional and exhortatory parts with retention of the Latin in the essential formulas, in the Canon of the Mass and the like...Thus, while we should be happy to see the Church go as far as she deems fit in introducing the vernacular into her Liturgy, our personal opinion is that the complete use of the Latin should always be retained, say in seminaries or colleges, solemn parish celebrations...We cannot imagine that anyone would advocate the use of the vernacular to the extent of wishing to drop the Latin altogether.[95]

---

[92] Cf. P. Marx OSB, *Virgil Michel and the Liturgical Movement,* pp. 256-257.
[93] Ibid., p. 56.
[94] Cf. *OF* vol. IX p. 331; vol. X pp. 183-184; vol. XII p. 378.
[95] "The Liturgy in the Vernacular" in: *OF* vol. XII pp. 172-173.

> ...We ardently hope and humbly pray for a more liberal adoption of the vernacular in public worship.[96]

And, certain that "there is no doubt that during the first century the sacrifice was quite commonly celebrated either in the late afternoon or in the evening,"[97] he suggested the possibility of the celebration of Mass in the evening:

> In the history of the Church, wherever accommodation to the exigencies of human nature and human life could be exercised without the compromise of any basic principle, the Church has acted in imitation of God's own way with man. The very legitimate question therefore continues to impose itself: Why not an evening Mass?...This may be an idle dream. But dreams may also be visions of constructive possibilities.[98]

Michel's proposals then, are not all that "considerable" in the light of the liturgical changes of the second half of the twentieth century. Michel is advocating prudent reforms taking into account what he perceives as the needs of his day, which do no radical violence to the rites themselves. His acceptance of (implicitly total) papal authority in liturgical matters is somewhat unquestioning, but very much in keeping with the spirit of uncritical obedience and of Roman centralism prevalent in the late nineteenth and early twentieth centuries. Michel does not advocate an antiquarian or enlightened recasting of the whole Liturgy, nor, one suspects, would he envisage that authority would sanction such.[99]

"Orate Fratres'" Discussion of the Principles of Liturgical Reform

Before Michel's death, a discussion of the principles of liturgical reform began in *Orate Fratres*. Roger Schoenbeckler opened it with an article that set forth a rationale and principles for future reform:

> With the growth of the Liturgical Movement and the consequent increase of liturgical understanding and appreciation, many suggestions have been made for reforms that would bring about a deeper and a fuller living of the liturgical life. These suggestions are not only of our day, although in recent years they have been offered

---

[96] "With Our Readers" in: *OF* vol. XII pp. 566-7. R.W. Franklin and R. Spaeth's selective use of Michel's writing in: *Virgil Michel: American Catholic* distorts his meaning and their references are incomplete: cf. pp. 83, 89.

[97] "The Evening Mass" in: *OF* vol. IV p. 90.

[98] "Why not the Evening Mass?" in: *OF* vol. XII pp. 30, 31.

[99] Michel also pioneered the social, cultural, philosophical and educational implications of liturgical piety: cf. P. Marx OSB, *Virgil Michel and the Liturgical Movement*, chapters 7-10 & K. Pecklers SJ, *The Unread Vision*, chapters 3-5.

> with a greater frequency and with a better appreciation of the spiritual values of the Liturgy, of its essential nature as the life of the mystical body of Christ, in which all members should share as much as possible...
>
> In general, the suggestions have arisen out of the laudable desire to increase and intensify the liturgical life of the faithful, priests and laity. They are moreover in harmony with the Tradition of the Church, in so far as the Church has periodically instituted reforms in her liturgical life, for the better spiritual participation and growth of her children...
>
> We shall state briefly the basic principles according to which all liturgical reform must be broached or discussed.
> 1. First of all, there is no need of reform in essentials. As a whole the Roman Liturgy is the product of the selective growth of ages of Christian life.
> 2. All reform in principle must be conservative. No changes should be considered except where change is really necessary, e.g., if a present rite has lost its meaning on account of changing historical conditions and background and the like.
> 3. Desirable changes will therefore always be small as compared to the Liturgy as a whole, even though individual items of change may be numerous.
> 4. Simplification and concentration must not be advocated without reference to past forms. All reforms must have a high regard and esteem for the traditions of the past, for that which now exists and which has been. Such respect will preclude the introduction of subjective inventions. This principle is also followed in other fields, e.g., the restoration or repairing of a church or a painting; or even the civic remodelling of an ancient city like Rome with its many monuments and traditions.
> 5. Reforms need not be a literal going back to the old, or a restoring of ancient rites and ceremonies, although they should always be of a traditional spirit. Many rites have been discarded in the past for good reasons, and there has always been development and evolution in liturgical practices.[100]

The rationale for liturgical reform is clearly that of the Movement: to increase liturgical piety. The principles enunciated are not new: they are open to necessary development yet careful to conserve objective liturgical Tradition as an organic whole. The analogies provided in the fourth principle are most illustrative.

Schoenbeckler continues, suggesting practical reforms. They include "the use of the vernacular in sacramental administrations" and "in the Mass of the Catechumens." He mentions that "the vernacular has also been suggested for the sacrificial banquet," but adds "we know of no

---

[100] "On Liturgical Reforms" in: *OF* vol. X pp. 562-3.

instance where the same suggestion has been made for the preface and the Canon of the Mass." He mentions reform of the calendar, including the possibility of a fixed date for Easter, the simplification of octaves and the perennial need for the pruning of the calendar. He suggests that the Holy Saturday Vigil "could again take place on the evening itself." Simplification of the Mass rite so that "the priest would no longer say those parts of the Mass text that are officially said or sung by the assistant ministers or choir," and by removing the *Confiteor* before the reception of Holy Communion are envisaged. A reform of church architecture to facilitate "participation of the faithful" which includes giving the altar "a more prominent and more central position." Making it possible for the priest "to stand facing the people while celebrating Mass" is advocated. Schoenbeckler goes as far as to suggest an abbreviated breviary, though he is quick to "recall that similar abbreviated breviaries in the past were met with decisive and universal rejection," noting that he has the reform of Quignonez in mind.[101] Little ritual change is envisaged, and that which is proposed is in accordance with the principles outlined.

At this point we must note the proposal of celebrating Mass facing the people. This became somewhat fashionable in the Liturgical Movement, yet the assumptions behind this practice—that early Church architecture indicates that facing the people was the norm, and that participation is best promoted when the celebrant faces the people—have been shown to be decisively flawed.[102] Godfrey Diekmann OSB, Michel's successor as editor of *Oratre Fratres,* though himself keen on "facing the people," admitted as early as 1957:

> An altar facing the people is, obviously, not essential to any liturgical apostolate. Recent scholars incline to the view that originally this position of the altar was due not so much to pastoral reasons of better participation, as rather to the desire for proper orientation (i.e., that the celebrant faces the East).[103]

As Diekmann admits, the proper orientation of the celebrant (and the people) from the offertory onward[104] is what is found in Christian

---

101 Cf. ibid., pp. 563-5.

102 K. Gamber states: "The idea that the priest standing facing the congregation during the celebration of Mass is…nowhere to be found in the literary sources before the time of Luther, and nor can the archaeological evidence be called in support of this conception;" *The Modern Rite,* p. 31. Cf. also his *The Reform of the Roman Liturgy,* part II "Facing the Lord: On the Building of Churches and Facing East in Prayer;" and U.M. Lang Cong Orat, *Turning Towards the Lord: Orientation in Liturgical Prayer.*

103 "Liturgical Briefs" in: *Worship* vol. XXXI p. 612.

104 Celebrating the whole of Mass at the altar, as in Low Mass, emerged with the growth of private Masses; cf. Jungmann, *The Mass of the Roman Rite,* vol. I pp. 212-233. Reforms giving to Low Mass celebrated with a congregation the rites present

antiquity. That this was not thoroughly appreciated by the Liturgical Movement, and that this erroneous fashion persists still, is a timely reminder that peremptory reforms risk the loss, albeit unwittingly, of important theological components of liturgical Tradition.

The next contribution on liturgical reform pointed out that "essential participation was not always deemed to be visible participation;"[105] the application to the desire for Mass facing the people is clear. The author was reacting against all-encompassing enthusiasms such as the blanket imposition of Gregorian chant, however badly performed, the rejection of all things gothic, and other fads.[106] His is also a timely reminder of the foolishness of sudden and ill-thought-through reforms:

> When one beholds the destruction that has begun in our churches in the name of liturgical reform and then considers the inner significance of the Liturgy, veritable terror seizes heart and mind. Priceless gold and brass chandeliers designed in the imperial style are junked so that lanterns like those in any depot can be suspended as liturgical symbols. The Baroque wood carvings of a cathedral are discarded as old lumber so that a rayon drape can hang behind its altar, and the walls are painted like those of any living room. Peculiar chalices and monstrances which are in reality the embodiment of individual eccentricities in craft are preferred to normal shapes and designs in the name of Liturgy. And most deplorable of all, a type of picture representation, done in flat lines, often grotesque and intrinsically disproportionate, will immediately be called liturgical, simply because it is hard to look at. These and many instances of barbarous individualism are daily doing damage to the true cause of the Liturgy, because first principles have been lost to sight in an eagerness to change.[107]

He concludes: "reform to be prudent must be one of positive substitution and not legal suppression."[108]

The English Jesuit C.C. Martindale was the next contributor. He argued for simplifying the ranking of feasts, abolishing commemorations, rendering some of the epistles more intelligible and, in spite of personal preference, for the Mass of the Catechumens in the vernacular.[109] He too

---

in High Mass where the lessons are chanted away from the altar, and even those of Pontifical Mass where the throne or faldstool is used for the collects, may be said to be in harmony with the Roman rite.

105 F. Falque, "Liturgical Spirit in Reform," in: *OF* vol. XI (1936/7) p. 211.

106 Cf. further: P. Anson "Fads and Fashions" in: *OF* vol. XVI pp. 454-457.

107 F. Falque, "Liturgical Spirit in Reform" p. 212.

108 Ibid., p. 213.

109 A printed "Manifesto of the Catholic Laity" dated Pentecost 1943, found in the Archives of the Archbishop of Westminster, suggests that one cannot assume that

suggests a simplification of the breviary.[110] Martindale disclaims any pretence to being a liturgical scholar, making practical proposals based on his experience, and upon the assumption that "the Liturgy itself could be 'better' than it is;"[111] a not unreasonable assumption given the growth of the Liturgy in history.

William Busch, certainly a scholar, responded promptly. He objected not to the *minutiæ* of Martindale's suggestions nor to the possibility of development, but "to all undue haste in proposals for 'liturgical reform.'"[112] He was not at all convinced of the need to change the traditional Liturgy, and held up the Augustinian Canon Pius Parsch as an example of one who, by publishing editions of the breviary with parallel Latin and vernacular texts, demonstrated "a 'reform' measure which does not introduce the slightest change in our present Liturgy."[113]

---

the laity were united in a desire for the vernacular. Its concept of liturgical Tradition and piety, and the abuse to which it alludes are of interest: "We, the undersigned Catholic Layfolk, desire...to make known our true feelings with regard to the present controversy concerning the language used by the Church in her public worship. We utterly repudiate the subversive efforts that are being made to discredit the use of the Latin Liturgy, a precious heritage brought to the English people by St Augustine of Canterbury from our glorious Apostle, St Gregory the Great, and which we are proud to have preserved intact these fourteen hundred years, even throughout the hardships and dangers of the penal times. We therefore protest that we are opposed to all attempts to tamper with this venerable Liturgy, or to substitute for it a copy of any non-Catholic rite, however beautiful and impressive. We strongly resent the implication that we and our children are not sufficiently intelligent to understand the simple Latin of the Mass, and we declare our readiness to do all we can to equip ourselves with the necessary knowledge so as to be able to take a more active and intelligent part in our parochial Mass. We also respectfully petition our bishops to use their authority to make the teaching of simple liturgical Latin obligatory in all our Catholic schools, since we are convinced that such instruction would be of immense spiritual and intellectual value to our children and would help them to realise more vividly the supra-national character of our faith. Finally we very humbly beg our Clergy to help our efforts by a distinct and deliberate enunciation of all of the words of the Liturgy, so as to make it possible for every one of us to become more at home with the spiritual language of our Holy Mother Church, and thus to assist at her public worship with greater understanding and devotion." Notwithstanding, *The Tablet* of July 17th 1943 announced a liturgical summer school at which the question of the extension of the vernacular, even as far as the Mass, was to be discussed "in all its aspects, not even omitting the most controversial" cf. pp. 33-34. *The Tablet* (September 18th 1943, p. 143) reported the subsequent formation of "The English Liturgy Society."

[110] Cf. "Liturgy Reform," in: *OF* vol. XI pp. 241-245.

[111] Ibid., p. 241.

[112] "On Liturgical Reforms," in: *OF* vol. XI p. 353.

[113] Ibid., p. 354.

He examined the arguments made in favour of evening Masses, concluding incisively:

> We will not secure the desired understanding of [the Mass] and active and devout popular participation by a simple mechanical device such as turning the hands of a clock. The question that ought to concern us is how we are to restore a deep and general consciousness that the eucharistic Sacrifice is the centre and compendium of the Christ-life in the Church...[114]

He also observed that in Catholic liturgical Tradition, Vespers is "the evening sacrifice,"[115] praising efforts towards its promotion.

His article is an important recapitulation of the principles of liturgical reform. "The elder statesman of the Liturgical Movement"[116] warned:

> We should be on our guard against a disposition to suit the Liturgy to modern temporary circumstances, a disposition which is apt to manifest itself among those who are newly interested in the liturgical revival and who, with a limited understanding of it, wish to utilise it for some particular and immediate purposes...
>
> We should not wish to change in haste what we are only beginning to revive. Let us take time to learn what the Liturgy is, and then we shall be in a position to judge what adaptations to modern circumstances may be desirable—perhaps not so many as we first imagined...if modern life finds Liturgy difficult, is it the Liturgy that should be changed? Ought we not adjust ourselves to the Liturgy, rather than wish to adjust it to our liking? I mean that the process should be that way more than the other. I do sympathise with the desire for such "reforms" as a return to the better customs of the past, and I think we are capable of more adjustment to the traditional Liturgy than Father Martindale seems to think possible...
>
> Worship is not merely a God-ward movement on our part. It is the reciprocal action of God and man through Christ. The Liturgy is the prayer of the mystical Christ. Certainly the largest amount and the best quality of subjective effort on our part is desirable. And therefore it is desirable that the forms of the Liturgy be appropriate in some measure to our circumstances. But this is not the only consideration.

---

[114] Ibid., p. 355.

[115] Ibid.

[116] K. Hughes RSCJ, *How Firm a Foundation: Voices of the Early Liturgical Movement*, p. 53. Hughes' selection of Busch's writings omits the article studied here. A fairer synopsis of his work may be found in: G. Sperry-White "William Busch: Educator" in: R. Tuzik, *How Firm a Foundation: Leaders of the Liturgical Movement*, pp. 200-206, though, curiously, he regards Busch's "attitude toward liturgical revision" as "ambiguous."

> The Liturgy has also its objective value above and beyond whatever we may contribute. To this objective element also its forms must be appropriate. And here it is that modern individualistic piety has been neglectful, inclining too much on the subjective side. The present liturgical revival aims to restore the right balance of the objective and the subjective. And as the Liturgy regains attention there is, I think, a real danger that individualistic piety may seek to impose itself and to introduce modifications in the Liturgy without sufficient understanding of its objective nature and without due effort to acquire such understanding.
>
> It is true that at various times in the past the Liturgy has been "reformed," but always the process has aimed to safeguard the traditional objective heritage. It is also true that at the present time some modifications are desirable, but they should be guided by the same conservative spirit.[117]

Busch's description of the relationship of the objective and subjective components in liturgical development is thoroughly grounded in liturgical history and is of permanent value as a philosophical explication of the principle of organic development.

Over a year passed before *Orate Fratres* turned again to the question of liturgical reform. The English Lancelot Sheppard offered "a way in which some of those things pointed out by Father Martindale might be done and at the same time the traditional Liturgy of the Church preserved from innovation."[118] His suggestion is simple and traditional: reform the calendar of the saints, as was done often in the past, to allow the seasons and more important feasts to predominate. It is a reasonable proposal.

Sheppard introduces a principle not hitherto articulated. He claims:

> Whenever there has been any question of reforming the Liturgy there has always been a conflict between the great liturgical Tradition of centuries and the reforming spirit. In the past the result of this conflict has generally been a compromise...This spirit of compromise must be borne in mind in attempting to elaborate any scheme of reform.[119]

By way of example he cites the "compromise" of the breviary reform of St Pius X, regarding it as satisfactory. And yet he notes, without complaint, the rejection of the reform of Quignonez.

As a principle of reform, "compromise" contains a radical flaw. We have seen in Busch's elaboration of liturgical reform, well grounded in liturgical history, the primacy held by the objective traditional Liturgy

---

[117] "On Liturgical Reforms," in: *OF* vol. XI pp. 353, 356.
[118] "Reform of the Liturgy: Another View" in: *OF* vol. XII p. 538.
[119] Ibid., pp. 535, 536.

as it is received by each age. Compromise, however, risks equating the subjective and objective and depriving the traditional Liturgy of its primacy. It could require that each abandon part of their nature in order to produce a new reality. This would not be organic development.

Certainly, organic development does involve, at times, the leaving behind of some practices, and it must be open to persuasion by contemporary needs. However, as Busch made clear, the subjective and objective are not equal partners in dialogue: the objective is of "value above and beyond whatever we may contribute."[120] And we must note that up until St Pius X's reform of the breviary, "conflict" between "the great liturgical Tradition of centuries" and "the reforming spirit," of which the protestant reformation was the apotheosis, has met with rejection in the history of the Roman rite.

The emergence of Sheppard's principle of compromise is illustrative. He departs from the principles enunciated hitherto, and risks doing violence to the objective traditional Liturgy. His is an over-emphasis on subjective concerns. This was a particular danger facing the Movement as it began to discuss reform. Others would express similarly flawed proposals. The principles outlined by Schoenbeckler and Busch, though, were thoroughly traditional. Theirs, we suggest, is the position that is in harmony with the nature of the Liturgy and with its organic development in history.

In 1936 H.A. Reinhold fled to the USA to escape Nazi persecution. He brought with him first hand experience of the European Liturgical Movement,[121] and quickly became a contributor to *Orate Fratres.* A passionate writer, Reinhold's motivation was the promotion of true liturgical piety, to combat "a secularist puritanism on one hand, and...Jansenist spiritualism and individualism on the other."[122] Yet, his earliest contributions include the question:

> If we consider our existing Liturgy, changed and developed through the centuries, can we claim that it is perfect? Could it not be better?[123]

Practically, he argued:

> Our Roman Mass...has lost much of its beauty and even its clearness through the introduction of some prayers outside the Canon and the suppression of the psalms in the introit, offertory and communion songs, leaving often but incoherent and obscure fragments...

---

[120] "On Liturgical Reforms," in: *OF* vol. XI p. 356.

[121] Cf. *H.A.R., The Autobiography of Father Reinhold,* esp. pp. 38, 40-41, 44-45, 56-57. Reinhold was a persistent promoter of facing the people and of the dialogue Mass. Also: R. Tuzik, "H. A. Reinhold: A Timely Tract for the American Church" in: R. Tuzik, *How Firm a Foundation: Leaders of the Liturgical Movement,* pp. 174-183.

[122] "More or Less Liturgical (continued)" in: *OF* vol. XIII p. 217.

[123] Ibid., p. 213.

> These atrophies and deletions have done harm to the fullness of prayer and to the intelligibility of the whole. The introit and the communion verse without their psalm often make no sense, or at least not the sense they would make if the old practice were introduced.[124]

He knew that "the Liturgy has grown like a natural plant"[125] throughout history, and argued that it should continue to do so:

> There is no reason why the Holy Ghost should have deserted the liturgists after the year 700 AD It is un-Catholic to deny development and Tradition and to choose a period after which the wheel of Church history is supposed to have stood still. Choosing of periods or doctrines is heretical. To choose in Greek is *haireo*, the root word of heresy. To limit the period of liturgical inspiration and growth, therefore, is imprudent, nay silly, because it would give people the idea that those who work for a liturgical revival are nothing else than esthetes, antiquarians and esoterics, who shun the reality of their own time and try to escape into their self-made dream church.[126]

Reinhold believed that the twentieth century should influence the liturgical form as had past ages:

> Our form will be liturgical if we have enough faith to "consecrate" our contemporary beauty and then go right ahead and use what we find. Of course this does not mean admission of the less desirable elements of modern invention: movie effects, neon tube crosses, record music, or similar things which would make the Sacred Liturgy a conglomeration of stage effects. We have to consecrate our age by eliminating all products that are unreal, untrue, false and calculated only to play on our emotions.[127]

We can say that Reinhold's principles: restoring parts of the tradition that have been lost to the detriment of the rite (the offertory and communion psalms to their antiphons); the realisation that the Liturgy is a living organic reality open to development ("like a natural plant"); and that the twentieth century should affect the Liturgy, are acceptable in the light of liturgical history, with one reservation: he risks giving the twentieth century a disproportionate influence. His analogy of the plant is apposite. But we must remember that just as plants will die without water and fertiliser, should one particular age prune or graft disproportionately, the living organism would suffer harm.

We know what Reinhold had in mind with regard to reform of the Mass from his "radical dream" published in 1940 as "My Dream

---

124 Ibid.

125 Ibid., p. 217.

126 Ibid., p. 215.

127 "More or Less Liturgical" in: *OF* vol. XIII p. 153.

Mass."[128] He says that "it is the dream of the ideal parish Mass, the outcome, as I see it, of all these years of effort of the liturgical revival in Germany, Italy, France, England, Switzerland and these United States."[129]

He describes a church in which the priest faced the people over a stone table, with the people "close to the altar, lined up in fan formation with the altar as the centre."[130] There were no pews and "the whole place looked more casual and ready for action and change;"[131]

> The priest and the assistants vested in the sacristy...While vesting they recited the prayers which we used to say at the foot of the altar. Then the procession was formed...When they entered the rear of the church the schola sang a beautiful antiphon adapted from the Gregorian, and intoned a psalm...the whole thing was in English...the whole populace respond[ed] with a short verse. This happened after every psalm verse...
>
> The priests incensed the altar, walking all round it...I noticed all through the Mass that the priest did not read the things which had been sung by somebody else...The priest intoned the *Kyrie*...he had a tremendous response from the people who sang mightily, helped by a fine schola of men and boys...
>
> The people sang the "and with thy spirit" and the "Amen" every time the priest or deacon greeted them or finished a prayer. I was especially amazed at the beautiful "thanks be to God" at the end of the epistle (in English of course, because it had been read to the people from the ambo), and the "Glory to Thee O Lord" and "Praise to Thee, O Christ" at the beginning and end of the solemn gospel. For the gospel the deacon stood on the ambo, the subdeacon beside him and the candle and the censer bearers slightly in the rear...
>
> When I had entered the Church I had noticed that there were trays...on which people deposited money, food in bags, linen, clothes, bottles with wine, bread and even packages containing altar breads and candles. At the offertory a few men and women took up these trays...and brought them to the gates of the sanctuary. There servers in albs accepted them and deposited them at the foot of the altar...All during the offertory the schola sang one of the old offertorial verses...The people took up the short responses. I was told...that the priest's offertory prayers were in Latin and that the whole sacrificial part would be in this sacred language of the Mystery...I noticed that the *Benedictus* had returned to its old organic place before the

---

128 *OF* vol. XIV pp. 265-270.

129 Ibid., p. 265.

130 Ibid., p. 265.

131 Ibid., p. 266.

> consecration, since it was short and Gregorian. So the deepest silence enhanced the supreme moments of the consecration...
>
> The sacred banquet started with the Our Father, again in English. The deacon recited the communion prayers with the faithful, after the triple "Lamb of God." ...Rome had abolished the second *Confiteor*...While the priest and deacon gave holy Communion, schola and people alternated a common verse and psalm in an adapted Gregorian melody in English...
>
> At the end the priest and assistants recited the last gospel on their processional way out, while the people, led by the marching schola, sang the *Salve Regina*...[132]

This is indeed radical for 1940. Yet, with the exception of the questionable practice of facing the people from the offertory onward, the modifications are either the arguably apposite restoration of lost practices (returning the prayers at the foot of the altar to the priest's private preparation, the offertory procession, the removal of textual duplication by the priest) or are arguably reasonable adaptations (the use of the vernacular in some parts of the Mass).[133] The traditional Roman rite is intact, albeit developed. The proposed reforms do no violence to objective liturgical Tradition. Thus, whilst his principles as they stand on paper may give us pause, his most radical practical application of them illustrates a development that enables the Liturgy to provide for the spiritual needs of the people in a manner consonant with Tradition (save one or two errors).[134]

Orate Fratres' discussion of liturgical reform from 1936-1940 demonstrates the emerging commitment of the Liturgical Movement to development of the Roman rite along traditional lines, consonant with the principles of reform found in liturgical history. The contribution of Sheppard to this debate is certainly an exception: one that indicates that some advocates of liturgical reform operated from questionable principles as early as before the second world war.

---

132 Ibid., pp. 267-270.

133 In his autobiography, Reinhold comments upon his founding of the Vernacular Society of America: "I consider it my only real contribution to the American Liturgical Movement;" *H.A.R., The Autobiography of Father Reinhold*, pp. 140-141.

134 Similar proposals may be found in Reinhold's article "Desiderata to be Prayed For" in: *OF* vol. XX pp. 234-235. See also his 1960 *Bringing the Mass to the People*, considered below.

Pius Parsch

Parsch, the leader of the Liturgical Movement in Austria,[135] a canon of the Augustinian monastery at Klosterneuberg near Vienna, was deeply motivated by the lack of liturgical piety he experienced amongst soldiers during the first world war:

> I spent four years at the front as a chaplain. It was in the course of this work that I began to realise the importance of the Bible for both priests and layfolk. I realised too how important it was that people should learn to understand the Liturgy and take an intelligent part in it. I returned home from the war full of these two discoveries and resolved to devote the rest of my life to propagating these ideals.[136]

He obtained the use of Saint Gertrude's, an old chapel nearby, and began over thirty years of liturgical formation and celebration with ordinary people, earning himself the epitaph "an apostle of 'active participation.'"[137] Ernest Muellerleile observed the Liturgy at Saint Gertrude's in 1950. Parsch had re-ordered the building (to include an altar for celebration *versus populum*) in 1935:

> It is early Sunday morning…At a quarter of seven Fr. Parsch enters to prepare the altar for the Sacrifice. Then, seated at the throne with a few ministers about, he leads the small group that are present in morning Matins, in the German…After the *Te Deum* the organ intones the opening sunrise praises of Lauds. By now there are many more present and this prayer hour is in large part sung. Already one realises that there are no on-lookers. All are participants. During the *Benedictus,* incensing is done around the entire altar. Following Lauds the ministers retire to the sacristy…Then all stand when the main procession enters—a cross-bearer carrying candles [sic!] leading some thirty to forty ministers and singers clad in white tunics with red clavi stripes…The large church bells ring out and the people sing with full voice, alternating with the chanters…The *Kyrie* is threefold—the first part sung by the young men chanters, the second *Kyrie* by the young women, and the third by all the faithful. The *Gloria* is sung in phrases alternating between schola and community. During the collect a lector

---

[135] On the origins of the Liturgical Movement in Austria see: P. Parsch, "Liturgical Action in Austria" in: *OF* vol. V pp. 126-130, and "Liturgical Action in Austria (Cont.)" in: *OF* vol. V pp. 176-182.

[136] Parsch continues: "Gradually, however, I began to realise that another idea was involved. The Bible and the Liturgy were after all only sources. The important thing was grace...They must not be cultivated for their own sakes, for they are but means to something spiritual. Their whole purpose is to bring us the wonderful gift of grace;" *Seasons of Grace,* p. 7.

[137] Cited by C. Howell SJ, "Introduction" in: P. Parsch, *The Liturgy of the Mass,* p. viii.

> reads the same prayer in German for the people. Another lector reads the Epistle to the seated congregation.
>
> After the Epistle, a chanter standing on the step (*gradus*) of the ambo, sings the gradual in German. The congregation responds with the first verse as a refrain... [The celebrant] having finished the Latin Gospel [at the altar] the procession is now formed and the same chanter leads the congregation in the *Alleluia*...
>
> The cross-bearer leads the way...followed by ministers bearing candles and the smoking censer. At the end is the celebrant holding high the Gospel-book, while all is accompanied by the ringing of the church-bells and the singing of the *Alleluia*...the celebrant announces the Holy Gospel in German from the topmost step of the ambo...
>
> During the *Credo* which is sung alternately like the *Gloria,* an Offertory table is prepared...for the gifts. As the choir chants the Offertory psalm and the community sings the refrain, the Offertory procession begins...At the conclusion a lector reads in German the great offering prayer—the Secret.
>
> After the Preface, the *Sanctus* and *Benedictus* are sung by all. Then follows the holy silence of the Canon-action. There is not a sound...During the consecration all kneel. The great bell in the Church tower rings out...
>
> During the *Pater Noster* the offertory gifts are removed and the same table is prepared for Communion...with communion plates (lay-patens), wine glasses and two burning candles. After the *Agnus Dei* the kiss of peace is given. By means of the pax-board it is passed on to the community...the faithful come in procession to communion, singing the Communion verse alternately with the chanters' psalm. The Eucharist is received standing and is followed...with a purification of wine...
>
> A lector reads the Post-Communion prayer in the German. All respond to the *Ite Missa Est* and kneel for the last blessing. As the last Gospel is being read at the altar the community again sings the Introit-verse...All recite the "canticle of the Three Children" as the procession returns through the centre of the church.[138]

Muellerleile describes Saint Gertrude's as "the cradle of folk-liturgy." In so doing he emphasises the active participation in the traditional Liturgy, not what the term "folk-liturgy" came to connote later in the century.[139]

---

138 *At The Cradle of Folk-Liturgy: The Story of the Life Work of Father Pius Parsch.* There is no page numeration: this quotation is from what would be pp. 22ff.

139 In the author's opinion Parsch, along with practically all the leaders of the Liturgical Movement of the twentieth century, would repudiate the excesses and abuses committed under this banner following the Second Vatican Council.

Klaus Gamber praises this, noting that Parsch "in his time...opened up for many people a new world, namely that of joining in together with the prayer and the sacrifice of the priest at the altar," though he cautions that such could distort true liturgical participation, saying that Parsch's Mass "was often transformed into a prayer spoken by priest and people in alternation, and enlivened by a few hymns. Hardly a trace remained of the celebration of a mystery."[140]

Whilst it is questionable whether Parsch's adaptations such as celebrating the Mass *versus populum* or standing to receive Holy Communion in fact enhance active participation, and whilst it is true that liturgical participation is not exclusively verbal, we can see that Parsch was attempting, rather boldly, particularly in the extent of his use of the vernacular, to bring the people to the traditional Liturgy. He reformed the Liturgy in so far as he revived customs that had fallen into disuse (the offertory procession and the taking of a purification of wine after receiving Holy Communion), though he did not touch the texts or the structure of the rites. Very few, if any, churches offered their people the possibility of *participating in* Matins and Lauds on a Sunday, and of singing those parts of the Mass that are properly theirs, particularly the introit, offertory and communion antiphons. Is this not a revival that opens up the textual treasury of the traditional Liturgy for the people? His revival of processions, his use of lights and incense, do these not enhance the participation of mind *and* heart? Does not kneeling at the consecration and the "holy silence of the Canon-action," or the *solemn* passing of the kiss of peace contribute toward the same end?

Thus, whilst those raised on a low-Mass diet and with a rubricist's mentality may see Parsch as excessive and as unruly, he may rightly be said to be a proponent of participation in the traditional Liturgy, even though one may argue that some of his reforms were ill-considered and that he placed too much emphasis on verbal participation.

Parsch's apostolate grew beyond Saint Gertrude's principally by means of his publications.[141] He was not simply another promoter of

---

[140] *The Modern Rite*, p. 11.

[141] In 1922 a booklet explaining the Sunday Masses was produced. This quickly developed into the thousand page *Das Jahr des Heils* (The Year of Grace), translated into many languages. C. Howell SJ declares that it "won more adherents to the Liturgical Movement than any other book;" "Introduction" in: P. Parsch, *The Liturgy of the Mass*, p. ix. The English edition, *The Church's Year of Grace*, was published by the Liturgical Press, Collegeville, in five volumes between 1953 and 1959. The other arm of Parsch's wider apostolate was the periodical *Bibel und Liturgie* (Bible and Liturgy) that appeared in 1926, intended for the formation of the parochial clergy. For a contemporary account of Parsch's

liturgical piety: his emphasis on the fundamental relationship between Sacred Scripture and the Church's Liturgy was itself a significant development in liturgical theology.[142]

In 1934 Parsch began to speak of reform, suggesting the restoration of the Paschal Vigil to the evening. He also promoted the use of the vernacular: a vernacular ritual (for the administration of the Sacraments) was granted to Austria in 1935.[143] In the 1949 foreword *The Liturgy of the Mass* Parsch argued for reforms to the Mass. His motivation was noble:

> Sometimes our conclusions have prompted me to make certain proposals regarding the possible future development of the Liturgy of the Mass...
>
> I am impelled not by profitless disaffection, but by an ardent love of holy Church. I long to see this jewel in her crown, the Eucharist, shine forth in as perfect a setting as is possible.[144]

---

earlier work cf: G. Ellard SJ, "Liturgy for the common man in Austria," in: *OF* vol. III pp. 17-22.

142 L. Bouyer Cong. Orat., underlines this: "The advance caused by this development cannot be too greatly emphasised. First, it enabled men to grasp the full significance of the Liturgy itself by uniting it once more with its chief source, this source also now being valued in its fullness. At the same time the Liturgical Movement came in this way at last to promote that direct and abundant use of God's Word in all forms of Christian spirituality which for so long had been rendered suspect in the eyes of Catholics rather than effectively promoted by the sixteenth century reformers. This particular effect of the Biblical movement was accomplished by giving the Bible that living commentary without which it cannot be properly understood. For it is in the Liturgy that the Church best prepares us to understand God's Word, both by means of the light thrown on the texts of Holy Scripture by one another as they are placed together in the Liturgy, and also by the way in which the Liturgy itself handles the inspired themes which make up the unity of Revelation itself. This widening of the scope of the Liturgical Movement is a fact of the very greatest significance in the history of its development, for the importance of this biblical renewal inside the Liturgical Movement goes far beyond the sphere of practical methods, and involves theological implications of the greatest value... How close...the interrelation between Revelation and the Liturgy [is], or, more exactly, between the Divine Word and the congregational worship of the Church. To realise this interrelation and to grasp its full significance will prove to be one of the decisive factors in our attaining a true and renewed understanding of the nature of the Church itself. And such an understanding is certainly the supreme aim of the whole Liturgical Movement...it is only in and through each other that the Mystery of Christian worship and the living Word of God can both be rightly understood in the living Church;" *Life and Liturgy*, p. 66.

143 Cf. C. Howell SJ, "Introduction" in: P. Parsch, *The Liturgy of the Mass*, p. ix.

144 *The Liturgy of the Mass*, pp. xi-xii.

The proposals he makes, radical enough in his day, are moderate and are well argued from liturgical history: vernacular readings, the restoration of the offertory procession, an increase in the number of prefaces, frequent communion from hosts consecrated at the same Mass,[145] an improvement in the quality of the bread used at Mass and the reception of Holy Communion under both species. Significantly, he does not envisage the vernacularisation of the Mass, and far from calling for any reform of the Roman canon, he underlines the value of its silent recitation in a most beautiful passage.[146] Parsch does not call for a restoration of the *preces,* and admires the last Gospel. His calls for the reform of the number of collects at Mass and of the ranking of feasts had been implemented before the publication of the English edition of the book.[147]

Parsch knew well that the Liturgy had developed over time, and believed that it ought to continue to do so. His desire for reform respected the principle of the organic development of the Liturgy, indeed he enunciated this principle eloquently:

> Our Eucharistic rite may be compared to an ancient and magnificent cathedral. It is a structure of prayers and ceremonies that has been nineteen hundred years in building. Clearly, therefore, every age and style will have made its contribution, and it would be a grave mistake to ignore the later elements in its construction and to seek to reduce the Mass to its ancient classic style. We must accept the Mass as it has developed through the ages. We may indeed prefer the ancient style—such an attitude is understandable—but to condemn outright everything that is of later origin would be petty and unworthy.[148]

Parsch is another example of the Liturgical Movement's openness to prudent reform that sought to respect objective liturgical Tradition according to the principles of liturgical reform.[149]

---

145 Encouraged by Benedict XIV: *Certiores effecti,* 1 September 1742; cf. *Papal Teachings: The Liturgy,* 22.

146 Cf. P. Parsch, *The Liturgy of the Mass,* pp. 67-71, 145, 178-9, 226, 257, 311-313.

147 Cf. ibid., pp. 131, 146.

148 Ibid., p. 325.

149 The author visited Saint Gertrude's Klosterneuberg on Holy Saturday (11th April) 1998. Information regarding Parsch, and Saint Gertrude's following his death, was provided by Frau Krasny of Klosterneuberg who had known him. Parsch was buried in 1954 in front of his *versus populum* altar in St Gertrude's. The Church has been redundant since 1996. It stands today, exactly as Parsch designed it, his tasteful vestments and furnishings unused, perhaps something of a mausoleum to his ideals?

The North American Liturgical Weeks

A resolution of the first Liturgical Week, held in 1940, explained its purpose:

> It is designed primarily to serve as a representative national forum in which liturgical leaders can discuss their problems, exchange ideas and generally act to co-ordinate their efforts toward a common goal. It is only a forum, and has not been conceived as a body competent to recommend or propose liturgical reforms...[150]

By "reforms" here, we should understand changes to the ritual: the vernacular,[151] the offertory procession, evening Mass and Mass facing the people, were certainly discussed.[152]

The published proceedings of the Liturgical Weeks are a testimony to their endeavours in the promotion of liturgical piety, faithful to their original purpose, throughout the USA. A detailed survey of this literature lies beyond our scope. However we shall have recourse to it in other contexts, and examine the work of one prominent person in the life of the Liturgical Weeks from their inception.

Martin Hellriegel

Hellriegel was a convent chaplain in O'Fallon, Missouri for over twenty years up to 1940, and pastor of the parish of Holy Cross, St Louis, from 1940 onward. His work illustrates the practical application of the ideals of the Liturgical Movement and of the reforms it envisaged at the local level. At the 1942 Liturgical Week Hellriegel related the genesis of his ideals:

> Although I was born into a liturgically inspired home in 1890, I was baptised into the Liturgy...in 1909...but my *conversio morum* took place at Maria Laach. That was in 1922, when I made a memorable visit there. Ever since I have been drawing copiously on that rich source of liturgical inspiration...[153]

---

150 Benedictine Liturgical Conference, *National Liturgical Week (USA) 1940*, p. 233.

151 The 1944 week included a scholarly paper by Dom Rembert Sorg OSB, "The Language of the Roman Liturgy," the conclusion of which, given the overwhelming favour shown by the Liturgical Movement to the use of the vernacular, is of interest: "...it is quite unnecessary, from the standpoint of active participation, and altogether regrettable for disciplinary and theological reasons, to substitute a vernacular for the Latin of our Roman Liturgy;" in: The Liturgical Conference, *National Liturgical Week (USA) 1944*, p. 144.

152 Cf. "Secretary's Report" in: The Liturgical Conference, *Christ's Sacrifice and Ours: National Liturgical Week (USA) 1947*, pp. 132-134.

153 Discussion at the National Liturgical Week (USA), 14 October 1942, in: Benedictine Liturgical Conference, *National Liturgical Week (USA) 1942*, p. 142.

At O'Fallon, Hellriegel introduced the dialogue Mass, "prepared the sisters to celebrate fully the solemn seasons of the church year," and placed "particular emphasis...on making the daily holy sacrifice, especially the Sunday high Mass, the greatest experience of all." He also introduced the offertory procession.[154] A novice at O'Fallon during the 1930s recalls:

> Hellriegel helped the community of sisters to see itself in the light of the Church's Tradition. The postulants and novices were carefully trained to find their spiritual life grounded in the Sacred Liturgy...The life of the religious was seen to be the flowering of the baptismal life and its growth always was in keeping with the life of the church.[155]

The agenda for liturgical reform he set himself as pastor at the 1940 Liturgical Week is impressive:

> (1) We must do away with all slovenliness and routine. *Sancta sancte,* God's things must be done in God's way!
> (2) Back, therefore, to a holier and worthier celebration of the Christ-life-carrying and the Christ-life-imparting mysteries, the Holy Sacrifice, the sacraments and the sacramentals.
> (3) Back to the Sunday High Mass, 52 times a year. It is the ideal way of celebrating the Lord's death, particularly on the Lord's day.
> (4) Back to an active participation by every member of the parish in the prayers and the chants of the Church.
> (5) Back to a more earnest preparation and a more joyful announcement of the living word of God. Back to the "homily" patterned after the homilies of the Fathers.
> (6) Back to the Sunday and feastday Vespers...
> (7) Back to a fitting celebration of the patronal feast...
> (8) Back to our cassock and surplice for the administration of the sacraments to the sick. The time has come for the "embryo" of a stole put over the civilian coat to make room for vestments that are a "worthy frame around God's picture."
> (9) Back to Advent, Lent, and ember days cleansed from lottos, bingos and buncos.
> (10) In short: Back to a *sentire cum Ecclesia* for the purpose of restoring true Catholic parochial life in the cell of Christ's Mystical Body, the parish.[156]

---

154 Cf. M.P. Ellebracht, "Martin Hellriegel: Pastor," in: R. Tuzik, *How Firm a Foundation: Leaders of the Liturgical Movement,* pp. 185-186.
155 Ibid., p. 187.
156 "The Parish and Divine Worship," in: Benedictine Liturgical Conference, *National Liturgical Week (USA) 1940,* pp. 32-33.

A year later he could present a no less impressive list of nineteen liturgical achievements (including the *versus populum* celebration of the Holy Thursday Mass) in his first year as pastor.[157]

In 1941 Hellriegel published an article in *Orate Fratres* in which he discussed proposals for the reform of High Mass. He suggests celebrating it earlier on Sunday mornings so that it is the main Mass rather than the late one, and so that the people could communicate from hosts consecrated at that Mass. He insists that the people sing "all the responses," and gives practical suggestions for this.[158] Not once does he suggest that the rite itself is in need of reform: rather it is the celebration and participation in it that stand in urgent need of reform.

Hellriegel continued his involvement in the North American Liturgical Weeks, and contributed "Towards a Living Parish" for *Worship* for many years. His work witnesses to the sound aims of the Liturgical Movement, and to their successful practical application.[159] The reforms he promoted were pastoral, albeit in one instance mistaken.[160] His work as a liturgical pastor remains exemplary.[161]

---

157 Cf. "A Pastor's Description of Liturgical Participation in His Parish (Continued)," Benedictine Liturgical Conference, *National Liturgical Week (USA) 1941*, pp. 82-90.

158 Cf. "Merely Suggesting" in: *OF* vol. XV pp. 393-394.

159 Sister Mary Gabriel Burke's Master of Education essay, the field of research for which was Hellriegel's parish, indicates, some ten years later, how Holy Cross' liturgical life was underpinned by a far reaching educational philosophy: "Unless children have come to appreciate the Liturgy by actual and consistent participation, they will live the 'way of the world.' It is essential that teachers understand the sacrificial and transforming character of Liturgy and see the Liturgy as a reflection of Catholic philosophy;" *Liturgy at Holy Cross: In Church & School*, pp. 50-51. For a detailed exposition of the educational philosophy of the Liturgical Movement see: E. Athill, *Teaching Liturgy in Schools.*

160 On celebrating Mass *versus populum* ("facing the people"). The mistaken assumption behind this practice is seen, when, at a demonstration of Low Mass at the 1951 Liturgical Week, Hellriegel explained "The altar has been set up here facing you, so as to enable all to follow the rite without difficulty, as well as to promote a better sense of participation. A similar arrangement...exists in Rome in St Peter's Basilica, as well as in other great churches of the world; and this was the arrangement that obtained throughout many centuries of the Church's history..." *The Priesthood of Christ: National Liturgical Week (USA) 1951*, p. 3.

161 In the preface to the 1995 edition of *The Recovery of the Sacred*, p. 9, J. Hitchcock reported, not without significance, that "the Liturgical Movement...turned sharply leftward immediately after the Council, so that some of its pioneers, such as Msgr Martin B. Hellriegel...were quickly estranged from the Movement they had laboured so long to bring to fruition." Hitchcock adds: "Before Msgr Hellriegel died in 1981, the author had several candid conversations with him in which America's greatest pastoral liturgist expressed his deep disappointment at the post-conciliar developments." In a letter to the author dated 15th November

Dom Odo Casel OSB

Casel, a monk of Maria Laach and probably the Movement's most significant theologian, advocated a reform of the theological *perception* of the Liturgy itself. In the light of the development of the theology of the Church as the Mystical Body of Christ, Casel developed his theology of worship, of the *Mysterienlehre*. He taught:

> The content of the mystery of Christ is...the person of the God-man and his saving deed for the Church; the Church, in turn, enters the mystery through this deed...
>
> The Christian thing, therefore, in its full and primitive meaning of God's good Word, or Christ's, is not as it were a philosophy of life with religious background music, nor a moral or theological training; it is a *mysterium* as St Paul means the word, a revelation made by God to man through acts of God-manhood, full of life and power; it is mankind's way to God made possible by this revelation and the grace of it communicating the solemn entry of the redeemed Church into the presence of the everlasting Father through sacrifice, through perfect devotion; it is the glory that blossoms out of it...
>
> What is necessary is a living, active sharing in the redeeming deed of Christ...For this purpose the Lord has given us the mysteries of worship: the sacred actions which we perform, but which, at the same time, the Lord performs upon us by his priests' service in the Church. Through these actions it becomes possible for us to share most intensively and concretely in a kind of immediate contact, yet most spiritually too, in God's saving acts.[162]

1997, Hitchcock explained: "I can testify to my own experience. I knew Msgr Hellriegel—not intimately—beginning about 1955 and lasting until his death in 1981, when he was 91. Especially between about 1970 and his death I would talk with him once or twice a year. He was never bitter or angry about liturgical change, but he was what I would call melancholy. He would say sadly things like, 'this is not what we had in mind when we advocated liturgical reform.' He was fairly scathing about balloons, secular readings at Mass, and other such abuses. He also thought the idea of 'participation' had been skewed in a bad way. For him, participation meant prayerful, knowledgeable entry by the laity into the inner meaning of the Liturgy as it was being celebrated. He favoured congregational responses and singing, offertory processions, etc. But he disliked informality, 'spontaneity,' overly intrusive priests, etc. He had always taken a somewhat neutral position towards the vernacular. He was not opposed to it, nor did he think it was crucial to authentic reform...He did on a number of occasions specifically tell me that he was very disappointed in the way in which the 'reform' had gone."

[162] *The Mystery of Christian Worship and other writings*, pp. 12-15.

Casel included the celebration of the sacraments and of the entire liturgical year in this teaching: Christ acts today through the mystery of the Sacred Liturgy. This innovative theology left little room for a-liturgical piety, and implicitly claimed a theological primacy for the Liturgical Movement, the likes of which few of its proponents dared to imagine in the 1930s.[163]

This provoked controversy. Casel's use of material drawn from pagan mystery cults caused astonishment, and has, in retrospect, been said to betray "a certain naïveté" by imposing Christian and New Testament concepts onto his study of Graeco-Roman mystery cults.[164] Some read Pius XII's 1947 encyclical *Mediator Dei* as a condemnation of his theories, whilst others claimed that the encyclical vindicated his theological stance.[165] Casel did not live to see his stance vindicated. His friends saw his death in 1948, as the result of a fatal heart attack suffered in the very act of proclaiming the paschal mystery during the paschal vigil, as an apposite consummation of his life's work.

What is significant is that Casel, as an eminent theological reformer of the Liturgical Movement, placed little if any importance on the possibility of ritual reforms so often desired by his contemporaries. As a monk of Maria Laach he was certainly well acquainted with such.[166] However his theology of worship which he implemented in the convent to which he was chaplain[167] placed little importance on subjective ritual reforms. He spoke rather of "the 'givenness,' the objectivity of Liturgy,"[168] in a manner which put subjective concerns into sharp relief:

> The Church not only stretches far beyond all national boundaries of one age, but from the beginning of the world to the end, from penitent Adam the just man, to the last saint at the world's end. All pray and work in the building of our Liturgy. There are times when it grows in lively fashion, springs up, when life in the spirit of Christ and the body is so strong that it creates a forceful artistic expression for itself; the first centuries particularly were an age of this kind. There are other ages which have been less fresh, less rich; they keep the truth and

---

163 Pius XII's 1947 encyclical *Mediator Dei* can be said to begin to go down this theological path. *Sacrosanctum Concilium* is heavily indebted to the liturgical theology of Casel; cf. A. Nichols OP, "Odo Casel Revisited" in *Antiphon* vol. III no. 1 p. 18. Cf. also: Arno Shilson, "Liturgy as the Presence of the Mysteries of the Life of Jesus According to Odo Casel" in: *Communio* vol. XXIX no. 1 pp. 39-46.

164 Cf. Malloy, "Odo Casel," in: Tuzik, *How Firm a Foundation: Leaders of the Liturgical Movement*, p. 54.

165 Cf. A. Nichols OP, "Odo Casel Revisited" in: *Antiphon* vol. III no. 1 pp. 15-18.

166 Maria Laach was an early practitioner of the dialogue Mass and of Mass *versus populum*.

167 Holy Cross Abbey, Herstelle. Cf. H.A. Reinhold "Dom Odo Casel" in: *OF* vol. XXII pp. 366-372.

168 O. Casel OSB, *The Mystery of Christian Worship and other writings*, p. 76.

> goodness they have inherited, cultivate and hand it on. In no case is it 'historicism' on the Church's part when she holds fast to the ancient and traditional fashion of her worship; rather, this love of what she has received comes from her very nature, from the timeless personality which we have seen, belongs to her; in a fashion she shares God's everlastingness. The Church does not belong to yesterday; she need not be always producing novelties; she has treasures which never grow old. Therefore she is happy with Tradition. Men, creatures of a single day, come and go, with no joy in antiquity; the Church can wait. Other generations will come to be grateful for her conservatism.
>
> When, therefore, the Church of our time makes her celebration one of rigid pattern this follows from her loyalty to Tradition and a love for real value which rests upon here everlastingness. The deepest realism, however, rests not on a mere adherence to traditional forms, but in the mind of Christ and the Church, which reaches beyond all individuals. The discipline of the Church, of course, prefers to hold fast to the rites and texts which were created in Christian antiquity, and does so in the belief that those ancient times created what they did with a peculiarly high awareness of the Church's mind. Realism and a sense of form here protect not merely inner reality: exterior discipline serves inward order and proceeds from it...
>
> Thus Catholic worship has strongly objective lines: they are expressed in its form. Nothing subjective or arbitrary, no personal enthusiasm, momentary ecstasy or expressionism are to mark it; what it seeks are clarity beyond the limits of any single person, roots for a content that is divine and everlasting, a sober peaceful and measured expression of what belongs to it, in forms which give direction to the over-flow of thought and emotion, which put nature and passion within its bonds.[169]

Organic, developed reality is, for Casel, the objective norm. His is not the position of a romantic immobilist, although some regard him thus. Rather, Casel views the Liturgy as a living, organic reality, which does not exclude the possibility of development. It is fair to say that the importance he gives to objective liturgical Tradition would clearly exclude any radical restructuring of the traditional Liturgy in the light of subjective contemporary concerns. Casel thus enunciates most clearly the principle seen already, that the objective has priority over the subjective in liturgical development.

Charles Davis deprecated this stress on the objectivity of the Liturgy in an article, which prefaces the 1962 English edition of Casel's works:

---

[169] Ibid., pp. 76-77, 78.

> I think it is true to say that Casel was out of touch with the pastoral problems of the liturgical revival and, further, that there is a definite tinge of romanticism in his approach to the Liturgy. By romanticism I mean a failure to see and admit the reality, often defective, of liturgical forms and practice in the actual life of the Church, both past and present. His view on the use of Latin[170] and his dismissal of the desire for intelligibility—which, unfortunately, are sure to be seized upon and exploited—are only the more visible symptoms of [his] attitude...the Liturgy he describes does not seem to be the growing and changing thing that it actually has been. He has fixed it in an imagined moment of classical perfection and isolated it from the ups and downs of its history...[171]

Davis' criticism appears not to take account of Casel's belief that "all pray and work in the building of our Liturgy" cited above. Casel did not live to discuss the liturgical changes of the late twentieth century, though his importance as "*the* great father of the twentieth century Liturgical Movement" has recently been underlined.[172]

Anton Baumstark

Baumstark, a layman, died in 1948. In 1952, prefacing a new edition of Baumstark's *Comparative Liturgy,* first published in 1939, Botte declared:

> At the present time when there is much talk of the reform and adaptation of liturgies, it is more than ever needful to be informed about their traditional history. The Liturgical Movement may put forward some very bold reforms and may well set aside the letter. But it should always keep the spirit of the Tradition. From this point of view, Baumstark's work is important.[173]

---

170 Casel saw no need for the vernacular, placing great value on a sacred language in worship: cf. ibid., p. 79.

171 Cf. ibid., pp. xi-xii. Chapter 5 of Davis' *Liturgy and Doctrine* explains Casel's views without making this criticism.

172 A. Nichols OP, "Odo Casel Revisited" in: *Antiphon* vol. III no. 1 p. 18. Nichols is speaking of Casel's influence over the Second Vatican Council's *Sacrosanctum Concilium* and beyond: "...the reluctance to treat Dom Odo Casel as one of the great fathers, indeed I would say *the* great father of the twentieth century Liturgical Movement made it easy for those who had quite different agendas for the future of that Movement, and appealed to other, less crucial, sections of the Conciliar constitution—those, namely, dealing with the pastoral adaptation of the rites—to push the entire liturgical life of Western Catholicism in a direction which, I do not think it excessive to say, Casel would abhor." The Society of Saint Pius X's *The Problem of the Liturgical Reform* severely critiques the use made of Casel's insight by the Conciliar reformers.

173 *Comparative Liturgy,* p. xi.

His book, the research for which is grounded in Eastern as well as Western liturgical history, devotes a chapter to "The Laws of Liturgical Evolution." Baumstark writes descriptively not prescriptively: his "laws" describe liturgical evolution in history.

In the Roman rite Baumstark observes up to and following Trent a tendency towards a "uniformity" in the "substance of forms and texts" which tolerates "divergent practice" in "secondary customs." The "*propria* of the dioceses and religious orders of our own days," he says, bear witness to this substantial unity which permits a certain degree of diversity.[174]

Baumstark speaks of two laws "which determine liturgical evolution." The first is the law of organic development. Noting its association with a tendency towards abbreviation in liturgical prayers and readings, he describes it as:

> 'Organic' and therefore 'Progressive.' In general, because the primitive elements are not immediately replaced by completely new ones, the newcomers at first take their place alongside the others. Before long they assume a more vigorous and resistant character, and when the tendency to abbreviation makes itself felt it is the more primitive elements which are the first to be affected; these disappear completely or leave only a few traces.[175]

His second law is that "primitive conditions are maintained with greater tenacity in the more sacred seasons of the liturgical year."[176] The Roman Holy Week rites demonstrate this.

The relationship between legitimate liturgical diversity in the Roman rite, even in what is regarded as the post-Tridentine liturgical dark ages, and substantial unity, is noteworthy.[177] So too is the fact that liturgical development is not a matter of radical innovation ("primitive elements are not immediately replaced by completely new ones"), and that any displacement of extant liturgical forms is a gradual phenomenon. In conjunction with this we may also note that the losses inherent in the "tendency to abbreviation" of which Baumstark speaks, however lamentable to the liturgical historian or archaeologist, is nevertheless a part of the progression of the living Liturgy in its growth throughout the ages.[178] Finally, we notice in Baumstark's second law that the Liturgy itself has accorded an importance to particular customs in

---

[174] Ibid., p. 19.
[175] Ibid., p. 23.
[176] Ibid., p. 27.
[177] The Second Vatican Council would speak of "substantial unity;" cf. *Sacrosanctum Concilium* no. 38.
[178] Transplanting or restoring such practices does not occur to Baumstark.

certain seasons, preserving them almost in spite of other liturgical developments.

For Baumstark, then, the Liturgy is an objective Tradition that is a progressing and developing organism.

Gerald Ellard SJ – "The Mass of the Future"

In 1948 this popular American writer published *The Mass of the Future.* It "attempts a full-length account of the aims and objectives...of the Liturgical Movement."[179] Assuming developments in the Mass rite are going to occur, Ellard enunciates the following principles:

> In the Catholic Church nothing can be said to have a future, save in so far as it has a past and is deeply rooted in Tradition...
>
> On those marginal areas...where the Mass is reckoned as our joint worship, Christ's and ours, its offering, it is clear, is capable of a good and a better, of stagnation or of growth, of loss or of gain...
>
> Every single period in the Church's history has contributed to enrich these rites, and the twentieth century will want to go on making its contribution, too, all in orderly and proper fashion, *sentire cum Ecclesia, agere cum Ecclesia.* In putting its hand to the task the twentieth century will be guided by that cognate law traced by the great Cardinal Newman for appraising dogmatic growth: "There is no violent break with the past, development must be true to, and consonant with, its own immediate background." So whatever study and prudent zeal may prompt twentieth century Catholics to contribute to the Eucharistic heritage of the ages, they will carefully avoid casting overboard any value a previous age brought with it.[180]

Ellard's principles are in harmony with liturgical Tradition and provide another example of the Liturgical Movement's concern that liturgical development be organic. His use of Newman in this respect is particularly illustrative.

He also manifests the increasing importance of "study" on the question of liturgical reform. Whilst scholarship served the reform of St Pius V, to establish the authentically developed objective liturgical Tradition, the antiquarian position of scholar-reformers has been consistently rejected. Ellard identifies himself with the rejection of the latter by Pius XII.[181]

Ellard's principles are applied in section three of the book. He argues that the Mass could be renamed the "Eucharistic Sacrifice"[182] and

---

179 *The Mass of the Future,* p. vii.

180 Ibid., pp. vii-ix.

181 Cf. ibid., p. ix.

182 Cf. ibid., pp. 241-248.

calls for increased permissions for the vernacular.[183] Calendar revision, a codification of the rubrics of the missal to include authoritative clarifications and directives, and the inclusion of some new biblical *pericopæ* are suggested, as are some minor ceremonial improvements based on precedents already in the Roman rite.[184] A re-ordering of churches is envisaged which tends to favour, but which does not insist upon, Mass celebrated facing the people.[185] Communal singing, in the vernacular as well as in Latin, is hoped for.[186] Meaningful offertory processions are seen as integral,[187] as is more frequent sacramental communion.[188] Mass propers for different categories of lay people, festivals and occasions are hoped for.[189] Priestly concelebration of the Mass is recommended.[190] The rationing of votive requiem Masses is called for to allow the faithful access to the weekday liturgical texts.[191] The celebration of Mass at more convenient times, including the evenings, is wanted.[192]

In their application, Ellard's proposals are consonant with his principles. He gives weight to the needs of modern man and to desirable revivals that do no radical violence to objective liturgical Tradition.[193] He does, though, fall for the 'facing the people' fad. Yet the *Ordo Missæ* is respected intact. It is, rather, primarily people's attitudes and practices that Ellard seeks to reform. Again we see the Movement's sense of Tradition and its prudent desire for organic development.

The Holy See and Liturgical Reform up to 1948

The Liturgical Movement originated and grew primarily through the efforts of monastic centres and other key individuals. It arose from a desire to nourish the whole Church once again with the substantial food of liturgical piety. In this it was thoroughly and positively traditional.

Whilst the Holy See did not produce the Liturgical Movement, nor closely direct its activities, neither did it stand aloof from it. We have

---

183 Cf. ibid., pp. 249-257.
184 Cf. ibid., pp. 258-265.
185 Cf. ibid., pp. 266-273.
186 Cf. ibid., pp. 274-279.
187 Cf. ibid., pp. 280-289.
188 Cf. ibid., pp. 290-296.
189 Cf. ibid., pp. 297-308.
190 Cf. ibid., pp. 309-321: including an extraordinary plan for a "Concelebration Church" on pp. 316-320.
191 Cf. ibid., pp. 322-330.
192 Cf. ibid., pp. 331-344.
193 Regarding 'facing the people' cf. supra p. 91. *Post factum* reservations about the abuse of the vernacular and of concelebration ought not to colour any assessment of Ellard's desire that they be considered.

seen how the kernel of liturgical piety was articulated and authoritatively promoted by St Pius X.[194] In 1915 the Cardinal Secretary of State communicated the "cordial satisfaction" and "joyful expectations" of Benedict XV with regard to the regional liturgical conference being held at the abbey of Montserrat, once again restating the importance of liturgical piety.[195]

Such papal encouragement continued. Pius XI's 1928 Apostolic Constitution *Divini Cultus*, marked the twenty-fifth anniversary of St Pius X's seminal *Tra le sollecitudini*. It insisted upon St Pius X's reform of liturgical music—which suggests that hitherto it had not been sufficiently implemented—and asserted the "close connection between dogma and the Sacred Liturgy, and between Christian worship and the sanctification of the faithful."[196] In a passage explaining the relationship of popes to the Liturgy, Pius XI goes on to say:

> No wonder, then, that the Roman pontiffs have been so solicitous to safeguard and protect the Liturgy. They have used the same care in making laws for the regulation of the Liturgy, in preserving it from adulteration, as they have in giving accurate expression to the dogmas of the faith.[197]

The original speaks of the pope's rôle as custodian of the Liturgy: "sollicitudinem in liturgia tutanda et custodienda."[198] This, in the author's opinion, is a singularly important statement by a reigning pope on the competence of the Bishop of Rome with regard to liturgical reform. It makes clear that the pope is the custodian of the (living) objective liturgical Tradition and, by implication, is not its proprietor.

Whilst *Divini cultus* was Pius XI's most solemn approbation of the Liturgical Movement, it was not an isolated instance. His pontificate is permeated by encouraging remarks addressed to groups and

---

194 Cf. supra pp. 64ff. It should be noted that whilst St Pius X was speaking authoritatively, the liturgical piety he elucidated was the product of neither himself as Pope, nor of any curial agency. He was recalling the Church to fundamental principles and ratifying and promoting universally the work of the nineteenth century liturgical pioneers, of which he himself was one. In an ultramontane age, this was a most apposite exercise of the Petrine office.

195 Cf. "Pope Benedict XV and the Liturgy" in: *OF* vol. IX p. 325.

196 K. Seasoltz OSB, *The New Liturgy*, p. 58. "Hinc intima quædam necessitudo inter dogma et liturgiam sacram, itemque inter cultum christianum et populi sanctificationem;" A. Bugnini CM, *Documenta*, p. 60.

197 Ibid., (Seasoltz) p. 59.

198 "Ex his intelligitur cur Romani Pontifices tantam adhibuerint sollicitudinem in liturgia tutanda et custodienda; et quemadmodum tam multa erat eis cura in dogmate aptis verbis exprimendo, ita liturgiæ sacræ leges ordinare, tueri et ab omni adulteratione præservare studuerint;" A. Bugnini CM, *Documenta*, p. 61.

individuals engaged in the liturgical apostolate,[199] including, in December 1935, a private audience accorded to Dom Capelle, Abbot of Mont-César.[200]

Pius XII, who as Secretary of State to Pius XI had conveyed the latter's encouragement on a number of occasions, himself continued to support the Movement in addresses[201] and in two seminal encyclicals: *Mystici Corporis* in 1943,[202] which laid the ecclesiological foundation for the growth of liturgical piety, and what was regarded as its specifically liturgical "second chapter,"[203] *Mediator Dei,* considered below.

We also find the Holy See developing the Liturgy during this period. In 1919 two new prefaces (of St Joseph and of the Requiem Mass) were added to the missal: the first in many centuries. Another two were added, in 1925 (Christ the King) and in 1928 (the Sacred Heart) respectively. In 1922 the Sacred Congregation of Rites admitted the permissibility of the dialogue Mass.[204] Pius XI had himself celebrated a dialogue Mass in St Peter's on May 27th.[205]

In 1919 and 1924 Benedict XV and Pius XI authorised the restoration of the traditional Liturgy of the rite of Braga, the ancient Portuguese use of the Roman ritual family originating between the eleventh and thirteenth centuries.[206] Since the sixteenth century various untraditional elements (spurious legends of saints, the breviary hymns of Urban VIII, ritual practices from the Roman missal, etc.) had crept into the Liturgy. The Roman rite had itself increasingly displaced the traditional Braga Liturgy until the traditional Liturgy was "restricted to a comparatively few churches in the diocese."[207] The reform of the early twentieth century expunged untraditional incursions and reasserted the obligation of the traditional rite, and revised it to bring it in line with the structural reforms of St Pius X to the breviary.[208]

---

199 Cf. "Two Papal Documents on the Liturgy" in: *OF* vol. IX pp. 167-170; "Pope Pius XI and the Liturgical Movement" in: *OF* vol. X pp. 377-378; G. Ellard SJ, "Pope Pius XI on Corporate Worship" in: *OF* vol. X pp. 553-561; "The Liturgical Movement as Approved by Pius XI" in: *OF* vol. XVIII pp. 324-328.

200 Cf. B. Capelle OSB, "The Holy See and the Liturgical Movement" in: *OF* vol. XI pp. 1-8; and: "The Holy See and the Liturgical Movement (2)" *OF* vol. XI pp. 50-61.

201 Cf. G. Ellard SJ, *The Mass in Transition*, pp. 348-354; also J. Ford "Teaching Liturgy in the Seminary" in: *OF* vol. XXI pp. 294-295.

202 E. Koenker, *The Liturgical Renaissance in the Roman Catholic Church*, p. 20, describes it as presenting "a fundamental doctrine of the Movement."

203 G. Ellard SJ, "At Mass with my Encyclical" in: *OF* vol. XXII p. 241.

204 Cf. A. Bugnini, CM, *Documenta*, p. 55.

205 Cf. G. Ellard SJ, *The Mass in Transition*, p. 341.

206 Cf. A.A. King, *Liturgies of the Primatial Sees*, pp. 190ff.

207 Ibid., p. 204.

208 Cf. ibid., pp. 204-206.

The initiative for this restoration lay with the Archbishops of Braga. The pope ratified their initiative. Benedict XV's 1919 Apostolic Constitution *Sedis huius* approving of the new edition of the Braga breviary affirmed the legitimate ritual diversity within the Roman rite, referring to the veneration to be shown to such rites by virtue of their antiquity, and of the opportuneness of reviving this rite "dating from remote antiquity."[209] Pius XI expressed a similar respect for liturgical Tradition in his 1924 Bull *Inter multiplices* approving of the new edition of the missal[210] which, whilst acknowledging the contribution of the growth in studies of ancient liturgical sources, includes a significant passage on their risks:

> However, in these studies concerning ancient rites the due preparation of knowledge must not be overlooked, which should have as its companion piety and docile and humble obedience. And if these be lacking, any investigation whatever about ancient liturgies of the Mass will turn out to be irreverent and fruitless: for when the supreme authority of the Apostolic See in liturgical matters, which deservedly rejects puffed-up learning, and, with the Apostle, "speaks wisdom among the perfect" (1 Cor. 8:1, 2:6), has been spurned, whether through ignorance or a proud and conceited spirit, the danger immediately threatens that the error known as modernism will be introduced also into liturgical matters.[211]

If we interpret this statement of Pius XI in the light of his understanding in *Divini Cultus* of the pope as "custodian" of the Liturgy, what we have here is not purely an ultramontane assertion of papal authority over the Liturgy, but a salutary warning lest the Liturgy, and liturgical reform, fall prey to a modernist reductionism which rejects organic development as illegitimate: what Pius XII would later proscribe as antiquarianism. Thus, in the context of the restoration of the rite of Braga, Pius XI asserts the legitimacy of developed liturgical Tradition against antiquarian enthusiasms.

The significance of the restoration of the rite of Braga in the history of liturgical development is twofold. In the first place it

---

209 "a remota gaudet antiquitate;" C. Braga CM, *Documenta*, pp. 275.

210 Cf. *Missale Bracarense*, pp. vii-ix. Both Bugnini's *Documenta* and Braga's *Documenta* fail to include this document.

211 "Hisce tamen de antiquis Ritibus studiis præmittenda est debita scientiæ præparatio, quæ comitem habeat pietatem ac docilem humilemque obedientiam. Quæ si deficerent, profana evaderet et sterilis quævis de antiquis Missæ Liturgiis investigatio: contempta enim, sive ob ignorantiam, sive ob elatum inflatumque animum, suprema in rebus liturgicis auctoritate Sedis Apostolicæ, quæ merito scientiam repudiat inflantem et cum Apostolo sapientiam loquitur inter perfectos (1 Cor. 8:1, 2:6), periculum prorsus immineret ne error ille, qui modernismus audit, in res quoque liturgicas induceretur;" ibid., p. viii. [Translation: A. Paver]

demonstrates, as did the liturgical reform following the Council of Trent, precisely how late "venerable liturgical antiquity" may be found: in this case we are speaking about a rite formed in the first centuries of the second millennium. Thus, what we understand as "venerable liturgical antiquity" is not necessarily a liturgical rite or form having a very early date of origin. This would be an archaeologist's understanding. Rather, by "venerable liturgical antiquity" we understand the worth of, and the respect to be shown to, a liturgical rite because of its having a place in living liturgical Tradition which, over a sufficient period of time, has come to be regarded as "venerable" no matter how late it originated. We recall that St Pius V accorded such status to liturgies having a tradition of at least two hundred years.

Secondly, in the restoration of the rite of Braga we see the Bishop of Rome confirming the action of a local bishop, recognising and restoring a traditional rite that had largely fallen into disuse. The venerable rite of Braga, corrupted and almost totally discarded, was reclaimed and reasserted, albeit with some developments. Here we find a confirmation of the right of local churches to their truly traditional liturgies, even when the events of history may have displaced them,[212] as part of the legitimate diversity of the Roman ritual family.

---

212 In 1996 "The Society of Saint Osmund for the preservation of the Sarum Rite in the Catholic Church" was formed in Oxford. The Sarum rite, together with those of the Religious Orders, is "the Roman Liturgy previous to the fourteenth century, with a few rare local customs added to it;" F. Cabrol, *The Mass of the Western Rites,* p. 191. It was the ancient Salisbury use of the Roman ritual family that thrived throughout much of England, parts of Scotland and Ireland until the Protestant Reformation. With the consent of the local bishop, Archbishop Maurice Couve de Murville of Birmingham, the Society organised two solemn Masses according to the Sarum rite at Merton College, Oxford, on February 10th 1996 and February 1st 1997. These celebrations ceased when the Congregation for Divine Worship rapidly responded to an inquiry from a private person dated 21st February 1997 saying: "Such celebrations are not lawful and the reasons advanced to justify them are spurious. As a Catholic in good standing you should have nothing to do with such activities. The celebration of the Liturgy is a most serious matter and is not to be subjected to esoteric whims;" Msgr Carmelo Nicolosi, 18 March 1997. A letter from the Secretary of the Congregation directed the local bishop to "ensure that the abuse committed is not repeated;" Archbishop G. M. Agnelo, 18 March 1997. Another celebration according to the Sarum rite, independent of the Society of Saint Osmund, occurred on 1 April 2000. Bishop Mario Conti (then) of Aberdeen celebrated it in King's College Chapel, Aberdeen, on the occasion of the chapel's quincentenary. Seemingly Bishop Conti was unaware of the earlier intervention of the Congregation. In a letter to the author dated 28th July 2000 Bishop Conti states: "Permission of the Holy See was not sought, and I judged that it was not needed, since the Mass is substantially that of the so-called Tridentine Rite, the central eucharistic prayer, or canon, being almost word for word that of the Roman canon still in use

In 1930 Pius XI established the *Sectio Historica* of the Sacred Congregation of Rites, part of whose mandate was to prepare for reform, emendation and the issue of new editions of liturgical texts and books.[213] In doing so we see his intention to continue the reform spoken of by St Pius X in 1911.[214] Before 1948 this *Sectio* issued only one consultation document on the reform of the rite of Confirmation.[215] It did not manage the publication of new editions of the liturgical books. Annibale Bugnini CM mentions of a draft for liturgical reform or codification in 1942 drawn up for the consideration of the Sacred Congregation of Rites, which came to nothing.[216]

In 1945 Pius XII permitted, though he did not impose, in the public or private use of the breviary a new translation of the psalter prepared by the Jesuits of the Pontifical Biblical Institute.[217] In doing so he acceded to the desires of scholars and of some clergy for a translation that was considered more accurate in the light of developments in the historico-critical method of Biblical scholarship. Given the integration of the text of the psalter into the texts of the missal, pontifical, ritual, chant, the writings of the Fathers and in many other aspects of the life of the Church, this was no small reform. Furthermore, the reform was not limited to improving the accuracy of the text; like the reform of breviary hymns authorised by Urban VIII, the style of the Latin text was also 'improved.'

---

throughout the Latin rite." In the author's opinion, in the light of the principles operative in the reinvigoration of the traditional rite of Braga, both the Archbishop of Birmingham and the Bishop of Aberdeen acted within their competence, in harmony with liturgical Tradition, and in accordance with the precedent of the Holy See by allowing, and in the case of the latter, by personally celebrating, Mass according to the Sarum rite. Further consideration of the restoration of the Sarum use needs to examine the discussion of the desirability of its restoration at the time of the restoration of the Catholic hierarchy in England in 1850, and the discussion of its possible adoption for Westminster Cathedral at the beginning of the twentieth century.

213 "Per evidenti ragioni di utilità la Sezione storica dovrà essere consultata per le riforme, emendazioni e nuove edizioni di testi et di libri liturgici;" A. Bugnini CM, *Documenta*, p. 67.

214 Cf. supra, p. 67.

215 Sacra Rituum Congregatio, Sectio Historica no. 12, *De Pontificali Romano Iussu Sanctissimi Domini Nostri Pii Papæ XI Emendato: I De Confirmandis.*

216 Cf. *TRL* p. 7. Cardinal Ferdinando Antonelli's papers contain a hand-written draft, dated 20th June 1945, signed by Archbishop Alfonso Carinci, Secretary of the Sacred Congregation of Rites, of a document "for the consideration of the Holy Father" outlining possibilities for reform of the breviary, and a further three hand-written pages by Archbishop Carinci on breviary reform, dated July 1945; Fondo Antonelli, Archive, Congregation of the Causes of the Saints.

217 Cf. *In cotidianis precibus,* 24 March 1945, in C. Braga CM, *Documenta,* pp. 531-533. Translation: K. Seasoltz OSB, *The New Liturgy*, pp. 104-107.

The Tablet commented two years later:

> We are strongly of the opinion that it is in the main an enormous improvement on the old, though we regret that the revision was not confined to changes of meaning and wish that no alterations had been made for the sake of Latinity. Only mistaken sense, surely, justifies departure from the venerable Vulgate text.[218]

A French Canon complained:

> It is the language chosen for this work which disturbs me, and the deliberate use of the Latin of Cicero-Caesar, of a Latin, consequently, anterior by nearly a century to Christianity...
>
> The psalms of the *Vulgate* are witnesses *par excellence* of [the] taking over of Old Testament ideas by the New. The senilities of stiff-necked Israel were charged with fresh and profound resonances as they fell from the lips of Christ and entered the Church's Liturgy, and these words sounded in ears and hearts alike a note which was at first unprecedented *but is now become traditional.*
>
> There is then a sort of historical absurdity in trying to translate, in a book of Christian prayers, the Latin of the Vulgate by the Latin of Cicero. In this literary exercise which might well serve as an occasion for the ingenuity of the humanists, but which has no place in the choir of the Church, one runs the risk of making the worst of both worlds.[219]

Reinhold wrote in 1948:

> Fr Bea's group of scholars struck light with bold strokes…few of us dared hope for such a bold solution. We did expect…a few corrections of our present text with a lot remaining uncorrected for dogmatic and traditional reasons. Criticism of the new text has been very outspoken, especially in France, where recognised scholars are all out to prove that one could do better with the original and better with the Latin...
>
> On principle, Father Bouyer's claim, that there is a Christian Latin, that of the Fathers and of the Liturgy, seems justified, and his wish to see the revision revised again in favour of a consistent application of the vocabulary and usage of the great Fathers appears reasonable.[220]

In 1961 he returned to the "problem of the psalter of Pius XII:"

---

218 From an unsigned report entitled "The Divine Office in France," in *The Tablet* 14th June 1947, p. 303. The report is based on a study of the Office in France by Hyacinthe Paissac OP in: *La Vie Spirituelle,* January 1947. It continues: "For the public Office many priests would like the use of French…The nuns are far more conservative. They are all for Latin and for the Vulgate Psalter."

219 E. Masure, "About the New Psalter" in: *Liturgy* vol. XVII pp. 9, 10-11.

220 "Towards the Breviary Reform" in: *OF* vol. XXIII p. 75.

> Gregorian musicologists, first rate experts of the late Latin, as it was developed by the Fathers and by the Church at the time of Pope Damasus I and St Jerome have protested that the psalter is unsuitable for Gregorian chant and is an academic Latin of pseudo-ciceronian hue and vocabulary...All I have read against the new psalter has its value, and it seems that a sort of high-school Latin has taken the place of a language organically wedded to Tradition. But that is not the question at all.
>
> The question really: does the new psalter come closer to the original Hebrew text?[221]

In the *motu proprio* promulgating it, Pius XII makes the use of the new psalter optional.[222] He thus shows a measure of respect for the objective traditional Liturgy, in this case for what the *Tablet* called "the venerable Vulgate text," and Reinhold, "a language organically wedded to Tradition." A tentative positing of new material, which we have also seen in the Carolingian reform, does at least mitigate the charge of absolute reform by edict and does give some scope for integration or evaluation over time. However, when papal authority has introduced a reform, it may be argued that many will accept it uncritically regardless of its consonance with objective liturgical Tradition. Catholic ultramontanism was certainly healthy in the 1940s and 1950s.

This reform also raises an important question: the place of scholarly insight and desires in liturgical reform. We shall return to it below when considering the later reforms of Pius XII.

Up to 1948 the Holy See increasingly granted permission for the use of the vernacular in some rites. The occasional use of the Czech language was permitted from 1920.[223] A new edition of the Roman missal for use in Dalmatia was published in 1927.[224] The text was entirely Slavonic (with the Canon printed in ancient Glagolitic characters in parallel). The use of a non-Latin Roman missal in this region has a history dating back at least to the seventeenth century.[225] A Croatian edition of the Roman ritual, which also traces its origin to the seventeenth century, was republished in 1929.[226] In 1933 the Sacred Congregation of Rites

---

[221] *The Dynamics of Liturgy*, p. 126. B. Avery OSB discusses the question further in his 1962 article "The Vulgate Psalter: A New Revision" in: *Worship* vol. XXXVI pp. 626-636.

[222] Pius XII allows its use "si libuerit," C. Braga CM, *Documenta*, p. 533.

[223] Cf. C.R.A. Cunliffe, *English in the Liturgy*, p. 4.

[224] Cf. *Rimski Missal Slověnskim Jesikom Prěsv. G. N. Urbana Papi VIII Povelĕnjem Izdan-Missale Romanum Slavonico Idiomate* (1927); also: C. Korolevsky, *Living Languages in Catholic Worship*, pp. 85-87.

[225] Cf. *Missale Romanum Slavonico Idiomate* (1631).

[226] Cf. C. Korolevsky, *Living Languages in Catholic Worship*, pp. 88-89.

approved a ritual in Slovenian.[227] A mostly German-language ritual was approved in principle in 1943.[228] A mainly French edition followed in 1946 and bilingual rituals were approved for Liège in Belgium in 1948.[229]

Rome also exercised vigilance over the Liturgical Movement. In response to some controversy over the Movement's orthodoxy and practices in Germany,[230] the German bishops established a liturgical commission under their direct supervision in 1940.[231] Towards the end of 1942 Archbishop Groeber of Frieburg circulated a memorandum amongst the bishops detailing seventeen criticisms of the Movement.[232] By January 1943 Rome asked for a report, which was sent under Cardinal Bertram's signature the following April.[233] Of concern was the possible diminution of devotion to the Sacred Heart and to the Blessed Virgin, the introduction of German at Mass, as well as the celebration of Mass *versus populum.*

Cardinal Bertram defended the *Gemeinschaftsmesse* (where some responses were made by the people in German, and the epistle and gospel were read over in German), the *Bet-Sing-Messe* (where a low Mass was said totally in Latin over which the people sang hymns in German), and the *deutsches Hochamt* (sung Mass where people sang the parts proper to them in German), arguing that for historical and, significantly, for pastoral reasons the German people should be allowed to continue such use of the vernacular at Mass.[234] He insisted that priests were using the Latin text of the missal and that the devotions mentioned above were not suffering. He petitioned for a new and simpler Latin psalter for the breviary, for further use of the vernacular in the ritual, and for the celebration of the Maundy Thursday and Easter Vigil ceremonies in the evening.[235]

---

[227] Cf. ibid., p. 89.

[228] Cf. A. Bugnini CM, *Documenta*, pp. 80-82.

[229] Cf. G. Ellard SJ, *The Mass in Transition,* p. 354; also SRC Decree P. 16/946.

[230] For a more detailed and highly critical account of these events cf. D. Bonneterre, *The Liturgical Movement,* pp. 39-44.

[231] Cf. E. Koenker, *The Liturgical Renaissance in the Roman Catholic Church*, pp. 18-20. Also: B. Neunheuser, "Report on Germany" in: *OF* vol. XXI pp. 114-122; G. Diekmann OSB, "Movement in Germany" in: *OF* vol. XXIII pp. 471-474. D. Bonneterre claims that this commission was skilfully comprised of "none other than the leading lights of the German movement;" *The Liturgical Movement*, p. 39.

[232] A translation appears in: T. Richstatter OFM, *Liturgical Law Today,* pp. 2-4.

[233] Cf. T. Maas-Ewerd, *Die Krise der Liturgischen Bewegung in Deutschland und Österreich,* pp. 634-646.

[234] Cf. H.E. Winstone, "Sunday Mass in a German Parish Church" in: *Liturgy* vol. XXVII pp. 9-18.

[235] Cf. T. Maas-Ewerd, *Die Krise der Liturgischen Bewegung in Deutschland und Österreich,* pp. 634-646.

The Secretary of State, Cardinal Maglione, communicated the Holy See's "most benign toleration"[236] of the use of German at Mass, adding that the question of the psalter was being studied further. Bertram's other requests remained unanswered.

Significantly, Maglione's letter speaks of:

> The fruits which can flow into the salvation of souls from the liturgical action, constrained by the just limits of Tradition and of prudence;

and of:

> The dangers, those either to Christian discipline or to the life of the Church in Germany, which can threaten the faith itself if straying individuals, 'by way of experiment' as they say, introduce aberrant novelties into the Liturgy.[237]

This explicit recognition of limits upon liturgical reform, only twenty years before the opening of the Second Vatican Council, is important. With regard to the petition of the German bishops, and in the light of its activity in the preceding twenty years it can certainly be said that the Holy See was open to, and indeed engaging upon the gradual development of the rite, to the preparation of new editions of the liturgical books and even to the increasing use of the vernacular according to pastoral need. It is certainly not true to say that the Holy See was rigid, or closed to the possibility of liturgical reform. Yet it explicitly recognised the limits upon development and reform imposed by liturgical Tradition and prudence.

Thus, whilst the Holy See welcomed and supported the sound aims of the Liturgical Movement, it exercised a supervisory rôle to safeguard liturgical Tradition and to guard against imprudence. Such a rôle is, in the light of the history of liturgical reform, properly that of the Bishop of Rome and of his officials. However, with the introduction of the psalter we have seen the emergence of a problem when reforms based on scholarly desires win the approbation of papal authority. To this we shall return.

---

236 "benignissime toleretur;" ibid., p. 694.

237 "licet fructus parvi non perpenderint qui ex actione liturgica, iustis traditionis ac prudentiæ coarctata limitibus, in animorum salutem permanare possunt, nihilo tamen secius opinati sunt fundamento minime caruisse timorem...ob pericula, quæ sive christianæ disciplinæ, sive Ecclesiæ vitæ in Germania, ipsique fidei imminere possint si a singulis 'via facti' uti aiunt, in rem liturgicam aberrantes inducantur novitates;" ibid., pp. 692-693. [Translation: A. Paver]

Beauduin's 1945 Norms for Liturgical Reform

The inaugural issue of *La Maison-Dieu* opened with Beauduin's article "Normes pratiques pour les réformes liturgiques," written as a charter for the work of the French *Centre de Pastorale Liturgique.* Given the author, the principles articulated are of wider import.

Beauduin recognises the existence of a grave situation: zealous liturgists who, operating on the assumption that the current Liturgy of the Church is an impoverishment and a deformation of Christian worship which has long since lost its ancient evangelical dynamism, can become audacious reformers.[238]

In response Beauduin outlines three norms. The first:

> The Church has received from our Lord the power of regulating divine worship and the supreme legislative authority over the administration of the sacraments, the conditions for their validity and the manner in which they are performed. Liturgical law, established by the Church in her liturgical books, is given full justification in virtue of the priestly power which she has received from her divine Founder.[239]

Having spoken of reprobate reforms, including those of Wycliffe, Huss and those of Jansenist and enlightenment inspiration,[240] Beauduin concludes:

> The Church has not received the institutions of the sacraments, any more than she has also received Sacred Scripture, as a fixed and dead treasure which she must guard without change, but as a living deposit which she continually develops according to the many and varied needs of successive generations. This is a good which pertains to the Church and is given to her to administer; she does not bury these talents, but causes them to bear fruit. This is the Catholic concept of the economy of salvation.[241]

---

[238] Cf. "Normes pratiques pour les réformes liturgiques," in: *LMD,* no. 1 p. 10.

[239] "L'Église a reçu de Notre-Seigneur le pouvoir d'organiser le culte divin et de légiférer souverainement sur les institutions sacramentelles, les conditions de leur validité et de leur emploi. Le droit liturgique, établi par L'Église dans ses livres liturgiques, est donc pleinement justifié en vertu du pouvoir sacerdotal qu'elle a reçu de son divin Fondateur;" ibid., p. 11.

[240] Cf. ibid., pp. 11-13.

[241] "L'Église n'a pas reçu les institutions sacramentelles, pas plus d'ailleurs que le Sainte Écriture, comme un trésor scellé et mort qu'elle doit garder immuable, mais comme un dépôt vivant qu'elle met constamment en valeur selon les besoins multiples et changements des générations qui se succèdent. C'est un bien qui lui appartient et dont elle a l'administration; elle ne doit pas enfouir ses talents, mais les faire fructifier. Telle est la conception catholique de l'économie rédemptrice;" ibid., p. 13.

The second principle:

> Since the Council of Trent the Holy See has reserved to herself exclusively the power of legislating in the domain of the Liturgy.[242]

The third:

> *Liturgical* law, by an exceptional dispensation, is constrained by legitimate custom, which in this case is not without the power of abrogating the law and of rendering licit that which, literally, would otherwise be illicit.[243]

The first principle, which in context is a restraint upon the desire for unauthorised reform, locates authority in liturgical matters. Its explication demonstrates that the Liturgy is subject to organic development. The second, which explains the historical reservation of this authority to the pope, ought to be read in conjunction with the third, which underlines that liturgical law is not purely a collection of positive law; custom, or Tradition, is integral to it. Whilst Beauduin does not say this, the respect shown by authority for these constraints is fundamental in discerning the integrity of positive acts of liturgical law (reforms).

The article's conclusion restates the aims of the Movement Beauduin fathered, and demonstrates that in 1945 his agenda for reform was not one that sought substantial change in liturgical ritual. Rather, whilst recognising the possibility, if not the necessity, of the organic development of objective liturgical Tradition, Beauduin still sought the spread of liturgical piety:

> The C.P.L. intends to work in a profoundly catholic and disciplined spirit, avoiding all initiative or innovation which does not conform to existing liturgical law.
>
> At the same time it intends to use freely the liberty which is given by ecclesiastical authority, and to employ all the legitimate and approved means to make of the Liturgy that which it should be: the voice and the very life of the people of God.[244]

---

242 "Depuis le concile de Trente, le Saint-Siège se réserve d'une façon exclusive le pouvoir de légiférer dans le domaine liturgique;" ibid.

243 "Le droit *liturgique*, par une disposition exceptionelle, est soustrait au jeu de la coutume légitime, laquelle sans cela a la force d'abroger la loi et de rendre licite ce qui, littéralement, pourrait être illicite;" ibid., p. 14.

244 "le C.P.L. veut travailler dans un ésprit profondément catholique et discipliné; en dehors de toute innovation ou initiative qui ne soit pas conforme au droit liturgique actuel. En même temps il veut user largement de la liberté que laisse l'autorité ecclésiastique, et s'employer par tous les moyens légitimes et approuvés à faire de la liturgie ce qu'elle doit être: la voix et la vie même du peuple de Dieu;" ibid., p. 22.

Didier Bonneterre regards Beauduin's article as "the charter of the deviated Liturgical Movement" which contained "a method of subversion to be adopted in the Church" to effect a liturgical revolution.[245] As we shall consider in chapter three, in the years following the second world war pressure for liturgical reform was certainly applied by some, including by individuals associated with the *Centre de Pastorale Liturgique,* and at times on the basis of highly questionable principles. However, the principles articulated above are neither deviant nor subversive, and, as the Liturgy and the exercise of ecclesiastical authority stood in 1945, it is difficult to see that they were envisaged as containing the seeds of radical reform.

Pope Pius XII – Mediator Dei

The relationship between the Liturgical Movement and the Holy See was consummated by the promulgation of Pius XII's encyclical *Mediator Dei* dated November 20th 1947. Beauduin asserted that it was:

> A solemn, unique document by which the supreme authority rehabilitates the Liturgy—yesterday's Cinderella—in its rights and claims of primacy. To be sure, Popes Pius X and Pius XI had spoken decisive words, but our Holy Father Pius XII is the first to explain in a magisterial document, vibrant with apostolic ardour, the basic prerogatives which entitle the Liturgy to a post of the first order in the spiritual life.[246]

"Life can have few moments of deeper thankfulness than attended my reading of *Mediator Dei,*" Ellard exclaimed.[247] *Orate Fratres* was grateful that the Liturgical Movement "finally has been granted official Catholic status,"[248] and declared that it had "come of age."[249] "*Mediator Dei* is a beacon light. It makes the liturgical endeavour now not a matter of choice but a *must,* an apostolate incumbent upon all,"[250] the 1948 U.S. Liturgical Week heard. However, as the official summary issued by the Secretariat

---

245 *The Liturgical Movement,* p. 47.

246 "la Cendrillon d'hier, est rétablie dans ses droits et ses titres de primauté par l'autorité suprême, par un document solennel, unique. Sans doute les papes Pie X et Pie XI avaient-ils prononcé des phrases décisives; mais pour la première fois, notre Saint Père le Pape Pie XII expose dans un document magistral, tout palpitant d'ardeur apostolique, les titres fondamentaux qui assignent à la liturgie, dans le domaine de la vie spirituelle, une place maîtresse;" in "L'Encyclique *Mediator Dei*" *LMD,* no. 13 p. 7.

247 *The Mass of the Future,* p. xi.

248 "Liturgical Briefs" in: *OF* vol. XXII p. 90.

249 "Liturgical Briefs" in: *OF* vol. XXII p. 139.

250 J.E. Kelly, "The Encyclical, *Mediator Dei*" in: The Liturgical Conference, *The New Man in Christ: National Liturgical Week (USA) 1948,* p. 11.

of State indicates, the purpose of the encyclical was also to "restrain the imprudent"[251] amongst enthusiasts of the Liturgical Movement.

It defines the Sacred Liturgy,[252] and locates liturgical piety at the heart of Christian life. The fourth and fifth chapters of part one treat of liturgical development. *Mediator Dei* is seen today as the "Magna Carta" that prepared for the general reform called for in *Sacrosanctum Concilium*,[253] The pertinent paragraphs form appendix I of this book.

In them we find five principles of reform. The first is that of authority. Legitimate ecclesiastical authority may enrich and modify the Liturgy for latruetic, catechetical and edificational reasons.[254] Such authority is seen as vested in the pope, and the Sacred Congregation of

---

251 "Mediator Dei" in: *The Tablet* vol. 190 p. 359. T. Richstatter OFM (*Liturgical Law* p. 4) regards *Mediator Dei* as strongly influenced by the concerns of the German bishops discussed above.

252 "The Sacred Liturgy is, consequently, the public worship which our Redeemer as Head of the Church renders to the heavenly Father, as well as the worship which the community of the faithful renders to its Founder, and through Him to the eternal Father. It is, in short, the full, public worship rendered by the Mystical Body of Jesus Christ, namely Head and members." "Sacra igitur Liturgia cultum publicum constituit, quem Redemptor noster, Ecclesiæ Caput, cælesti Patri habet; quemque christifidelium societas Conditori suo et per ipsum æterno patri tribuit; utque omnia breviter perstringamus, integrum constituit publicum cultum mystici Iesu Christi Corporis, Capitis nempe membrorumque eius." English translations differ in paragraph numeration; the Latin original contains none. Here the numeration contained in the text on the Vatican web site and published in: A. Reid OSB, *A Pope and a Council on the Sacred Liturgy*, is followed; cf. no. 20.

253 Bishop Luca Brandolini observes: "ampiamente riconosciuta come la "magna carta" di quel rinnovamento destinato poi a sfociare nella costituzione *Sacrosanctum Concilium* del Vaticano II e nella riforma generale della liturgia da essa promossa nell'ambito più vasto dell'aggiornamento della vita della Chiesa voluto da Giovanni XXIII;" preface to: Centro Liturgico Vincenziano, *50 Anni alla Luce del Movimento Liturgico*, p. 5. This connection is developed in A. Catella's chapter "Dalla Constituzione Conciliare *Sacrosanctum Concilium* all'Enciclica *Mediator Dei*" in pp. 11-43 of the same volume. A. Nichols OP distinguishes between the principally theoretical nature of *Mediator Dei* and the practical orientation of *Sacrosanctum Concilium*, noting also that "*Mediator Dei* is set against a background of liturgical conservatism...a moderately reformist document... *Sacrosanctum Concilium* is set against a background of growing liturgical radicalism, a largely traditional document—though at the same time it carried within it, encased in the innocuous language of pastoral welfare, the seeds of its own destruction;" "A Tale of Two Documents: *Sacrosanctum Concilium* and *Mediator Dei*," in: *Antiphon* vol. 5 no. 1 p. 24.

254 Para. 49.

Rites is his organ for vigilance and legislation.[255] Bishops are to supervise the observance of their directives: others have no authority.[256]

The second is that the Liturgy, in its human elements, is capable of evolution. This admits of gradual growth and even the recall of long discarded liturgical practices according to the needs of the Church.[257]

Thirdly, *Mediator Dei* accepts the legitimacy of influences throughout ecclesiastical history on liturgical development: doctrinal development,[258] changes in the manner of administering the sacraments,[259] and (late) popular devotions, including pilgrimages.[260] The influence of the fine arts is noted without deprecation.[261]

The fourth is that the use of the vernacular "in several of the rites" may be advantageous when done with due authorisation.[262]

Fifthly, it specifically excludes liturgical antiquarianism.[263]

Note that the absolute authority of the Holy See in liturgical matters is presented first. This is a strong refrain running throughout the encyclical and can be explained by the Holy See's view that part of the encyclical's function was to restrain the imprudence of some liturgists. Let us also recall that the "time immemorial" which *Mediator Dei* claims for this liturgical authority goes back only to the Council of Trent.

We ought also to note the absence of the explicit mention of liturgical Tradition. We know that the Holy See spoke to the German bishops some four years before *Mediator Dei* of the "just limits of Tradition" in matters of liturgical development. However there is no such mention in *Mediator Dei*.[264]

---

255 Para. 57.

256 Paras. 58 & 65. The impact of counter-reformation centralism and post-enlightenment ultramontanism is apparent.

257 Para. 50: "...inde progrediens incrementum profiscitur, quo peculiares excolendæ religionis consuetudines ac peculiaria pietatis opera pedetemptim evolvuntur, et quorum tenue dumtaxat indicium superioribus ætatibus habebatur; atque inde etiam interdum evenit, in pia hac in re instituta, temporis decursu oblitterata, interim in usu revocentur, iterumque renoventur." Para. 59: "Ecclesia procul dubio vivens membrorum compages est, atque adeo in iis etiam rebus, quæ ad sacram respiciunt Liturgiam, succrescit, explicatur atque evolvitur, et ad necessitates rerumque adiuncta, quæ temporum decursu habeantur, sese accommodat atque conformat, sarta tamen tectaque servata suæ doctrinæ integritate."

258 Para. 52.

259 Para. 53.

260 Paras. 54-55.

261 Para. 56.

262 Para. 60. Cf. also "Liturgical Briefs" in: *OF* vol. XXII pp. 235-236.

263 Paras. 62-64.

264 The word "tradition" occurs four times in the encyclical: "traditi" is used in para. 11 in reference to the liturgies of the Eastern Churches; "traditio" in para.

This is of some importance. While authority acts to safeguard liturgical Tradition (as well as being open to its organic development), all is well. But all might not be well were authority, on the basis of its (or of its advisers') theories, preferences or ideologies, to authorise reforms without sufficient respect for liturgical Tradition. We have argued that this was at least in part the case with the breviary reform of St Pius X. Yet we have seen that authority and Tradition must be in harmony in liturgical development and that reform by means of innovations imposed from above is foreign to the fundamental principle of organic development. *Mediator Dei* does not explicitly advocate such one-sided reform. However, we may say that it is deficient in its exposition of the priority of liturgical Tradition in liturgical development, and that its one-sided emphasis on the rôle of authority is capable of interpretation that would permit any reform provided it was duly authorised.

The third and fourth principles present little difficulty. They admit of growth in the Liturgy throughout history and, in respect of the vernacular, admit of development. Significantly Pius XII underlines the legitimacy of some relatively recent liturgical developments (those arising from medieval or post-reformation devotions, etc.).

This goes hand in hand with his deprecation of antiquarianism, the fifth principle. We have seen this rejected as foreign to liturgical development throughout history. That it is resolutely excluded by Pius XII in 1947 attests his continuity with liturgical Tradition. The antiquarian excesses he proscribes in paragraph 61 and his explicit mention of Pistoia in paragraph 63 leave little room for doubt about his meaning.

That *Mediator Dei* was received so warmly by the Liturgical Movement as a whole, especially given the excesses it condemned, is itself a testimony to the overall equanimity of the Liturgical Movement at this time and of its well-founded place in the life of the Church. It was, in the words of Crichton, "a new incentive to further efforts and a safe guide to follow in all our work."[265]

Conclusion

Underpinned by *Mediator Dei*, the Liturgical Movement was poised to have even greater impact. One of its more free-speaking sons, Reinhold, writing in 1947, stated:

> The modern Liturgical Movement is obedient, orthodox, modest. The *first thing* it demands is that all of us, we ourselves, perform the

---

113 explaining the teaching of the Council of Trent on Holy Communion; "traditum" in para. 130 in defending adoration of the Holy Eucharist outside of Mass; and "traditæ" in para 163 referring to doctrinal Tradition.

265 "The New Encyclical on the Liturgy" in: *Liturgy* vol. XVII p. 40.

> Liturgy as it is in the books and conform to it. Self-reform and perfection. In the *second place* we expect this to open our eyes to niceties and rediscoveries that will transform our thinking into greater dogmatic correctness, proportionality and joy. The *third thing* will be to see the Liturgy restored to simplicity and originality. Only in the *fourth degree* will we prostrate ourselves at the feet of the Holy Father and ask for reforms.[266]

The priority Reinhold gives to each of his steps is significant and underlines the fact that the Liturgical Movement was not primarily reformist. So does his realism: "I have a sneaking feeling that none of us will ever reach station four and that most of us will be lucky to attain some modicum of stage one."[267]

Reinhold's distinction between restoring and reforming the Liturgy is also important. He was, and would continue to be, a strident advocate of change yet he was well aware that restoration (purifying and reinvigorating the rite, after the manner of the Council of Trent) is quite another matter from its reformation (producing a new Liturgy).

A theological and less strident account of the Movement's position was expressed by Yves Congar OP in *Orate Fratres* in 1948:

> There are in the Church invariable realities, because they are of divine institution and represent the very foundations on which the Church is built: dogma, the sacraments, the essential constitution of the Church. Other realities, without being so essential, are nevertheless so bound up with the essence of the Church that it would be extremely difficult to change them basically, and it is fitting to touch them only with extreme circumspection. We must not be hasty in judging and wishing to change things, the appreciation of which calls for mature prudence, a broad experience like that of the Church herself. We ought to reflect a long time in an attitude of great docility to the Tradition of the Church before condemning a form of life within the Church in the name of development; too hasty judgements are exposed to errors, the superficial character of which are revealed by a more attentive consideration.
>
> But there are also in the Church many human institutions. Even the essential elements which no one can touch have taken on in the course of history modality and forms which are contingent, historic, and subject to change. Christianity is eternal, but the forms in which Christian civilisation is realised...even the celebration of her cult...these forms are in one sense bound to history, conditioned by a given state of development. To wish to assimilate them in value and permanence to Christianity itself, would be to make the relative

[266] "Jubé d'Asnières" in: *OF* vol. XXI p. 516.
[267] Ibid.

> absolute, which is an idolatry akin to that which consists in making the absolute relative; and this would be, moreover, a grave fault of intellectual perspective and perhaps marks narrowness and lack of culture...
>
> Development, which is the law of this life, requires respect for forms of the past, fidelity, and deep-rooted continuity. But it also demands movement, growth, adaptation...[268]

The Liturgical Movement, then, approached its fortieth birthday—if we take Beauduin's appeal at the 1909 Malines conference as the moment of its birth—in good health and with a largely traditional and moderate mentality with regard to reform. In the first half of the twentieth century it was certainly not a movement that worked for or achieved "a more comprehensible, subjective and meaningful Liturgy," as has been argued recently.[269] Even though some reprobate practices arose, the Movement's essence was to comprehend objective liturgical Tradition in order to give shape and meaning to Christian life, and indeed to society. As Dom Benedict Steuart stated in 1946:

> What the Liturgical Movement is aiming at in these days is to overcome the *dichotomy,* the division or 'sundering,' between liturgical and individual life and prayer—a dichotomy which does exist still in this country, and in others too. The Movement aims at bringing about a real union and mutual assistance between the Christian individual and Christian society. This aim is intended and desired by the Church herself whose work is to make each and all of her children 'one body with Christ.'[270]

The root of this problematic dichotomy, according to Steuart, was that:

> Mental prayer, under the usual title of 'meditation,' has become since the end of the Middle Ages a spiritual practice apart, in itself, and quite distinct and different from liturgical practice.[271]

---

268 "True and False Reform in the Church" in: *OF* vol. XXIII pp. 258-259.
269 Cf. D. Torevell, *Losing the Sacred,* p. 126.
270 "The Meaning of Liturgical Worship" in: *Liturgy* vol. XV p. 69. A. Thorold develops this theme: "the purpose of [the Liturgical Movement] is to reanimate the Catholics of today with a *corporate* sense of their responsibility as members of one another in Christ; to remind them that they form part of…our Holy Mother, the Church…The deep purpose of the Liturgical Movement is to baptise the genuine but groping movement of mankind towards some kind of unifying principle…What has hampered the Church from influencing the mental atmosphere of the twentieth century is not only the persecution of her enemies, but also the narrow religious outlook of so many of her children. The Liturgical Movement was instituted to correct this outlook…" "The Liturgical Movement and the Social Forces of Our Time" in: *Liturgy* vol. XVIII pp. 72, 73.
271 Ibid.

J. Fitzsimons, speaking more specifically of people's involvement in the Liturgy itself, asserted in his 1945 article "The Future of the Liturgical Movement in England" that:

> Our aim is that all Catholics should take an intelligent and active part in the Sacred Liturgy...The two operative words are 'intelligent' and 'active.'...
>
> We should not think of it [the Movement] as a revival. A revival implies bringing back to life something which is dead. It is not dead but sleepeth...[272]

Fitzsimons, whose article exemplifies the sane, practical and traditional aims of the Movement, adds a warning: "The Liturgical Movement...has to become a vast popular surge—if it does not it will have failed."[273]

The words of Dom Oliver Rousseau, written in 1945, also sounded a note of caution:

> How important it is for the future that the Liturgical Movement, while continually advancing and developing, should ever have a sense of Tradition, without which, sooner or later, it is destined to failure.[274]

These words might profitably be kept before us as we examine the next phase of the Liturgical Movement and its impact upon the Liturgy.

---

[272] *Liturgy* vol. XV pp. 17, 18.

[273] Ibid., p. 19. Fitzsimons concludes with the statement "we are adapting something which is age-old to the exigencies of modern life;" p. 23. In the context of the article published in 1945 this cannot be seen as a reformist stance.

[274] *The Progress of the Liturgy*, p. 172.

Chapter 3

The Liturgical Movement and Liturgical Reform from 1948 to the Second Vatican Council

Introduction

A 1949 article, "Obsolete or Obsolescent?" posed a question that captures the predicament of those working to achieve the aims of the Liturgical Movement in a world where even Catholics were riddled with post-reformation individualism and enlightenment rationalism. It asks:

> How shall these build a basilica when they know not what a church is for; a sanctuary when they are ignorant of worship; an altar to a God unknown?[1]

Addressing his readers, who, given the nature of the periodical in which the question was posed, one may presume did not share such debilitating ignorance, the author pointed out the existence in the missal of a seemingly obsolete rubric, requiring a candle to be lit on the altar at the consecration. He observes:

> Low Masses, often at side altars, are celebrated perhaps more frequently than before. The passing worshipper wonders: 'Ought I to genuflect'? Should the extra candle be burning, he bends his knee and adores our Blessed Lord present on the altar; or, in the absence of the third light, bows his head to the Cross and passes on. Were it not a pity that this flickering flame of courtesy towards our Divine Lord should be finally extinguished. Its fate rests with this generation, with you and me. It is in our power to tend it or to quench it utterly.[2]

This "power" to tend or to quench, is at the heart of our study of the Movement's impact on reform from 1948 onward.

William Busch observed that *Mediator Dei* marked "the beginning of a new stage" for the Liturgical Movement.[3] Charles Davis calls this the "stage of liturgical reform:"

---

[1] D. Chute, "Obsolete or Obsolescent?" in: *Liturgy* vol. XVIII p. 93.

[2] Ibid., p. 94.

[3] "About the Encyclical *Mediator Dei*" in: *OF* vol. XXII p. 156.

> What happened was that the historical, doctrinal and pastoral work brought the realisation that our present Liturgy was not in a healthy state. Historical studies laid bare the evolution of the Liturgy and showed the reasons why the Liturgy had ceased to play the part in the ordinary Christian life that it should. One conclusion became clear: if vitality was to be restored to the liturgical life of the Church, changes must be made. Historical studies made it possible to discern what changes would be foreign to the Liturgy and due to some unfounded modern fashion.[4]

Note again the importance given to historical studies. We shall return to this, particularly in examining J.A. Jungmann SJ, of whom Davis was a particular admirer, and whose ideas were to prove singularly influential.[5]

J.D. Crichton recalls:

> The next phase came during the second world war. There was a vast, forced movement of workers from France into the factories in Germany. Some priests went with them. And they realised once again as Beauduin had realised that the Liturgy, the Mass as it was, was remote from these people who were risking their lives, and so out of this situation came the phase of the Liturgical Movement which has been absolutely decisive, which was the foundation, which was the coming together of the German and the French liturgists and others...And so the *Centre de Pastorale Liturgie* was set up in 1943 in Paris and the emphasis was on the *pastoral* nature of the Liturgy, that the Liturgy must be available to the people and accessible to the people. There was also an immense propagation of the knowledge of the Liturgy and of the history of the Liturgy, education in the Liturgy, in France especially but also in Germany, and this was the truly pastoral Liturgical Movement.[6]

The fundamental tenet of proponents of the "pastoral" Liturgical Movement, to which Crichton alludes, is that wherever necessary the Liturgy is to be adapted in order to accommodate the perceived needs of the people. This view would grow in popularity. We shall consider its relation to the organic development of objective liturgical Tradition. Crichton continues:

---

[4] *Liturgy and Doctrine*, p. 15.

[5] Cf. ibid., p. 81. Cf. Davis' enthusiasm for Jungmann expressed in his preface to the English edition of the work of Casel's *The Mystery of Christian Worship*, p. xii: "An historian, he has unequalled mastery of the complex changes in liturgical forms, but he has a wonderful sense for the abiding values of the Liturgy. With fine discrimination he is able to assess the gains and losses through the centuries and to suggest reforms that will restore to traditional values their pastoral efficacy. A deep pastoral concern pervades all his work."

[6] Interview by the author of J.D. Crichton, 24th August 1994.

> The third phase of the Liturgical Movement was reform, and it was going on before the Council. The third phase is the pressure for reform.[7]

Indeed, amongst liturgical scholars a number held that the time had in fact come for reform to meet pastoral ends. As *Worship* (the new name for *Orate Fratres*) reported in 1952:

> In January 1948 the editors of the Roman *Ephemerides Liturgicæ* addressed a circular to its collaborators in which they expressed their conviction that the time had come to continue the revision of the liturgical books begun by Blessed Pius X in 1911, and discontinued (or rather postponed) in 1914 because of the absence of the necessary critical textual studies. That deficiency, the editors felt, had in the meantime been largely supplied. The thirty years which the Sacred Congregation of Rites had suggested as an interval of study had long passed; and the Holy Father himself had, in recent years repeatedly urged that the question of reform, more particularly of the breviary, be again taken up. Accordingly the editors invited scholars to submit plans of revision. A number of these were published in the *Ephemerides*. And in March 1949 Fr Bugnini CM, one of the editors, summarised the plans, adding that the question could not be restricted to the breviary but must embrace the other liturgical books as well.[8]

Bugnini describes the questionnaire as "a bold move...a free—and risky—undertaking by the young editor-in-chief of the periodical,"[9] (i.e., himself). It was, he said, "the first alarm signal that something was stirring."[10]

The resultant 1949 article, which he says profited from the approach taken in the *Memoria sulla Riforma Liturgica,*[11] indicates the assumptions and desires of advocates of liturgical reform at the time. They sought a lessening of the burden of the Liturgy, and an adaptation of it that would make the Liturgy more realistic in the concrete circumstances in which the clergy and laity found themselves in the

---

[7] Ibid.

[8] "Liturgical Briefs" in: *Worship* vol. XXVI pp. 201-202. Cf. "In Annum 1948 Præloquium" in: *Ephemerides Liturgicæ* vol. LXII pp. 3-4, & A. Bugnini CM, "Per una Riforma Liturgica Generale" in: *Ephemerides Liturgicæ* vol. LXIII pp. 166-184.

[9] *TRL* p. 11; "Fu un'audacia...fu una libera, diciamo pure richiosa, iniziativa del giovane direttore del periodico;" *La riforma liturgica* [hereafter *LRL*] p. 26. In an interview by the author on 31st May 1996 in Toulouse, France, A.G. Martimort observed that the first edition of *LRL* contained inaccuracies which he, amongst others, corrected for the second edition, subsequently published in Italian in 1997. A corrected English edition has not yet been published.

[10] Ibid., p. 10; "fu il primo segnale d'allarme che qualcosa cominciava a muoversi;" ibid.

[11] Cf. ibid. p. 11. Examined below.

changed conditions of 'today;'[12] a complete revision according to the spiritual needs of modern Christianity.[13] It was assumed that since the eleventh century the state of the Roman rite was one of unacceptable compromise. The Liturgy as it stood was compared to a mosaic or an ancient building, built by different hands using different materials in different times. Because to take away or to modernise but one part of the edifice would cause the rest to crumble and fall, or result in a lack of congruence in the Liturgy,[14] a complete modernisation was thought necessary.

We have observed the periodic recurrence of the desire to lighten the 'burden' of the Liturgy, from the reform of Quignonez through to that of St Pius X. Such desires, in so far as they substantially subject objective liturgical Tradition to the tastes of any passing age are, as we have noted, not organic developments of the Liturgy and as such are to be rejected. So too are transient desires to subject objective liturgical Tradition to a complete revision according to the perceived spiritual needs of any particular age. To accept such a principle of reform is radically to subjectivise the Liturgy.

It is illustrative that Bugnini's article should use the analogies of an ancient building and of a mosaic in describing the Liturgy as received from Tradition. Both exemplify the organic nature of the Liturgy and its gradual development throughout the centuries. That they also demonstrate the incongruence of desired reforms with the existing Liturgy, and assert the purported need for a radical reconstruction according to the supposed needs of the time, is revealing. Thus, as early as 1949, reconstruction and innovation according to the perceived needs of modern man, conceived as clearly distinct from the development of the objective liturgical Tradition, was part of, if not the very basis of, the agenda of some (key) liturgists. *Ephemerides Liturgicæ*, published in Rome and printed on the Vatican Press, whilst editorially independent, was no fringe publication. The rubrician J.B. O'Connell described it as

---

12 "un alleggerimento dell'apparato liturgico e d'un adeguamento più realistico alle esigenze concreto del clero e dei fedeli nelle mutate condizioni d'oggi;" "Per una Riforma Liturgica Generale" in: *Ephemerides Liturgicæ* vol. LXIII p. 166.

13 "*una revisione pienamente adeguata* ai bisogni spirituali della cristianità moderna;" ibid., p. 167.

14 "Dal secolo XI almeno noi viamo su un compromesso, impropriamente detto 'rito romano'...la liturgia è un mosaico, o, se più piace, un vecchio edificio, costruito a poco a poco, in tempi diversi, con diversi materiali e da diverse mani. Se ora si vuol togliere o cambiare («modernizzare») l'una o l'altra parte, tutto il resto comincia a sgretolarsi o a non convenire più con la parte restaurata;" ibid., p. 167.

"authoritative."[15] Bugnini himself described it as "the semi-official voice of Roman liturgical circles."[16]

We ought to underline the centrality of Annibale Bugnini, then editor of *Ephemerides Liturgicæ*. He was behind the consultation that resulted in his 1949 article and was to become and remain *the* key figure in liturgical reform until 1975.

Bugnini's article also reports principles of reform suggested by respondents. One is to conserve Tradition without being afraid to simplify the Liturgy.[17] Another is to return to primitive liturgical Tradition, prior to its later compromise, which would include a purification of the calendar, which amongst other reforms would give predominance to the temporal cycle over the sanctoral.[18] Finally, Bugnini advocates a codification of liturgical customs following the basic principles of the reform.[19]

The first attempts to synthesise the two antithetical positions of innovation and conservation. It is, in effect, a principle of compromise. However, as we have maintained, compromise is not a sound principle of liturgical reform. The second, to return to primitive liturgical Tradition, is clearly antiquarian and rejects the organic development of Liturgy throughout history. Whilst Bugnini's article associates this principle mainly with calendar reform, and one may argue that reform of some of the colliding feasts and seasons is both desirable and in harmony with objective liturgical Tradition, as a principle of reform it is defective. Bugnini's desire for an overall codification of liturgical customs is, in effect, a practical desire for a certain harmonisation of the rubrics of the liturgical books. Such practical reform would not itself do violence to objective liturgical Tradition, though it could involve the relatively minor adjustment of traditional rites in order to achieve harmony between them. Alternatively, a reform based on untraditional principles could use a codification to whitewash the Liturgy according to an ideology.

---

[15] *Simplifying the Rubrics of the Roman Breviary and Missal*, p. 10.

[16] *TRL*, p. 1; "voce ufficiosa degli ambienti liturgici romani;" *LRL*, p. 26.

[17] "a) principio tetico: «melior est conditio possidentis», cioè della tradizione, che si deve presumere buona, finchè non sia dimostrata cattiva, cioè meno utile; b) principio antitetico: bisogna attenersi alla brevità e semplicità del comando divino: «Sic orabitis: Pater noster...»; c) principio syntetico: bisogna fare una cosa e non tralasciare l'altra, cioè conservare la tradizione e non temere la semplificazione;" "Per una Riforma Liturgica Generale" in: *Ephemerides Liturgicæ* vol. LXIII p. 168.

[18] "la riforma dev'essere concepita come un ritorno alla tradizione primitiva della celebrazione del mistero cristiano piuttosto che come un compromesso tra questa celebrazione in sott'ordine e le superfetazioni devozionali che l'hanno disarticolata nel corso del secoli..." ibid.

[19] Contrary to the opinion held by some: "una riforma generale debba necessariamente esser preceduta da una «codificazione metodica»;" ibid.

Concluding his article, Bugnini asserts that amidst the variety of proposals and projects proffered, one common wish shines through: the intimate desire to renew and to adjust the Liturgy according to the actual spiritual needs of the clergy and laity.[20] This is his fundamental assertion. It is the fundamental principle behind the desire for a so-called 'pastoral' Liturgy.

The question is whether this principle is valid, or whether it is not the re-emergence of the error of Quignonez, of the enlightenment liturgists, of the Gallicans, etc.? This is crucial in assessing the work of liturgical reform carried out in the twenty years, and beyond, following Bugnini's article. The tone of his recollection of the 1948 questionnaire and the ensuing article some thirty-five years later is itself not without interest. Bugnini wrote in 1983: "In this case, the proverb was proved true: 'Fortune favours the brave.'"[21]

The Pian Commission for Liturgical Reform

The *Sectio Historica* of the Sacred Congregation of Rites formally commenced the work of reform in 1946 with a *Promemoria intorno alla riforma liturgica.*[22] This was presented to Pius XII in May, with the result that, with papal approval, the Austrian Redemptorist, Joseph Löw, began to draft a plan for a general reform. This was completed at the end of 1948 and published[23] as *Memoria sulla Riforma Liturgica* the following year. A papal commission for liturgical reform was established in 1946, but it was May 1948 before its members were appointed. Bugnini, its secretary until its absorption into a pre-Conciliar commission, observes that it "worked in absolute secrecy" and "enjoyed the full confidence of the pope."[24] Nicola Giampietro OFM Cap appends to his doctoral work on Cardinal Antonelli's rôle in liturgical reform both the *Promemoria sull'origine della Commissione Pontificia per la Riforma Liturgica e sul lavoro*

---

[20] "Proposte e progetti, nella loro multiforme varietà, riflettono una identica luce: l'intimo desiderio di rinnovamento e di adeguamento della «laus perennis» alle attuale esigenze spirituali del clero e della «plebs Dei»;" ibid., p. 184.

[21] *TRL* p. 11; "E quella volta si verificò il proverbio: *audaces fortuna iuvat;*" *LRL* p. 26.

[22] Cf. N. Giampietro OFM Cap., *Il Card. Ferdinando Antonelli e gli sviluppi della riforma liturgica dal 1948 al 1970*, p. 274.

[23] For private circulation amongst those whom the Sacred Congregation of Rites wished to consult. Only three hundred copies were printed; cf. A. Bugnini, CM, *TRL* p. 7ff.

[24] *TRL* p. 9; "lavorò nel più assoluto segreto...godeva della piena fiducia del Papa;" *LRL* p. 25. Torevell suggests, somewhat incredibly given the fact that the commission was set up by the pope and that its members were curial officials or papal appointees, that this secrecy was "possibly because of the fear of Rome;" cf. *Losing the Sacred*, p. 126.

da essa compiuto negli anni 1948-1953, and the minutes of the eighty-two meetings it held up until July 1960.[25]

The *Memoria* gives the rationale for beginning a general reform. Firstly, the state of the Liturgy was seen as problematic; overcrowding in the calendar and the increased number of octaves in particular. The complexity of the rubrics was another: this was seen as diminishing the love of many priests for the Liturgy. Thus, "a desire for a reform which would bring about a sensible simplification and a greater stabilisation of the Liturgy" had arisen.[26] The significant development of studies in liturgical history was seen as putting the commission in a better position for "a solid revision of the Liturgy on a broad and secure basis in [liturgical] science."[27] The state of the Liturgical Movement was seen as having given rise to "a greater sensibility in liturgical matters and hence a more conscious desire to see the Liturgy freed from certain accretions which obscure its beauty and diminish in a certain sense its efficacy."[28] The *Memoria* regarded the practical situation of the clergy, their occupation with pastoral duties in the changed circumstances of the modern world, and their dissatisfaction with the complications of the Liturgy, the breviary in particular, as a "most serious reason to hasten liturgical reform."[29] The clergy are said to want the whole Liturgy simplified from an exuberant calendar and complicated rubrics and returned to its original Christo-centric basis. Finally, the *Memoria* says that, in the light of these considerations, it is a most opportune, if not necessary, time to carry on the work of reform begun by St Pius X.[30] The reform is envisaged as being able to be completed in "a relatively short time."[31]

Much of the rationale in the *Memoria* is familiar. In liturgical history we have seen the desire to prune the overgrown calendar, or to lighten the burden of the breviary on the clergy. (It is interesting that the burden of the breviary should again be seen as too great only thirty-five years after its reduction in the reform of St Pius X.) We have seen that those charged with the reform of the liturgical books following Trent used the scholarship available at the time to assist them in restoring the

---

25 *Il Card. Ferdinando Antonelli e gli sviluppi della riforma liturgica dal 1948 al 1970,* pp. 274-277, 278-388. Giampietro's pararaph numeration [x] is used hereafter.

26 *Memoria,* no. 5; "un vivo desiderio di una riforma che porti finalmente ad una sensibile semplificazione e ad una maggiore stabilizzazione della Liturgia."

27 Ibid., no. 6; "Insomma, è certo che oggi siamo in grado di poter fare una solida revisione della liturgia su di una base scientifica larga e sicura."

28 Ibid., no. 7; "una maggiore sensibilità in materia liturgica e quindi un desiderio sempre più cosciente di vedere la liturgia liberata da certe superfetazioni, che ne oscurano la bellezza e ne diminuiscono in un certo senso l'efficacia."

29 Ibid., no. 8; "una ragione molto seria per sollecitare la riforma liturgica."

30 Cf. ibid., nn. 9-13.

31 Ibid. no. 13; "un tempo relativamente ristretto."

Liturgy to its purity in antiquity (remembering that by "antiquity" was understood the organically developed Roman Liturgy of the eleventh century).

The importance given to liturgical science in the *Memoria's* rationale does, however, indicate the emergence of a mindset which disproportionately elevates scholarly findings, and which, if allowed to predominate, or if uncritically accepted by authority, could result in reform which fails to respect objective liturgical Tradition. Given the exaggeration in *Mediator Dei* of the extent of papal authority in matters of liturgical reform, such a risk may be said to have been real.

Yet in the *Memoria's* rationale we have seen a concern not to lose the beauty of the Liturgy and to preserve its efficacy. There is no explicit desire for a major structural reform or recasting of the Liturgy itself at the prompting of scholars.

Following its rationale, the *Memoria* outlines fundamental principles for the reform. The introduction observes:

> For several decades, many devout and also learned priests have made countless proposals in this direction, more or less complete, regarding a reform of the Liturgy. Those who take the trouble to examine those proposals seriously…very soon notice that, unfortunately, there is lacking in them the foundation of a solid scientific preparation and a sense of healthy balance, which would enable one to discern the good *old* from the inopportune *new*. One notes frequently thè marked tendency of the modern mentality to systematise, classify, quantify, everything; or the subtlety of the specialist who is lost in minutiae; or the spirit of a pure subjectivism; or the reflection of local, contingent and ephemeral situations and movements. Consequently many plans, even if well studied and amply expounded, are vitiated at their roots, precisely because they are either devoid of a scientific basis, or are too alien to the spirit of the Church, which[32] is always even and objective, and always inclined to harmonise proven traditions with the new exigencies of the times.[33]

---

32 "Which" refers to "the Church," not the "*spirit* of the Church," as the Italian makes clear.

33 *Memoria*, no. 14. "Da vari decenni a questa parte, molti sacerdoti pii e anche dotti hanno fatto innumerevoli proposte più o meno complete intorno ad una riforma della liturgia. Chi si applica ad esaminare seriamente quelle proposte…si avvede ben presto, che spesso manca in esse, purtroppo, il fondamento di una solida preparazione scientifica e il senso di un sano equilibrio, che faccia discernere il *vecchio* buono, dal *nuovo* inopportuno. Si nota frequentemente l'inclinazione spiccata della mentalità moderna a tutto sistemare, classificare, totalizzare; o la sottigliezza dello specialista che si perde nelle minuzie; o lo spirito di un puro soggettivismo; o il riflesso di situazioni e movimenti locali, contingenti ed effimeri. Molti progetti pertanto, anche se ben studiati e largamente esposti, sono viziati in radice, proprio perchè, o destituiti di base

The *Memoria* is, then, well aware of the need to respect the objective liturgical Tradition in the face of contemporary excesses. The considerable weight given to "scientific" bases for liturgical reform is tempered by a harmony and objectivity which the Church (presumably papal authority) provides.

The fundamental principles articulated in the *Memoria* are:

> 1. The opposed claims of the conservative tendency and the innovative tendency must be balanced.
> 2. Given that the Liturgy is by its nature eminently latreutic, the worship of *dulia* must be subordinated to that of *latria*; consequently, in the liturgical Calendar, the *Temporal* and the *Ferial* must predominate over the *Sanctoral*.
> 3. Given that the Liturgy is a unitary and organic complex, it is necessary that reform also be unitary and organic.[34]

The first and third principles are most directly relevant to our study. The second, the content of which is uncontroversial, illustrates the matter of most concern at the time to those planning reform. Indeed, the *Memoria* gives over 148 of its 342 pages to the development of the second principle alone, before devoting its remaining pages to the breviary. The second principle also makes clear the *Memoria's* liturgical theology, which is entirely consonant with that of the Liturgical Movement. Thomas Richstatter OFM, in a comment betraying a heavy post-conciliar bias, notes that the second principle demonstrates that:

> The Liturgy is something the Church *does;* it is not yet considered as a self-expression of the Church itself. Also the Liturgy is considered to be directed to God; there is no mention of its educative dimension.[35]

In interpreting the principles of the *Memoria,* we should keep in mind the prescriptions and proscriptions of *Mediator Dei.* The two documents were published within thirteen months of each other, the former with the explicit authority of the author of the latter. Indeed, the *Memoria* emanated from the same Roman dicastery that was presumably

---

scientifica, o troppo lontani dallo spirito della Chiesa, sempre equa e oggettiva, e sempre tesa ad armonizzare le tradizioni provate con le nuove esigenze dei tempi." [Translation of nn. 14-20 & 314-316: Rev Dr Peter Joseph]

[34] Ibid., no. 15. "1. Si devono equilibrare le opposte pretese della tendenza conservatrice e della tendenza innovatrice. 2. Dato che la liturgia è per natura sua eminentemente latreutica, il culto di dulia dev'essere subordinato a quello di latria; conseguentemente, nel Calendario liturgico, il *Temporale* e il *Feriale* devono predominare sul *Santorale*. 3. Dato che la liturgia è un complesso unitario e organico, conviene che la riforma sia anche unitaria ed organica."

[35] *Liturgical Law,* p. 29. The theological shift demonstrated by Richstatter here has been repudiated in writings such as J. Ratzinger, *The Spirit of the Liturgy,* chapters 1-3.

responsible for drafting or at least commenting upon *Mediator Dei* before its publication.

The *Memoria* elucidates its principles. Of the first it explains:

> There are some liturgists and promoters of the Liturgical Movement who sin by archaeologism; for them the most archaic forms are always and of themselves the best; those later ones, even if of the High Middle Ages, are always to be set after those more ancient. They would like to take the entire Liturgy back to a state closest to its origins, excluding all successive developments, regarded as deteriorations and degenerations. In short, listening to them, the Liturgy would be reduced to a species of a precious mummy, to preserve jealously as in a museum.
>
> There are others, instead, of precisely the opposite tendency, who would actually like to create a new and modern Liturgy; we no longer understand, they say, the forms, gestures, chants, created in now distant ages; the Liturgy must be a manifestation of current religious life; hence, the language, pictorial and sculptured art, music, dramatic action and so on, ought to be completely new, in conformity with modern culture and sentiments.
>
> Naturally, these are the extremes, but unfortunately they exist and have already been reproved in the Encyclical *Mediator Dei*. However, as always, there is a nucleus of truth at the basis of the two extremist tendencies. Now, a wise reform of the Liturgy must balance the two tendencies: that is, conserve good and healthy traditions, verified on historico-critical bases, and take account of new elements, already opportunely introduced and needing to be introduced. Since the Liturgy is a living organism—like the Church herself, which is ever ancient and ever new—so the Liturgy, which is a continuous manifestation of her religious vitality, cannot be something set in stone, but must develop, as in fact it has developed, in parallel line with all the other vital manifestations of the Church.
>
> Hence, it is the task, certainly very delicate and very difficult, of a liturgical reform, to balance, with discretion and wise discernment, the just demands of the opposed tendencies, in such wise as not to change through sheer itching for novelty, and not to mummify through exaggerated archaeological valuation. To renew, therefore, courageously what is truly necessary and indispensable to renew, and to conserve jealously what one can and must conserve.[36]

---

[36] "Ci sono alcuni liturgisti e fautori del movimento liturgico che peccano di archeologismo; per essi le forme più arcaiche sono sempre e di per sè le migliori; quelle più tarde, anche se dell'alto medioevo, sono sempre da posporre a quelle più antiche. Vorrebbero essi ricondurre tutta la liturgia ad uno stato più vicino alle origini, escludendo tutti gli sviluppi successivi, considerate come deterioramente e degenerazioni. Insomma, dando ascolto ad essi, la liturgia si

Here we find an elucidation of the principle of organic development of the Liturgy in response to the extremes of the day. Given that this is found in the first official document preparing for a general liturgical reform of the Roman rite, it is of quite some importance. It repudiates archaeologism and excludes the creation of Liturgy according to the contemporary tastes. The *Memoria* speaks of balancing, or more properly of finding an equilibrium amidst, these tendencies. Whilst some may find in this the first step toward accepting reform by compromise, this elucidation is more probably an expression of the realities and difficulties with which a general liturgical reform would have to deal.

Again we see that "historico-critical bases" emerge. They are regarded as *the* criteria by which liturgical traditions to be retained are to be verified. Whilst it would be wrong to exclude advances in historico-critical studies from consideration in liturgical reform, to elevate what (at least in Catholic circles) was in 1948 a relatively new discipline to the status of being *the* decisive criteria was a radical step indeed.

Furthermore, claiming such a decisive rôle for historico-critical factors risks compromising the organic growth of the Liturgy, in which authority is more passive (ratifying developments that are harmonious with objective liturgical Tradition). It also lends authority to a rationale which would then be able to precipitate liturgical reform. Thus, scholarly

---

ridurrebbe ad una specie di mummia preziosa, da conservare gelosamente come in un museo.

Ci sono altri invece di tendenze talmente opposta, che vorrebbero creare addirittura una liturgia nuova e moderna; noi non comprendiamo più, essi dicono, le forme, i gesti, i canti creati in epoche ormai lontane; la liturgia dev'essere una manifestazione della vita religiosa attuale; quindi, la lingua, l'arte pittorica e scultoria, la musica, l'azione drammatica e via dicendo, dovrebbero essere completamente nuove, conformi ai sentimenti e alla cultura moderna.

Questi, naturalmente, sono gli estremi, ma che purtroppo esistono e sono stati già riprovati nella Enciclica *Mediator Dei*. Come sempre però, c'è alla base delle due tendenze estremiste un nucleo di vero. Ora, una sapiente riforma della Liturgia deve equilibrare le due tendenze: conservare cioè le buone e sane tradizioni, accertate su base storico-critica, e tener conto degli elementi nuovi, già opportunamente introdotti o da introdurre. Poichè la Liturgia è un organismo vivente: come la Chiesa stessa, che è sempre antica e sempre nuova, così la Liturgia, che è manifestazione continua della sua vitalità religiosa, non può essere qualcosa di pietrificato, ma deve svilupparsi, come di fatto si è sviluppata, in linea parallela con tutte le altre manifestazioni vitali della Chiesa.

Compito quindi, certamente delicatissimo e gravissimo, di una riforma liturgica, è di equilibrare, con discrezione e sapiente discernimento, i giusti postulati delle opposte tendenze, in modo da non cambiare per solo prurito di novità, e non mummificare per esagerata valutazione archæologica. Rinnovare quindi coraggiosamente quanto è veramente necessario e indispensabile rinnovare e conservare gelosamente quanto si può e si deve conservare;" *Memoria*, no. 16.

consensus emerges not as a component of liturgical reform that has to take its place in due relation to other factors. Nor, as in the work of the commission following Trent, is it a tool with which to identify and conserve authentic developed liturgical Tradition. Rather, it has become the decisive basis for reform. As such it is capable of a disproportionate impact on reform, and of overriding the principle of organic development.

The *Memoria* lauds Pius XII's reform of the psalter:

> The sovereign gesture that the Holy Father Pius XII showed in the approbation of the new version of the Psalter provides us with a gauge of how the Church knows how to make courageous innovations when the supreme good of Christian life demands it.[37]

This clearly combines and unreservedly accepts the legitimacy of the action of papal authority at the prompting of historico-critical scholarship in liturgical reform. It is doubtful, though, that "the supreme good of Christian life" *demanded* the Pian reform of the psalter: the literature of the period simply contains no evidence that the Vulgate was perceived as a major obstacle to Christian life! Were it so, one might accept that authority had the right, if not indeed the duty, to intervene. However, this was not the case. Furthermore, it must not be forgotten that Pius XII posited this reform optionally, alongside the traditional psalter: the language used in the *Memoria* does not reflect this. Further still, our study of liturgical history has shown us that "courageous innovations" are foreign to the organic development of the Liturgy.

The elucidation of the third principle:

> The Liturgy is a real organism, co-ordinated and organic; whence, whenever one touches one part, by natural reflex the effects of it are felt in the other parts also. Hence it follows that we cannot think of partial re-touching, without first having established an organic and general plan. Of this, all those competent in Liturgy are convinced. It is not enough, for example, to touch up the Calendar here and there, eliminate some feasts, fix up some rubrics, prepare a critical edition of some books or some historical reading. It is necessary to embrace in a general vision the whole complex of the reform: rites, formularies, rubrics, feasts, liturgical year, etc., and to arrange in advance, wisely and with accurate knowledge of the function of the single parts, the measures necessary to balance the individual provisions.

---

37 "Il gesto sovrano che il Santo Padre Pio XII ha avuto con l'approvazione della nuova versione del Salterio, ci dà la misura del come la Chiesa sappia fare innovazioni coraggiose, quando il bene supremo della vita cristiana lo richieda;" ibid.

> In the realisation then of the general plan, one will be able to proceed *by stages*,[38] something simple if the principles and the fundamental bases are clearly established from the outset. Only thus will one have the certainty of an ordered progress and of a happy arrival at the goal.
>
> Executed finally the reform itself, it will be necessary to have a final element to guarantee the stability of the reform and the organic nature of future developments of liturgical life; all this will be attained through the much spoken about *Codex liturgicus*, which should represent the crowning of the Reform and assure its application and stability.[39]

Much of this is of a practical nature and illustrates wise planning. We ought to note, however, the recurring identification of the Liturgy as an organism, and the presence of a desire to make "ordered progress" and to achieve a state of stability in the Liturgy which would itself be open to future organic development.

Overall, these principles, whilst in part consonant with those we find in liturgical history, nevertheless accord an unjustified primacy to the findings of scholarship, not hitherto seen. In this, the work of the Pian commission was askew from the outset.

The *Memoria* also makes clear that a reform of the whole of the Liturgy was conceived. Indeed, chapter three opens with a proposed order for the reform, indicating its scope:

I. The gradation of feasts, and the Calendar
II. The Roman Breviary
III. The Roman Missal

---

[38] *per partes* (by parts).

[39] "La liturgia è un vero organismo, coordinato e organico; onde qualora si tocchi una parte, per riflesso naturale se ne risentono gli effetti anche nelle altre parti. Di qui la conseguenza che non si può pensare a ritocchi parziali, senza avere prima stabilito un piano organico e generale. Di ciò tutti i competenti in liturgia sono convinti. Non basta, per esempio, ritoccare qua e là il Calendario, eliminare alcune feste, rifondere qualche rubrica, curare l'edizione critica di alcuni libri o di qualche lezione storica. Occorre abbracciare in una visione generale tutto il complesso della riforma: rito, formulari, rubriche, feste, anno liturgico ecc., e predisporre sapientemente e con accurata conoscenza della funzione delle singole parti, le misure necessarie per equilibrare i singoli provvedimenti.
Nell'attuazione poi del piano generale si potrà procedere *per partes*; cosa facile se i principi e le basi fondamentali sono chiaramente stabilite in partenza. Solo così si avrà la sicurezza di un avanzamento ordinato e di un felice arrivo alla meta.
Eseguita finalmente la riforma stessa, occorrerà un ultimo elemento per garantire la stabilità della riforma e l'organicità dei futuri sviluppi della vita liturgica; tutto ciò si otterrà con il tanto invocato *Codex liturgicus*, che dovrebbe rappresentare il coronamento della Riforma e assicurarne l'applicazione e la stabilità;" *Memoria*, no. 19.

IV. The Roman Martyrology
V. The *libri cantus*
VI. The Roman Ritual
VII. The Ceremonial of Bishops
VIII. The Roman Pontifical
IX. The *Codex Iuris Liturgici* [40]

The reform of the missal was discussed towards the end of the *Memoria's* third chapter:

> The multiple reforms proposed hitherto for the gradation of feasts, the re-ordering of the calendar and the breviary, will have a direct repercussion on the Roman missal also, accomplishing a sensible renewal and a considerable simplification.
>
> All of that, however useful and necessary, is confined to the *material* content of the missal; but one must look at Holy Mass, the central act of Catholic worship, from broader aspects.
>
> For this purpose it is necessary to give attention to the enormous work accomplished in recent decades in the whole Catholic world through the Liturgical Movement, with the interest aroused not only among the clergy but also among the laity regarding the Holy Sacrifice, the understanding of it, and active participation in it. Hence some problems of an especially liturgical-pastoral character have arisen, of a gravity and a delicacy, which not all take into account; problems which obviously are not resolved by simply denying their foundation or importance. It is enough to mention the use of *modern languages* in the Liturgy, the forms and methods of *participation at Mass*, the various forms of the *celebration of Mass*: private, parochial, social, solemn, concelebrated, etc., the *internal structure* of the Mass itself. All of these are brought to the forefront today, are studied and treated with enthusiasm in journals and conventions, in academies and in liturgical and pastoral institutes, advanced also by numerous prelates in their ordinances and recently by the Holy Father Pius XII in his great encyclical on the Liturgy. A whole world is in movement, part of it in a preparatory and preliminary stage, part of it in possession of noteworthy results. In different places people are trying to actuate, in different ways and according to different points of view, the experiences had and the multiple possibilities in restoring to the Mass the place which belongs to it as the central mystery of divine worship.
>
> Considering attentively this state of things, the seriousness of the questions presented and the responsibility of the decisions to be taken, in a matter so fundamental for the Liturgy and the life of the Church, we judge it opportune to defer the detailed treatment of the missal and the Mass to a second stage of the Commission's work. On the one

[40] Ibid., no. 21.

hand, as we have already mentioned, the definitive arrangement of the missal will depend in a great part on the decisions that will be taken concerning the major principles of the reform and concerning the definitive lay-out of the ecclesiastical year and feasts. On the other hand, the questions which affect not so much the missal, as the Mass in its external form of celebration and the modes of assisting at it, with all the concomitant questions, will demand further and deeper study. Indeed, we will be able to think perhaps of the possibility and the opportunity of direct research into the major questions of 'pastoral Liturgy' regarding the Holy Mass, as they are truly felt and thought in the various centres of the Liturgical Movement. It would be enough to send to these centres, or even to some of the more qualified experts in this matter, a well formulated questionnaire, so as to have an objective idea on the concrete state of the problems and desires which exist in this regard. It is indeed certain that everyone is awaiting from a future liturgical reform, the solution in principle to so many questions which for decades now have occupied the minds of zealous pastors and priests.[41]

---

41 "Le moltiplici riforme proposte finora per la gradazione delle feste, il riordinamento del calendario e del Brevario, avranno la loro diretta ripercussione anche sul Messale Romano, compiendone un sensibile rinnovamento e una notevole semplificazione.

Tutto ciò, per quanto utile e necessario, si limita al contenuto *materiale* del Messale: ma bisogna considerare la santa Messa, l'atto centrale del culto cattolico, sotto più vasti aspetti.

A questo proposito è necessario porre attenzione all'enorme lavoro compiuto negli ultimi decenni in tutto il mondo cattolico, per mezzo del Movimento liturgico, con l'interessamento suscitato non solo tra il clero, ma ance tra i laici in favore del santo Sacrificio, della sua intelligenza e della partecipazione attiva ed esso. Di qui sono sorti dei problemi di carattere sopratutto liturgico-pastorale, di una gravità e delicatezza, di cui non tutti si rendono conto; problemi che evidentemente non si risolvono negandone semplicemente il fondamento o l'importanza. Basti accennare all'uso delle *lingue moderne* nella Liturgia, alle forme e ai metodi di *partecipazione alla Messa,* alle varie forme della *celebrazione della Messa*: privata, parrochiale, sociale, solenne, pontificale, concelebrata, ecc., alla *struttura interna* della Messa stessa. Tutte cose portate oggi in primo piano, studiate e trattate con entusiasmo nelle riviste e nei convegni, nelle accademie e negli istituti liturgici e pastorali, prospettate anche da numerosi prelati nelle loro ordinanze e recentemente dal Santo Padre Pio XII nella sua grande Enciclica sulla Liturgia. È tutto un mondo in movimento, parte nella fase preparatoria e preliminare, parte in possesso di notevoli risultati. In vari luoghi si tenta di attuare, in diverse maniere e secondo differenti punti di vista, le esperienze fatte e le molteplici possibilità di ridare alla Messa il posto che le compete come mistero centrale del culto divino.

Considerando attentamente questo stato di cose, la gravità delle questioni prospettate el la responsibilità delle decisioni da prendersi, in una materia tanto fondamentale per la Liturgia e per la vita della Chiesa, stimiamo opportuno

The envisaged impact on the missal of calendar reform reflects the organic nature of the Liturgy, and as such presents no *a priori* difficulty. Nor do the consideration of the possible use of the vernacular or of enhancing the people's participation: neither is of itself inconsistent with respect for objective liturgical Tradition.[42]

The question of reforming "the *internal structure* of the Mass itself" arises here, without further explication. The *Memoria's* reticence with regard to the missal is clear, and it cannot be accused of advocating a reform that is inconsistent with objective liturgical Tradition. What it does is put the question on the agenda and call for further research "in a matter so fundamental for the Liturgy and the life of the Church."

This extract also makes clear the impact made by the Liturgical Movement on the Holy See's considerations of reform. Of particular interest is the emergence of the term "pastoral Liturgy." We shall return to it below.

Chapter four outlines the way forward for the Commission. The *Memoria* was first to be discussed in order to establish and stabilise the fundamental principles of the liturgical reform, after which a generic approbation was to be sought from the pope so that the Commission could continue its work on a secure and stable basis. This work was to proceed in the nine-fold order outlined above, with seven sub-comissions (biblical, patristic, historical, hymnological, chant, rubrical and rhetorical) contributing. The resultant liturgical books were to be submitted to the pope for approbation and promulgation.[43]

---

rimandare la trattazione particolareggiata del Messale e della Messa in un secondo tempo di lavoro della Commissione. Da una parte, come abbiamo già accennato, l'assestamento definitivo del Messale dipenderà in gran parte dalle decisioni che saranno prese circa i grandi principi della Riforma e circa la sistemazione definitiva dell'anno ecclesiastico e delle feste; onde sarà più prudente attendere queste soluzioni. Dall'altra parte, le questioni che toccano non tanto il Messale, ma piuttosto la Messa nella sua forma esterna di celebrazione e nei modi di assistervi, con tutte le questioni concomitanti, richiederanno ulteriori e più approfonditi studi. Anzi, si portrà pensare forse alla possibilità e opportunità di indagini dirette circa le maggiori questione della «pastorale liturgica» intorno alla santa Messa, come esso sono realmente sentite e pensate nei vari centri del movimento liturgico. Basterebbe inviare ai detti centri, o anche ad alcuni fra gli studiosi più qualificati in questa materia, un questionario ben formulato, per avere così un'idea oggettiva sullo stato concreto dei problemi e dei desideri che esistono a questo proposito. È certo infatti che tutti si attendono da una futura Riforma liturgica, la soluzione di principio su tante questioni che occupano ormai da decenni la mente di zelanti pastori e sacerdoti;" ibid., nos. 314-316.

[42] However all three may certainly occasion difficulties *a posteriori*.

[43] Cf. *Memoria*, nos. 334-341.

Following initial discussion of the *Memoria,* in November 1949 copies of it were sent *sub secreto,* with the explicit permission of Pius XII, to three eminent liturgists: J.A. Jungmann, Dom Capelle, and Mario Righetti. These liturgists were asked to comment in the margin of the text and to return the annotated volume. The annotations were collated and published for the commission in 1950.[44] We confine our study to pertinent annotations made to the paragraphs of the *Memoria* examined above.

Capelle's letter accompanying his annotations expresses his opinion of the first of the *Memoria's* principles, and his overall stance with regard to liturgical reform:

> I cannot but admire the solidity of the principle set forth in no. 16 of the *Memoria.* It is a monument of clear and of conscientious information, and the solutions it proposes to most of the problems satisfactorily resolve the issues for me...It seems to me that in the reform of a thing so sacred, it is a thousand times better to keep to the minimum than to risk going beyond it.[45]

Capelle's annotation of the fundamental principles (only he makes any) clarifies his stance. After the words "to renew therefore courageously what is truly necessary and indispensable to renew, and to conserve jealously what one can and must conserve," summarising the *Memoria's* discussion of the first principle, he writes:

> From this we are to deduce that nothing is to be changed unless it is a case of indispensable necessity.
>
> This rule is most wise: for the Liturgy is truly a sacred testament and monument—not so much written but living—of Tradition, which is to be reckoned with as a locus of theology, and is a most pure font of piety and of the Christian spirit.
>
> Therefore:
> 1. That which serves [well] at the present time is sufficient unless it is gravely deficient.
> 2. Only new things which *are necessary* are to be introduced, and in a way that is consonant with Tradition.
> 3. Nothing is to be changed unless there is comparatively great gain to be had.

---

[44] Sacra Rituum Congregatio, Sectio Historica, *Memoria sulla Riforma Liturgica: Supplemento II – Annotazioni alla "Memoria,"* no. 76.

[45] "Je ne puis qu'admirer la fermeté du principe posé au n. 16 de la *Memoria.* Celle-ci est un monument de claire et consciencieuse information et les solutions qu'elle propose, pour la plupart des problèmes, me paraissent heureuses...Il me semble que dans la réforme d'une chose si sacrée, il vaut mille fois mieux rester en deçа que de risquer d'excéder;" ibid., p. 6.

4. Practices that have fallen into disuse are to be restored if their reintroduction would truly render the rites more pure, and more intelligible to the minds of the faithful.[46]

This is, of course, the principle of the organic development of the objective liturgical Tradition applied to the project of reform under consideration: it is essentially conservative but open to truly necessary growth.

Capelle was thoroughly steeped in the ideals and work of the Liturgical Movement, to the origins and development of which he was both a witness and a contributor. Had not Capelle championed the ideals of the Liturgical Movement in the presence of Pius XI in 1935?[47]

In the author's opinion, in Capelle's principles we find a mature consideration of liturgical reform. His was not the zeal of a recent convert. Nor was he primarily fired by a thirst for historical research—though he was himself an accomplished liturgical historian. Capelle was a monk who lived and loved the Liturgy, and who sought the return of liturgical piety to its rightfully central place in the life of the Church. As he stated plainly to Pius XI in 1935: "I would not concern myself about the Liturgy, unless I believed that it is such an important, essential and sacred thing."[48]

His principles are all the more important given that they appear at the beginning of the Holy See's work on a general reform. He was, after all, one of only three experts invited to comment upon the *Memoria*. Given their sound origin in Capelle's person, and their consonance with the organic development of the Liturgy, they serve well as an evaluative tool for liturgical reforms enacted prior to the Second Vatican Council.

There are no further annotations to the paragraphs from the *Memoria* we have quoted, save that Jungmann annotates paragraph 337 (which proposes the formation of the seven different sub-comissions to assist in the practical application of the reform), suggesting that before official promulgation "there should be a phase of using the new rite *ad*

---

[46] "Ex quo deducitur nihil immutandum esse nisi in casu indispensabilis necessitatis. Sapientissima quidem regula: Sacra enim liturgia testis est et monumentum—non tantum scriptum sed vivum—Traditionis, adeo ut annumeretur inter loca theologica, et purissimos fontes pietatis et spiritus christiani. Quare: 1. Servetur quidquid servari potest sine *gravi* damno. 2. Introducantur tantum quæ *necesse est* introducere; et modo traditioni consentaneo. 3. Nihil immutetur nisi magnum ex immutatione comparetur emolumentum. 4. Restaurentur obsoleta, si *vere* per instaurationem puriores reddantur ritus, magisque fidelium mentibus perspicui;" ibid., p. 9.

[47] B. Botte OSB recounts Capelle's contribution first as a monk of Maredsous and then as Abbot of Mont-César: cf. *From Silence to Participation*, esp. pp. 41-49.

[48] "The Holy See and the Liturgical Movement" in: *OF* vol. XI p. 7.

experimentum conceded to certain qualified centres..."[49] The remainder of the annotations concern themselves with practical questions pertaining to the proposed reform of the calendar and of the breviary.

The achievements of the Pian commission are of interest because of their application of the principles outlined above. Also, it can be maintained that the reforms brought about by the commission in the 1950s and early 1960s were important precedents for the Fathers of the Second Vatican Council.

So too, the principles the commission articulated, or its subsequent published documentation, laid foundations for future reform. Giampietro reports that at the insistence of Cardinal Bea, who, like Antonelli, was a member of the commission throughout its existence, the *Memoria* and its five printed supplements were distributed to the members and *periti* of the conciliar liturgical commission,[50] underlining the significance of the *Memoria* beyond the commission itself. Whilst it is true that it is a working plan, and that its principles and proposals were not authoritatively promulgated, the *Memoria* was, nevertheless, the basis of the work of this commission. This formed the immediate background to the consideration of liturgical reform by the Fathers of the Second Vatican Council.

Accordingly, we examine the reforms of the commission alongside contemporary events and literature generated by the Liturgical Movement, with an eye on Capelle's fourfold list. Before doing so, however, it is appropriate to consider the principles of reform in Jungmann's work, who, as we have already seen, was highly regarded by the Holy See, and whose influence was significant.

Josef Andreas Jungmann SJ

In 1948 Jungmann published his monumental two-volume work *Missarium Sollemnia*.[51] Joseph Crehan SJ acclaimed it: "no existing work by a single writer can compete with this exhaustive discussion of the historical evolution of every single feature of the Mass as we know it today."[52] "This book is an event!" exclaimed Reinhold. It had particular value, Reinhold argued, in the light of the "great desire all over the world…to raise claims for adaptations" to the Liturgy. Jungmann's book

---

49 "Prima della promulgazione ufficiale ci dovrebbe essere anche una fase di uso del nuovo rito «*ad experimentum*» concesso a certi centri idonei…;" *Memoria sulla Riforma Liturgica: Supplemento II – Annotazioni alla "Memoria,"* p. 62.

50 Cf. *Il Card. Ferdinando Antonelli e gli sviluppi della riforma liturgica dal 1948 al 1970*, p. 52.

51 Verlag Herder, Vienna. English: *The Mass of the Roman Rite: Its Origins and Development.*

52 "Fashioning the Liturgy" in: *The Month* vol. CLXXXVI p. 314.

was seen as making available "sound Tradition" which should inform them.[53]

Jungmann was accorded an immense authority by his contemporaries. In 1958 Clifford Howell SJ extolled him:

> There is mighty little that he holds that anybody would be inclined to dispute; for he seems to come as near to omniscience on this subject as is humanly possible...Jungmann's conclusions are pretty well universally accepted by the pundits. He is THE great man of the day.[54]

Given this, his appointment as a consulter to the Sacred Congregation of Rites early in the 1950's, his influence on the reforms before and after the council,[55] and given the extent of his influence on modern liturgists,[56] Jungmann's principles of liturgical reform are of particular importance.

In *The Mass of the Roman Rite* we read: "the monumental greatness of the Roman Mass lies in its antiquity..."[57] This was Jungmann's fundamental tenet. He deprecated liturgical embellishments after the Peace of Constantine, most particularly those of the medieval[58] and baroque periods.[59] Accordingly, Jungmann distinguished "secondary"[60] developments in liturgical history. These were "distortions of the original ethos of Christian eucharistic worship" rather than "providential and beneficial gains in the organic development of the

---

[53] "Missarium Sollemnia" in: *OF* vol. XXIII p. 126. Significantly, Reinhold notes the limits of such historical research, rejecting—with *Mediator Dei*—liturgical historicism as a fundamental principle of reform: "An appeal to history and Tradition is therefore not a conclusive argument, apart from the fact that the encyclical on the Liturgy makes very short shrift of any appeals to extinct traditions;" p. 127.

[54] "The Parish in the Life of the Church" in: Living Parish Series, *Living Parish Week,* p. 23.

[55] According to Balthasar Fischer, "Probably more than any other single book, *Missarium Sollemnia* prepared the way for the conciliar reform of the Liturgy;" cf. R. Peiffer "Joseph Jungmann: Laying a Foundation for Vatican II" in: Tuzik, *How Firm a Foundation: Leaders of the Liturgical Movement,* p. 62.

[56] Cf., J. Pierce & M. Downey, *Source and Summit: Commemorating Josef A. Jungmann, SJ.* This *Festschrift* goes so far as to rejoice in Jungmann's "ideal of pastoral Liturgy" which is seen as foundation for such things as the "feminist Liturgical Movement;" cf. Marjorie Proctor-Smith ""The 'We' of the Liturgy:" Liturgical Reform, Pastoral Liturgy and the Feminist Liturgical Movement," p. 156.

[57] Vol. I p. 165.

[58] Cf. supra, p. 24.

[59] Cf. his seminal 1960 essay, "The Defeat of Teutonic Arianism and the Revolution in Religious Culture in the Early Middle Ages" in: *Pastoral Liturgy,* pp. 1-101; also: *The Sacrifice of the Church: The Meaning of the Mass,* pp. 48-51.

[60] Cf. *Pastoral Liturgy,* p. 286.

Liturgy."[61] Put simply, Jungmann was a liturgical antiquarian,[62] proposing a "corruption theory of liturgical history" that is "widely accepted today as fact,"[63] and who advocated what came to be called "pastoral Liturgy:" Liturgy that is fashioned to meet the needs of contemporary man.

Addressing the First International Congress of Pastoral Liturgy at Assisi in 1956, he declared:

> The living Liturgy, actively participated in, was itself for centuries the most important form of pastoral care. This is true particularly of those centuries in which the Liturgy was developed in its essentials. In the later middle ages, the Liturgy was indeed celebrated with zeal and much splendour in numerous collegiate and monastic churches, and was also further developed in its various forms. But unfavourable circumstances brought it about that something like a Fog Curtain settled between and separated Liturgy and people, through which the faithful could only dimly recognise what was happening at the altar…
>
> The Liturgy has become a succession of mysterious words and ceremonies, which must be performed according to a fixed rule, and which one tries to follow with a holy reverence—but which themselves finally harden into rigid and unchangeable forms.
>
> Perhaps this rigidity was necessary—as a protection against heretical attacks upon the Sacrifice of the Church. It may also have been necessary to safeguard the sacred heritage for future times, for a time of greater need and of more grave decisions, such as we experience in

---

61 G. Hull, *The Banished Heart*, p. 210. Hull also asserts that Jungmann's "formidable scholarship was vitiated by the subjective assumption that the analysis of a thing necessarily implies its reform;" p. 55.

62 He himself applied this term to early twentieth century liturgical romantics; cf. *Pastoral Liturgy*, p. 90.

63 T. Day, *Why Catholics Can't Sing*, p. 92. J. Baldovin SJ's contribution "The Body of Christ in Celebration: On Eucharistic Liturgy, Theology, and Pastoral Practice" to Pierce & Downey's *Festschrift*, admits: "The criticism does have a point, at least with regard to those who took Jungmann's historical presuppositions and brought them to their logical conclusion;" p. 51. Jungmann's account of the corruption of Vespers in "Vespers and the Devotional Service" in: W. Leonard SJ, *Liturgy for the People*, pp. 170-172 fails to account for the presumably not untypical liturgical practice of the French village of Undervelier described in Belloc's *Path to Rome*: "A bell began tolling and it seemed as if the whole village were pouring into the Church…I then saw that what they were at was Vespers. All the village sang, knowing the psalms very well, and I noticed that their Latin was nearer German than French…My whole mind was taken up and transfigured by this collective act, and I saw for a moment the Catholic Church quite plain..." pp. 141-142. Nor does it account for the popularity of Latin-English editions of Vespers, of which a *ninth* edition was published in London in 1812: cf. *Vespers: or the Evening Office of the Church in Latin and English according to the Roman Breviary*.

> our own day, when the faithful in an especial manner need that same guidance by the Liturgy which was the privileged lot of the Christians of the first centuries.
>
> Today the rigidity is beginning to lessen. Forms which appeared petrified have come to life again. Just as the Church under Pius XI, by the Lateran Treaties, surrendered that external protection which, in the more crude times of the middle ages, had seemed so necessary to her as a world power, so now under Pius XII she has begun to loosen the protective armour which till now has encased the sacred forms of her Liturgy.[64]

And in the introduction to *The Early Liturgy* in 1958, he explained:

> The Liturgy of the Catholic Church is an edifice in which we are still living today, and in essentials it is the same building in which Christians were already living ten or fifteen or even eighteen and more centuries ago. In the course of all these centuries, the structure has become more and more complicated, with constant remodellings[65] and additions, and so the plan of the building has been obscured—so much so that we may no longer feel quite at home in it because we no longer understand it.
>
> Hence we must look up the old building plans, for these will tell us what the architects of old really wanted, and if we grasp their intentions we shall learn to appreciate much that the building contains and even to esteem it more highly. And if we should have the opportunity to make changes in the structure or to adapt it to the

---

64 "The Pastoral Idea in the History of the Liturgy," The Liturgical Press, *The Assisi Papers* [hereafter *AP*] pp. 29-31. In 1957 Bishop François Charrière of Lausanne, Geneva and Fribourg took exception to Jungmann's use of the Lateran Treaty as an analogy appropriate to the reform of the Liturgy: "Ajoutons à ce propos encore que la comparison dont le Père Jungmann s'est servi à Assise à propos du pouvoir temporel des Papes ne me paraît concluante. Bien sûr que les accords du Lateran ont trouvé une solution libératrice à une crise qui durait depuis longtemps au sujet du pouvoir temporel des Papes. Mais précisément les accords du Latéran on retenu une solution *territoriale,* minime bien sûr mais réele quand même, alors que la plupart des théologiens du commencement du vingtième siècle insistaient sur l'impossibilité d'une solution territoriale quelconque! En réalité, les accords du Lateran représentent bel et bien une solution *dans la sens* de la tradition, de la *nécessité d'un territoire,* si petit soit-il pour marquer visiblement l'independence du Saint Siège. La comparison du Père Jungmann me paraît donc aller à fin contraire;" *Memoria sulla Riforma Liturgica: Supplemento IV—Consultazione dell'Episcopato Intorno alla Riforma del Breviario Romano (1956-1957) Risultati e Deduzioni,* p. 100.

65 In the author's opinion liturgical history does not bear witness to "constant remodellings" of the Liturgy.

> needs of our own people, we will then do so in such a way that, where possible, nothing of the precious heritage of the past is lost…
>
> We are going to deal, therefore, with that period of liturgical history that surpasses all others in importance because it is concerned with the basic outlines, the very ground-plan of the structure, namely the period up to Gregory the Great.[66]
>
> The discovery of the origins of our worship holds a special attraction…a knowledge of the original text, or of the original form used in the primitive Church, while of considerable value, is not our only interest…we now realise that other forms, which developed in the years that followed, also proceeded from the life of the Church. In the same way as the original, or at least in a similar way, they are derived from the inspiration and activity of the Holy Spirit…they form the links of a chain connecting our present-day worship with the life and worship of the primitive Church. All the links in that chain are important, for only when we possess them all do we have a complete explanation of the present-day forms of our divine worship. But it remains true that the first links are the more important, for they determined the course that succeeding forms were to take.[67]

There are two questions to be raised. The first is whether Jungmann's assumption that his own period is indeed "a time of greater need and of more grave decisions" is apposite, and whether it may lay, at least in part, a sound foundation for liturgical reform? But is it not a temptation of each age, particularly of those that have experienced a renaissance such as that enjoyed by liturgical historians in the past two centuries to regard itself as particularly enlightened? Was this not also the temptation of Quignonez, of Jubé and of Ricci, of the Gallicans?

The second question, the answer to which will clarify the issue raised by the first, is: how does Jungmann account for the principle of organic development?

He certainly recognises the organic development of the Liturgy:

> The Liturgy is like a tree, which has grown in the changing climate of world history and which has experienced stormy as well as flourishing times. Its real growth, however, comes from within, from those life forces whence it took its origin.[68]

His distinction, which may have its origins in elements of post-reformation Jesuit spirituality,[69] between the observable tree-like growth of the Liturgy and what we may call the interior growth (more properly

---

66 *The Early Liturgy*, p. 1.

67 Ibid., pp. 4-5.

68 "The Pastoral Idea in the History of the Liturgy," The Liturgical Press, *AP* p. 19.

69 For a critique of its impact on the Liturgy, cf. G. Hull, *The Banished Heart*, pp. 145-147.

the "value" or "effect") of the Liturgy, enables Jungmann to dismiss external forms not found in antiquity.[70] Organic growth for Jungmann is thus an historical phenomenon, but not a—let alone the—principle of liturgical reform. Hence he says:

> It is always necessary, therefore, to observe and recognise in Liturgy, the law of continuity. And this not merely from psychological considerations...Of its nature Liturgy is conservative. Man is caught up in constant change but God never changes and His revelation too, which is committed to the Church, and the scheme of Redemption, given in Christ, is always the same. Prayer and worship are a constant flowing back and homecoming of the souls of restless, wavering men, to the peace of God...
>
> Religious sentiment is very much disinclined to change liturgical forms except for very grave reasons.[71]
>
> But like every living organism, the Liturgy has to adapt itself to the present conditions of life. As a rule this is achieved by silent growth: but there are times of almost complete standstill, and there are times of stormy advance...
>
> Towards the end of the middle ages growth became a wild and unhealthy profusion and so the Council of Trent and Pope St Pius V called a halt...and a period of standstill was inaugurated...
>
> For three and a half centuries things went on under this regime until Pius X...began to speak once more of reform...
>
> Certainly, after so long a pause an imperceptible growth could not suffice. A jerk—more than a jerk—was clearly necessary...
>
> Thanks to the emergence of historical theology, and Christian archaeology, too, the world of the Fathers and that in which our Liturgy found its origin has been brought near once more. The ancient Christian world has revived. Much knowledge has become available to us...
>
> The religious situation of our time also demands forms of Church life such as will be found in a meaningful, corporately celebrated

---

70 In the author's opinion, this distinction is false: one cannot have the "effect" or "value" of the Liturgy without its external forms. (Though one can certainly have its external forms without its value—hollow ritualism.) To follow Jungmann's analogy, if you have no tree you have no sap. This distinction, taken to its logical conclusion, also risks spiritualising Catholic Liturgy and denying its, and therefore the Christian faith's, incarnational nature.

71 In *Public Worship* Jungmann writes: "Liturgical formulation has, of its very nature, a tendency to assume a character independent of time and respectfully hesitant ever to touch sacred things; this is manifested in the retention of prescribed forms..." p. 7.

> Liturgy...Like its architecture, the thinking of our time has become practical...
>
> The Liturgy itself is on the move. This does not please everyone. It is as though the walls of an ancient building were beginning to totter; as though an axe were being laid to a thousand-year-old oak.[72]

The weight put on the demands of "the religious situation of our time" is significant. These, and the new insights of historical theology and Christian archaeology, are seen to justify reform by "jerk." Organic development is regarded as insufficient, to the obvious peril of the "thousand-year-old oak."

In 1949 Jungmann told the German liturgical commission that, because of a lack of available historical sources:

> Pius V's reform was only half a reform. Nowadays...the reconstruction of the Mass would present no difficulties. If this was what one aimed at, the following elements would disappear: the multiplication of opening prayers, the disorder in the closing parts of the prayers, the repeated kissing of the altar, the Pax Domini being in the wrong place, all genuflections, the emphasis on the Words of Institution as consecration, and many other things. Obviously, such a radical reform would not be desirable. Reform of the missal needs to be undertaken less in accordance with some principle, so that we make cuts, and more like the work of an architect who has some plan in his mind, and who takes account not only of what has come down from history, but also of the needs of today and of tomorrow, and who is able to construct a well-ordered new building, using both old elements and new, and with more variety than there is at present, so that above all the basic structure of the Mass becomes more easily visible.[73]

---

[72] *Pastoral Liturgy*, pp. 91-94.

[73] "So war die Reform Pius' V. nur eine halbe Reform. Heute aber würde die Rekonstruktion der Messe keine Schwierigkeiten bedeuten. Würde man sie erstreben, dann fielen weg: die Häufung der Orationen, die Unordnung der Orationsschlüsse, die Häufung des Altarkusses, die Unordnung der Pax Domini, alle Kniebeugen, die Hervorhebung der Wandlung und vieles andere. Offensichtlich wäre eine solch radikale Reform nicht erwünscht. Die Missalereform verlangt weniger nach einem Prinzip, um Abstriche vorzunehmen, als vielmehr nach einem Baumeister mit einem Plan im Herzen, der sowohl den historischen Bestand wie auch die Bedürfnisse der Gegenwart und Zukunft berücksichtigt und einen wohlgeordneten Neubau aus Altem und Neuem, von mehr Relief, als es der jetzige hat, zu errichten weiß, so daß vor allem die Gliederung der Messe deutlicher hervortritt;" J. Wagner, *Mein Weg Zur Liturgiereform 1936-1986*, p. 143; [translation: H. Taylor]. Jungmann's further proposals in this document include the reform and shortening of the Roman canon.

Jungmann's principle of reform thus combines antiquarianism with pastoral expediency. It is an historical and pastoral principle which, precisely on historical grounds, fails to accord sufficient respect to the organic development of the Liturgy beyond antiquity, and indeed rejects organic development as the fundamental principle of liturgical reform, in favour of a 'jerking' of the Liturgy into suitable shape for modern man, using objective liturgical Tradition, in the words of Duffy, "as an inexhaustible resource and a universal panacea."[74] In this he has certainly, to return to our first question, attributed a disproportionate weight not only to his own period, but also to antiquity.

Jungmann saw his principle as having immediate practical implications. These clearly move beyond the fundamental aim of the Liturgical Movement to foster liturgical piety:

> Not only amongst the people but at the altar, within the Liturgy in the narrowest sense, things require to be done. There is no lack of proposals which seek to do justice both to the spirit of Tradition and to pastoral needs. They aim at making the shape of the Mass as celebrated by the priest more straightforward. Many accessories are to be reduced or must disappear altogether. Thus the Mass for the revived Easter Vigil has had parts omitted at the beginning and the end; in a similar mood the decree of March 23, 1955, has reduced the number of prayers at Sunday Masses.
>
> The construction of the Mass ought to be made more obvious. The chief sections, Proanaphora, Offertory, Canon and Communion should be easily distinguished; and various details should be made more intelligible...the symbolic handwashing could be brought forward to the beginning of the Offertory. Scripture readings ought to be enriched by the introduction of a cycle covering several years. Popular intercession which was supplied at the end of the last century by prayers after Mass ought now to come fully into its own through the revival of the prayer of the faithful as an organic part of the Mass immediately after the Scripture readings and sermon. Sunday Prefaces should once more take up the note of Easter joy, and the thanksgiving after Communion could be re-fashioned so as to allude to the Communion of the people.[75]

Such suggestions are not of themselves deleterious: none wields an axe to the thousand-year-old oak except, perhaps, the proposal to

---

[74] "*Rewriting the Liturgy: The Theological Implications of Translation*," in: S. Caldecott, *Beyond the Prosaic*, p. 98. In 1956 G. Ellard SJ's review of the English volume II of Jungmann's book emphasised the view of Creehan reviewing the German originals in 1948: "If these [liturgical experiments] are to be renewed, what better guide than these books into the storehouse of the past?" "Jungmann's Volume Two" in: *Worship* vol. XXX p. 217.

[75] *Pastoral Liturgy*, pp. 99-100.

"enrich" the readings from Sacred Scripture—we consider such poposals, and the 1955 decree, below. Indeed, they resonate with the *desiderata* of Parsch, and may be said to be prudent suggestions for pastoral reform that organic development, albeit induced, might encompass. However, we must maintain our concern with regard to Jungmann's assumptions and his principle, which are, nevertheless, capable of underpinning root and branch reforms that move well beyond moderate proposals and the organic development of the Liturgy.[76]

The 1951 Reform of the Paschal Vigil

Dominica Resurrectionis vigiliam of 9th February 1951[77] reformed the solemn paschal vigil for one year *ad experimentum,* restoring the time for the celebration of the vigil to the night preceding Easter Sunday: it had hitherto been celebrated on the *Saturday* morning, "not without detriment to the original symbolism"[78] of the rite. According to Bugnini, the publication of this, the first concrete fruit of the Pian commission, "caught even officials of the Congregation of Rites by surprise."[79] It is clear that its preparation was rushed.[80]

The Holy See had received numerous requests for this restoration over a number of years.[81] To the possibility of its celebration at night, raised in 1948 in the *Memoria,*[82] Jungmann and Righetti responded

---

[76] In addition to our critique of Jungmann's approach to liturgical reform, recent scholarship has also questioned the assumption of Jungmann's *The Place of Christ in Liturgical Prayer* that "people up to the fourth century did not pray to Jesus Christ but only to the Father;" J. Ratzinger, *A New Song for the Lord,* pp. 7ff, and finds in this a "deficient Christology" and an "æsthetically impoverished liturgical horizontalism" that "unwittingly affected the Liturgy adversely by insinuating a humanistic Christ no longer capable of inserting the temporal into the eternal in his own person;" A. Nichols OP, *Christendom Awake,* p. 26.

[77] Cf. *Ordo Sabbati Sancti Quando Vigilia Paschalis Instaurata Peragitur,* p. 5.

[78] *Dominica Resurrectionis vigiliam:* "non sine originalis symbolismi detrimento;" ibid.

[79] *TRL* p. 9; "colse di sorpresa gli stessi ufficiali della Congregazione dei Riti" *LRL* p. 25.

[80] The commission only finished discussing the reform on January 30th: cf. N. Giampietro OFM Cap., *Il Card. Ferdinando Antonelli e gli sviluppi della riforma liturgica dal 1948 al 1970,* nos. [152]-[186]. The publication of the *Ordo* left less than a month before Easter Sunday (25th March) cf. pp. 56-57.

[81] Cf. *Ordo Sabbati Sancti Quando Vigilia Paschalis Instaurata Peragitur,* p. 5: "His itaque suffulti rationibus, multi locorum Ordinarii, fidelium cœtus religionisque viri, supplices ad Sanctam Sedem detulerunt preces, ut ipsa restitutionem antiqu vigiliæ paschalis ad horas nocturnas inter sabbatum sanctum et dominicam Resurrectionis indulgere vellet."

[82] Cf. no. 74.

positively; Capelle enthusiastically.[83] This reform recognised authenticity as a principle of reform; that is, a liturgical vigil should truly be a vigil and therefore be celebrated at night. That the Holy See should intervene to correct an inauthentic development, indeed a certain liturgical decadence and contradiction, whereby the liturgical texts proclaimed the "truly blessed night" during the previous morning, is, in the opinion of the author, an apposite use of authority in liturgical reform which shows profound respect for the objective traditional Liturgy.

As well as restoring the authentic time of celebration, ritual changes were made.[84] Amongst these we may distinguish two types. Firstly, those which were simply the logical consequence of the restored time of the vigil's celebration, principally to the rubrics for the recitation of the office and for the purification of the chalice.[85]

Of the second type—reforms unrelated to the time of celebration—there were eleven significant changes. The principles from which these operate are of particular interest:

1. The reduction of the three prayers for the blessing of the fire to one.[86] Antonelli states that eliminating repetition was part of the motivation behind this reform. However he also says that there was a straightforward desire "to abbreviate."[87] Abbreviation was envisaged neither by the *Memoria* nor by Capelle.

2. The reordering of the blessing of the candle, including the abolition of the triple candle so that the Easter candle is lit directly from the fire and then itself taken into the Church in procession.[88] This may be said to render the rites surrounding the candle more pure in order to promote the participation of the faithful. The loss of the triple candle in this purification is unfortunate and, arguably, unnecessary.

---

83 Cf. *Memoria sulla Riforma Liturgica: Supplemento II – Annotazioni alla "Memoria,"* pp. 21-22.

84 For a comprehensive account, including subsequent modifications up to 1953, cf. B. Steuart OSB, *The Development of Christian Worship*, pp. 273-280.

85 Cf. *Ordo Sabbati Sancti Quando Vigilia Paschalis Instaurata Peragitur*, "De Officio Divino" nos. 1-4, and "De Missa Solemni Vigiliæ Paschalis" nos 6-7.

86 Cf. *Ordo Sabbati Sancti Quando Vigilia Paschalis Instaurata Peragitur*, "De Vigilia Paschali" no 3.

87 "Solo che delle tre lezioni si usa solo la prima. Ragione: per abbreviare e perché le altre due erano pezzi di ricambio;" N. Giampietro OFM Cap., *Il Card. Ferdinando Antonelli e gli sviluppi della riforma liturgica dal 1948 al 1970*, pp. 24-26.

88 Cf. *Ordo Sabbati Sancti Quando Vigilia Paschalis Instaurata Peragitur*, "De Vigilia Paschali" nos. 5-7. According to Giampietro, Antonelli stated that there was a conscious desire to restore the paschal candle to its place as the material and symbolic centre of the whole liturgical action; cf. *Il Card. Ferdinando Antonelli e gli sviluppi della riforma liturgica dal 1948 al 1970*, p. 60.

3. The restoration of the incision of the Easter candle with the Greek letters A and Ω.[89] This is a restoration of a liturgical form lost in history: a small restoration when one considers the vigil as a whole, and an enrichment of the rite both symbolically and theologically, consonant with Tradition.
4. The introduction of candles carried by the clergy and the people lit from the Easter candle.[90] This reform may be described as pastoral reform promoting active participation in the rite. Its novelty is offset by its powerful paschal symbolism and profound theological content. It may be regarded as a healthy pastoral development.
5. The deletion of the reference to the (Holy Roman) Emperor from the *Exsultet* and the insertion of a newly composed prayer for those in authority.[91] This can be said to be necessary due to a change in the reality to which the liturgical prayer relates, and thus ecclesiastical authority rightly acts to develop the liturgical text and to render it authentic by updating it to correspond with the reality with which it deals.
6. The reduction of the twelve prophecies to four.[92] This is abbreviation, justified because four prophecies were the practice in the time of St Gregory the Great and because twelve prophecies in Latin were regarded as too onerous for the people.[93] The *Memoria* envisaged reducing the number, but it is hard to see how this is more than an example of antiquarianism, traces of which we have noted in the *Memoria*. One might reflect that, if actual participation was desired, granting permission for reading the prophecies in the vernacular[94] would be more in keeping with Tradition than their arbitrary and substantial reduction from twelve to four.[95] And it is difficult to see how actual participation is enhanced if that in which one is supposed to participate is reduced by two-thirds! However, the structure of the twelve prophecies was not without its own

---

[89] Cf. ibid., no 5.
[90] Cf. ibid., no 11.
[91] Cf. ibid., no 13.
[92] Cf. ibid., nn. 14-17.
[93] "ai tempi di S. Gregorio Magno erano quattro. Certo è che il numero di 12 non è di una necessità assoluta; ed è anche certo che oggi, la lettura in latino delle profezie è un vero onere specialmente per il popolo assistente;" *Memoria* no. 72.
[94] In 1952 A.G. Martimort argued in *LMD* that "there are very serious reasons to consider the formulation of this new rubric *sedentes auscultant* [the seventh reform in this study] to be able to be legitimately interpreted as a discreet but certain invitation to draw such a pastoral conclusion" as to read the prophecies in the vernacular; cf. T. Richstatter OFM, *Liturgical Law*, p. 33.
[95] In what may be regarded as an irony of liturgical history the missal of Paul VI increased the number of prophecies to a maximum possible of seven; however only three are compulsory.

theological import—the loss of which is clearly an impoverishment.[96] Capelle opposed any reduction in number, though he thought that for smaller churches some reduction might be possible.[97]

7. The instruction that the celebrant sit and listen to the prophecies rather than reciting them himself at the altar.[98] This reform eliminates the priest's repetition of the texts read by other ministers, restoring a certain authenticity to the rite in harmony with that renewal envisaged by the *Memoria.*

8. The insistence on a time of silent prayer between the *flectamus genua* and the *levate* following the prophecies.[99] Again, here, we have the restoration of the original purpose for this liturgical action, rendering the rite more authentic and pure and enhancing the actual participation of the faithful.

9. The directive that blessing of the water be done in the sight of the faithful.[100] Here again we see an explicit desire that the faithful be able to participate (in this case visually), in the rite. The rite does retain the possibility of a procession to a baptistery separate from the Church building for the blessing of the water should there be one. Where this procession does not occur, one might express concern at divorcing the blessing of the paschal water from the annual blessing of the baptismal font, which this reform made possible.

10. The renewal of baptismal vows by the people, permitted in the vernacular.[101] This may be regarded as *the* major innovation of the reform. Capelle objected to it vehemently on the grounds that there was no necessity for its introduction, that it was theologically deficient (he argued that the vigil was not primarily a commemoration of baptism and that the reception of the Holy Eucharist is *the* act of participation for the faithful in the paschal mystery: neophytes participate in this by receiving baptism which is then consummated in the reception of the Eucharist), that this restoration was not in line with the stated intention of wisely and discretely restoring the Liturgy to a purer state, that it was utterly inopportune to introduce rites that not only lack a solid and longstanding

---

[96] Cf. J. Parsons, "A Reform of the Reform?" in: T. Kocik, *The Reform of the Reform?* pp. 254-256.

[97] "De prophetiis nihil immutandum in ipso missali, aliter forte in *Memoriale Rituum.* Videant periti;" Sacra Rituum Congregatio, Sectio Historica, *Memoria sulla Riforma Liturgica: Supplemento II – Annotazioni alla "Memoria,"* p. 21.

[98] Cf. *Ordo Sabbati Sancti Quando Vigilia Paschalis Instaurata Peragitur,* "De Vigilia Paschali" no 15.

[99] Cf. ibid., no 16.

[100] "in medio chori, in conspectu fidelium" ibid., no 20.

[101] Cf. ibid., nos 24-26.

tradition but are also totally novel, and that such a change would harm the equilibrium of the rite.[102]

11. The omission of psalm 42, the *Credo, Agnus Dei* and the last gospel from the Mass of Easter which follows the vigil.[103] These abbreviations are varied. The omission of psalm 42 and the last gospel, the private and devotional preparation and thanksgiving of the priest,[104] are historically understandable, and one may argue that vigil itself is the preparation for the first Mass of Easter. One could suggest that a purer restoration would have the priest once again reciting the last gospel after leaving the altar as his thanksgiving. The omission of the *Credo* is the logical avoiding of repetition in the light of the introduction of the renewal of baptismal promises. However the omission of the *Agnus Dei* is peculiar, particularly in the light of its relation to the liturgical action of the fraction of the Host, itself integral to every celebration of the Mass, and considering its specifically paschal symbolism.[105] No sources indicate a reason for this abbreviation.

---

102 "I. *Nulla habetur necessitas cur introducatur hæc renovatio.* Vigilia enim paschalis duplicem finem habet: 1: Commemorandi Christi resurrectionem, sicut in aliis festivitatibus commemorantur cetera Domini mysteria. Activæ quidem sunt et efficaces hæ commemorationes, ut docetur in encyclica *Mediator.* 2. Neophytos particeps reddendi resurrectionis Christi per baptismum. Quoties vero desunt baptizandi, celebratio paschalis altera quidem significatione privatur, *non autem primaria,* commemorativa scilicet, quæ omnino sufficit, sicut sufficit in ceteris festivitatibus, Natalis Domini, Ascensionis Domini, Pentecostes, etc. Immo, melior est conditio Sabbati Sancti: tunc enim fideles per communionem paschalem particeps fiunt supremi Doni initiationis christianæ, sacramentaliter Christo viventi communicando. II. Ut opus Liturgiæ reformandæ finem intentum attingat, studio informari debet redeundi sapienter et discrete ad fontes puriores. Ergo *inopportunissimum esset inductio rituum* non solum haud diuturna traditione probatorum, sed *ex toto novorum.* Quod intolerabile præsertim apparet quando agitur de antiquioribus et sacratioribus solemniis. III. *Renovatio promissorum* quæ proponitur, *non apte substitueretur ritibus baptismi...* IV. Tandem, festum tam perfecti decoris, si nequit ex integro celebrari, saltem ne alteretur!" Sacra Rituum Congregatio, Sectio Historica, *Memoria sulla Riforma Liturgica: Supplemento II – Annotazioni alla "Memoria,"* pp. 21-22. Jungmann and Righetti raised no objection.

103 Cf. *Ordo Sabbati Sancti Quando Vigilia Paschalis Instaurata Peragitur,* "De Missa Solemni Vigiliæ Paschalis" nos 1, 2, 5.

104 The popularisation of the Low Mass through the so-called "dialogue Mass" obscured their nature as preparatory and thanksgiving prayers and created what may be called a hyper-liturgical devotion by focussing the people's attention on private prayers. As C. Howell SJ, said in 1958, "the prayers at the foot of the altar do not pertain to the people. There are no historical...pastoral...[or] practical grounds for it. Keep the people out of it;" "The Parish in the Life of the Church," in: Living Parish Series, *Living Parish Week,* p. 18.

105 The missal of Paul VI corrects this omission.

In these eleven reforms four operative principles may be distinguished. *Restoration of rites lost in liturgical history* may be seen in reform three. *Liturgical authenticity* is found in the fifth, seventh and eighth reforms. As with the restoration of the vigil to the evening, these reforms can hardly be said to be contrary to liturgical Tradition. Rather, they are a revivifying of it. Reforms one, two, six and eleven may be described as reforms operating from the principle of the *simplification of the rite*. Of these, reforms two and six may be said to have a directly pastoral motivation,[106] and as such overlap somewhat with the next principle of reform, which we call *pastoral expediency*. This includes both innovation and abolition of liturgical forms according to perceived pastoral need. Reforms four, nine and ten are examples of this. The evaluation of such reforms is complex.

Following Capelle's interpretation of the *Memoria's* principles, we need to be convinced of "grave deficiency" in a rite before expunging it, and we must only introduce new material because of necessity "in a way that is consonant with Tradition."

There is no doubt that the organic growth of the Liturgy over time can include occasional pruning: we have seen this time and time again with the calendar. In the liturgical rites themselves, it is possible that clearly repetitive prayers that have no further symbolic purpose could be reduced from three to one without detracting from the objective traditional Liturgy. The Roman rite's hallmark has been a ritual sobriety in comparison with Eastern rites; what Dom Cabrol called in 1934 a "solidity, grandeur, strength, and a simplicity which excludes neither nobility nor elegance."[107] We have seen Fortescue argue in 1917 for the repression of Byzantine tendencies in the Liturgy, saying that "some measure of simplification is desirable."[108] This is not, however, the same as a modern desire for abbreviation which operates from the assumption that 'shorter (quicker?) is better.' Nor do we find abbreviation articulated

---

[106] *Dominica Resurrectionis vigiliam* emphasised the pastoral motivation behind the reforms, including the restoration of the time of the vigil: it was considered that more people could participate in it if celebrated at night, and indicated that studies in liturgical history had contributed to them: "Nostra autem ætate, succrescentibus de antiqua liturgia investigationibus, vivum obortum est desiderium, ut paschalis præsertim vigilia ad primitivum splendorem revocaretur, originali eiusdem vigiliæ instaurata sede, ad horas videlicet nocturnas, quæ dominicam Resurrectionis antecedunt. Ad huiusmodi instaurationem suadendam, peculiaris quoque accedit ratio pastoralis, de fidelium scilicet concursu fovendo; etenim cum sabbati sancti dies, non amplius, ut olim, festivus habeatur, quampluri fideles horis matutinis sacro ritui interesse nequeunt;" *Ordo Sabbati Sancti Quando Vigilia Paschalis Instaurata Peragitur*, p. 5.

[107] *The Mass of the Western Rites*, p. 182; cf. E. Bishop's "The Genius of the Roman Rite," in: *Liturgica Historica*, pp. 1-19.

[108] *The Ceremonies of the Roman Rite Described*, p. xix.

in the general principles of reform articulated either in the *Memoria* or in its discussion of the reform of the vigil.[109]

There is also no doubt that organic development includes the introduction of some new practices: an immobilist stance with regard to liturgical reform is simply a-historical. The crucial factor with such introductions is, as Capelle has said, their consonance with Tradition. One may also add that due proportion is an important criteria in admitting rites, new or restored, into the organism that is the Liturgy, as a disproportionate introduction would displace the equilibrium of the rite as a whole, and render it a substantially new rite. In the 1951 reform, the changes cannot be said to have displaced the substance of, or changed the nature, of the objective traditional Liturgy, and therefore could be welcomed as part of its organic development, albeit again, induced by ecclesiastical authority. However we must stand with Capelle's objection to the untraditional and theologically impoverished innovation of the renewal of baptismal vows.

Thus, we are able to rejoice in the liturgical authenticity and in the restoration of some rites lost in liturgical history in the 1951 reform of the paschal vigil, which are clearly organic and in harmony with the objective liturgical Tradition. Yet we note with concern the activity of liturgical archaeologism, untraditional innovation and the abolition of elements of the rite, which we have called pastoral expedience and a desire for abbreviation.

We have seen St Pius X rearrange the objective traditional Liturgy from a pastoral motivation. However he did not innovate. With the introduction of the renewal of baptismal promises, Pius XII did. This use of papal authority, exalted if not exaggerated by the same pope in *Mediator Dei* in relation to the objective traditional Liturgy, may be said to be the liturgical face of ultramontanism.

However that was not the assessment of most liturgists of the time. *La Maison-Dieu,* in an issue devoted entirely to the reform of the vigil, claimed that the horizons had been opened to hope for further progress "certainly in the line of traditional Liturgy but oriented toward the legitimate needs of the people of God."[110] In the USA, Hellriegel recorded his profound gratitude to Pius XII,[111] and Diekmann hailed the "generosity" of the reform noting that it "exceeds any requests voiced."[112] The 1952 North American National Liturgical Week was devoted to its

[109] Cf. nos. 67-74.

[110] "il ouvre des horizons pleins d'espoir à d'autres progrès dans la ligne d'une liturgie traditionelle, certes, mais orientée vers les besoins légitimes du peuple de Dieu;" "Editorial" in: *LMD*, no. 26 p. 7-8.

[111] Cf. "The New Papal Permission" in: *OF* vol. XXV pp. 225-229.

[112] "The Easter-Eve Celebration" in: *OF* vol. XXV pp. 279.

discussion.[113] The English journal *Liturgy* published a more sober welcome.[114] Almost thirty years later Bugnini spoke of this reform as a change "which elicited an explosion of joy throughout the Church. It was a signal that the Liturgy was at last launched decisively on a pastoral course."[115]

The father of the Liturgical Movement, Beauduin, writing in *La Maison-Dieu* in 1951, described the reform as a "point of arrival" and a "point of departure," saying that it was "certainly made in a traditional and an historical spirit and opened horizons that the most daring of optimists could not hope to see."[116] Beauduin, whose article demonstrates a profound respect for liturgical Tradition, both in its origins and in its living reality, calls for reforms to be made in the order of Mass in the spirit of the reform of the vigil that would, in his opinion, restore its authenticity. He proposes seven:

1. To remove the anomaly of the celebrant reading texts whilst others sing them.[117]
2. To make the Liturgy "sensible and living,"[118] by extending the authenticity of the vigil's rubric requiring a period of silent prayer between *flectamus genua* and the *levate.* Beauduin suggests that the reform be extended to the penitential seasons, and to other rites that have lost significance.[119]
3. To restore the communal significance of the "Amen," and to enhance the active participation of the people, particularly at the end of the Secret and of the Canon, by a simple change of the rubrics.[120]
4. To ensure that the faithful receive Holy Communion from Hosts consecrated at the Mass at which they assist, at the appropriate liturgical time, and not ordinarily outside of Mass.[121]
5. To restore the *Ite missa est* to its true place, at the end of the rite.[122]

---

[113] Cf. The Liturgical Conference, *The Easter Vigil: National Liturgical Week (USA) 1952.*

[114] Cf. J. Connelly "The Restored Paschal Vigil" in: *Liturgy* vol. XX pp. 73-81.

[115] *TRL,* p. 10; "che prevocò un'esplosione di gioia in tutta la Chiesa e fu il segnale che, finalmente, la liturgia imboccava decisamente la via pastorale;" *LRL* p. 25.

[116] "un point d'arrivée...un point de départ;" "faite dans un esprit si traditionnel et si historique, ouvre des horizons que les plus optimistes osaient à peine entrevoir;" "Le décret de 9 Février 1951 et les espoirs qu'il suscite" in: *LMD,* no. 26 p. 100.

[117] Cf. ibid., pp. 106-107.

[118] "raisonnable et vivante;" ibid., p. 107.

[119] Cf. ibid., pp. 107-108. The "Oremus" before the commencement of the offertory is an example.

[120] Cf. ibid., p. 108.

[121] Cf. ibid., p. 109. It is significant that Beauduin should still include this as a desire four years after it had been called for in *Mediator Dei.*

[122] Cf. ibid.

6. To omit the last gospel in public Masses, retaining it for private Masses.[123]
7. To omit the Leonine prayers after Mass.[124]

Beauduin's *desiderata* arise from the principle of liturgical authenticity, which encompasses the restoration of some rites lost in liturgical history and a small measure of simplification of the rite. His authenticity is certainly pastorally motivated; however his is not a principle of pure pastoral expediency. Significantly, in this article in which he explains the hopes raised by the 1951 reform, Beauduin calls for no innovations, and for no substantial restructuring of the rite to meet contemporary pastoral needs. Nor does he argue for the vernacular. In Beauduin's wishes for reform, as in Capelle's explication of the *Memoria's* principles above, we find a mature desire for reform, a true fruit of the Liturgical Movement (in Beauduin's case in the very words of its father), motivated by a profound respect for the objective traditional Liturgy.[125] The principle of authenticity is grounded in this very respect. So too is Beauduin's understanding that the traditional Liturgy is capable of development along authentic lines.

The reform of the vigil was experimental and local ordinaries were required to report on the experiment to the Holy See. The English Bishop of Brentwood required those priests availing themselves of the permission for the new vigil to furnish a report. His archives contain eleven replies, all of which are positive. Typical reports indicate that "the number of persons attending...was considerably in excess of the number of those who would have been able to attend at the traditional hour,"[126] and that there was "great enthusiasm...for the whole idea [expressed] by all those who were present."[127] The renewal of baptismal vows was popular.[128] One commented "the new rite was a great success but that the prophecies should be read in English facing the people. The reading of

---

[123] Cf. ibid., p. 110.

[124] Cf. ibid., p. 111. Beauduin states that Leo XIII regarded them as a temporary measure introduced for a specific purpose, which had by then been obtained.

[125] D. Bonneterre's *The Liturgical Movement*, which is scathingly critical of Beauduin, fails to study this 1951 article.

[126] Archives of the Diocese of Brentwood, Parish Reports on 1951 Easter Vigil, Report: Rochford, Essex, dated April 2nd 1951.

[127] Ibid., Report: Frinton-on-Sea, Essex, no date.

[128] The report: Canning Town, no date, says: "The comparatively large number present on this 'blessed night' assisted with intense interest in every part of the service, showing a special enthusiasm for the renewal of their Baptismal Vows. This outspoken declaration of faith in their own tongue seemed a really fitting prelude to the reception of their Easter communion, and the joy and true peace brought by the Resurrection seemed to be written on every face;" ibid.

them in Latin is meaningless to 99%."[129] According to the published extracts of bishops' reports to the Holy See, this local enthusiasm was reflected world-wide,[130] though it is clear that in some places the adoption of the new vigil was the exception rather than the norm.[131]

In 1952 the Holy See extended the experiment for three further years. Some adjustments in the rite were also made, which do not alter our assessment: it was permitted as early as 8.00p.m. on the Saturday evening where the bishop judged this suitable; the rules for how many Masses a priest might say on Easter Sunday, on fasting, and on how often a person might receive Holy Communion were relaxed slightly; the people were allowed to re-light their candles for the renewal of baptismal promises; it was decreed that participation in the vigil would take the place of Saturday Compline and Sunday Matins for clergy, and that Lauds of Easter Sunday would be inserted at the end of the Mass following the vigil.[132] In 1953 Joseph Löw CSsR, Vice-Relator of the Historical Section of the Sacred Congregation of Rites, published an article encouraging its celebration.[133] People's editions of the rite were published to facilitate their actual participation.[134] The experiment was

---

[129] Archives of the Diocese of Brentwood, Parish Reports on 1951 Easter Vigil, Father Martin Hancock, Report: Ilford, Essex, no date.

[130] Cf. Sacra Rituum Congregatio, Sectio Historica, *De Instauratione Liturgica Maioris Hebdomadæ: Positio*, pp. 21-42, 64-93. These extracts include reports on the vigil up to 1954.

[131] This was certainly the case in the USA: cf. "Liturgical Briefs" in: *Worship* vol. XXVI p. 374.

[132] Cf. *Instaurata vigilia paschalis,* 11 January 1952 in: C. Braga CM, *Documenta,* pp. 733-734ff. J.A. Jungmann SJ expressed his delight and those of the German liturgical commission in a typewritten letter to Antonelli dated 30 March 1952: "Con molto gioia ho ricevuto le coppie del nuovo "Ordo Sabbati Sancti," che così generosamente ha voluto farmi inviare…Anche il contenuto, cioè le modificazioni del nuovo Ordo, ci ha piaciuto molto. La settimana scorsa sono stato a Würzburg, dove abbiamo avuto una conferenza della Commissione Liturgica tedesca; e s'intende, abbiamo parlato anche del nuovo Ordo. Tutti erano assai contenti. Ci pareva una via eccellente, che si metteva il "Benedictus" al luogo del "Magnificat" della messa. Anche la possibilità di anticipare per le nostre regioni è di gran valore;" Fondo Antonelli, Archive, Congregation of the Causes of the Saints.

[133] Cf. "We Must Celebrate the Easter Night" in: *Worship* vol. XXVII pp. 161-171. This emphasises the pastoral benefit of the reform, and stresses that it is a "restoration of the ancient, original state of things," without discussing the origins of specific reforms.

[134] Cf. *Easter Eve: A Manual for the Faithful Attending the New Service of the Paschal Vigil.*

permitted for one more year in 1955[135] before the Holy See promulgated a definitive reform of Holy Week in 1955, which is considered below.

Louis Bouyer's 1951 Criticisms of the Liturgical Movement

The French Oratorian Louis Bouyer, a convert from Lutheranism, began publishing on liturgical topics in the 1940s. *The Paschal Mystery* (1949) opens with a fresh definition of the Liturgy:

> Liturgy is the life reflected in the pages of the Bible, concretised in a devotional action, the liturgical text being hardly more than an application of the biblical original set in vivid relief.[136]

Over the subsequent three decades Bouyer would apply his energies to awakening people to this reality, and to correcting distortions of it.[137]

In 1951 Bouyer published an article which, in part, was severely critical of reforms being made in the name of the Liturgical Movement.[138] H.A. Reinhold reports:

> He objects to the para-liturgies[139] in their motivation, to the "bending over backwards" of the apostolic zeal of many among those who want reform; to the liturgists' overemphasis on the "transfigurative" task of nature (instead of death and cross); and to the blindness of the liturgists who have cut themselves loose from Tradition and are now drifting on external currents with no end in sight but chaos.[140]

Bouyer recalled basic principles which he believed were ignored by certain groups and individuals at the time:

> Above all, and this is the essential point, in the urgent effort of translation and adaptation, in the field of the Liturgy just as in others, one must never become too caught up in eclectic and hasty constructions, showing contempt (often simply through ignorance) for the traditional heritage of the Church, and throwing oneself uncritically and without discernment upon whatever appeals to the fashion of the day.[141]

---

135 Cf. *Instauratæ vigiliæ paschalis,* 15 January 1955, C. Braga CM, *Documenta,* p. 802.

136 *The Paschal Mystery,* p. xxi.

137 His two principal works, *Life and Liturgy* (1956) and *Rite and Man* (1963), are cited elsewhere in this study.

138 Cf. "Où en est le Mouvement liturgique?" in: *LMD* no. 25 pp. 34-46.

139 Devotional services composed by individuals drawing on the Liturgy and Scripture, assuming that the Liturgy was not sufficiently intelligible or sufficiently adapted for modern needs; particularly popular in France.

140 "Past and Present" in: *Worship* vol. XXVI p. 183.

141 "Surtout, et c'est là le point essentiel, l'effort urgent de traduction et d'adaptation, dans le champ de la liturgie comme dans les autres, ne doit jamais

> A Liturgical Movement which forgets or refuses to acknowledge frankly that the Liturgy is traditional in its essence, that the Liturgy is a the property of the Church, that the Liturgy transmits to man the gifts of God, before it is able to offer to man any expression of himself…such a movement would be liturgical only in name.[142]

He articulates the nature of living (liturgical) Tradition:

> This is the whole problem of true reform in the Church, which is always *and at the same time* a return to the sources, fidelity to the Church of today, and open to the possibility of creating something new in response to contemporary needs. This is of the nature of the Church, which assures the continuity of the same supernatural life through the course of the ages in realising not only a permanent equilibrium, but the profound union of these three necessities.[143]

In response, Capelle published an article asking whether the Liturgical Movement was not in crisis?[144] Capelle agreed with Bouyer's assessment of the development of para-liturgical celebrations and with his articulation of the traditional nature of the Liturgy, describing it as "a received gift."[145] Capelle identifies a crisis, but not in the objective liturgical Tradition. He asserts that the practical mentality of modern Christians has, at least in part, weakened the capacity of the Liturgy to nourish piety. The extent of the envisaged crisis is indicated by Capelle's poignant question: "Do the majority of priests have an intense liturgical faith?"[146] His response to this crisis was to call for better liturgical

---

se confondre avec un effort de construction hâtive et hétéroclite, faisant fi (le plus souvent par simple ignorance) du donné traditionnel de l'Église et se jetant sans critique ni discrimination sur tout ce qui paraît a goût du jour;" "Où en est le Mouvement liturgique?" in: *LMD* no. 25 p. 42.

142 "un movement liturgique qui oublierait ou refuserait d'admettre franchement que la liturgie est traditionnelle dans son essence, que la liturgie est chose de l'Église, que la liturgie transmet à l'homme les dons de Dieu avant de pouvoir offrir à l'homme aucune expression de lui-même…un tel mouvement n'aurait plus de liturgique que le nom;" ibid.

143 "C'est tout le problème de la vrai réforme dans l'Église, qui est toujours *en même temps* retour aux sources, fidélité à l'Église d'aujourd'hui et sens de ce qu'elle doit créer de neuf pour répondre aux besoins contemporains. C'est le propre de l'Église que d'assurer la continuité d'une même vie surnaturelle au cours des âges en réalisant non seulment l'équilibre permanent, mais la jonction profonde des ces trois nécessités;" ibid., p. 43.

144 "Crise du Mouvement liturgique?" in: *Questions Liturgiques et Paroissiales,* no. 32 pp. 209-217.

145 "un don reçu" ibid., p. 213.

146 "La majorité des prêtres a-t-elle une intense foi liturgique?" ibid., p. 214. Almost fifty years later—in 1999—J.D. Crichton lamented "the bad, slovenly and

formation for seminarians, arguing that courses in rubrics were insufficient in themselves, and that what was needed was an integration of liturgical, scriptural and theological formation. It follows that, according to Capelle's view, a properly formed clergy would see the intrinsic flaws behind putting energy into para-liturgical celebrations, and would concentrate on the liturgical formation of their people.

Capelle does not entertain the possibility of adapting the Liturgy to suit the modern mentality. Nevertheless, he is open to the organic development of the objective liturgical Tradition within certain limits:

> Certainly, that which one hands on is not a dead thing: "To rediscover a tradition and to give it a new life, is one and the same thing. Here below, he who speaks of life speaks of change."
>
> It appertains to the Church to keep watch over the necessary alterations she wishes to make, and to see that they are inspired by true criteria. She alone is able to situate reforms "between a dead rigidity and an evolutionism which is nothing but another name for decomposition."[147]

Both Bouyer's and Capelle's positions are familiar. Their articulation in 1951, as discussion about, and the work of, liturgical reform was gaining momentum, was a timely reminder of the nature of objective liturgical Tradition.

The trends that they censure are also noteworthy. It is clear from Bouyer's criticism of the para-liturgies that, at least in places, a desire for creating popular services, which showed scant regard for liturgical Tradition, had surfaced. Capelle's identification of the impact of the mentality of the age, particularly of its effect upon clergy, and of the effects of their defective liturgical formation, may be seen to be at least remotely causal here.

It is significant that this tension, between what we may call the desire for popularising or modernising the Liturgy to accord with the perceived needs or desires of contemporary man, and fidelity to objective liturgical Tradition, arises in the 1950s. Would the former eventually come to predominate over the latter? In the mind of Bouyer and of Capelle there is a divide between the two.

---

even idiosyncratic way many priests celebrated Mass" and added "plus ça change, plus c'est la même chose;" *As it Was*, p. 14.

147 "Certes ce que l'on transmet n'est pas une chose morte: 'Retrouver une tradition et la rendre à nouveau vivante, c'est une seule et même chose. Or, ici-bas, qui dit vie dit changement.' Il appartient à l'Église de veiller à ce que les retouches indispensables se fassent, et qu'elles s'inspirent des vrais critères. Elle seule saura situer les réformes 'entre une fixisme mortel et une évolutionisme qui n'est qu'un autre nom donné à la décomposition;'" ibid., p. 217. Capelle is quoting Bouyer.

Yet we must maintain, with these eminent fathers of the Liturgical Movement, that objective liturgical Tradition, whilst having priority, is living and that it is capable of development. Throughout this study we have called that development "organic" precisely to specify the growth of objective liturgical Tradition as it has been shaped by different ages. However, it has never been legitimately abducted or corrupted by the 'spirit' of a particular age, and attempts so to do have met with repudiation.

The Maria Laach Conference, 1951

Alongside the ongoing work of the commission, liturgical scholars initiated a series of international study meetings to consider reform.[148] Frederick McManus is clear that "certainly the 1948 [Pian] commission was influenced in succeeding years by the meetings of (mostly) European scholars...with which Antonelli, Löw, and Bugnini were in contact."[149] Jungmann states that the meetings:

> Assumed great importance, for it was here that the fruit of experiences gathered and of scholarly work, conducted with heightened fervour, was brought together and, encouraged more and more by the authorities in Rome, the concrete aims of a possible reform were debated.[150]

The first was held at Maria Laach in July 1951,[151] with forty-eight invited scholars in attendance. It discussed the recent reform of the paschal vigil, which had "fulfilled, and in some respects surpassed, long-cherished hopes."[152] A number of further modifications were proposed,[153] some of which were realised in the 1952 revision. The meeting concluded that:

> It would seem desirable that the entire *Triduum Sacrum* be revised to correspond to the Easter nightwatch: in particular, the Holy Thursday Mass should be an evening Mass, and Good Friday should be transferred to the afternoon.[154]

---

[148] The most comprehensive study of these meetings, and of their eventual impact on *Sacrosanctum Concilium,* which includes lists of participants, summaries of discussions and an extensive bibliography, is by Siegfried Schmitt, *Die internationalen liturgischen Studientreffen 1951-1960.*

[149] Letter to the author, 24 April 1994.

[150] "Constitution on the Sacred Liturgy" in: H. Vorgrimler, *Commentary on the Documents of Vatican II,* vol. I p. 2.

[151] Cf. S. Schmitt, *Die internationalen liturgischen Studientreffen 1951-1960,* pp. 75-95.

[152] "Liturgical Briefs" in: *Worship* vol. XXVI p. 202.

[153] Cf. ibid., pp. 202-203.

[154] Ibid., p. 203.

The latter suggestion, a request for a return to liturgical authenticity in the time of celebration, is, as we have argued above, in complete harmony with liturgical Tradition.

The scholars also discussed reforms that could be made to the missal. The influence of Jungmann was considerable,[155] and he read a paper proposing the construction of a penitential rite for the people at the beginning of Mass, because he believed it to be pastorally expedient, as well as the reform of the silent prayers of the priest (outside of the Canon). In the latter part of the paper we find a clear articulation of his theory of liturgical corruption and of the impact his principles of antiquarianism and pastoral expedience would have:

> The silent prayers (outside the Canon) are no older than the Carolingian era of the Roman Liturgy. In any revision of the missal according to Pius V's principle of reform (*"secundum ss. Patrum normam ac rituum"*) they would really all have to vanish (including the prayers at the foot of the altar). At a minimum we would have to say today: In order that any of these prayers be retained, a justifying reason must, in each single case, be adducible.[156]

In other words: such rites are corrupt because they are late developments, therefore they must be abolished unless they are currently seen as pastorally expedient. Jungmann even goes so far as to claim the authority of St Pius V for such a position.

However it must be said plainly that Jungmann's use of a principle of reform from St Pius V's commission is staggering in its revisionism. We have seen that Trent, in both its breviary and its missal, accepted as legitimate components of the Liturgy dating from Carolingian times and later. Whilst it is true that scholars of Jungmann's period had access to the findings of more historical research than those implementing the reform of Trent, it is only an antiquarianism that finds in this justification for disregarding elements of developed liturgical Tradition.

Furthermore, those elements Jungmann insists "have to vanish" (the prayers at the foot of the altar, the *Oramus te Domine,* the continuation of the *Lavabo* psalm, the *Suscipe Sancta Trinitas,* and the last Gospel),[157] are in fact present in the *Missalis Romani editio princeps* of 1474 *and* the 1570 *Missale Romanum* of St Pius V (with the exception of the last Gospel which was first universally mandated by St Pius V's missal).[158]

---

[155] *Worship* reports that the conclusions "for the most part...follow the logic of Jungmann's *Missarium Sollemnia;*" ibid.

[156] "Problems of the Missal" *Worship* vol. XXVIII p. 155.

[157] Cf. ibid., pp. 155-156.

[158] Cf. J.A. Jungmann SJ, *The Mass of the Roman Rite,* vol. II pp. 448-449.

This fact renders his assertion that their abolition is in accordance with St Pius V's principle unsupportable.[159]

The emergence of such flawed reasoning at this first international meeting of liturgical scholars is a cause for concern. In the history of twentieth century liturgical reform this may be regarded as a critical moment. Should Jungmann's stance prevail, liturgical reform would no longer be, as in history, the organic development of the objective liturgical Tradition, but the refashioning of the Liturgy according to prevailing scholarly opinion and the perceived needs of the day.

The conference formulated twelve conclusions, which were forwarded to the Holy See at its request:

> 1) All duplications ought to be eliminated: that is, the celebrant himself ought not be obliged to recite the scriptural lessons read by a Reader, nor the proper parts sung by the choir or the ordinary parts sung by the congregation. Rubric 15 of the new *Ordo Sabbati Sancti* offers reason to look forward to the early realisation of this hope, which is likewise a generally accepted demand of contemporary liturgical science.
>
> 2) The present beginning of Mass, i.e., the prayers at the foot of the altar, need some revision. Would it not be preferable to restore them to their former place and use, and merely conclude these prayers briefly at the altar after having begun them in the sacristy? Or should the model of the new *Ordo Sabbati Sancti* on this point be followed, and these prayers be eliminated altogether?
>
> 3) The Fore-Mass—a better name for which would be "the Liturgy of the Word"—should take place, not at the altar, but *"in choro,"* analogously to what happens in a pontifical Mass, or at Vespers (cf. the new *Ordo Sabbati Sancti*, n. 12).
>
> 4) The number of orations at Mass should be reduced to a minimum. As a general rule there should be only one. The addition of a commemoration should be possible only in exceptional cases.
>
> 5) The present arrangement of the scriptural pericopes would seem urgently to require a serious re-examination, in which, moreover, a clear distinction should be made between the cycle of readings for the Sundays, that for special solemnities and feasts of the saints, and that for ordinary weekdays. For the Sundays after Pentecost and after Epiphany especially, a three or four-year cycle seems desirable. The present arrangement could perhaps remain as the first year of such a cycle.

---

[159] Cf. A. Ward SM & C. Johnson OSB, *Missalis Romani Editio Princeps*, nn. 963, 967, 984 & 985; M. Sodi & A. Triacca, *Missale Romanum*, nn. 1391, 1398, 1427, 1429 & 1552. The possibility of reform or of development of the prudential decisions of St Pius V is not being excluded here.

The scriptural readings for the Sundays and holy days of obligation should be so chosen that a Christian who attends Mass only on these days would nevertheless, in a few years, come to know the essential passages of holy Scripture, particularly that of the New Testament. The readings for weekdays, on the other hand, would serve to give a profounder knowledge of Scripture to a more restricted group of zealous faithful; perhaps in this case the ancient practice of continuous reading would be in place, or even permission for the celebrant to select appropriate passages.

In order that the reading of the Bible fulfil its function of communicating the word of God to the faithful more effectively, all present at this congress express their unanimous and most urgent hope that in every Mass at which the people assist the scriptural readings will be done directly and exclusively in the mother tongue.

6) The recitation of the Creed should occur much less frequently, and not at all in octave Masses.

7) After the "Liturgy of the Word," there follows an isolated *Oremus* before the offertory: here belong the Suffrages (*prex fidelium*). It would seem that for ordinary use in a litany form, enumerating the intentions and needs of the congregation to which the people respond with a set formula, would be preferable to the *Orationes solemnes* form. Moreover, it should be, at least facultatively, in the mother tongue.

8) As in a solemn Mass, so in every parish Mass the table of the altar should be prepared only immediately before the offertory: i.e., the sacred vessels, and more especially the elements of sacrifice, should not be brought to the altar until this moment.

9) There should be a greater number of prefaces (especially for Sundays), and they should, as in ancient times, be more inspired with the idea of the *memoria passionis* than has been the case in some of the newer prefaces.

10) The celebrant should begin the *Te Igitur* only after the sung *Sanctus* and *Benedictus* have been completed. Within the Canon, at least the *Amen* that occurs several times (if not the *Per Christum Dominum Nostrum*) should be eliminated.

11) When holy Communion is distributed during Mass, the *Confiteor* and its following prayers should be dropped: they are appropriate only for the distribution of Communion outside of Mass.

12) Mass ought to end with the blessing by the priest without the addition of the last Gospel—as is already provided for in the new *Ordo Sabbati Sancti*.[160]

These conclusions operate from principles almost identical to those seen in the reform of the solemn paschal vigil. Conclusion one, three and eight are clearly a call for liturgical authenticity. The suggestion made in the second that the prayers at the foot of the altar be restored "to their former place and use," and that made in conclusion eleven are also proposals seeking a return to authentic practice. As such they can be seen to be in harmony with objective liturgical Tradition.

Simplification of the rite motivates conclusions four and six, the latter part of the tenth (where the *Amen* and the *Per Christum Dominum Nostrum* of the Canon are considered) and even partially, conclusion eleven. The simplification of excesses of liturgical growth is found in liturgical history, and there is no reason to say that they were not necessary in the 1950's, particularly given the state of the calendar and the number of commemorations possible on some days.

We can welcome the proposal to restore elements lost in liturgical history in conclusion seven, noting that it is combined with a proposal motivated by pastoral expediency when it proposes that the *preces* be given a simpler form than those traditional to the Roman rite, and that they be permitted in the vernacular. The call for the enrichment of the rite in conclusion nine is a legitimate call for development, undoubtedly of pastoral motivation, but no less legitimate for that.

Conclusion twelve advocates the abolition of the last Gospel. Such severity is also partially present in conclusion two where the outright abolition of the prayers at the foot of the altar is postulated. One can argue, as does Jungmann, that because these are secondary and late developments they may be discarded without real loss. In the author's opinion such abolition denudes the rite of prayers that have become part of the rite in its organic development. Far better to restore them to their authentic use (as indeed does part of conclusion two), than to jettison them. Neither (a priest's preparation or his thanksgiving) is clearly inappropriate or detracts from the central meaning or actions of the rite. Their restoration to authentic use would respect and indeed refine objective liturgical Tradition of which even secondary and late developments form a part.

Conclusion five advocates the radical restructuring of the scriptural readings from a stance of pastoral expediency. This is no small proposal, as it cannot be considered an organic development of the received Liturgy. One can appreciate the pastoral reasons advanced for it.

---

160 "Conclusions of the First Congress, Maria Laach, 1951" in: *Worship* vol. XXVIII pp. 157-159.

Jungmann's account of the formation of the Roman lectionary emphasises the historical exigencies of its formation.[161] Archdale King, however, relates that:

> The arrangement of pericopes in the missal is of great antiquity, but it is difficult to discover a fixed system, and it probably represents a fusion of various systems. The organisation of the liturgical lessons, with their distribution for Mass and Office, seems to have been completed by the 9th century, and the pericopes for the gospels as early as the 6th century.[162]

A certain respect is shown for the antiquity of the lectionary in conclusion five's suggestion that "the present arrangement could perhaps remain as the first year of such a cycle." But this does not solve the problem of the abandonment of the traditional one for the other two or three years of the proposed new cycle. The construction of an entirely new lectionary raises even greater difficulties.

In the author's opinion such reform of the lectionary would do unprecedented violence to the objective traditional Liturgy in the name of pastoral expediency. In the history of liturgical reform this is the first instance of the proposal of such a radical reform of texts so central to the missal on such a scale. Expanding the lectionary, and perhaps substituting more apposite passages in some instances would be legitimate paths to follow in the development of the rite in response to pastoral concerns. However sidelining the traditional lectionary (by rendering it an option for one year out of three or four), or discarding it and constructing a new lectionary, radically contravene the principle of organic development, and the continuity that is at the same time open to development, which is of the essence of this principle.

Conclusion five also calls for the "exclusive" use of the vernacular for the scriptural readings. This proposal is again motivated by pastoral expediency, but is also in part a call for liturgical authenticity: the readings are intended to be immediately comprehensible. Such a reform is in harmony with the nature and purpose of the rite and can be welcomed. However, proposing that this reform be "exclusive" goes too far, as it would result in the abolition of the solemn Latin chanting, particularly of the Gospel, in communities where Latin was comprehensible (of which there were not a few in the 1950s), or where by means of the people's missal the scriptural text would be no less intelligible.[163]

---

161 Cf. *The Mass of the Roman Rite*, vol. I pp. 399-403.

162 *Liturgy of the Roman Church*, p. 247.

163 In times of increased literacy and the advance of printing technology it is hard to see how this can be excluded on the grounds of incomprehensibility. Indeed,

The Maria Laach meeting also formulated questions which were recommended for further and more intensive study:

> 1) It is desirable that the Secret prayer again be called by its proper name of the "Prayer over the offerings," and that, as the terminating prayer of the offertory, it be sung aloud together with its conclusion—as is done with the collect and the postcommunion.
>
> 2) It is desirable that the great doxology at the end of the canon (*Per ipsum,* etc.) be sung in its entirety (using the *tonus antiquus orationis*). The five signs of the cross should drop out, and the "small elevation" take place during the entire doxology, and the genuflexion (if at all) only after the concluding *Amen.*
>
> 3) Highly desirable would be a re-arrangement of the section after the *Pater Noster,* in such a way that the prayers and ceremonies fit together better; and some adaptation of a reconciliation rite (*Pax*) should be introduced for the congregation—but what specific form should it take?
>
> 4) Some amplification of the after-Communion part of the Mass is desirable, perhaps by inserting a prayer, or several, or a song between the Communion verse and the postcommunion, which would more clearly express sentiments of praise and thanksgiving. This would, as is the case in other liturgies, give us a less abrupt conclusion to the Mass after Communion.
>
> 5) It is desirable that the present rubric about the use of the *Ite Missa Est* and *Benedicamus Domino* be altered: let the *Ite* be used in all public Masses, and the *Benedicamus* in private Masses. (The Requiem Mass would not come into question.)[164]

In questions one and five we find a call for liturgical authenticity, as also in the first part of question two. These present little difficulty. In the latter part of the second question we see a combination of a desire for simplification and innovation.[165] Question three seeks a reconstruction from the standpoint of pastoral expediency, and question four seeks to innovate, again from pastoral expediency. How consonant such simplifications, reconstructions and innovations are with Tradition is questionable. Indeed, in these proposals which, taken by themselves are not substantial, we nevertheless find the emergence of a mentality that, in order to create a liturgical rite that will speak to the perceived needs of the day, will simplify, rearrange, abolish and innovate in order to achieve

---

the use of Latin chant (where all have access to a translation) may serve to focus people's attention.

164 Ibid., pp. 159-160.

165 Though not explicitly, the proposals for the reform of the *Per ipsum* appear to presume the celebration of Mass *versus populum.*

its end: that which came to be called "pastoral Liturgy." These are illegitimate means to an end.

The Maria Laach meeting also gives rise to a new consideration in the history of liturgical reform. Even if it is clear that the reforms envisaged in its large number of conclusions and questions are themselves in harmony with or would not do violence to objective liturgical Tradition, and are desirable, what effect would the introduction of such a number of them have on the organic reality that is the Liturgy? Should they be introduced wholesale, or gradually? Could this be in harmony with the principle of the organic development of the Liturgy? Could a rite thus reformed be said to be in continuity with that which preceded it? And, even though the objective traditional Liturgy is capable of assimilating new rites, can it sustain substantial rearrangement of its elements, or the abolition of the same and subsequent substantial innovation?

In the author's opinion, the nature of the Liturgy and the history of liturgical reform underline these questions as identifying significant problems with the course of reform desired by the scholars meeting at Maria Laach. It may be true that they were making bold proposals in the hope that an ever-cautious Rome would accede at least to a few of the more moderate amongst them. However such a strategy does not mitigate the flaws inherent in the proposals themselves.

In fact, Maria Laach considered going even further. In his memoirs, Bernard Botte OSB, a participant, adds a detail that was not made public in the contemporary accounts: the question of the reform of the Roman canon was discussed. Botte explains the significance of its discussion:

> The Ordinary of the Mass such as it was then, had been formed during the Middle Ages—between the ninth and thirteenth centuries by the addition of the celebrant's prayers to a much older nucleus. That is the canon, just as it had been established at the end of the sixth century at the time of Saint Gregory. It is not an inspired text, to be sure, but it has to be treated with special respect. The theologians of the Middle Ages did not try to make it agree with their speculations. They considered it as a given element of Tradition and commented on it like a sacred text. One can pass judgement on this exaggerated respect, but what would have happened if the theologians had used the text of the Mass as the jousting field for their quarrels? Could it be imagined that a text, which for thirteen centuries had been at the centre of Western Christian piety and which had survived theological controversies unscathed, would finally succumb to a liturgical reform? This didn't concern minor details, like the lists of saints, but a reform of structure. All the critiques would have to be well-founded and the proposed corrections backed up by evidence. But this was far from being the

case. The corrections proposed were arbitrary, and they disfigured the text without making up for its real defects.[166]

Thus the Roman canon escaped inclusion in Maria Laach's conclusions or questions for further study, but simply due to a lack of diligent homework on the part of those who would reform it. That the reform of a text, regarded for most of liturgical history as "a given element of Tradition," and "a prayer unaltered and unalterable,"[167] could be considered by at least some of these scholars is a clear indication that, in their view, objective liturgical Tradition placed few limits upon the possibilities of reform. According to Botte's account, the only necessary criteria are well-founded proposals backed up by evidence. The primacy he thus gives to contemporary scholarship, present in other of Maria Laach's proposals, is evident. We have already noted that such a primacy is disproportionate.

The Mont Sainte-Odile Conference, 1952

A second private meeting of scholars, convoked by German and French liturgical institutes was held at Mont Sainte-Odile in Alsace in October 1952[168] taking "Modern Man and the Mass" as its subject. Botte relates a telling incident from the eve of the conference:

> Since the location was not easy to reach we were told to meet in a hotel in Strasbourg...It was there I made the acquaintance of Msgr Andrieu...We had time to speak for an hour, but when the cars came to pick us up, Msgr Andrieu remained in Strasbourg. He was the best historian of the Roman Liturgy...We would have liked him to come, but a position he had taken was an obstacle: the Liturgy could not be reformed; it was a given element of Tradition which had to be accepted. He was allergic to the idea that the Liturgy could be modified for pastoral goals.[169]

---

[166] B. Botte OSB, *From Silence to Participation,* pp. 80-81. As late as 1964 Bouyer would speak of "the great eucharistic prayer, which in the Western Tradition remains always substantially the same;" *The Liturgy Revived,* p. 95.

[167] I. Schuster, OSB, *The Sacramentary* vol. I p. 317.

[168] Cf. S. Schmitt, *Die internationalen liturgischen Studientreffen 1951-1960,* pp. 95-123.

[169] B. Botte OSB, *From Silence to Participation,* p. 81. "Mais comme l'endroit est peu accessible, on nous avait donné rendez-vous dans un hôtel de Strasbourg...C'est là que j'ai fait la connaissance de Monseigneur Andrieu...Nous avons eu le temps de causer pendant une heure, mais quand les voitures sont venu nos chercher, Monseigneur Andrieu est resté à Strasbourg. C'était le meilleur historien de la liturgie romain...Nous aurions aimé qu'ils nous accompagne; mais on se heurta à une position qu'il avais prise: on ne pouvait pas réformer la liturgie, c'était une donné traditionnel qu'il fallait accepter. Il était allergique à l'idée qu'on puisse la

It is clear that the motivating principle was indeed that objected to by Andrieu: pastoral expediency. One participant, the Oxford Dominican, Illtud Evans, related that the meeting:

> Considered the obstacles in the existing Liturgy which make a true participation in it more difficult than it need be. And here it must be emphasised that the liturgical rites have never, in the economy of the Church's life, been considered as untouchable ancient monuments ...the complex structure of word and gesture in which rites are in practice transmitted may well need to be modified so that they may more effectively achieve their purpose.
>
> Thus there is a twofold approach to the work of reform: that of liturgical scholarship, with its exact analysis of the history of the sacred rites and its concern to see that modifications should be in the line of the Church's Tradition, and that of the pastoral mission of priests anxious to give to the liturgical mystery its fullest efficacy in the often unfavourable climate of our time.[170]

Evans' rationale for liturgical reform, and its re-publication[171] as *Worship's* account of the conference, indicates that his thinking was by no means marginal, and patently assumes that the Liturgy is to be changed to accord with contemporary man. It also accords disproportionate weight to the "exact analysis" of liturgical scholarship. The assumption behind this rationale is flawed in that it would render the Liturgy the subject of the perceived needs of each generation, save only the consensus of scholars. This was not the aim of the Liturgical Movement in its origins: man and his mindset were to be changed (formed in the Liturgy and in liturgical piety) that he might participate in the Sacred Liturgy. Evans does recognise the right of ecclesiastical authority to decide upon reform, but as we have asserted, it is possible for authority to be used to impose reforms based upon a defective rationale. What is missing from Evans, and we may infer that it is missing also from the mindset of the Sainte-Odile conference, is precisely that respect for objective liturgical Tradition, which is paramount throughout liturgical history. This is likely to have been the very point that led a scholar of the calibre of Andrieu to refuse to participate in such an endeavour.

The conference resolved:

> 1) It is to be hoped for that in the rubrics of the missal too, as in the 1952 *Ordo Sabbato Sancti,* pastoral directives be added.
>
> 2) It is to be hoped for:

---

modifier dans un but pastoral;" *Le Mouvement Liturgique: Témoignage et souvenirs,* pp. 104-105.

[170] "The International Conference at Mt. Ste. Odile" in: *Worship* vol. XXVII p. 150.

[171] Originally published in *Blackfriars* vol. XXXIII pp. 513-517.

a) That permission be granted for the doxology of the Canon (*Per Ipsum* etc.) to be sung in a *Missa cantata* and pronounced aloud in a *Missa lecta*.
b) That the five signs of the cross be dropped.
c) That the celebrant hold Chalice and Host elevated during the entire doxology, and until the people have responded *Amen*.
d) That the celebrant makes his genuflection (if at all) only after the *Amen*.

3) It is to be hoped for:
a) That the *Amen* after the *Pater noster* be omitted.
b) That the embolism (the *Libera* prayer) after the *Pater noster* with its doxology be sung in a *Missa cantata* and recited aloud in a *Missa* lecta.
c) That the signs of the cross with the paten, the kissing of the paten, as well as the genuflection be omitted during this *Libera*.

4) It is to be hoped for that the prayer for peace (*Domine Jesu Christe, qui dixisti Apostolis tuis...*), if it is retained at all, be inserted immediately after the *Libera*. Then only should the celebrant sing or speak the *Pax Domini*, and without any accompanying ceremony. Thereupon would follow the usual kiss of peace.

5) It is to be hoped for that the rite of breaking and commingling the Host follow upon the kiss of peace, but without any accompanying ceremony. During the breaking, the congregation could sing the *Agnus Dei*; in a *Missa lecta* the priest could say it after the breaking. Only now would follow the two preparatory prayers for holy Communion—if they are kept at all.

6) It is to be hoped for that, if holy Communion is distributed, the priest retain only half of his Host for his own Communion; the other half he would break into pieces and place with the small hosts, and distribute them first of all, preferably to the servers.

7) It is to be hoped for:
a) That the *Confiteor, Misereatur* and *Indulgentiam* be omitted before the distribution of holy Communion during Mass.
b) That, if there are many communicants, the priest be permitted to use a shorter formula for distribution: e.g., *Corpus Christi*, or *Corpus Domini*.

8) It is to be hoped for that the pastors be encouraged to have the communion verse sung during the distribution of holy Communion at parish Masses, and if possible, in a more solemn fashion. This could be done by singing the corresponding psalm, and inserting the verse at regular intervals as a refrain. In every case, text and melody should be such that the people are able to have a part in the singing. For this reason, the use of the mother tongue would here be especially appropriate.

9) It is to be hoped for that in parishes (apart from Requiems) the *Ite Missa Est* be the exclusively used formula of dismissal, to which the people would answer aloud *Amen*.[172]

These resolutions take up the unresolved questions from Maria Laach. Again we may welcome the liturgical authenticity desired in conclusions 2a, 6, and 8. Evans' account of the conference ascribes these proposals to a paper read by Capelle, though in fact Capelle's paper did not advocate conclusion eight.[173] Evans judges them, in the author's opinion rightly, as "rooted in the most authentic liturgical Tradition" as well as "stressing an intelligent and intelligible participation."[174] Capelle's paper is in fact an example of the use of historical scholarship in the service of liturgical authenticity. He does not advocate a wholesale return to ancient practices, but minor reforms that will give a greater measure of authenticity to objective liturgical Tradition. He argues for the perfection of the Liturgy as it stood. Capelle is also well aware of the delicate nature of adjusting even small parts of the rite, and in one instance expresses a preference, for this very reason, to leave what might be an anomaly in the opinion of liturgical historians well enough alone.[175]

To the three proposals already mentioned, we may add 2c, 3b, 7a, and 9 as harmonious with Tradition and seeking to restore a measure of authenticity where it had, perhaps, been lost. In these we have proposals that again aim to perfect the traditional Liturgy, certainly drawing upon scholarship and with a pastoral goal in mind, but without doing violence to it.

However, this is not necessarily the case with the various proposals for simplification: 2d, 4, 5, and 7b. The 'time-saving' rationale behind 7b shows just how far this conference was prepared to go to accommodate 'modern man'! Nor is it the case with proposals seeking abolition amongst which we may number 2b (though this would need to be accepted were 2c implemented), 3a and 3c. In these, pastoral expediency and scholarly archaeologism appear to have combined to produce a reformist mentality which operates from a rule which is applied to any so-called "late" liturgical development or to any considered pastorally inexpedient: 'If it is to be kept at all, simplify it

---

172 "Conclusions of the Second Congress, Ste. Odile, 1952" in: *Worship* vol. XXVIII pp. 160-161.

173 "Fraction et Commixtion: Aménagements souhaitables des rites actuels" in: *LMD* no. 35 pp. 79-94.

174 "The International Conference at Mt. Ste. Odile" in: *Worship* vol. XXVII p. 152.

175 Discussing the historical origins of the rite of the small elevation at the *Per Ipsum* at the end of the Canon, and various implications of reforming it, Capelle concludes: "Pour toutes ces raisons il semble préférable de laisser la petite élévation telle qu'elle est;" in: *LMD* no. 35 p. 85.

radically, but if possible abolish it.' Such a mentality is fundamentally alien to that which seeks the organic development of objective liturgical Tradition.

The Lugano Conference, 1953

A third international congress was held at Lugano, Switzerland, in September 1953, taking "Active Participation" as its theme, in honour of the fiftieth anniversary of St Pius X's *Tra le sollecitudini*.[176] Two days of private meetings in which twenty scholars participated were followed by two days open to the public. This resulted in Lugano being a more international gathering than its predecessors. The hundred and forty participants included three cardinals[177] and several bishops, though Anglo-Saxon participation was limited to five Americans and one Englishman.[178]

J.D. Crichton acclaimed it as marking "an epoch in the history of the Liturgical Movement."[179] *Worship* eulogised that Lugano heralded "a new era of creative reform based on the best norms of Tradition."[180] However, Reinhold's report makes it clear that the predominant sentiment was that objective liturgical Tradition was to be subjected to pastoral expediency:

> No one was silenced, and no one "pulled his rank." All were inspired by the one thought: where it is in fact impossible to bring the people to the Liturgy, the Liturgy must be brought to the people.[181]

Active participation was discussed in the light of the experience of the 1951 reform of the vigil, and in relation to a prospective reform of the whole of the Holy Week Liturgy.[182] The conference resolved:

---

[176] Cf. S. Schmitt, *Die internationalen liturgischen Studientreffen 1951-1960*, pp. 123-161.

[177] Including the Pro-Prefect of the Holy Office, Cardinal Ottaviani. Botte ascribes his attendance to family considerations; cf. *From Silence to Participation*, p. 82. Reinhold observes of him: "No bishop sang the ordinary of the pontifical Mass on the first morning of the main congress with more obvious relish and spirit. No "grand inquisitor" ever displayed such vivacious cordiality or watched with greater sympathy the stately and in some details novel rite around the holy altar—which of course faced the people, as goes without saying in these quarters;" "A Turning Point: Lugano" in: *Worship* vol. XXVII pp. 557-558.

[178] Cf. ibid., p. 560. The Englishman was Crichton, who relished the sight of a cardinal celebrating at an altar facing the people; cf. Interview by the author of J.D. Crichton, 24th August 1994.

[179] "More About the Lugano Congress" in: *Liturgy* vol. XXIII p. 111.

[180] "The Lugano Conference" in: *Worship* vol. XXVIII p. 28.

[181] "A Turning Point: Lugano" in: *Worship* vol. XXVII pp. 559-560.

I. Gratefully recalling the words of Blessed Pius X concerning the active participation in the sacred Mysteries to be striven for by the faithful, words which were solemnly confirmed by subsequent pontifical documents, this congress wishes to voice its full awareness that such participation is the most fruitful source from which the faithful are to draw the life of Christ more abundantly; nor is it to be doubted that this holds true in our time, and will hold true in the future also, and in fact more patently, in mission areas and in those regions separated from the unity of the Church, or the so-called diaspora.

II. Recalling the apostolic concern of the Sovereign Pontiffs, made manifest by the decrees of Blessed Pius X and by the more recent constitution of our Most Holy Father Pope Pius XII, that the faithful be nourished with the eucharistic Bread by more frequent participation at the holy Table, this congress expresses the wish that the nourishment of the divine word may similarly be made more easily available to the minds of our people—and this result would seem to be obtainable if the family of God could hear the scriptural lessons in Mass directly and immediately from the mouth of the celebrant in its own mother tongue whenever the number of people would warrant it.

III. In order that the people may participate more easily and more fruitfully in the Liturgy, this congress most humbly asks that the local Ordinaries be empowered to permit the people (if they so judge opportune) not only to hear the word of God in their own tongue, but also, as it were, to respond to it, by praying and singing in their own tongue even during a *Missa Cantata.*

IV. Since it is clearly evident that most precious fruits resulted from the very opportune restoration of the Easter Vigil by the Sovereign Pontiff Pius XII, this congress wishes to express its gratitude for the pastoral solicitude of the Holy See, and to ask that the celebrations of the entire Holy Week too be submitted to a similar reform.[183]

These resolutions are more general, moderate and deferential than are those of 1951 and 1952. This may be explained by the participation of larger numbers, and indeed of many of the hierarchy: the resolutions are no longer solely the specific desiderata of scholars. However, they do not rescind the earlier resolutions: the commentary accompanying them specifically links these with the earlier specific requests.[184] Yet their tone gives to the meeting an air of docility that is,

---

182 Cf. Crichton's summary of the Italian volume of proceedings: "More About the Lugano Congress" in: *Liturgy* vol. XXIII pp. 111-113.
183 "Conclusions of the Third Congress, Lugano, 1953" in: *Worship* vol. XXVIII pp. 162-163.
184 Cf. ibid., pp. 163-167.

perhaps, lacking in the published conclusions of Maria Laach and Sainte-Odile.

Nor do these resolutions reflect the 'inspiration' which Reinhold asserts was that of all. This may be explicable by Reinhold's inclusion in the private meeting of scholars, which was far more free in its discussion than the public sessions, considering the revision of the Missal and the order of Mass, and the expansion of the reading from Sacred Scripture at Mass.[185] Of the former, Archdale King would write in 1957:

> A revision of the solemn Mass, little short of revolutionary, was discussed...with the intention of simplifying the rite, removing what is redundant or superfluous, and giving the faithful a more active part in the Liturgy. There is, however, no certitude that Rome will accede to all these changes, and in any case her innate conservatism and caution would preclude any immediate acceptance.[186]

An English popular liturgical historian, King's attitude is illustrative of at least some of those outside the circles of scholars and enthusiasts "inspired" by the thinking outlined by Reinhold above.

And in 1955 another Englishman, Father Coyne of Oscott, expressed reservations in the light of these resolutions. His questions, even when read *a posteriori*, are not without significance:

> We may be allowed to express a doubt as to whether, in our particular circumstances, the suggested changes are desired by any considerable body of the faithful, or whether, in the event of their being granted, they would have any visible results? This surely must be the touchstone by which we are to judge each and all of the many changes now presented to us: do they make practising Catholics better? Do they effectively stem the leakage? Do they win converts in notably larger numbers to the Church?
>
> ...whatever may be urged against the form of the Mass as we know it, it is at least something that has developed naturally, and there ought to be paramount reasons for acceding to requests for what appear to many to be radical reforms. It is easy to decry what has been termed the ossification of the Liturgy since Trent, but there is nothing very wrong with a Liturgy which has produced so many saints in every walk of life.[187]

---

[185] Cf. S. Schmitt, *Die internationalen liturgischen Studientreffen 1951-1960*, pp. 134-142.

[186] *Liturgy of the Roman Church*, p. 45. In a manuscript letter of 26 July 1970 King remarks: "I do not like the new Mass."

[187] J. Coyne "The Traditional Position" in: C.R.A. Cunliffe, *English in the Liturgy*, pp. 96-97.

In both King and Coyne there is a distinct distaste for the reforms advocated by Lugano. That both men—educated people immersed in the liturgical life of the Church—share such a disdain is evidence that the pressure being applied for ritual reform did not necessarily have its origin in the widely felt needs of the Church.[188] Its origin is more likely to be found, we suggest, in the desire of some, perhaps many, influential liturgical scholars.

Yet Crichton reassured Englishmen that, although "the word 'reform' in connection with the Liturgy is offensive to many people," and in spite of:

> The fear that the ancient and venerable Liturgy of Holy Church which has been the vehicle of sanctity to countless souls throughout the centuries, should be treated violently, that barbarous hands should be laid on it and immortal treasures lost;

nevertheless:

> It should be a great relief to know that the Holy See is taking a very active part in this reform of the Liturgy. And perhaps we may say at this point that if 'reform' sounds too strong a word, what the Church is seeking to do is to *adapt* certain parts of the Liturgy so that the people may take their rightful part in it more fully and with greater profit.[189]

Moreover, Crichton assured, such an opportunity for "both scholars and the pastoral clergy to get together" as at Lugano "guarantees that any changes made will not be merely archaeological restorations."[190]

Two reservations may be expressed about Crichton's assurances. Firstly, the authority of the Holy See may not be sufficient guarantee that liturgical reforms it mandates are indeed organic developments. The breviary of Quignonez was both approved and proscribed by papal authority. Certainly, Crichton's portrait of the Holy See's paternal supervision may accord with the attitudes of those officials of the Holy See present at Lugano. However, it does not account for the possibility that authority could, if persuaded of their expediency by liturgists, scholars or others, authorise reforms that go well beyond an adaptation of "parts" of Liturgy, and in fact re-form, in the distasteful sense of the word alluded to by Crichton, "the ancient and venerable Liturgy of Holy Church." In an age of ultramontane and largely uncritical obedience this was certainly possible.

---

188 A case could be made that there was a widely felt need for permitting some use of the vernacular.

189 "Rome and Liturgical Reform: The Lugano Congress, September 1953" in: *Liturgy* vol. XXIII p. 32.

190 Ibid., p. 34.

Secondly, Crichton's faith in the dialogue between scholars and the pastoral clergy seems naïve. The palpable sense of excitement in the reports of the participants in this dialogue from which we have cited suggests the emergence of a momentum which would itself contribute to the pressure for reform. And again, in this dialogue, the equation is somewhat disproportionate: the findings of scholars and the desires of pastoral clergy are not the only, or even the fundamental, components of liturgical development, though one could be forgiven for thinking that this was the case from Crichton's account. It is true that they are factors that can induce liturgical development, but only in accordance with the components encapsulated in Capelle's 1950 principles, indeed that of organic development.

Furthermore, if changes were not to be *merely* "archaeological restorations," what did Crichton envisage? It is clear that he would subject archaeological proposals to the test of pastoral expediency before agreeing to a reform. Yet in this the question of the organic development of the objective liturgical Tradition does not arise.

We may agree that Lugano marked an epoch in the history of the Liturgical Movement, and that it heralded a new era of creative reform. However the question remains as to what extent reforms inspired by the momentum generated at Lugano would or would not be organic developments?

The Mont-César Conference, 1954

In 1954 a private meeting of scholars was held once again, at Mont-César.[191] Wagner accounts for the need for privacy, saying that following the previous conferences, "themes insufficiently studied among too many participants were now able to be discussed in order to resolve disputable problems."[192] Botte, the organiser of the conference, relates that there were two topics considered: the readings of the Mass and concelebration.[193] The former was a continuation of discussion of the resolutions from 1951-1953.

Concelebration, the full, sacrificial participation in the offering of one ritual celebration of Holy Mass by more than one priest, was a new item on the agenda for reform, occasioned principally by the difficulty of arranging private Masses whenever large numbers of priests met. The

---

191 Cf. S. Schmitt, *Die internationalen liturgischen Studientreffen 1951-1960*, pp. 174-199.

192 "Themen in einem nicht allzu großen Kreis zu diskutieren, ungelöste Probleme herauszustellen und zu ihrer Klärung anzuregen;" *Mein Weg Zur Liturgiereform: 1936-1986 Erinnerungen*, p. 206.

193 Cf. *From Silence to Participation*, p. 83.

topic was a sensitive one. The conference received a letter from Rome containing:

> A warning regarding concelebration. We were reminded that we had no competence for making a decision in the matter and that our rôle was solely to give information.[194]

Diekmann reported in *Worship:*

> The number of participants was limited to forty, from about thirteen countries...
>
> A study on the Mass pericopes of the Christmas cycle was presented by Dom Bernard Botte, and on those of the Sundays from Septuagesima to Pentecost by Prof. Chavasse and Dr. Heinrich Kahlefeld; some pastoral principles on the question from the missionary standpoint were added by Fr Hofinger SJ. General discussion followed each paper.
>
> The problem of eucharistic concelebration was first treated historically: Prof. Raes SJ spoke of its tradition in the Eastern Churches, and Dom Adalberto Franquesa analysed its developments in the West. Two opposing currents of speculative theological thought on the subject were represented by Msgr Davis of Birmingham and Dr Karl Rahner SJ of Innsbruck. Finally, the liturgical aspects were discussed by Fr Joseph Jungmann SJ and Canon A G Martimort.[195]

The meeting was in favour of the restoration of concelebration, however in the end there was an impasse between German scholars, who maintained that silent concelebration was sufficient, and the French, who held out for concelebrants pronouncing a minimal sacramental formula. In the words of Botte:

> It was thus impossible to draw up a document which would have had some chance of being approved by Rome. If the Germans had relented, the restoration of concelebration would probably have been attained ten years sooner.[196]

---

[194] Ibid. Diekmann's contemporary report puts a quite different slant on Rome's attitude to the meeting: "In the course of the Louvain meeting, a telegram was received from Msgr Montini announcing the papal blessing imparted to all participants, and expressing the Holy Father's satisfaction that these two actual themes were being competently studied and discussed from the historical, theological and pastoral points of view—though any such change of discipline falls of course solely within the competence of the Holy See itself;" "Louvain and Versailles" in: *Worship* vol. XXVIII p. 543.

[195] Ibid., p. 538.

[196] *From Silence to Participation*, p. 84.

Thus the conference produced no resolutions, as had its predecessors. Wagner reports: "A complete record was not made. Only a short synopsis was actually published."[197] Diekmann states that "areas of agreement and disagreement were drawn up...to be submitted to the competent authorities in Rome."[198]

Mont-César is, however, of interest for two reasons. Firstly, it demonstrates the existence of some Roman concern at the possible extent of the scholars' understanding of their own rôle. Secondly, it demonstrates again the rôle that scholarly consensus had in liturgical reform: as Botte makes clear, if the scholars could agree on a proposal, Rome would in all likelihood have accepted the proposal.

Furthermore, in Diekmann's report of the conference which, given the sensitivity of the matters under discussion at the time, he calls "some general remarks about the problems under study with some personal reflections,"[199] we find a clear articulation of the understanding of liturgical Tradition prevalent amongst liturgical scholars in this period. Diekmann, discussing the composition of a several-year cycle of scriptural readings for Mass, asserts:

> In any eventual choice, considerable weight should also be given, obviously, to tradition: i.e. to what selections of Scripture were thought important by the Fathers and in the earlier collections for Mass use. The new development would then be in the best sense of the word "traditional," for it would represent the mind of the Church in an era when the unquestionably desirable goal of abundant Scripture reading and teaching was still being realised.[200]

What precisely is meant by "tradition" here? There can be no doubt that he means the liturgical practice of the early Church, roughly, the patristic era. Thus, liturgical Tradition is regarded as something lost to the Church at the present time, but which, thanks to the development of liturgical studies, it is now possible to retrieve through reform. Therefore, in the period when many in the Liturgical Movement were, to use Crichton's phase, engaged in "pressure for reform," liturgical Tradition is seen as a rich mine of practices that can be quarried in the construction of a liturgy suitable for modern man. The inherent archaeologism of such a position is clear. So too is its acceptance, indeed its reliance, on Jungmann's theory of the corruption of liturgical development.

---

[197] "Eine umfassende Niederschrift wurde nicht verfaßt, lediglich eine knappe Zusammenfassung veröffentlicht;" *Mein Weg Zur Liturgiereform: 1936-1986 Erinnerungen,* p. 206. Cf. also pp. 30-33.

[198] "Louvain and Versailles" in: *Worship* vol. XXVIII p. 538.

[199] Ibid., p. 538.

[200] Ibid., p. 539.

The defect of this position is that it ignores the essence of Tradition itself (that something precious is faithfully handed on), and of liturgical Tradition in particular (that the living entity that is the Liturgy develops organically throughout the ages). Diekmann's stance, which is that of Jungmann and that of many if not most of those engaged in pressuring for reform at this time, is tantamount to denying the living nature of objective liturgical Tradition beyond the patristic age.[201] As we have maintained throughout this study, this is an unacceptable basis upon which to ground liturgical reform, as it leaves the objective liturgical Tradition to the mercy of whatever scholars can pressure authority into approving.

This is not to deny that elements of liturgical practice lost in the course of its history can be restored to the Liturgy, but as we have seen Capelle assert above, these must be truly necessary and must be effected in a way that is consonant with Tradition (understood as living objective liturgical Tradition as it has been received). Such restorations would be developments of the living organism, not a new construction according to contemporary desires using ancient practices and whatever might be seen as salvageable from the purportedly dead liturgical hulk in current use.

There was no international meeting in 1955. The next was the 1956 Assisi Congress, considered below.

Evening Mass

In his 1953 Apostolic Constitution *Christus Dominus*, Pius XII, in the light of "new, serious continuing and sufficiently general causes which make it exceedingly difficult in many circumstances both for priests to celebrate the eucharistic sacrifice and for the faithful to receive the bread of angels fasting," permitted the celebration of Mass in the evening on condition that a three hour fast was observed by the priest and by those who intended to communicate.[202]

Ellard, who had championed such a reform since the 1930s[203] commented:

> Epiphany of 1953 can go down in history as the day the Holy Father, by a stroke of his pen, or rather, by the kind prompting of his fatherly heart, gave us all some wonderful presents when he changed the ages-old provisions for the reception of Communion.[204]

---

201 Theologically, one could ask whether this position does not imply that the Holy Spirit ceased to guide the Church's development after this time.

202 Cf. K. Seasoltz OSB, *The New Liturgy*, pp. 178-185. Latin text: C. Braga CM, *Documenta*, pp. 758-765.

203 Cf. *Men at Work at Worship*, pp. 222-236.

204 *Now Evening Mass: Our Latest Gift*, p. 1.

The 1953 North American Liturgical Week was told that "the Eucharistic springtime fostered so graciously by Blessed Pius X has turned into summer under the paternal hand of Pius XII."[205] Reinhold exclaimed: "one of the oldest causes has won a victory."[206]

Reinhold defends the reform from the charge that the reason for the reform was to be found in the desires of liturgical scholars:

> The very words of the Constitution lift the whole complex out of the level of repristination and archaism...whether or not the apostles had evening Eucharist makes very little difference. What the Holy See is concerned about is the "good of souls" in 1953.[207]

Indeed, this was clearly a pastoral reform in the light of the needs and changed circumstances of modern man. It was a reform of the *time* of celebration and of the attendant fasting regulations, not of the rite. If looking for a precedent in the restoration of the time of the celebration of the paschal vigil to the evening, we must remember that that reform was a return to liturgical authenticity, whereas the permission for evening Mass was partially innovative (there is nothing *essentially* vesperal about the celebration of the Eucharist) and partially a return to an earlier discipline, judged by Pius XII to be expedient.

Thus, the traditional Liturgy was made more accessible to the people who henceforth had greater opportunity to participate in it in the fullest manner (by receiving Holy Communion). Such pastoral liturgical reform is, in the author's opinion, an apposite use of papal authority in liturgical matters showing both pastoral solicitude and respect for objective liturgical Tradition. It is a salient example of the sound desire for reform that arose from the fundamental tenets of the Liturgical Movement.[208]

Ernest Koenker's 1954 Assessment of the Liturgical Renaissance

In 1954, Koenker, an American protestant, published his doctoral study *The Liturgical Renaissance in the Roman Catholic Church.* His assessment of the achievements and prospects of the Liturgical Movement, written from the perspective of one "determined by Holy Scriptures as these were rediscovered through the Lutheran Reformation" is of interest.[209]

---

205 B. Ehman, "The Inevitability of Evening Mass" in: The Liturgical Conference, *St Pius X and Social Worship: National Liturgical Week (USA) 1953*, p. 190.

206 "The New Eucharistic Decrees" in: *Worship* vol. XXVII p. 187.

207 Ibid., p. 189.

208 For a contemporary discussion of the reform's impact: G. Garrone "The Pastoral Import of Christus Dominus" in: *AP* pp. 139-148.

209 *The Liturgical Renaissance in the Roman Catholic Church*, p. vi.

We have noted Koenker's overly harsh assessment of the impact of Guéranger.[210] This assessment identifies his assumptions. He writes:

> Though Guéranger envisaged a return to the official prayer of the Church rather than remain with the meagre nourishment of devotional books then popular, his work did not involve bringing the Liturgy to the masses as does the work of the modern Movement. It did not aim at general participation or recognise as its ideal the ancient Christian Church, nor did it embrace the all-pervading social concern of the modern apostolate.[211]

For Koenker then, the fundamental question is: how can the Liturgy be adapted to come closer to "the masses," preferably drawing on practices of the early 'uncorrupted' Church, in order to serve the evangelical needs of the modern apostolate? His question is not: how can "the masses" be brought to nourish their Christian lives from the received Liturgy? In other words, Koenker rejects the priority of objective liturgical Tradition and the legitimacy of its organic development in history. His is a straightforward protestant stance. Koenker is right in asserting this was not the stance of Guéranger. Nor was it that of the Liturgical Movement in its origins. The Catholic Liturgical Movement operated from fundamentally different assumptions.

His conclusions follow from his assumptions. Hence he pays "tribute to the liturgical reformers" whom he says have a "vital, Christ-centred faith" which "animates them and frees them from the accretions of many centuries" as they gradually free "the Roman rite from the sclerosis under which it has suffered for centuries."[212] Koenker rejects the charge of antiquarianism, and defends the promotion of the offertory procession, *versus populum* altar, and the restoration of the paschal vigil to the evening on the grounds that they are "intimately bound up with the desire for participation of the faithful." With this we may largely agree.[213] However, he goes on to assert that:

> The Movement must now enter new areas of everyday life and create new symbols, worship forms, ceremonies, and sacramentals which will speak to our own day and form a more contemporary, living, Liturgy.[214]

Furthermore, "a maximum use of the vernacular" is said to be essential to attaining participation.[215] And Koenker joins Karl Barth in

---

210 Cf. supra, p. 55.

211 *The Liturgical Renaissance in the Roman Catholic Church*, p. 11.

212 Cf. ibid., pp. 195-196.

213 Cf. ibid., p. 196. As has been asserted, with the exception of the altar *versus populum* there are sound reasons for accepting these.

214 Ibid., p. 197.

215 Cf. ibid.

standing aloof from a position that accepts "the sanctifying virtue of the objective liturgical act,"[216] and proclaims that "the time is ripe for a restudy, free and critical, of the symbolism on which Christianity has lived for centuries."[217] He rejoices in "the nearness" of the work of modern liturgical reformers "to the basic principles of the Reformation,"[218] and concludes his entire study by expressing the opinion, if not the hope, that:

> The Movement may go on to personalise, to individualise, and to Christianise the sacraments and sacramentals in such a way that the old magic sacramentalism of the Roman Catholic Church will be completely overcome. A new, evangelical spirit may be infused into the relationship between priest and people and their bishop; even the concept of the papacy may be spiritualised and Christianised. If the renaissance can continue unhindered, there may be a new "Liturgical Springtime" of the Roman Catholic Church—an awakening, the importance of which many would not now dream.[219]

There is no doubt that Koenker's desire is for a liturgical revolution based upon protestant theological principles. He does not pretend otherwise. The significance of his study is that his conclusions are, in a number of areas, shared with some prominent Catholic proponents of liturgical reform. This raises the question of whether the fundamental assumptions of such Catholic would-be reformers were theologically erroneous?

We have already noted the defective theology of Tradition, which is the foundation of the liturgical archaeologism evident in Diekmann's comments following the Mont-César conference. A similarly defective theology may be said to be at the basis of Jungmann's archaeologism and of his corruption theory. Diminishing the theological value of objective liturgical Tradition in this way certainly enables such proponents of reform to advocate the creation of "new symbols, worship forms, ceremonies, and sacramentals which will speak to our own day and form a more contemporary, living, Liturgy." Such proposals, often made by Catholic liturgists under the banner 'pastoral Liturgy,' may well be similarly defective.

---

[216] Ibid., p. 198.
[217] Ibid., p. 199.
[218] Cf. ibid.
[219] Ibid., p. 201.

The 1955 Australian Liturgical Week

January 1955 saw Australia hold its first (and only) national Liturgical Week in Melbourne, under the patronage of its then ninety year-old Archbishop Daniel Mannix, who attended in person.[220]

Its proceedings were unspectacular. Calls for ritual reform, foremost on the lips of northern European scholars in the preceding years, and heralded in the columns of *Worship,* are conspicuously absent.

In fact, the week was a promotion of the essence of the Liturgical Movement: liturgical piety. The Week's resolutions call for the study of *Mediator Dei,* the restoration of the religious significance of Christmas and Easter, the observance and fostering of the Lenten and ember fasts, the promotion of the dialogue Mass and congregational singing,[221] the distribution of Holy Communion from particles consecrated at the same Mass, the greater use of blessings and sacramentals in the daily life of the faithful, fostering knowledge and love of the Liturgy through the promotion of an altar servers' guild, integration of teaching on the Liturgy and on liturgical arts in schools, the promotion of Gregorian chant and liturgical publications, and the integration of school pupils into the liturgical life of their parishes.[222]

This list echoes the writings of Beauduin, Parsch, Hellriegel and other leaders of the Movement. The reform it seeks is primarily one of attitude from which a better use of the Liturgy will flow.

The Apostolic Delegate to Australia, speaking in the name of the Holy Father, assured the participants:

> The Liturgical Movement is neither a blind return to practices of the past nor an attempt to change our entire manner of worship of Almighty God. Instead, it is an effort to know and use better what we have, and to modify or change such details as have become less suited for the main purposes of the Liturgy.[223]

Archbishop Carboni's concept of liturgical modifications or changes falls well within the bounds of the organic development of the Liturgy. If there are to be any it is to be to "details," within a continuity ("our entire manner of worship" shall not be changed), and the value, if not the priority, of objective liturgical Tradition clearly recognised (we

---

220 J.D. Crichton asked "Is it not time that we in England had a really *national* congress under as high a patronage as this one?" "Notes and News" in: *Liturgy* vol. XXIV p. 23.

221 Resolution five adds the caveat: "but hymns should be chosen that are worthy in words and melody and are appropriate to the particular Liturgical Movement;" cf. Melbourne Diocesan Commission for the Liturgy and Sacred Music, *Australian Liturgical Week,* p. 218.

222 Cf. ibid., pp. 218-219.

223 R. Carboni, "The Liturgical Movement" in: ibid., p. 13.

are "to know and use better what we have"). His exclusion of antiquarianism is significant, as is the absence of any suggestion that the Liturgy itself is in a state of overall decay.

Given the date of this conference, the absence of any resolution calling for, or supporting European calls for, ritual reform, is perhaps significant. It is certainly evidence that the pressure for reform actively being applied by scholars in another hemisphere did not reflect a widely expressed need throughout the Liturgical Movement in the Catholic Church. Indeed, the proceedings of the contemporary North American National Liturgical Weeks, whilst welcoming reforms that occur, do not themselves resolve that further ritual reform is necessary. This most probably reflects the docility towards ecclesiastical authority that was a hallmark of the period, and perhaps also higher Mass attendance rates in Australia and North America in comparison to some parts of Europe. In the latter case pastors were probably not looking for liturgical reasons to explain the absence of so many, nor for liturgical 'solutions' to the problem. Nevertheless, our observation that pressure for liturgical reform was not a *sine qua non* of the Liturgical Movement at this time stands.

The 1955 Simplification of the Rubrics

The publication in May 1955 of the decree *Cum nostra*[224] of the Sacred Congregation of Rites was regarded by Bugnini as "constituting another chapter of the general liturgical reform."[225] It effected a simplification of the rubrics of the breviary and missal, principally with regard to the ranking of feasts and the number of prayers to be said on different occasions. The Pian commission had been considering the question of calendar reform for some years.[226]

Richstatter summarises the decree:

> With regard to the calendar: the degree and rite of semi-double is suppressed. Liturgical days which up to now were celebrated as semi-doubles will be celebrated with the rite of simplex. However, the Sundays which were formerly semi-doubles now become doubles. What this means in practice is that the Sunday Liturgy will be replaced by a saint's feast much less frequently, in accord with the general principle stated in the *Memoria*...

---

[224] Cf. K. Seasoltz OSB, *The New Liturgy*, pp. 203-209, C. Braga CM, *Documenta*, pp. 805-814.

[225] "alterum constituit caput instaurationis liturgicæ generalis;" A. Bugnini CM & I. Bellocchio, *De Rubricis ad simpliciorem formam redigendis*, p. 7.

[226] Cf. Sacra Rituum Congregatio, *Memoria sulla Riforma Liturgica: Supplemento III – Materiale Storico, Agiografico, Liturgico per la Riforma del Calendario*, published in 1951; N. Giampietro OFM Cap., *Il Card. Ferdinando Antonelli e gli sviluppi della riforma liturgica dal 1948 al 1970*, nos. [771]-[793] and earlier.

> The number of "facultative" or optional rubrics is increased. The priest is given the freedom to choose what Mass text he will use on certain days...Also, the celebrant can choose to celebrate the ferial office or the feast of the saint of double rank on the weekdays of Lent.[227]

This had the practical effect of reducing the number of commemorations made at each Mass, the frequency with which the Nicene and Athanasian Creeds, as well as the *Dies Iræ,* were used, and of lessening the number of octaves and vigils observed. The length of the Office was shortened by suppressing introductory and concluding prayers that were extraneous to the liturgical texts themselves and which were of devotional origin, by abolishing many commemorations of feasts impeded by higher ranking ones, and by reducing the occasions on which the *preces* were recited.

There is no doubt that such a reform was needed.[228] Crichton, who welcomed this "further stage in the reform of the Roman rite" as "an immense boon," commented that:

> For a long time many have felt they [the rubrics] were too complicated and the multiplication of commemorations and the interweaving of octaves have not made for a devout recitation of the Divine Office.[229]

J.B. O'Connell commented:

> No reform will be more heartily welcomed than the simplification of the rubrics of the Roman breviary and missal—a reform long overdue. Clergy and laity will be truly grateful to the Pope and to the liturgiologists whose profound knowledge and devoted labours have achieved such excellent results.[230]

He lauded it as a decree that has:

---

[227] *Liturgical Law,* pp. 33-34.

[228] A.S.E. Burrett's "Breviary and Calendar Reform" in: *The Clergy Review* vol. XXXV p. 225, describes the state of the Calendar as "like a garden tastefully planted out with flowers of divers colours, which has been allowed to develop in such a way that the flowers of one colour have so increased that the others have got somewhat smothered." The concurrence of different octaves was one problem, exemplified in the 1940's by J.B. O'Connell's directive for the feast of St Paul (June 30): "The Celebrant bows his head slightly at the name 'Paul' in the collect, in the *Alleluia* verse, in the Secret and in the post-communion...He bows at the name 'Peter' (because within the octave of SS. Peter and Paul) in the three prayers of commemoration, in the Epistle and in the Gradual, and throughout the Canon. He also bows at the name 'John' (because within the octave of the feast of St John Baptist) in the collect and post-communion prayers of commemoration, and in the prayer *Nobis quoque peccatoribus* (where this saint's name is mentioned), and in the last Gospel;" *The Celebration of Mass Vol. II The Rite of the Celebration of Low Mass,* p. 29.

[229] "The Recent Changes in the Missal and Breviary" in: *Liturgy* vol. XXIV p. 73.

[230] *Simplifying the Rubrics of the Roman Breviary and Missal,* p. 7.

> Freed the Liturgy of the Divine Office and the Mass from certain formalistic and complicated elements of comparatively recent introduction. The general result of the reform will bring that sense of relief and joy that arises when some noble building is cleared of ornaments and furnishings of doubtful value—the gifts over a long period of a genuine but misguided piety—enabling its outlines, in all their original beauty of form, proportion, and colour to be seen to full effect.[231]

O'Connell saw the reform, then, as "one of simplification, without touching the texts of the breviary or the missal or altering the traditional, essential structure of the Divine Office or the Mass."[232]

O'Connell's analysis is of interest. He does not balk at the abolition of some later liturgical developments: the prayers before and after the Office were certainly devotional accretions, yet some of the abolished octaves or vigils are, arguably, organic developments of the rite itself. O'Connell frequently asserts that this reform is "a simplification of the rubrics without any change in the essential structure of the Mass and the Divine Office, and leaving untouched the texts of the Mass and the Divine Office."[233] His position is not immune from antiquarianism, but it is limited by respect for what he calls the "essential structure" of the Liturgy. We must remember that O'Connell was a rubrician—probably the foremost Anglophone one—for whom the fundamental concern was what is permitted by authority, not what authority should permit.

Nevertheless, his acceptance of the reform is based on precedents in liturgical history: the pruning of the calendar and the insertion or abolition of celebrations has always been seen as well within the competence of ecclesiastical authority, and that it has indeed often been done without altering the essential structure of the Liturgy (excepting part of the breviary reform of St Pius X).

If we apply Capelle's principles, we can agree that there were grave deficiencies in the concurrence, and at times collisions, of the various octaves and feasts of calendar as they stood. We can observe that nothing new was introduced in this reform. We can argue about whether the gain brought about by these changes was "great." However it would certainly appear that O'Connell, by no means a man without respect for objective liturgical Tradition, considered it to be so. He would certainly argue that, considering their effect on the Liturgy as a whole, they were not disproportionate.

This reform was fundamentally motivated by pastoral concerns—though in this instance for "pastoral" one could equally read

---

231 Ibid., p. 76.

232 Ibid., p. 8.

233 Ibid., p. 72.

"practical"—for the 1953 papers of the Pian commission include principles that make clear that from the outset this reform was planned as a measure to reduce the burden of the Liturgy on the clergy by simplifying in areas where this was easiest and necessary.[234] Bugnini's commentary states that the principle pastoral reasons were the busyness and decreasing numbers of the clergy.[235] Bugnini also makes clear that this "second chapter" of the liturgical reform proceeded from the same basic principles as the "first chapter," the 1951 reform of the paschal vigil.[236] It is also clear that this reform was seen as provisional.[237] A complete reform of the rubrics was to come later in the general liturgical reform envisaged in the *Memoria,* being worked towards by the Pian commission.

This reform may be said to have abolished some legitimate developments. Quantitatively, the demotion of so many vigils and octaves did impoverish the Liturgy: perhaps a more traditional option would have been to restore at least some to their original importance? On the other hand, their abolition may simply be an appropriate example of authority formalising the desuetude into which some vigils and octaves had long since fallen. This, too, may be seen as part of the organic development of the Liturgy.

It is clear that much of this reform's content had long since been advocated within the Liturgical Movement.[238] By pruning the Liturgy of dubious accretions the Liturgy is purified, and by reasserting the priority of the temporal cycle over the sanctoral, an important element of objective liturgical Tradition that had certainly become obscured was

---

[234] Cf. Fondo Antonelli.

[235] Cf. *The Simplification of the Rubrics,* p. 19. On. p. 117 Bugnini outlines some other practical concerns addressed by the reform.

[236] "Primum caput exaratum est a. 1951, cum instauratione solemnis vigiliæ paschalis. Bina documenta procedunt ex iisdem principiis instaurationis;" A. Bugnini CM & I. Bellocchio, *De Rubricis ad simpliciorem formam redigendis,* p. 7.

[237] Cf. Commissione per la Riforma Liturgica, typescript: "Progetto per la semplificazione delle rubriche" 24 giugno 1953. This lists three principles: "Primo principio: La semplificazione non deve importare cambiamenti di testi liturgici, ma soltanto, eventualmente, omissioni. Secondo principio: La semplificazione non può abbracciare tutti i settori che meriterebbero, di per sè, una riforma, ma per il momento, solo le cose più facili e più ovvie, e con un immediato effetto sensibile. Terzo principio: Se con questa semplificazione si raggiunge anche una riduzione del "pensum," tanto meglio; ma una tale riduzione come scopo *principale,* al momento, non pare opportuna (per es. una riduzione del "pensum" nelle domeniche, o nelle feste con concorso di popolo, come si desidererebbe da molte parti)."

[238] Cf. P. Parsch, *The Liturgy of the Mass,* pp. 131, 146.

restored. A return to liturgical authenticity[239] is to be welcomed, and, on the whole we may regard this pastoral reform as one which respects Tradition without subjecting the Liturgy to radical innovation or to disproportionate structural change. As such, we may assert that it is an apposite use of authority largely within the limits of organic development, save perhaps its severe treatment of vigils and octaves.

Annibale Bugnini CM's Rationale for Liturgical Reform

In November 1955 *Worship* published an article by Bugnini entitled "Why A Liturgy Reform?"[240] It may be said to articulate some of the rationale behind the decree *Cum nostra*. However, Bugnini also enunciates principles he regards as applicable for a general reform. He asserts:

> Liturgical reform is something that is needed if the Liturgy is to preserve its vitality and splendour…
>
> The act of the Church [the liturgical rites]…bounded by time, by space, by the ministers who perform it, is necessarily linked in its exercise to the changeableness of human matters.
>
> On this account the Liturgy in its structure has required a corpus of formulas, gestures, rites and ceremonies which make of it a living organism, exposed like all organisms to outside influences, to luxuriant vitality and, sometimes, to decay.[241]

Bugnini's opening sentence betrays his agenda. He is writing in the "age of reform." As Crichton related, pressure was being applied to achieve reform at this time. And, according to Bugnini, reform is a necessity. Yet whilst one must accept that liturgical *reform* is indeed part of the life of the Church, surely reform must be subservient to the *development* of the Liturgy, in which there is a dialogue between Tradition and adaptation, wherein it is Tradition that must be persuaded. The distinction is important.

Bugnini rightly notes the changeableness of the human elements of the Liturgy, but his account is defective. He does not give any indication that liturgical elements of human origin, the Roman canon for example, are integral parts of liturgical Tradition that have never been regarded as changeable. His account of the nature of objective liturgical Tradition is therefore limited. We also note that in his account of the

---

239 In his commentary, Bugnini calls this the "vital, dynamic principle" or the principle of "dynamic simplification;" *The Simplification of the Rubrics*, p. 116.
240 "Why a Liturgy Reform?" in: *Worship* vol. XXIX pp. 562-569; also published in Bugnini's *The Simplification of the Rubrics*, pp. 9-16.
241 Ibid., p. 562.

organic nature of the Liturgy (he does not speak of liturgical reform as organic), Bugnini proffers the possibility, popular in his circles, that the Liturgy may be decayed.

He continues, stating that:

> The present Liturgy...is the result of many factors, among them the contributions of individual piety, the development of dogma, the constantly increasing number of saints, and the adaptations of the forms of worship to the necessities of the times and the needs of souls.[242]

Bugnini considers each of these four influences.

Discussing the influence of piety, he asserts the existence of a "sacred deposit which is the Liturgy" which "represents the most marvellous conceptions that have arisen in the mind of man in contact with God and in the presence of the Mystery." This is indeed an account of liturgical Tradition: however it too is defective. Bugnini would have us believe that this "liturgical patrimony" was fixed early in the life of the Church. Thus liturgical Tradition can be seen as something to be uncovered by an archaeologist and recovered by a reformer, rather than something living, developed in the course of the centuries, to be received with reverence and to be reformed only with the greatest respect.[243] According to Bugnini, the liturgical patrimony:

> In the course of its history often encountered the danger that the luxuriant and sometimes uncontrolled growth of "devotions" would get the upper hand over "devotion," meaning total and irrevocable consecration of the creature to God.
>
> Hence the Church, besides exercising a continual control, must sometimes set itself to a labour of restoration and alleviation, that the superadded elements may not disfigure the beauty of the primitive line or alter its sober, majestic aspect, but may be added into the harmonious whole of the Church praying.[244]

Again we have the erroneous assertion of the priority of a supposed "primitive" Liturgy. Nevertheless, it is true that the removal of devotional accretions (such as the abolition of the prayers before and after the Office in the 1955 decree) is legitimate. So too is ensuring that new developments are in harmony with the whole of the Church's prayer.

Dogmatic development in the history of the Church, Bugnini points out, was always followed by liturgical development. He quotes Righetti:

---

242 Ibid.

243 Cf. ibid., pp. 562-563.

244 Ibid., p. 563.

> When dogma is made precise in scientific speculation and doctrinal teaching, or when it issues victorious after a theological controversy, a formula quickly becomes the echo of it or a ceremony translates it and fixes it in the ritual.[245]

Bugnini, rightly, accepts this doctrinal influence, which he calls "the whole grand development of the worship of the most holy Eucharist with its related formulas,"[246] and makes no explicit case for its reform here.

Again, Bugnini rightly asserts the need for periodic reform of the calendar of saints, which we have often discussed. Bugnini's reasoning, however, sets out along a path that would have the Liturgy conform itself to the modern age. He asserts:

> The Church should choose the *types* of sanctity to be proposed for imitation and example, according to the times and the spiritual needs of the faithful.
>
> Hence arises once more the necessity of a revision of her prayer-texts in which some saints, whose spiritual features have lost contact with the modern soul, may be replaced by others more typical, more present-day, closer to us.[247]

Whilst agreeing that the periodic pruning of the calendar is simply inevitable given the growth of the sheer numbers of saints throughout history, reasoning such as the above is open to an interpretation which could lead to eroding the objectivity of the witness of the saints of the calendar, and to its reconstruction according to perceived "modern" needs. Surely the calendar should include "saints, whose spiritual features have lost contact with the modern soul," precisely in order to challenge modern souls? Otherwise we risk replacing them with "others more typical, more present-day, closer to us" simply to confirm our own tastes.

This reasoning is conspicuous in the consideration of the fourth influence, which he calls the "*Equation* of forms of worship to the social and spiritual needs of the faithful."[248] That the Liturgy, that objective given which we reverently receive and develop only cautiously, should be "equated" with the subjective and changing situations of a particular age, is repugnant to its very nature as traditional. Admission of such "equation" risks rendering the Liturgy the construct of each passing generation.

Furthermore the distinction Bugnini makes in his assertion here that, "in its essence the Liturgy partakes of the divine immutability; in

---

245 Cited: ibid., p. 563.

246 Ibid., p. 564.

247 Ibid.

248 Ibid., p. 565.

outward form it shows the mark of the times,"[249] which underpins his desire to conform liturgical forms to the subjective situation of the current age, is false. Outward liturgical forms, which may indeed develop and change and even fall into disuse in the progress of time, are themselves subsumed into, and become privileged vehicles of, the divine immutability. Earthly things become entwined with the divine so as to render the divine present in and through the resultant liturgical forms. Rites, gestures, words, sounds and objects thus themselves become sacramental. The divine is not distinct from earthly forms in Catholic Liturgy. Indeed, Catholic Liturgy is essentially incarnational in a manner that is directly analogous to the Incarnation. Similarly, the "essence" of Liturgy cannot be detached from its "outward forms" without changing its very nature. Therefore, each age cannot adjust its external expressions according to their own desires without risking rendering the Catholic Liturgy essentially protestant and spiritualist. In short, such a distinction risks accepting the fundamental anti-liturgical error of the protestant reformers who constructed their liturgies anew to fit into their theological ideologies.

To justify his position, Bugnini briefly surveys some developments of the Liturgy in history, recalling how different periods have influenced it.[250] However his account, which does show the influence of different periods on the *development* of objective liturgical Tradition, fails to demonstrate that the Liturgy was *equated* "to the social and spiritual needs of the faithful" in any particular period. Except in one instance. Bugnini refers to the reform of Cardinal Quignonez:

> The attempt…to free the Church's prayer of its superstructures and give it a practical meaning and one more adapted to the pastoral life, had the fault of movements in the vanguard of breaking too sharply and suddenly with Tradition. But it was an indication. Three hundred editions of his breviary in twenty years showed the necessity of stripping down and simplifying the whole liturgical structure.[251]

Apart from the speciousness of judging such necessity on popularity, particularly given the contingencies of sixteenth century printing and publication, we have seen that the Quignonez' belief in the "necessity of stripping down and simplifying the whole liturgical structure" was authoritatively rejected not simply because his reform was effected too quickly, but precisely because it was untraditional. As Guéranger articulated, it contravened fundamental principles of reform.[252] It is a

---

249 Ibid.

250 Cf. ibid., pp. 565-568.

251 Ibid., pp. 566-567.

252 Cf. supra, p. 29.

matter of some concern that in 1955 Bugnini should regard Quignonez' reform as an "indication" of a "necessity."

Having surveyed the work of liturgical reform ending with the 1955 Simplification of the Rubrics, Bugnini ends his article with the statement: "It is a bridge which opens the way to a promising future."[253] Bugnini's principles however, at the heart of which we find an untraditional subjectivism akin to that of Quignonez, and indeed to those of the enlightenment liturgists, raise the question of precisely what promise such a future would hold? Any reform which realised Bugnini's principles as articulated above would seem to promise a break with Tradition, perhaps less sharply and suddenly, but nonetheless consistent with that of Quignonez. Such a reform was certainly not the aim of the Liturgical Movement's fathers.

The same issue of *Worship* also translates an extract of an article Bugnini published in *L'Ossservatore Romano* on 18th June 1955. He states:

> The Liturgy is not an uninhabited and open field upon which one can draw the outlines of a new city. Rather, there is question of 'restoration:' of patient, delicate labour, performed humbly and prayerfully. For the Liturgy is the praying voice of the centuries: it must speak to the souls of today and of tomorrow with the same vibrancy and immediacy with which it spoke to the Christian generations which its prayer-formulas created in the past.[254]

The first sentence is almost paradoxical in the light of the principles already articulated by Bugnini. However, given that *L'Osservatore Romano* is an official publication of the Holy See, there may have been good reason to take a more restrained stance here. Nevertheless, reading this in conjunction with "Why A Liturgy Reform?" we can see that what is meant by a "restoration" of the Liturgy so that it would "speak to the souls of today and of tomorrow," in Bugnini's mind, risks going well beyond the organic development of the Liturgy and could very well lead to the foundations of a radically new city. Indeed, in his booklet *The Simplification of the Rubrics* Bugnini states that the aim of reform is, in fact, "a new city in which the man of our age can live and feel at ease," albeit arrived at by reforming the existing Liturgy.[255]

The 1955 Reform of Holy Week

In July 1955 *Worship's* editor, Godfrey Diekmann OSB, wrote to Father Antonelli:

---

[253] "Why a Liturgy Reform?" in: *Worship* vol. XXIX p. 569.

[254] "Liturgical Briefs" in: *Worship* vol. XXIX p. 607. Bugnini's bibliography in *TRL* omits this article.

[255] Cf. *The Simplification of the Rubrics*, pp. 21-22.

It is extremely difficult, because of the vastness of America, to get anything like an adequate picture of the national observance of the Vigil. Unfortunately the unfavourable stand taken by Cardinal Spellman of New York is rather well known. So also is his unfavourable attitude toward the vernacular in our new ritual. From reports, it is certain that he has not yet allowed the Vigil, claiming that it was not meant for parish use but only for experiment in religious houses! To my knowledge, the new ritual has likewise not been permitted in his Archdiocese. May I speak frankly? Although Cardinal Spellman is undoubtedly the one member of the American hierarchy who is best known in other countries, I am sure that other members of the hierarchy are by no means unanimously inclined to follow his lead in all matters. Certainly the vast majority of the American Bishops heartily favour the new ritual; and the vast majority have likewise permitted the Vigil in their dioceses although only a few of them seem to have positively urged it upon their priests.

In Canada, the situation seems somewhat different. Two weeks ago I had occasion to speak to Archbishop Pocock of Winnipeg, concerning the Vigil. He suggested that he might bring up the matter at the annual meeting of Canadian Bishops this fall; and he felt convinced there would be almost unanimous support for the permanence of the Vigil. While of course encouraging him to take this step, I pointed out that it would be very useful if he would immediately write his own positive reaction to the Vigil to the Secretariat of State and the SCR. Within the past few weeks I have ventured to make the same suggestion to several members of the U.S. hierarchy whom I happen to know rather well.

The chief obstacle to obtaining enthusiastic support of the American bishops (as I personally mentioned to you at Louvain last fall) is the fact that the great majority of them are specialists in Canon Law and in administration, and have a correspondingly lesser interest in matters theological. This is borne out by the fact that up to the present, the Nat. Liturgical Conference has not been able to interest the American hierarchy sufficiently in its program, to convince them that they should undertake the official guidance and sponsorship of the program in the U.S. There has been a gradual change for the better in more recent years. But as a body, the American Bishops still do not consider the Liturgical Apostolate as being a normal part of their pastoral concern; despite *Mediator Dei* and all the rest, most of them consider the Liturgical Movement to be an affair of externals!...[256] I believe that one of the reasons for the gradual improvement has been that we have sent our magazine gratis to every bishop in the country for the past 3 years. (We should have done so from the outset, 29 years ago.)

---

256 This abbreviation is in the original.

> At present our magazine has about 9,000 subscribers, the majority of whom are priests. It likewise reaches every major seminary and very many of the mother houses of religious communities. If in any way we can be of service to you, in preparing the minds of American priests for pending liturgical reforms, please do not hesitate to suggest whatever steps you may think advisable. Perhaps you yourself may be inclined to write an essay or two concerning the recent Decree[257] and what it portends. Or perhaps you would prefer to inspire such an article to be signed by someone else. In any event, I wish to state that I am entirely at your service, and I hope that through our pages we may be instrumental in conditioning the thinking of American clergy for the promised reform of the missal and breviary.[258]

This reflection on the reception of the 1951 reform of the paschal vigil underlines the extent of the co-operation between officials of the Sacred Congregation of Rites and Liturgical Movement activists, and demonstrates that further reform was clearly on their somewhat political agenda.

The Pian commission had been working on the reform of the whole of Holy Week for some time.[259] It was complete by 1954, and presented to Pius XII who, on August 18th 1954 ordered that it be considered by the cardinals of the Sacred Congregation of Rites.[260] In the summer of 1955 the Congregation of Rites published a Positio compiled by Antonelli for their consideration.[261]

Part I of the *Positio* recounts the desire for a general liturgical reform from the time of St Pius X and acknowledges the importance of both the Liturgical Movement's pastoral impact (i.e. the promotion of liturgical piety) and of the advance in liturgical studies. The work of the

---

[257] The Simplification of the Rubrics.

[258] Typewritten letter 5 July 1955.

[259] Discussion began at the commission's sixth meeting, 27 January 1950: cf. N. Giampietro OFM Cap., *Il Card. Ferdinando Antonelli e gli sviluppi della riforma liturgica dal 1948 al 1970*, no. [106] seq. Antonelli's papers include: a typed document from 1952 "Sulla riforma della liturgica del Giovedi Santo e del Venerdi Santo" which has Löw's name and the date 29 X 52 written in pencil on the back by Antonelli; cyclostated documents pertaining to Holy Week reform dated 20 October 1952 and 15 October 1955, and proofs for the rites of Holy Thursday and Good Friday from 1953.

[260] Cf. N. Giampietro OFM Cap., *Il Card. Ferdinando Antonelli e gli sviluppi della riforma liturgica dal 1948 al 1970*, p. 82.

[261] Sacra Rituum Congregatio, Sectio Historica, no. 90, *De Instauratione Liturgica Maioris Hebdomadæ: Positio.*

Pian commission is recounted, and specific mention is made of the wishes (*voti*) expressed by the liturgical congresses held in recent years.[262]

The second part discusses reasons for restoring the rites of Holy Thursday and Good Friday to their ancient times, namely to the evening and to the afternoon respectively. The *Positio* is clear that this is not an antiquarian proposition and insists that such a reform would "above all" be to achieve a pastoral end, bringing the time of the celebration of the ceremonies into line with conditions that had radically changed since the seventeenth century.[263] As we have maintained, a return to liturgical authenticity where inauthentic practices exist within the objective liturgical Tradition is to be welcomed. Such reform is truly pastoral in its facilitation of the growth of liturgical piety.

The *Positio* holds the 1951 reform to be one that also removed inconsistencies from the "venerable texts and rites," and restored them to their primitive freshness. The innovation of baptismal promises is said to be fully justified.[264] This account is somewhat simplistic, failing to give a full justification for the innovation, or to account for the quite untraditional abbreviation of the vigil's readings. Nevertheless, its desire for liturgical authenticity and its respect for the "venerable texts and rites" in matters of liturgical reform are noteworthy.

The new vigil is said to have been a "large, universal success,"[265] particularly in the light of comments in liturgical publications and meetings throughout the world, and in view of communications sent to Rome by Ordinaries.[266] However, there is evidence that this was not necessarily the case in all places. In mid-1955 Coyne reflected on the impact of the 1951 reform of the paschal vigil:

> Now that the novelty is wearing off, parishes in many areas report dwindling congregations. In many places, also, the Easter Vigil

---

262 Cf. ibid., p. 10. The fourth resolution of the 1953 Lugano congress had explicitly called for a reform of the whole of Holy Week along the lines of the 1951 paschal vigil.

263 "Ma la proposta di un ritorno all'orario antico si basa piuttosto su di un dato di fatto, che ai fini soprattuto pastorali, ha un peso innegabile e che deve esser tenuto presente;" ibid., p. 13.

264 "Il nuovo *Ordo Sabbati Sancti* dal punto di vista liturgico liberava i venerandi testi e riti da varie incongruenze che vi si erano introdotte attraverso i secoli e ridonava al complesso liturgico la sua freschezza primitiva. Vi fu inserito anche un elemento nuovo, ma pienamente giustificato, quello della rinovazione pubblica delle promesse battesimali;" ibid., p. 16.

265 "un grand e universale successo;" ibid., p. 20.

266 "Che poi il nuovo rito abbia avuto una larghissima eco favorevole in tutto il mondo è provato dalle numerosissime pubblicazioni di carattere liturgico, dalle relazioni tenute in convegni, congressi e settimane liturgiche, e in modo particolare dalle copiose relazioni inviate dagli Ordinari alla S. Congregazione dei Riti;" ibid., p. 19.

congregation has never approached in numbers that of the Christmas midnight Mass. Nor has the new service always been adopted where we might most have expected to find it. In Westminster Cathedral, for example, it was not in use till 1955. St Peter's, Rome, has still to abandon the morning service.[267]

The *Positio* itself considers difficulties reported by bishops, though these are purely practical problems.[268] Other bishops responded negatively to the experiment, also for practical reasons.[269]

Requests from bishops for the reform of the liturgies of Palm Sunday, Holy Thursday and Good Friday are reported. Cardinal Liénart of Lille, who in 1950 had signed the petition for the restoration of the paschal vigil to the evening on behalf of the French episcopate,[270] asked in October 1951 that the remaining ceremonies might be completely renewed "in the same liturgical and pastoral spirit."[271] Others, however, including the then Patriarch of Venice, Cardinal Roncalli,[272] limited themselves to requesting the restoration of the Holy Thursday and Good Friday liturgies to their proper times, without calling for an overhaul of the rites themselves.

The *Positio* goes on to report that Pius XII gave permission for the study of a reform in 1952 which was carried out by the commission who used the 1948 *Memoria* as a starting point. By the first month of 1954 the commission's work was complete.[273] Antonelli, prefacing his summary of what is proposed, states that "the revisions...show the necessary respect to the formulas and to the rites throughout."[274]

For the reform of the Liturgy of Palm Sunday, a "light revision,"[275] of the blessing of palms and the subsequent procession is proposed that would restore the rite to its original simplicity and reverse medieval developments which had rendered the blessing a mini-Mass in itself. The procession to the honour of Christ the King was to be

---

267 J. Coyne "The Traditional Position" in: C.R.A. Cunliffe, *English in the Liturgy*, p. 97.

268 The ringing of bells late at night; the question of when priests could find time to bless homes given that the vigil was now on Saturday night; how to find sufficient clergy for the ceremonies; the excessive fatigue of clergy who have spent long hours in the confessional; and the precise hour at which to celebrate the vigil; cf. Sacra Rituum Congregatio, Sectio Historica, no. 90, *De Instauratione Liturgica Maioris Hebdomadæ: Positio*, pp. 29-35.

269 Msgr Bonomini, Bishop of Como, Cardinal Siri, Archbishop of Genoa, and Msgr Cuccarollo, Archbishop of Otranto; cf. ibid., pp. 35-42.

270 Cf. ibid., p. 15.

271 "renouvelés dans le même esprit liturgique et pastoral;" ibid., p. 43.

272 Elected Pope John XXIII in 1958; cf. ibid., pp. 44-46.

273 Cf. ibid., pp. 45-46.

274 "i ritochi che si stimano necessari intorno ai formulari e ai riti;" ibid., p. 46.

275 "lievi ritocchi;" ibid., p. 47.

emphasised. All the liturgists, Antonelli reports, were unanimous that this was necessary.[276] The reading of the Passion of Saint Matthew according to the ancient, simpler, arrangement is proposed. Otherwise, the Mass was left to be left as it was.

The principal element of the reform of the Holy Thursday rites was the return of the Mass *In Cœna Domini* to an evening hour of celebration. The *Missa Chrismatis,* which had been lost in the course of history (with the result that the texts for the consecration and blessing of oils were inserted into the Mass *In Cœna Domini*), was to be restored with new texts, to be celebrated in cathedral churches in the morning. One ritual innovation was proposed as an option: the moving of the *Mandatum* (the washing of the feet) to immediately following the gospel reading of the Mass: it had hitherto been performed, if at all, after the transfer of the Blessed Sacrament to the altar of repose. Antonelli also reports that the commission firmly rejected requests from priests for a private Mass to commemorate the anniversary of the institution of the priesthood on the grounds that this was contrary to Tradition.[277]

Antonelli notes that the Good Friday rites had been conserved substantially intact from antiquity and says that they comprise a most precious liturgical commodity of which we must take care with total veneration. In the light of this he asserts that only small revisions are necessary.[278] The first of these is the return of the hour of its celebration to the afternoon, approximating the time of the death of Christ upon the cross. The structure of the rite is to be left "substantially intact:"[279] an opening collect was proposed, the Passion reading was to be simplified in the same way as Palm Sunday, and the solemn intercession for the Emperor was to replaced with one for those in public office.

The exception to these moderate proposals for reform, which may be regarded as within the scope of organic development which leaves the rite substantially intact, was that proposed for what was known as the Mass of the Presanctified. Antonelli reports that this was a matter of disagreement in the commission[280] and that there was not always agreement with the liturgists on whether Holy Communion

---

276 "Tutti i liturgisti sono unanimi nel riconoscere la necessità di semplificare la benedizione delle palme;" ibid.

277 Cf. ibid., pp. 48-51.

278 "I riti del Venerdì Santo si sono conservati sostanzialmente intatti dal'antichità fino ad oggi e constituiscono un complesso liturgico preziosissimo che deve esser custodito con somma venerazione. I ritocchi necessari sono pochi;" ibid., p. 51.

279 "sostanzialmente intatti;" ibid., p. 52.

280 Cf. N. Giampietro OFM Cap., *Il Card. Ferdinando Antonelli e gli sviluppi della riforma liturgica dal 1948 al 1970,* no. [114]

should be distributed at all, and if so, to whom and with what rites.[281] Yet all the liturgists were agreed that what they regarded as the medieval superstructure of the Mass of the Presanctified, which included rituals from the offertory of the Mass, "introduced without reason"[282] was to be simplified or eliminated.[283] In the end, a compromise is proposed whereby, for pastoral reasons, Holy Communion is to distributed, but with the simple rite of the distribution of Holy Communion outside of Mass:[284] the Mass of the Presanctified is to be abolished.

The Pian commission's minutes reveal that the practice of blessing the people with the cross exposed for veneration, a practice of the Eastern Liturgy, was considered. However it concluded that it was not opportune to introduce this element "ex novo."[285]

The fundamental principles of the proposed reform are again: liturgical authenticity, simplification of the rite, and pastoral expediency. The proposed return to the authentic times of celebration presents no difficulty to the liturgical historian. Liturgical authenticity is to be welcomed. Some measure of simplification presents little difficulty either, provided it is proportionate.

Yet the proposals advocating truncating the blessing of the palms and the abolition of the Mass of the Presanctified are considerable. They demonstrate that the commission was prepared to cut significantly where they thought it pastorally expedient. The corruption theory underpins this stance. So too does a confidence, verging on faith, in the opinions of liturgical historians. Asked whether the reform of Palm Sunday did not contradict the norm of the amplification or growth of the Liturgy over the centuries, Antonelli responded that such a reform was fully justified from the point of view of liturgical history, as well as from its pastoral expediency.[286]

---

281 "Questo è l'unico punto su cui si concentrato le discussioni e i pareri non sempre concordi dei liturgisti;" ibid. Cf. *De Instauratione Liturgica Maioris Hebdomadæ: Positio,* pp. 53-54.

282 "introdotti qui senza ragione;" ibid. p. 59.

283 "Ora tutti i liturgisti sono concordi nel riconoscere che questa cosidetta Messa dei presantificati deve essere semplificata e che certi elementi impropri devono essere eliminati;" ibid. p. 54.

284 The commission's discussion of the reception of Holy Communion was itself wide ranging: cf. N. Giampietro OFM Cap., *Il Card. Ferdinando Antonelli e gli sviluppi della riforma liturgica dal 1948 al 1970,* nos. [380]-[391].

285 Ibid., [392]. An interesting precedent in the light of the use of Eastern sources following the Second Vatican Council.

286 To the question "An ritus benedictionis palmarum, decursu sæculorum abnorme amplificatus, ad simpliciorem formam reducendus sit?" Antonelli replied: "Per le ragioni sopra esposte, la Commissione per la Riforma liturgica è di parere che questa semplificazione, oltre al essere pienamente giustificata dal punto di vista della storia liturgica, sarà anche accolta con goia da tutti, perchè

However, this reform does reverse the development of the Liturgy. In the case of the Mass of the Presanctified, the proposed reforms were neither a return to ancient practice (which was that no-one received Holy Communion), nor a development of received Tradition (by extending Holy Communion to the people as well as to the priest). They were proposals to abolish the current rite and re-construct according to the pastoral and historical desires of the experts: pastoral expediency.

On the other hand, some developments proposed are in harmony with traditional principles of reform. It would be churlish to pretend that no development was desirable or that inertia could be a legitimate response to real pastoral needs. But the requirement of proportionate respect for objective liturgical Tradition cannot be abdicated.

It is interesting to note the appearance of the word "aggiornamento" in the 1955 *Positio*—the word that was to become the banner under which the Second Vatican Council was celebrated. Antonelli entitles the proposals for Holy Thursday "aggiornamento" but uses "riforma" for Palm Sunday and Good Friday.[287] Arguably, "aggiornamento" when used as distinct from "riforma," speaks of a renewal that is the perfection of the Tradition, which can involve simplification and development, but in harmony with Tradition. "Riforma," in contradistinction, can suggest more radical reconstruction.

The cardinals of the Sacred Congregation of Rites unanimously approved the reform as outlined in the *Positio* on July 19, 1955,[288] and with the decree of the same Congregation *Maxima redemptionis nostræ mysteria*, and its accompanying instruction, dated November 16th 1955, the reform of the entire Holy Week Liturgy was promulgated.[289]

The principles outlined in the decree are familiar: the correction of the timing of the ceremonies, which was to the "detriment to the liturgical meaning" of them, so that the people might participate in their "special sacramental force and efficacy for nourishing Christian life."[290] In other words, the reform is one that seeks liturgical authenticity in order to enhance liturgical piety. There is no rationale given in the decree for any reform of the rites themselves. The instruction notes only one rubrical change: the celebrant is to omit reading for himself those texts

---

darà modo di sveltire la funzione già di per sè lunga, e di mettere nuovamente nel dovuto risalto l'elemento principale di questa funzione particolare della Domenica delle Palme, vale a dire la processione quale omaggio pubblico a Cristo Re;" *De Instauratione Liturgica Maioris Hebdomadæ: Positio*, p. 55.

287 Cf. ibid., pp. 47, 48, 51.

288 Cf. J. Löw CSsR, "The New Holy Week Liturgy: A Pastoral Opportunity" in: *Worship* vol. XXX p. 99.

289 Cf. K. Seasoltz OSB, *The New Liturgy*, pp. 209ff; C. Braga CM, *Documenta*, pp. 821ff.

290 Cf. K. Seasoltz OSB, *The New Liturgy*, pp. 210-211.

spoken by other ministers—a felicitous and authentic simplification already previewed in the 1951 experimental reform.

The instruction makes clear the pastoral motivation of the reform:

> Local ordinaries should carefully see to it that priests, especially those who have the care of souls, be well instructed not only in the ritual observance of the restored *Ordo* of Holy Week, but also in its liturgical meaning and its pastoral purpose.
>
> They should likewise take care that the faithful also, during the holy season of Lent, be faithfully taught properly to understand the restored *Ordo* of Holy Week, so that they may both mentally and spiritually participate in the services.[291]

An authoritative commentary by Löw, promptly published in translation in *Worship*, says of the instruction:

> It is stated with the sharpest possible emphasis that the meaning and purpose of this liturgical restoration of Holy Week is *entirely pastoral*, inspired for concern for souls: it is not some kind of liturgical archaeology; nor is it meant to be a restoration of a museum piece. Which of course does not deny that, in the elaboration of this reform, thorough liturgical-historical studies and researches were consulted.[292]

What is meant by "pastoral" here is clearly that the faithful should be formed in liturgical piety so that the people can participate in the Liturgy "with mind and heart:"[293] a clear articulation of the inherently contemplative nature of liturgical participation as distinct from its activist interpretation.[294] To this end a significant and swift effort was made to publish people's editions of the new ceremonies, as well as commentaries and ceremonial guides for clergy.[295]

---

[291] Ibid., p. 213.

[292] "The New Holy Week Liturgy: A Pastoral Opportunity" in: *Worship* vol. XXX pp. 101-102.

[293] "ut eiusdem celebrationis mente et animo participes fiant;" C. Braga CM, *Documenta*, p. 825.

[294] Seen, for example, in the promotion of the dialogue Mass by some in the Liturgical Movement, and in the wave of liturgical activism that followed the Second Vatican Council.

[295] Cf. "Liturgical Briefs" in: *Worship* vol. XXX pp. 222-223; also: *Officia Nova Hebdomadæ Sanctæ*; G. Montague, *Ceremonies of Holy Week*; C. Howell SJ, *Preparing for Easter*; J.B. O'Connell, *The Ceremonies of Holy Week*; P. Murphy, *The Ceremonies of Holy Week: Guide to the Restored Order.* Antonelli reported to the Assisi Congress that "In the United States of America alone…there were twelve different editions of the *Ordo* for the faithful; and one of these…had a press run of 1,600,000 copies. Yet in spite of the many editions and copies, a few days before Holy Week all were completely sold out in the United States as well as in France, Germany and

Löw's semi-official use of the term "pastoral" may be distinguished from its use by some prominent liturgists at the time. Here it expresses no more than the desire of the Liturgical Movement since its inception: that the spiritual life of the faithful be nourished by the Liturgy of the Church. Ritual reform is a secondary concern. However in the words of Bugnini, Jungmann, Crichton, etc., we have seen that "pastoral" reform means primarily that ritual reform is to effect the change of the Liturgy to accommodate the perceived needs of people of the day.

Bugnini enunciates this principle in relation to the new provision which comprised part of the reform of Holy Week that enables a form of the ceremonies to be celebrated with the assistance of a deacon in the absence of a subdeacon, called the "semi-solemn" rite. Hitherto the rubrics had not permitted this. In bringing about this reform, Bugnini speaks of "a restoration that springs from motives that are purely pastoral," adding "I should almost say 'utilitarian,'"[296] and asserts that:

> The "restorers" showed very great courage[297] in overcoming traditional positions without delay when simple pastoral utility and not necessity required this step...pastoral interest presides over, guides and gives life to the present liturgical reform, even when, almost unnoticeably, it inspires the phrasing of a new rubric, the revision, and perhaps even the punctuation, of a formula, the pruning or the restoring of a rite.[298]

The strength of Bugnini's language leaves no doubt that pastoral utility was the motivation of this reform. Such a utilitarian disposition is foreign to the organic development of the Liturgy, and although its exercise did not in this instance compromise objective liturgical Tradition (the reform itself has much to commend it), the disposition itself was certainly capable of doing so.

The distinction between the two senses of "pastoral" is crucial. In the former conception the people are enabled to understand and penetrate the richness of objective liturgical Tradition, which itself may be somewhat simplified or adjusted to facilitate this encounter. The people's liturgical appetites are elevated and there is continuity, and possibly welcome development, of objective liturgical Tradition. In the latter stance objective liturgical Tradition is reconstructed to suit the

---

Italy;" "The Liturgical Reform of Holy Week: Importance, Realisations, Perspectives," in: *AP* p. 156.

296 "Mass with Deacon" in: *Worship* vol. XXXII p. 462.

297 In an interview by the author on 24th October 1996 in Rome, Carlo Braga CM, a confrère of Bugnini and member of the Pian commission from 1960, asserted that the reform of the vigil was "the only courageous point" of the work of the commission. Other reforms of the commission were, in contrast, simply "historical" revisions and simplifications.

298 "Mass with Deacon" in: *Worship* vol. XXXII p. 463.

perceived needs of the people: so that its rites 'speak to them.' There can be change without concern for continuity in the objective liturgical Tradition, and people's liturgical appetites are left as they stand. In the former, people are taught to comprehend the rich liturgical language of the Church. In the latter 'liturgical vocabulary' is reduced and restricted to that which reformers think people will grasp immediately. This is not consonant with the fundamental aims of the Liturgical Movement.

The *Ordo* for the reformed Holy Week was published early in 1956.[299] Antonelli underlined its historical significance, saying that it was "very probably the greatest liturgical reform since St Pius V's revision of the breviary and missal in the sixteenth century."[300] It contained the ritual reforms proposed in the *Positio,* and incorporated the simplifications in the Order of Mass found in the 1951 reform: the prayers at the foot of the altar are omitted or shortened; as mentioned above there is no duplication of texts; and the last gospel is omitted from the principal ceremonies. The homily is recommended for Holy Thursday. For pastoral reasons it is permitted to celebrate the paschal vigil earlier in the evening.

The reservations already expressed about truncating the rite of the blessing of the palms and abolishing the Mass of the Presanctified from motives of pastoral expediency and antiquarianism, and our earlier reservations about the reform of the paschal vigil, which is made obligatory in the 1956 *Ordo,* lead to the conclusion that this reform is a mixed blessing.[301] A return to authenticity and some simplification are certainly not repugnant to objective liturgical Tradition. Yet antiquarianism and unfettered pastoral expediency are. It is difficult to see how the abolition of the Good Friday Mass of the Presanctified is anything other than the latter.

Yet it may be argued that, taken as a whole, the innovations and abolitions contained in the reformed Holy Week rites are not sufficient to substantially displace the entire objective traditional Liturgy, and that there is an overall substantial continuity, with only a small proportion of liturgical forms being abolished, radically altered, or introduced. One may therefore assert that it is largely within the boundaries of both the organic development of the Liturgy and of the supervisory competence of the Bishop of Rome in respect of the Roman rite.[302]

---

[299] *Ordo Hebdomadæ Sanctæ Instauratus.*

[300] Quoted in "Liturgical Briefs" in: *Worship* vol. XXX p. 157.

[301] A 1960 conference by Msgr Gromier, one of Pius XII's Masters of Ceremony, makes a scathing assessment of the restored Holy Week rites; English translation: www.geocities.com/Athens/Styx/3121/gromier.html.

[302] Michael Davies states: "There were sound reasons behind all the reforms and the continuity with the previous ceremonies was evident;" *An Open Lesson to a Bishop,* p. 28.

Nevertheless, our concern is that the principles of antiquarianism and pastoral expediency are present in at least some elements of the reform. Were such principles to predominate, the substantial displacement of the objective traditional Liturgy could ensue.

The reception of the reform was mostly positive. Beauduin hailed it, offering his "unreserved congratulations"[303] to all those who had contributed to bringing about the reform. Yet he warned—and today we must admit, prophetically—that the concession afforded bishops to bring the hour of the celebration of the paschal vigil forward could result in a negation of the reform's restoration of it as a true vigil.[304] *Worship* stated that "only the decree of St Pius X, on frequent and daily Communion, rivals it in importance," and spoke of the realisation of "some of the great goals" for which its founder, Virgil Michel, had laboured.[305] McManus asserted that "no change thus far introduced is equal to [it]...in its extent and significance, and no change is of greater spiritual and pastoral worth."[306] Crichton welcomed it as a "far-reaching reform" of "epoch-making importance."[307] King, similarly, spoke of "far-reaching changes."[308] Reinhold rejoiced, with reference to the reform of the rite of Holy Communion on Good Friday in particular, that "all the sham has been cleared away and there is no longer a pretending or a substituting of anything alien or inappropriate."[309]

Antonelli's papers contain an appreciative letter from an American priest written only weeks after the promulgation of the decree:

> There is a group of us [who][310] meet regularly with Monsignor Tobin, Vicar General of the Archdiocese, to discuss pastoral and liturgical matters. Last night we studied the text of the new Holy Week Liturgy. Our first reaction was one of extreme pleasure and gratitude that we should be living in an age when such things can be done. There are so many individual features that pleased us that I could not begin to enumerate them. One thing that stood out is the fact that the active participation of the Laity is explicitly provided for. Another outstanding feature, we think, is the logical spirit pervading the rite. e.g., no duplication of the "Confiteor" on Holy Thursday...[311]

---

303 "nos félicitations sans réserve;" "Liminaire a Restauration de la Semaine Sainte" in: *LMD* no. 45 p. 5.
304 Cf. ibid., p. 7.
305 Cf. "Liturgical Briefs" in: *Worship* vol. XXX pp. 157, 158.
306 *The Rites of Holy Week*, p. vi.
307 "The Decree *Maxima Redemptionis Mysteria*" in: *Liturgy* vol. XXV pp. 45, 52.
308 *Liturgy of the Roman Church*, p. 45. The appendices in this work entitled "The Restored Order of Holy Week" and "Solemn Easter Vigil" are useful summaries of the changes in the rites.
309 "The Renewed Good Friday Liturgy" in: *Worship* vol. XXXI p. 256.
310 The typescript reads "you."
311 E. Bliven, typewritten letter: 23 January 1956.

However Crichton recounts, with some relish, that making the reform mandatory was:

> Much to the dismay of some bishops...The then Archbishop of Dublin[312] went to Rome...and said "Our people in Ireland will not understand it." And Rome said to him: "Then teach them!" Cardinal Spellman of New York was on his way to Rome to stop it and it had already been published while he was upon high seas![313]

Bugnini is explicitly critical of aspects of the texts of the Chrism Mass, reconstructed by the commission[314] of which he was secretary:

> Some were classical and beautifully constructed; others were less satisfactory. The liturgists [after the Second Vatican Council] were rather critical of the formulary as a whole. They found fault with its poverty of ideas...[315]

Giampietro comments that Bugnini's reflections, which go on to describe the further reform of the rites following the Second Vatican Council, serve to demonstrate that "the changes made in the 1955 reform are fairly marginal, the fruit of a natural process of evolution."[316]

The *Brentwood Diocesan Report on the New Holy Week Liturgy*,[317] and the returns from the parishes from which it draws, give an insight into the reception of the reform at a local level. The diocese was assiduous in its preparation for Holy Week: "an early and detailed instruction was issued," discussion amongst priests "was encouraged, and deanery conferences were allowed to substitute such discussion for their normal theological cases for...February and March. Two talks were given...by the Very Reverend Father Illtud Evans OP."[318]

Of the ceremonies themselves, the "shortening and simplification of the blessing of palms...were unanimously welcomed by the clergy." The procession resulted in "differences of opinion;" however the emphasis on the kingship of Christ was "appreciated as a happy feature of this day's Liturgy."[319] Holy Thursday's *Missa in Cœna Domini* was "one

---

312 Archbishop John Charles McQuaid.

313 Interview by the author of J.D. Crichton, 24th August 1994.

314 N. Giampietro OFM Cap., *Il Card. Ferdinando Antonelli e gli sviluppi della riforma liturgica dal 1948 al 1970*, no. [372] indicates that Bea presented the texts to the Commission.

315 *TRL*, pp. 116-117.

316 "le modifiche apportate alla riforma del 1955 sono piuttosto marginali, frutto di un naturale processo evolutivo;" N. Giampietro OFM Cap., *Il Card. Ferdinando Antonelli e gli sviluppi della riforma liturgica dal 1948 al 1970*, p. 99.

317 Dated 16 July 1956. Cf also: Archives of the Diocese of Brentwood, Parish Reports: Holy Week 1956.

318 Ibid., p. 1.

319 Cf. ibid., p. 2.

of the high-lights of the week" with "reports of very much larger congregations" everywhere. "The number of communicants was a source of amazement to many of the clergy." However the report says of the washing of the feet: "it would seem that, as it was optional, it was not carried out in many places." The watch at the altar of repose enjoyed only mixed success.[320] The report makes a significant observation about the impact of the reform of Good Friday:

> When a sudden change takes place in a devotion that has captured the popular imagination, there must needs be some regret from the conservative-minded. So it was with the relegation of the Stations of the Cross to second place in the Good Friday programme.[321]

However, "the Good Friday afternoon Liturgy attracted the biggest crowds in the whole week" and "the number of communicants was phenomenally large." The "striking method" of venerating the cross and "the solemn setting for it, were much esteemed, but the length of the whole service was found very fatiguing."[322] The report even mentions a suggested rearrangement of the service to save time.[323] The paschal vigil, which by 1956 was not such a novelty, occasioned a more sober assessment:

> Those places where the Easter Vigil has been kept in the new form for some years say, that, while the Mass congregation remains fairly constant, there has been a falling-off of the number attending the entire ceremonies from the beginning, and nowhere did the congregations, though large, equal those of Thursday or Friday.[324]

Part of the problem, it was thought, was the timing of the Mass for midnight. The possibility of its celebration at an earlier hour, or even at dawn, were proposed. In respect of the rite itself, "there was unanimous agreement among the clergy about the wisdom in the reduction in number of the prophecies," and "the solemn renewal of baptismal vows was singled out for special praise."[325]

The report concludes that "the laity…demonstrated an interest in the *triduum sacrum* that perhaps they have never before had the chance to manifest" and that congregations came "not merely to watch a spectacle, but to take an active part in the sacred action," as was evidenced by the demand for books "giving the text and explanation of the new *Ordo*."[326]

---

[320] Cf. ibid., pp. 2-4.

[321] Ibid., p. 4.

[322] Cf. ibid., pp. 4-5.

[323] "First part: prostration and bidding prayers; Second part: Unveiling of cross & adoration during which the Passion is sung; Third part: Communion;" ibid., p. 5.

[324] Ibid., p. 6.

[325] Ibid.

[326] Ibid., p. 7.

There is little reason to suspect this report as untypical, and in assessing the 1955 reform of the rites of Holy Week, it would be ungenerous to suggest that it did not succeed in its stated pastoral aims.[327] The decline in enthusiasm for the paschal vigil, however, is not without interest in that it suggests that a certain amount of the reforms' popularity may be accorded to their novelty. By 1959 one American commentator would claim that "the restored Easter Vigil meets with quiet but stubborn resistance."[328]

The 1955 reform of Holy Week was certainly seen as the climax of some years of significant events in liturgical history. *Worship* commented:

> On the first day of the Church's new year, our Holy Father gave to the Catholic world the great gift of the restored Holy Week. On Christmas Day, he issued his new encyclical on sacred music. And on January 1, the revised *Ordo* for Mass and breviary went into effect. Together they constitute almost an embarrassment of riches to be assimilated. Their cumulative force will undoubtedly make the year 1955 stand out in the Church's history as the year of liturgical form.[329]

One speaker remarked at the opening of the 1956 North American Liturgical Week:

> Here in 1956, eleven years after the introduction of the Pius XII psalter, five years after the introduction of the restored Easter Vigil, thirteen years after *Mystici Corporis*, nine years after *Mediator Dei*, three years after *Christus Dominus* and the decree on evening Mass and the mitigated Eucharistic fast, half way through the first year of the first breviary reform, in the great year when Holy Week was restored—here in 1956, it is hard to reconstruct the attitude that was abroad toward the Liturgy before these things were known.[330]

And, as Crichton reflected in *Liturgy*:

> There seems to be a general sense of satisfaction (to put it at its lowest) with the reform. What is equally certain is that this change has brought the importance of the Liturgy to the notice of both clergy and people in a way that it has never been brought to them before. If the restored Liturgy is largely the fruit of the Liturgical Movement, it will

---

[327] Cf. E. O'Hara, "The Observance of Holy Week in the United States in 1956" and O. Spüllbeck, "The Celebration of the Restored Holy Week in East Germany" in: *AP* pp. 167-175 & pp. 176-185. Also: "Four Reports on Holy Week in Ireland" in: P. Murray OSB, *Studies in Pastoral Liturgy*, pp. 267-277; J. Challis, "Holy Week in Australian Parishes" Living Parish Series, *Living Parish Week*, pp. 83-100.

[328] D. Geaney, "Guarded Enthusiasm" in: *Worship* vol. XXXIII p. 419.

[329] Cf. "Liturgical Briefs" in: *Worship* vol. XXX p. 221.

[330] T. Carroll, "Liturgical Week: What is it?" in: The Liturgical Conference, *People's Participation and Holy Week: National Liturgical Week (USA) 1956*, pp. 8-9.

> also be the most powerful means for spreading that Movement until it has reached the most remote corners of the Church. If it was always true that the Liturgical Movement was not some specialist thing or cult, if it has clearly appeared that it was part of the mounting spiritual revival in the Church, it is now in the forefront of the Church's preoccupations and must be the concern of all, priest and people alike. Some few years ago we wrote that the Liturgical Movement existed only to wither away, to be absorbed into the life of the Church. That prospect is much nearer now than we dared to hope. A revitalised worship in which the people always play their full part, a Liturgy which is the indispensable source of the spirit of Christ and the principal means for the living out of the Christian life in the circumstances of the modern world, seems to be within measurable distance of achievement in our own time.[331]

Furthermore, in January 1956, Crichton felt free to speak publicly of "the general reform of the Roman rite now in progress."[332] Yet, amidst such enthusiasm and expectation, Löw sounded a note of warning (in the light of varying proposals received by the Pian commission with regard to the number of readings desirable for the paschal vigil):

> There unfortunately still exists a widespread liturgical subjectivism, by which of course a solid and serious reform may and can not be guided.[333]

Such subjectivism, by giving a disproportionate priority to contemporary desires in liturgical reform, could indeed render the general reform in progress in the 1950s something other than "solid and serious."

The Encyclical 'Musicæ Sacræ Disciplina'

The decree effecting the reform of Holy Week was swiftly followed by Pius XII's second, and now largely forgotten, liturgical encyclical *Musicæ Sacræ Disciplina.*[334] Given that this was the third restatement of the Church's principles on sacred music in fifty-three years (following St Pius X and Pius XI), it is clear that there was papal concern about trends in liturgical music throughout most of the twentieth century before the Second Vatican Council.

---

331 "Pastoral Reflections on the Restored Liturgy of Holy Week" in: *Liturgy* vol. XXV pp. 92-93.
332 "Notes and News" in: *Liturgy* vol. XXV p. 40.
333 "The New Holy Week Liturgy: A Pastoral Opportunity" in: *Worship* vol. XXX p. 113.
334 K. Seasoltz OSB, *The New Liturgy,* pp. 218-233; C. Braga CM, *Documenta,* pp. 861-877.

The encyclical does not concern itself with ritual reform *per se*. However it does speak of the development of sacred music. The principles that it articulates, though, are correlative to those of ritual reform.

It insists that traditional heritage of liturgical music must be preserved:

> It is the duty of all those to whom Christ the Lord has entrusted the task of guarding and dispensing the Church's riches to preserve [the] precious treasure of Gregorian chant diligently and to impart it generously to the Christian people...
>
> If in Catholic churches throughout the entire world Gregorian chant sounds forth without corruption or diminution, the chant itself, like the sacred Roman Liturgy, will have a characteristic of universality, so that the faithful, wherever they may be, will hear music that is familiar to them and a part of their own home. In this way, they may experience, with much spiritual consolation, the wonderful unity of the Church.[335]

This heritage is open to development in harmony with received Tradition:

> If, because of recently instituted feast days, new Gregorian melodies must be composed, this should be done by true masters of the art. It should be done in such a way that these new compositions obey the laws proper to genuine Gregorian chant and are in worthy harmony with the older melodies in their virtue and purity.[336]

The encyclical also demonstrates an openness to the wider development of liturgical music which, it says:

> Has gradually progressed from the simple and ingenuous Gregorian modes to great and magnificent works of art. To these works not only the human voice, but also the organ and other musical instruments add dignity, majesty, and a prodigious richness.
>
> We hope that the noble art of sacred music—adapted to contemporary conditions and in some way enriched—may ever more perfectly accomplish its mission.[337]

Yet, it also finds it necessary to assert that:

> The Church must insist that [sacred music] remain within its proper limits and must prevent anything profane and foreign from divine

---

[335] Ibid., pp. 225, 226.
[336] Ibid., p. 226.
[337] Ibid., pp. 221, 219.

> worship from entering into sacred music along with genuine progress, and perverting it.
>
> The Church must take the greatest care to prevent whatever might be unbecoming to sacred worship or anything that might distract the faithful in attendance from lifting up their minds to God, from entering into sacred music, which is the servant, as it were, of the Sacred Liturgy.[338]

The encyclical notes that "for serious reasons, some quite definite exceptions have been conceded" to the norm of Gregorian chant, but insists that they "are not extended and propagated more widely," and that where they are in use Gregorian melodies should be taught so that "the unity and universality of the Church may shine forth more powerfully every day."[339] Also, the practice, "according to old or immemorial custom" of singing popular vernacular hymns *at Mass* is allowed to continue where it is judged that the custom "cannot prudently be removed."[340]

The principles enunciated are clear: the Tradition is to be preserved and is open to developments that enrich the Tradition and that are in harmony with it. Contemporary fashions are excluded if they are profane, that is, if they are discordant with the purpose of liturgical music to lift up minds and hearts to Almighty God. The vernacular may be tolerated, but not in a way that prejudices the Church's musical patrimony, the essence of which is Gregorian chant.

These principles summarise the efforts of the Liturgical Movement with respect to sacred music, though at the time some regret was expressed that the encyclical offered "only cold comfort" to liturgists "awaiting a change in the Church's attitude to the use of the vernacular" in the Liturgy.[341] In the light of such desires, one may indeed view the encyclical as an apposite delineation of the nature of sacred music in the Roman rite.

Published in the shadow of the reform of Holy Week, the encyclical's lack of explicitly "pastoral" language similar to that of *Maxima redemptionis nostræ mysteria*, and of its accompanying instruction, is of interest. Firstly, the encyclical was a papal document and not the work of the Pian commission, though there may have been some coincidence of personnel in drafting. Alternatively, it may be an indication of divergent thinking within the Holy See itself as the work of liturgical reform progressed.

---

338 Ibid., pp. 221, 223.

339 Ibid., p. 226.

340 Ibid. Vernacular hymns in other contexts were encouraged.

341 Cf. L. Bévenot, "De Musicæ Sacræ Disciplina" in: *Liturgy* vol. XXV p. 83.

Secondly, the encyclical betrays a refreshing lack of self-consciousness with regard to the concept of "pastoral" Liturgy current amongst many reformers at the time. Its assumption is that the facilitation of the God-man encounter that is the very purpose of sacred music (indeed of all Liturgy), is of the essence of the life and work of the Church, including anything that one may distinguish as pastoral—though in the author's opinion no such absolute distinction is possible. One does not need to be self-consciously "pastoral" in order to serve the pastoral mission of the Church. Furthermore, the Liturgical Movement did not have to be concerned to be explicitly pastoral to be so in fact. Those in the Liturgical Movement who so self-consciously spoke of the "pastoral Liturgical Movement" risked subjectifying objective liturgical Tradition and refashioning it according to contemporary desires.[342] Such a path is alien to Pius XII's *Musicæ Sacræ Disciplina.*

The Assisi Congress, 1956

Annibale Bugnini CM believed that the September 1956 "International Congress of Pastoral Liturgy was, in God's plan, a dawn announcing a resplendent day that would have no decline."[343] The Assisi Congress,[344] he explains, is foundational in the history of the liturgical reforms following the Second Vatican Council:

> Who would have predicted at that time that three years later the greatest ecclesial event of the century, Vatican Council II, would be announced, in which the desires expressed at Assisi would be fulfilled, and this by means of the very men who were present at Assisi?[345]

According to Jungmann the Assisi Congress "revealed the pastoral aim" at the bottom of the "attempts at renewal" of the Liturgy.[346]

The Archbishop of Birmingham led the delegation from the English and Welsh hierarchy which included one other bishop and six priests. In the light of Bugnini's grandiloquence, the hierarchy's discussion of the congress appears remarkably bland.[347]

---

[342] For a late twentieth century view, cf. D. Sartore CSJ, "Pastoral Liturgy" in: A. Chupungco, *Handbook for Liturgical Studies,* vol. I pp. 65-95.

[343] *TRL* p. 11; "Esso fu, nei disegni di Dio, l'aurora che annuncia il giorno splendente, che non conoscerà tramonto;" *LRL* p. 27.

[344] Cf. S. Schmitt, *Die internationalen liturgischen Studientreffen 1951-1960,* pp. 200-240.

[345] *TRL* p. 11.

[346] "Constitution on the Sacred Liturgy" in: H. Vorgrimler, *Commentary on the Documents of Vatican II,* vol. I p. 3.

[347] Cf. 1956 minute from a meeting of the hierarchy, in the Archives of the Diocese of Brentwood, "Item no 5: Liturgical Conference at Assisi: Report." The document records, presumably in the light of the report of the episcopal delegates to the

Apart from numerous members of the hierarchy, including several Cardinals, the congress brought together prominent players in the Liturgical Movement: Capelle, Antonelli and Löw of the Sacred Congregation of Rites, Jungmann and Bea, Rousseau and others. Furthermore:

> Additional weight was given to the significance of the congress by the presence of officers and representative members of various national and regional liturgical committees and institutes; of professors of theology, pastoral and Liturgy from numerous universities and theological faculties; of most of the editors of liturgical periodicals; and of the majority of the recognised scholars, writers and pastoral leaders in the liturgical apostolate.[348]

Bugnini draws particular attention to the papers of Jungmann and Bea, stating that "the principles set forth in these addresses would be found again in the Constitution on the Liturgy" of the Second Vatican Council.[349] We have examined Jungmann's paper, "The Pastoral Idea in the History of the Liturgy,"[350] noting that his fundamental principle is an antiquarianism which disparages the organic development of the Liturgy beyond the fifth century, and which calls for a refashioning of the whole of the Liturgy according to the perceived needs of contemporary man.[351]

Augustine Bea SJ's paper, "The Pastoral Value of the Word of God in the Sacred Liturgy,"[352] was a specific consideration of the pastoral reform of part of the Liturgy: the proclamation of the Word of God. Bea asserted that:

> It is...clear that liturgical reform must...take into account the important element of the reading of the word of God in the sacred liturgical functions, and must do what is possible that from this reading the most abundant fruit be derived by the participants.[353]

Whilst the paper does not explicitly advocate the reading of Sacred Scripture in the vernacular, Bea's pastoral principle, that from the readings the most abundant fruit be derived by the participants, is certainly fundamental to any such argument. Bea does, however, repeat

---

Assisi congress, that "The Hierarchy was of the opinion that no changes should be made in the present language of the Mass and that consideration be given to the use of the vernacular for the prayers surrounding the Sacraments. It was suggested that a further petition be made for a concession in the fasting laws for nurses and other night workers."

348 *AP* p. xiii.

349 *TRL* p. 12.

350 Cf. *AP* pp. 18-31.

351 Cf. supra pp. 153ff.

352 Cf. *AP* pp. 74-90.

353 Ibid., p. 75.

the call made at Maria Laach in 1951 for an extension of the cycle of readings, for an increase in "the number of 'preachable' pericopes...either by introducing a three or four-year cycle, or in some other manner appropriate to the special needs and particular conditions of our times."[354] His reason is purely pastoral: this part of the rite of the Mass is of its nature didactic, and "it is a fact that for very many people today the Sunday and feast day Mass is the sole occasion for a religious instruction of any depth."[355]

We have no reason to deny Bea's assumption or his logic. Indeed, his reasoning is persuasive. And his proposal would give a greater measure of liturgical authenticity to the "Mass of the Catechumens." Of course, it would be possible to effect a pastoral reform of the cycle of readings that substantially departed from objective liturgical Tradition, as distinct from developing it, particularly if the traditional arrangement of the gospel pericopes was discarded. Such a case would reveal a pastoral expediency foreign to organic development.

Yet, as his paper calls for a development or enrichment of the Liturgy in response to contemporary needs, and does not seek the subjectivisation of objective liturgical Tradition, Bea's proposals may fall within the bounds of the organic development of the Liturgy. Furthermore, Bea explicitly and effectively answers the objection that such a reform might deprive "the Sacred Liturgy of its sublime dignity" and put it "at the service of men," (i.e. subjectivise it), by asserting the consonance with Tradition of such a reform, and by making the crucial distinction between those parts of the order of Mass which are of their very nature latreutic and those which are didactic.[356] Bea makes no call for the reform of any other part of the Liturgy.

We may say, then, that Bea's pastoral principle has a validity that lies in its desire for liturgical authenticity and for the development of objective liturgical Tradition. As such it is consonant with the ideals of the Liturgical Movement, and indeed with the definition of pastoral Liturgy given by Cardinal Cicognani, Prefect of the Sacred Congregation of Rites, at the opening of the congress:

> The aim of pastoral Liturgy is precisely that of leading the faithful to form a closely-knit union in the Mystical Body of which Christ is the Head, and to participate *æquo modo,* according to one's station, in the liturgical rites.[357]

---

354 Ibid., pp. 85-86.
355 Ibid., p. 85.
356 Cf. ibid., p. 86.
357 Ibid., p. 5.

Of the other papers presented at Assisi, Dom Capelle's "The Pastoral Theology of the Encyclicals *Mystici Corporis* and *Mediator Dei*,"[358] is of importance. Capelle expounds the connection and the pastoral nature of the theology of the Church as the Mystical Body of Christ and liturgical piety. It is a classical presentation of the ideals of the Liturgical Movement at the beginnings of which, his audience is reminded, he was present.[359] Capelle speaks of the nature of the Liturgy and of liturgical reform:

> From the fact that the Liturgy is essentially a living reality, we must conclude that it would be intolerable if anyone, for merely archaeological reasons, were to set himself to eliminate all that has been added or changed through the centuries under the pressure of circumstances or of pastoral necessities; for the law of adaptation affects everything that, here below, wishes to remain alive.[360]

Again we see the possibility of development hand in hand with respect for past developments, however 'late' these developments are.

Capelle lauds the restoration of Holy Week, and the action of St Pius X in restoring the reception of Holy Communion to children. His emphasis on "restoration"[361] includes the assertion that authentic liturgical reform may even abolish what are in fact "abuses," even when such abuses or inauthentic practices have "become traditional over many intervening centuries."[362] Such purges from the Liturgy of longstanding practices that, given the nature of the Liturgy and of the essential place of liturgical piety in the life of the Christian, are indeed abuses (the celebration of the paschal vigil in the morning, or the widespread withholding of sacramental communion being prime examples), are consonant with the principles of liturgical reform, as they are corrections that restore to objective liturgical Tradition lost vitality. Such corrections truly serve the pastoral mission of the Church.

Johannes Wagner presented a paper "Liturgical Art and the Care of Souls,"[363] in which he asserts that:

> The Church's great liturgical services, such as the Mass-Liturgy (as a whole, even if not in all its details) or large parts of the divine office constitute splendid works of art, and that individually...include an astonishing wealth of true masterpieces of poetry and music...

---

[358] Cf. ibid., pp. 32-43.
[359] Cf. ibid., p. 32.
[360] Ibid., pp. 37-38.
[361] B. Capelle OSB refers to "the revealing title" of the "recent reform of Holy Week:" "Ordo Hebdomadæ Sanctæ *Instauratus*;" emphasis added. Cf. ibid., p. 38
[362] Cf. ibid.
[363] Cf. ibid., pp. 57-73.

> But not only the muses of the poetic and musical arts contributed to the unfolding and beautifying of the Liturgy. The muse of the dance, Terpischore, also had a contribution...the measured pomp of entrance and exit, the entire play of meaningful motion that characterises solemn liturgical functions, the processions and other movements around the altar and in the sanctuary.[364]

Wagner's appreciation of the developed beauty of the Liturgy does not prevent him from asserting that:

> It is not possible today without qualifications to praise the Liturgy as a whole and in all its parts as being in every respect a perfect work of art—as was customary, for instance, in liturgical textbooks of a not very distant past. As a result of more scholarly study...the conviction forces itself upon one that certain rites—particularly some of those in the pontifical and in the ritual—are not constructed in an especially artistic manner, nor even in a manner that aptly suits their pastoral purpose.[365]

This raises the question of whether liturgical scholarship's analysis of the components has destroyed the appreciation of the whole. Wagner, at least in speaking of the pastoral purpose of the rites, is advocating authentic reform along the lines of Capelle, and this is to be welcomed. However the weight he gives to "scholarly study" is significant, particularly since he became a key technician in the implementation of the Second Vatican Council.[366]

Missionary Bishop Wilhelm van Bekkum SVD, presented a paper "The Liturgical Revival in the Service of the Missions,"[367] in which a persuasive argument is put for the value to be gained from restoring the prayer of the faithful and the offertory procession to the rite of Mass, at least in mission countries.[368] He also argues for the possibility of further adaptation of the rite "penetrating more deeply into the entire communal and cultural life of the new converts." He adds:

> Let it be said at the outset that these adaptations and adoptions, as we envisage them, do not imply revolutionary changes in the Liturgy. The

---

364 Ibid., p. 61.

365 Ibid., pp. 60-61.

366 Wagner's paper also contains an assertion, accurate in 1956, which, given the state of liturgical art in the Roman rite today, is interesting: "In its actual historical development, the Liturgy has never been a tyrannical mistress of the arts, a mistress who according to whim will today compel her maids—slaves, rather than noble servants—to unwilling servitude, and tomorrow roughly dismiss them entirely from the house..." ibid., p. 59.

367 Cf. ibid., pp. 95-112.

368 Cf. ibid., pp.102-104.

> alterations which, in our opinion, would be concerned are of comparative insignificance.[369]

The alterations called for are: the use of the vernacular in the readings, the possibility of vernacular hymns for the people at Latin High Mass, a revival of the diaconate and a renewal of the minor orders, and the possibility of reflecting healthy elements of indigenous culture in vestments and architecture.[370]

Such proposals for what has become known as liturgical inculturation (though its contemporary proponents would be unlikely to be satisfied with these alterations, which nonetheless were of comparative significance in 1956!) raise few if any problems for the liturgical historian. As he makes clear, van Bekkum is not advocating a "revolutionary change" of the rite for mission countries. He seeks its adaptation, and indeed its enhancement, in some areas. It is possible that his proposals might well have lead to taking the first steps along paths leading to the development of new ritual uses for the liturgical family that is the Roman rite. Provided that substantial unity is maintained, the uses of Lyons, Milan, and Braga provide ample precedent for allowing the introduction of suitable local customs provided, in the words of van Bekkum, that "nothing must be allowed to get into the Liturgy which is not fitting."[371]

Dom Oliver Rousseau's paper, "Pastoral Liturgy and the Eastern Liturgies,"[372] recounted:

> A great promoter of pastoral Liturgy, but one who is perhaps too much inclined to do away with formulas and actions now lacking in immediate practical intelligibility for the people, confided to us a short time ago that a journey to Egypt and some contact with the ceremonies of the Eastern Rites had revealed to him a sense of mystery previously undreamed of.

To this revealing anecdote, Rousseau appended the following prophetic caution:

> Let us take care lest steps too hastily taken do not one day cause us to regret that we did not sufficiently take this sense into account.[373]

The essential point of Rousseau's paper, situated in the midst of the Movement's phase of "pressure for reform," can be said to be that the West must recover what he calls "the liturgical spirit," indeed, liturgical piety. He offers an eloquent account of its reality in the East:

---

369 Ibid., p. 104.
370 Cf. ibid., pp. 109-112.
371 Ibid., p. 108.
372 Cf. ibid., pp. 113-127.
373 Ibid., pp. 121-122.

> Their spiritual life is formed essentially by the Liturgy, by assisting at the unfolding of the drama of redemption, centred around the paschal mystery. Religious instruction is carried out almost entirely by way of infusing into their souls the dynamism of the Catholic life, of their having been baptised and having risen with Christ. The Liturgy has remained in these regions precisely what it should be according to the definition of Pius XI: the teaching (*didascalia*) of the Church, the concrete exercise of her magisterium. The people assist at the Liturgy simply by listening, without books, to the words of the prayers or the lessons recited aloud or chanted by the priest, the deacon and the ministers, and by responding: thus they take part in a sacred dialogue, and do so in a language often very close to their own...For them the Christian life is in a practical way liturgical life which, penetrating their hearts, forms their faith.[374]

As we have seen, Rousseau has a healthy distrust for reform that does away with "formulas and actions now lacking in immediate practical intelligibility for the people." For Rousseau, and we maintain for the Liturgical Movement properly so called, it is people and culture who must first be formed or indeed reformed to foster liturgical piety. Ritual developments are secondary, and are more judiciously posited when this priority is respected.

Father Antonelli's paper, "The Liturgical Reform of Holy Week: Importance, Realisations, Perspectives,"[375] discusses the principles behind the main achievement of the Pian commission, and its view of prospective reform. Of the reform of Holy Week, Antonelli acknowledges that:

> By their antiquity and the richness of their content these sacred rites and their formularies represent the most precious part of the whole liturgical patrimony. Hence we can readily suppose what a heavy responsibility weighed on those who were called upon to take action in regard to so venerable a liturgical heritage.

However, he continues:

> A revision was imperative. Over the course of centuries some precious elements were inevitably lost, many had been deformed, others were added or superimposed without adequate reason; besides, formalism had taken over the ceremonies, creating an artificial climate, quite the opposite of that immediate intuition of every liturgical function which is the indispensable condition for an active, enlightened participation of the faithful.[376]

---

374 Ibid., pp. 122-123.
375 Cf. ibid., pp. 149-166.
376 Ibid., p. 151.

To this, Antonelli adds the necessity of correcting the incongruity of the celebration of the liturgies of the Easter Triduum in the morning, before asserting that the reform carried out by the commission followed two criteria:

> Scrupulous faithfulness on the one hand to the best liturgical traditions, and on the other, sensitivity to pastoral interests.[377]

Antonelli manifests an awareness of the complexity inherent in fidelity to liturgical Tradition. This, he asserts, involves making use of "the advances in liturgical history and the critical edition of the principal ancient texts" to correct the situation whereby, "the rites and the texts" which "took shape in the classical period of the Liturgy:"

> Underwent modifications which were often unfortunate: precious elements were lost, others were deformed, more often superstructures were introduced that were out of proportion and out of place.[378]

There is no doubt that this position reflects the influence of Jungmann's corruption theory, and is capable of deprecating all liturgical development beyond whichever period scholarly convention declares "classical." However, if we recall the overall proportionality of the 1955 reform of Holy Week, and note that Antonelli speaks in his paper of the work of reform as being "a cautious revision of this whole complex reality,"[379] we see that, at least in this instance, the untraditional implications inherent in any unbridled application of such antiquarianism, have, on the whole, been guarded against.

"Sensitivity to pastoral interests" is the second of the criteria. The commission, Antonelli explains, held that:

> The Liturgy is not a museum of archaeological exhibits. It is the expression—very much alive—of the Church; and life is not static. Aside from being a worship of the majesty of God, the Liturgy is a school of Christian life; and in a school the pupil must be able to understand and follow the lesson. The Liturgy is also a religious pedagogy, and the layman must be helped by means of the gestures and formulas to penetrate and re-live the mysteries of the redemption.
>
> In short, that the Liturgy may be, as it should, both worship of God and a school of pedagogy of Christian life, it is necessary that the faithful be able to take an active, conscious part in it. In the liturgical action they are never mere spectators, but actors.[380]

---

377 Ibid., p. 152.

378 Ibid.

379 Ibid.

380 Ibid., p. 153. The context of this text rules out any interpretation that supports either the liturgical activism or the liturgical didacticism which have plagued the Roman rite following the reforms of Paul VI.

Antonelli states that actual participation is at the heart of the work of the commission:

> The reform of the Liturgy must aim in the first place at bringing back the faithful to an active, informed participation in the celebration of the sacred mysteries. To attain this end the people must be able to see, understand and follow the development of the action; their interest must be aroused and they must be led to perform their part. And this is precisely a return to antiquity.[381]

We can see, therefore, that the real intention of the reform, in Antonelli's mind, is to restore liturgical piety to its fundamental place in Christian life. This is not liturgical or ritual antiquarianism: it is recovering and restoring something essential to the life of the Christian. Matters of ritual reform are secondary, though correlative.

Antonelli's paper moves beyond consideration of the reform of Holy Week to speak of "the liturgical reform in general."[382] The reforms eliminating the priest duplicating texts read by another minister, and the insistence on a real pause for silent prayer after the deacon's invitation to kneel in the solemn intercessions of Good Friday, are said to be "examples indicative of the future" that "could be multiplied."[383]

But Antonelli does not see such laudable returns to an authenticity in liturgical practices as the aim of the general liturgical reform:

> The liturgical reform does not consist only, or even principally, in a revision of texts and rubrics, the search for worthier and more expressive aesthetic forms. Nor does the reform end with simplifications, abbreviations or emendations. The true aim of the liturgical reform looks much farther, beyond any outward expression, and wants to reach the soul, in order to work in its depths and incite a spiritual renewal in Christ, the High Priest, from whom every liturgical action acquires its value and efficacy.[384]

And, in a passage that might have been written by St Pius X, Beauduin, Guardini or Parsch, he maintains:

> The people have been separated, unfortunately, from the true liturgical life. A patient work of re-education, spiritual and technical, is needed to bring them back to an active, enlightened, personal, communitarian participation. This is a work that is not done in a year. It may require generations. But it must begin.[385]

---

381 Ibid., p. 154.
382 Ibid., p. 162.
383 Ibid., p. 155.
384 Ibid., p. 162.
385 Ibid., p. 165.

"Italy's nonconformist cardinal,"[386] Giacomo Lercaro, Archbishop of Bologna, presented a paper on "The Simplification of the Rubrics and the Breviary Reform."[387] He explains that in the 1955 reform, the intention of the commission:

> Was not to take immediately in hand a radical reform—which would have undoubtedly required a very long time—but to prune the complicated mass of the rubrics, by the suppression of adventitious elements less in tune with the spirit and the laws of liturgical style: in a word, by simplifying.[388]

Lercaro then employed a telling analogy to describe this simplification:

> The same thing had happened to the poem of the Divine Office as had happened so often to the fine Romanesque and Gothic basilicas, where the piety of succeeding generations had made additions which were also discordant and out of tune: to such an extent as to obscure the beauty of the simple and harmonious architectonic line and to clutter up the building with a farrago of decorations, of altars, of statues.
>
> Someone might think the removal of all this superstructure and the banishment of the statues and the altars an unseemly act when one considered the piety of those who had gathered them there and of those who had venerated them.
>
> But it is certainly reasonable and fitting to give back its beauty of line to the basilica, and to restore it to its native simplicity. In much the same way, it has appeared reasonable and fitting to remove from the Divine Office superstructures introduced very late without the guiding hand of vigilant liturgical sense, the effect of which was to crush its lines, and very often without the advantage, enjoyed perhaps at their introduction, of responding to a vital need of piety.[389]

It is clear from its context that this analogy refers to the simplification of the rubrics, the intention of which was to restore the predominance of the temporal cycle over the sanctoral, and to the pruning of late additions to the office, which we have considered above.[390] It does not refer to a substantial reform of the structure of the rites themselves.

Even so, the analogy goes much further than did the 1955 simplification of the rubrics, and for that may be said to be somewhat

---

386 P. Lesourd, *Giacomo Cardinal Lercaro,* p. 7. Lesourd continues: "Lercaro is ...identified with the critical, restless, *avant garde* in Italian Catholicism. He represents the 'advanced' line within the Sacred College."

387 *AP,* pp. 203-219.

388 Ibid., p. 204.

389 Ibid., pp. 204-205.

390 Cf. supra pp. 196ff.

inapplicable. Furthermore, the desire to clear out everything alien to its "native simplicity," is precisely that behind antiquarianism in its denial of legitimate organic development. Even considered in its context, one may ask whether Lercaro's zeal does not come dangerously close to ignoring this fundamental principle of liturgical reform. That this should emerge at the Assisi Congress from so prominent a speaker is a clear indication that, in contradistinction to those, like Antonelli above, who advocated the growth of liturgical piety through gradual reform, there were some at least implicitly advocating radical ritual reform. In this Lercaro must be grouped with Jungmann.

Lercaro's paper proceeds to apply this analogy, and in some ways goes beyond it, in a call for a comprehensive structural reform of the breviary. In Lercaro's vision, the breviary would differ according to the distinction between monastic and non-monastic office, and between the public or private celebration of the office.[391] Like many before him, Lercaro is motivated by a desire to lighten the burden of the office for the pastoral clergy by simplifying it. Some of his proposals arise from pastoral expediency: the possibility of making some hours optional in the office of pastoral clergy, a two or four week psalter, the abolition of the *capitulum* at the little hours, etc. Others seek to restore elements lost in liturgical history: the correction of Urban VIII's reform of the hymns, the solemn singing of the *Pater Noster* at Lauds and Vespers etc.

In so far as this is not simply a call for the removal of "superstructure" added in the course of centuries, or for a correction of inauthentic practices, its principle is more radical than that at the heart of his analogy. Lercaro shows little concern to *restore* the breviary. Rather, as did many from Cardinal Quignonez through to St Pius X, he is willing to *reconstruct* the office according to his perception of pastoral need.

Lercaro's paper was the most explicitly reformist of the Assisi Congress. In 1956 such words may not have been tolerated other than from the lips of a Cardinal. Yet they were uttered, giving eminent expression to a view of "pastoral Liturgy" which shows insufficient respect for the organic development of objective liturgical Tradition. In his view, the Liturgy is a pastoral tool, and its forms are subject to reconstruction in order to achieve pastoral ends. In the history of the Liturgical Movement, Lercaro was the most senior member of the hierarchy to express this view. That he should do so at Assisi would not have been without its influence. Given the office Lercaro would occupy in the future,[392] it is not without significance.[393]

---

[391] Cf. *AP* pp. 210-217.

[392] President of the Post-Conciliar *Consilium* from 1964-1968. Tracey Rowland has recently drawn attention to Lercaro's devaluation of the Church's cultural patrimony expressed in the Conciliar debate on *Gaudium et Spes*; cf. *Culture and the Thomist Tradition*, pp. 27-29, 175-176.

Assisi saw the unambiguous assertion of the authority of the Holy See in matters of liturgical reform. Cardinal Cicognani, Prefect of the Sacred Congregtion of Rites, declared in the opening address:

> The essential end of this congress is to pass in review the admirable initiatives of Pope Pius XII in the field of pastoral Liturgy and to pass them in review with the spirit of loyalty and reverence which every one of the faithful ought to nourish toward the Supreme Shepherd who guides us. The Liturgy demands precisely the direction of the Supreme Shepherd...
>
> Debates are not permitted by the very character of this congress, which is eminently hierarchical. Moreover, we have come together not to study problems or to propose reforms, but to put into relief, in their vast and many-sided frame, the laws and ordinances emanating from Pope Pius XII in his untiring activity as father and master. And when the armed forces pass in review, there are salutes and applause, especially when they are wonderfully equipped, as in the present case...
>
> Looking over the documents which integrate this liturgical period, we have been able to notice that His Holiness welcomes with delicate courtesy what the students of the Liturgy present or indicate; but in virtue of the supreme power which belongs only to him, it is the Pope who fixes the principles; giving secure and firm orientations to minds and spirits, he puts them on guard against opinions not in conformity with the aim of the spiritual life.[394]

This reflects the extent of the power accorded the papacy in matters of liturgical reform at the time. One may ask whether all participants, particularly those engaged in "pressure for reform," saw the congress as primarily an occasion for such ultramontane congratulation? It is true that Cicognani acknowledged that "various committees" at the congress may well engage in "private and unofficial discussions" and draw up "conclusions to be submitted to the ecclesiastical authority."[395] In the

---

393 In 1955 Lercaro read a paper "The Christian Church" in which he emphasises that liturgical Tradition should adapt itself to and express itself in the forms of the present age: "True Tradition allows the Liturgy to express itself in the language proper to every age...;" "the spirit of the Liturgy, while it maintains its principles unchanged, ensures that the prayer of man should reflect the continuous development of the human spirit;" cf. *The Furrow* June 1957, pp. 346-347. Lercaro's emphasis on the liturgical accommodation of "today" appears to go beyond a recognition that the Liturgy develops and risks propagating a naïvely optimistic anthropocentrism which subjectivises objective liturgical Tradition and allows for its reconstruction according to the preferences of each passing age.

394 *AP* pp. 6-7.

395 Ibid., p. 7.

light of his view of the nature of the congress, one wonders what the Cardinal made of Bea's, van Bekkum's, or Lercaro's explicitly reformist papers.

One of Cicognani's statements epitomises the extent to which ultramontanism and papal centralism had assumed absolute control of the development of the Roman rite: "it is the Pope who fixes the principles." Of course, no Catholic can deny the right and duty of the Bishop of Rome to make prudential judgements pertaining to the development of the Liturgy of the Western patriarchate, and indeed to supervise and even to initiate developments in accordance with the principles of liturgical development. However, as we have noted, it is only in the twentieth century that popes begin to perceive their authority with regard to liturgical reform as absolute and so extensive that it could stand above, and not in humble respect before, objective liturgical Tradition. Cicognani's address may be said to give this attitude its consummate expression. Pius XII's exercise of his authority, as we have maintained thus far, on the whole respected the limits imposed by the principles of liturgical reform. Yet, it must be repeated, such a distorted view of the extent of papal authority in matters of liturgical reform, and the uncritical acclamation it was accorded (there is no evidence of any dissent in liturgical writing of the time), was patently capable of manipulation and abuse.

Indeed, the congress was brought to a conclusion not in Assisi, but in Rome, where Pius XII delivered an allocution to its participants.[396] He is generous in his praise of the Liturgical Movement:

> If one compares the present state of the Liturgical Movement with what it was thirty years ago, it is obvious that undeniable progress has been made both in extent and in depth. The interest brought to the Liturgy, the practical accomplishments and the active participation of the faithful have developed to an extent unthought of at that time...
>
> The Liturgical Movement is thus shown forth as a sign of the providential dispositions of God for the present time, of the movement of the Holy Ghost in the Church, to draw men more closely to the mysteries of the faith and the riches of grace which flow from the active participation of the faithful in the liturgical life.[397]

Pius XII reasserts the authority of the papacy over the Liturgy, and the supervisory rôle of bishops:

> It belongs to the popes to examine current forms of worship, to introduce new ones and to regulate the arranging of worship, and to

[396] Cf. ibid., pp. 223-236.
[397] Ibid., pp. 223-224.

> the bishops to watch carefully that the canonical prescriptions relating to divine worship are observed.[398]

He also settled the debate about sacramental concelebration of the Mass which had emerged at the Mont-César Conference in 1954,[399] and deprecated the trend to separate the tabernacle from the altar at which Mass is celebrated as separating "two things which should remain united by their origin and their nature."[400]

The allocution concluded by speaking of the development of the Liturgy, carefully balancing what he called "two extreme attitudes with regard to the past: a blind attachment and a complete contempt,"[401] and stating that "the Liturgy today admits of a preoccupation with progress, but also of conservation and defence."[402] In other words, Pius XII regards the objective Traditional Liturgy as capable of development and enrichment, by way of restoring or drawing from past practices, whilst conserving its substance. Thus he is able to allow pastoral adaptations, along the lines of the reforms we have considered above. Yet his use of the term "defence"[403] makes clear, as in *Mediator Dei,* his awareness of tendencies that would do damage to the objective liturgical Tradition.

Diekmann's report, "Assisi in Retrospect,"[404] reported, somewhat enthusiastically:

> The presence of so many members of the hierarchy from so many countries, or Cardinals and their delegates, and of officials of the SRC, constituted the greatest single encouragement ever given to the Liturgical Movement—apart, of course, from *Mediator Dei* and the other papal initiatives.[405]

He observed that:

> The presence at Assisi of the Holy See's officially appointed committee for the revision of the missal and breviary, several of whom were on the programme, would seem to suggest, moreover, that the voice of Assisi may find some echo in the realisation of that revision. And yet the Holy Father himself did not speak to us of liturgical restoration in terms of future reforms. Instead, he referred us back to *Mediator Dei.* In that, he insisted, you will find your programme of action.[406]

---

398 Ibid., p. 227.
399 Cf. ibid., pp. 228-231.
400 Ibid., p. 234.
401 Ibid., p. 235.
402 Ibid., p. 236.
403 The original was French, and the word used is "défense;" cf. C. Braga CM, *Documenta,* p. 897.
404 *Worship* vol. XXXI pp. 48-52.
405 Ibid., p. 51.
406 Ibid.

Diekmann's report errs in one substantial point. The congress was not, as he asserted, "convoked by the Sacred Congregation of Rites."[407] As Löw of the Sacred Congregation of Rites makes clear in his own report, it:

> Was not "official" in the strict sense of the word; above all it was not officially convoked by the "Holy See," by the "Vatican" or by the "Congregation of Rites." The organisers...were the four "centres" of liturgical effort in Germany, France, Italy and Switzerland.[408]

Löw's article goes to some length to temper the enthusiasm about Assisi, of which Diekmann is an exemplar:

> The author of this essay is no prophet, and there would be very little sense in his stating boldly that the congress of Assisi will be the norm and guide of liturgical reforms through years and decades to come, that it has initiated a new era, that it indicates a new liturgical deal...
>
> Ultimately, the congress provided only a survey, a summary of all that through the years has been in the process of re-appraisal and change...The general Liturgical Movement, which is radiating ever more widely...is not a self-contained development. It is conditioned, obviously, by the leadership that papal authority has exercised in the field. And only from this authority and from its repeated directives which clearly indicate goals to be attained, has it achieved that impelling force which we see in action everywhere today.
>
> The congress of Assisi, therefore, was above all a rallying point which permitted a systematic survey of the whole vast domain of the Liturgy of the Roman Church, in order to become aware of what is planned, what attained, what already won, and also what is still to be striven for—not so much through *demands coming from without* but rather because of *insights derived from the Liturgy itself.* Such insights will clarify immediate tasks and goals, and once these have been achieved, new and further goals and tasks may be determined, in so far as the highest authority of the Church shall consider good and necessary.[409]

Löw's balance and reserve probably came too late to correct popular opinion, given that, as Diekmann reported, in the immediate wake of Assisi, "every Catholic paper in the country exploded with lengthy stories about the liturgical reform."[410] The generation of a climate of expectation, whereby reform could be seen as a response to "demands coming from without," posed a risk to an authoritative programme of gradual renewal where, in Löw's apposite words, reforms grew from

---

[407] Ibid., p. 49.
[408] "Assisi 1956 and Holy Week 1957" in: *Worship* vol. XXXI p. 236.
[409] Ibid., pp. 239-240.
[410] "Assisi in Retrospect" in: *Worship* vol. XXXI p. 48.

"insights derived from the Liturgy itself." This fundamental distinction was, perhaps, somewhat blurred following the Assisi Congress, at least in the popular mind. Indeed, such loud talk of reform may well have led to the Liturgical Movement being seen by those who had not previously studied it as primarily a movement for ritual reform, obscuring its fundamental aim of promotion of liturgical piety. This would, in part, explain Löw's corrective stance.

J.B. O'Connell, one of the English delegation at Assisi, spoke of reform in his report of the congress, but in measured tones:

> We trust, as we believe that [the congress']...labours will lead to an increasing knowledge, appreciation and love of the Sacred Liturgy on our part; on the part of the Church, in its supreme wisdom, to a continuation of the reform of the rubrics so well begun and to further measures to promote still more the active participation of the people in the worship of the Mystical Body, "the first and indispensable source of the true Christian spirit" (St Pius X).[411]

One voice was never heard at Assisi, that of a speaker whose sentiment reflects some of the equilibrium of the Liturgical Movement in its origins. It said: "the congress of Assisi must awaken an echo, not a revolutionary one, but one that will have enduring effects."[412] It is most ironic that Lercaro—the speaker advocating the most radical reforms—should have chosen to quote these words in his closing address.[413] This irony in some way reflects a dichotomy in the aspirations and work of the Liturgical Movement, which is visible at Assisi. Bugnini,[414] as we have seen above, referred to Assisi over twenty years later as a dawn announcing a resplendent day. The question remains: whether and to what extent did this dawn herald new growth, or revolution?

The 1957 Decree on the Tabernacle and the Altar

Following Assisi, and Pius XII's reference to the position of the tabernacle in his allocution at the close of the congress, a decree of the Sacred Congregation of Rites, *Sanctissimam Eucharistiam,* was published to clarify the regulations regarding the relationship between the tabernacle and the altar.[415] In one sense it is an un-noteworthy decree,

---

411 "The International Liturgical Congress at Assisi," in: *The Clergy Review,* vol. XLI no. 11, p. 649.

412 The words of Bishop Wilhelm Weskamm of Berlin who was to address the Congress but who died beforehand. Cf. *AP* p. xv.

413 Cf. ibid., p. 222.

414 Secretary of the Post-Conciliar *Consilium* of which Lercaro was President.

415 Cf. K. Seasoltz OSB, *The New Liturgy,* pp. 251-252; C. Braga CM, *Documenta,* pp. 908-909.

reasserting the ruling that the tabernacle must be fixed to the main altar of the Church—or to another suitable altar in Cathedral, collegiate, conventual or pilgrimage churches—at which Holy Mass must be habitually celebrated.

However, the decree specifically states that:

> In churches where there is only one altar, this may not be so constructed that the priest celebrate facing the people…
>
> Strictly forbidden are eucharistic tabernacles which are placed off the altar itself, for example in the wall, or beside or behind the altar, or in niches or columns separated from the altar.[416]

Löw, in a commentary published alongside the decree in *Worship*, explains the reason for the decree:

> The decree…very firmly indicates anew the regulations concerning the tabernacle already in force. And it does so because certain new trends in the building of churches and altars had finally to be met with a clear and authoritative statement of principles.
>
> Whoever has some acquaintance with recent churches or with older churches that have been renovated will very probably have sensed that everything is not quite as it should be in regard to the building of tabernacles. For one thing, there are at work certain speculative theological tendencies, sometimes associated with leftist pastoral-liturgical views. There is the desire, too, to be absolutely "modern" in church building, or rather, to create something never created before, lest one be tagged "traditionalist"…[417]
>
> Some persons give all too free reign to a desire for innovation or to a striving after "what has never been done before." The Church certainly does not deny genuine art its rights and she wants to progress with the times; she has given ample proof of that. But at the same time she insists on retaining certain sacred and legitimate forms and formulas based on sound Tradition, especially if there is a question of dogmatic content which may be endangered when translated into concrete external forms.[418]

Given that these are the words of an official of the Sacred Congregation of Rites, and a member of the Pian commission, they give this small decree a certain significance. We have seen that Löw is not opposed to liturgical reform, indeed here he speaks of "progress with the times." However he also speaks of the Church "retaining certain sacred and legitimate forms and formulas based on sound Tradition." In this

---

416 Seasoltz, ibid., p. 252.

417 "Tabernacle and Altar: Commentary" in: *Worship* vol. XXXI pp. 572-573.

418 Ibid., pp. 578-579.

instance it is the centrality of the cult of the tabernacle as opposed to the fashion to promote the celebration of Mass facing the people. The principle he enunciates is key. In the context of the publication of this decree we find an acknowledgement that liturgical development is possible, but that such development is limited by a respect for "sacred and legitimate forms and formulas based on sound Tradition:" objective liturgical Tradition. In other words, organic development is possible, but radical innovation is excluded.

That the Holy See should find it necessary to 'apply the brakes' in 1957 is itself evidence that the operation of "pastoral liturgists" without sufficient regard for objective liturgical Tradition was a significant and perhaps growing problem at the time. This decree, the details of which were found "puzzling" by Diekmann,[419] stands as a corrective amidst the continuing "pressure for liturgical reform."[420]

The 1957 Consultation on Breviary Reform

In 1957 the Sacred Congregation of Rites published *Supplemento IV* to the *Memoria* containing the results of a world-wide consultation of the episcopate (by means of a letter to 400 Metropolitan Archbishops), on the reform of the breviary.[421] Signed by Antonelli, the document is the result of the work of Bugnini and Braga, and drafting by Löw.[422]

The consultation, which asked for the bishops' suggestions but which offered no proposals for their evaluation, achieved an 85% response. The responses were wide-ranging, and a summary demonstrates that there was certainly no convergence of episcopal opinion in matters of breviary reform at the time. The most popular suggestion, which came from only 23.2% of the respondents, was for the simplification of breviary hymns. A desire for the use of the vernacular was expressed by 17.9%, however 11.1% of the respondents specifically requested the retention of Latin.[423] Other suggestions were quite varied.

The analysis published by the Sacred Congregation of Rites asserts the popularity of the 1955 simplification of the rubrics and calendar, and envisages further reform along these lines. It also points to

---

419 Cf. "Liturgical Briefs," in: *Worship* vol. XXXI pp. 611ff.

420 That Richstatter's *Liturgical Law* omits any reference to this decree results in a one-sided portrayal of the direction being taken by liturgical reform and liturgical law at the time.

421 *Memoria sulla Riforma Liturgica: Supplemento IV – Consultazione dell'Episcopato Intorno alla Riforma del Breviario Romano (1956-1957) Risultati e Deduzioni.*

422 Cf. ibid., pp. 56-57.

423 Cf. ibid., p. 13.

the desire ever present in liturgical history: to reduce the burden of the Office on clergy. It also details other suggestions.[424]

Significantly, the proposals for structural reform of the Office are analysed. Only 6% advocate radical structural reform, with a further 1.6% advocating some significant change. Over 52% wish the retention of the traditional structure of the Office, of which over 48% are open to making sensible or opportune adaptations. The silence of a further 39.4% on the question of structural reform is presumed to indicate their contentment with the existing form.[425] This leads the commission to conclude that the liturgical reform should follow the traditional structure of the Office and respect its nature, while preserving the necessary freedom to make minor adaptations and renewals in the light of the condition of the Office, the exigencies of modern times, and the proposals received.[426] This is yet another articulation of the principle of organic development, some six years before the opening of the Second Vatican Council, demonstrating respect for objective liturgical Tradition while at the same time being open to development.

A significant reference is also made to the need to reform the mentality of priests with regard to the Office. The attitude that regards it purely as an obligation to be discharged must be corrected so that the Office becomes the prayer of the priest throughout the day.[427] Such a reform, of attitude and not primarily of rite, reflects the primary objective of the Liturgical Movement. It is, perhaps, telling that such a reform should still be considered necessary as late as 1957.

The *Supplemento* includes extracts from the responses from the bishops. One, from Bishop Charrière of Lausanne, Geneva and Fribourg, stands out for its length and for his assertion of the need of continuity in liturgical reform. Charrière, while open to the use of the vernacular in parts of the Liturgy, warns against placing too much emphasis on it in the liturgical reform, and asserts the necessity of "strongly protecting the overall tranquillity of the Latin Liturgy."[428] He is critical of Lercaro's Assisi proposals for the reform of the Office as leading towards an untraditional division between the Office of the secular and of the regular clergy, and of beginning a trend of abbreviation that he believes will

---

[424] Cf. ibid., pp. 16-24.

[425] Cf. ibid., p. 36.

[426] Cf. ibid., p. 36; "*la Riforma liturgica in atto deve rispettare la natura e per conseguenza la struttura tradizionale dell Ufficio divino* nella sua sostanza, pur conservando la necessaria libertà di attuare quei minori adattamenti e aggiornamenti, che possano migliorare le condizioni generali dell'Ufficio divino di fronte all esigenze dei tempi moderni, cosa del resto già proposta nella *Memoria* e tenuta costantemente presente."

[427] Cf. ibid., pp. 38-39.

[428] "puissant garder en toute tranquillité cette liturgie latine;" ibid., p. 99.

snowball.[429] Charrière then adds a caution that recalls the fundamental nature and aims of the Liturgical Movement:

> In one word, on this point as on the others, we realise that, from many sides, more or less substantial changes are requested from Rome. *But those who are pleased with today's situation*, those who do live the Liturgy as given by the Roman Church, *are not complaining*, and do not say anything. Don't we also have to give large consideration to the majority who are content? *Isn't their number as great*, maybe greater, than the number of those who complain? We are being told of a desire, which then tends to become widespread, for a substantial modification of the Liturgy. What is really universal is the desire to see the faithful always participating in the Mass to a greater extent and to see the priests always living from their liturgical prayer. But as *for how this better participation of the faithful and priests can be achieved*, we do not believe that those who speak the more loudly, those who somehow impatiently keep asking for endless changes, do represent *the majority*. A general survey of all the bishops would perhaps let us know the thoughts of those who do not say anything but who are content to see the Liturgy kept in its present form…[430]

Charrière concludes his observations by recalling the teaching of St Thomas Aquinas, on change in law or discipline,[431] which is reflected in Capelle's principles and which underpins the principle of organic development's insistence on substantial continuity. The Bishop is not opposed to liturgical development and raises no objection to the reforms enacted in previous years. However he is concerned that the direction being taken by some proponents of liturgical reform is erroneous: his

---

429 Cf. ibid., pp. 100-101.

430 "En un mot, sur ce point comme les autres, nous nous rendons bien compte que, de divers côtés, on demande à Rome des changements plus ou moins substantiels. *Mais ceux qui sont contents de la situation actuelle*, ceux qui vivent vraiment la liturgie, telle que l'Eglise romaine nous l'a donnée, *ne reclamant pas*, ne disent rien. Ne faut-il pas tenir compte aussi, et largement, de ceux qui sont contents? *Leur nombre n'est il pas aussi considérable*, plus considérable peut-être que celui de ceux qui réclamant? On nous parle de désir qui tend à devenir universel en vue d'une modification massive de la liturgie. Ce qui est universel, c'est bien le désir de voir les fidèles participer d'une manière toujours plus active à la Messe, de voir les prêtres vivre toujours mieux leur prière liturgique. Mais quant à *la manière de réaliser cette participation* plus active des prêtres et des fidèles, nous ne croyons pas que ceux qui parlent le plus fort et le plus haut, ceux qui s'empressent avec quelque impatience parfois de solliciter sans cesse des changements, représentent réellement la *major pars*. Une consultation générale de tous les évêques permettrait peut-être de se rendre compte de la pensée de ceux qui ne disent rien, mais qui sont contents de voir se maintenir le plus possible la liturgie actuelle;" ibid., p. 101.

431 Cf. *Memoria sulla Riforma Liturgica: Supplemento IV*, p. 101 & supra, pp. 21ff.

response alludes to ideas put forward at the Assisi Congress.[432] His is a call to ensure continuity amidst the growing "pressure for reform:"

> As one can see through these notes, I am among those who are pleased with today's Liturgy, and who do think the kind of changes we were talking about above are not only undesired, but also dangerous. But I understand, as I said before, that in the completely 'de-Christianised' regions, Rome could grant permission. We are simply asking, that where the faithful fully live the present Latin Liturgy, we be authorised to keep this Liturgy.[433]

The 1957 consultation demonstrates that while there were numerous and diverse suggestions for the development and improvement of the breviary, there was no unanimity or indeed significant support for any particular reform or reforms. Furthermore, it demonstrates that the episcopate neither desired nor anticipated a radical structural reform of the breviary. No similar consultation was ever carried out on the question of the reform of the missal. There is little reason, however, to suggest that such a consultation would have produced different responses than those from the consultation for the breviary: suggestions for the pruning, adaptation or development of the objective liturgical Tradition, in line with the reforms enacted by the Holy See since 1951.

The 1958 Instruction on Sacred Music and the Liturgy

What O'Connell called "the last act of the great Pope of the Liturgy [Pius XII] on behalf of the Liturgical Movement,"[434] the Instruction on Sacred Music and the Liturgy, was published in October 1958, dated 3 September (the feast of St Pius X).[435] In a semi-official commentary originally published in *L'Osservatore Romano,* Antonelli states that the Instruction "takes account of the continuing marked

---

432 "Dans le lettre qui nous avons écrite au Saint-Père pour le remercier de son discours au congrès liturgique d'Assise, nous avons fait allusion à certaines remarques qui se font jour dans les milieux moins instruits et moins généreaux;" ibid., 102. Cf. his criticism of Jungmann's paper at Assisi: supra, p. 154.

433 "Comme on le voit par tout l'ensemble de ces notes, je suis du nombre de ceux qui sont satisfaits de la liturgie actuelle et qui estiment non seulement indésirable, mais dangereux qu'on y apporte des changements du genre de ceux auxquels nous avons fait allusion plus haut. Mais je comprends, ainsi que je l'ai dit plus haut, que pour les régions tout à fait déchristianisées Rome accorde de larges permissions. Nous demandons simplement qu'on nous autorise, là où l'ensemble des fidèles vit réellement la liturgie latine actuelle, à garder cette liturgie;" ibid.

434 *Sacred Music and Liturgy,* p. 13. Pius XII died on 9 October 1958.

435 Cf. K. Seasoltz OSB, *The New Liturgy,* pp. 255-282; C. Braga CM, *Documenta,* pp. 939-969.

development of the so-called Liturgical Movement in all countries," and that:

> The Sacred Congregation of Rites undertook to prepare this detailed Instruction at the Holy Father's own request, in order that the great principles set forth in the two encyclicals [*Mediator Dei* and *Musicæ Sacræ Disciplina*] might be effectively put into practice and that the practice might display a certain uniformity throughout the world.[436]

The Holy See was particularly concerned, Antonelli says, that this uniformity be found in diocesan liturgical "directories" or directives, and was worried by the fact that:

> There has been, here and there, some exaggeration and lack of restraint, due to a rather unenlightened zeal and an insufficient feeling of dependence and docility toward the hierarchy in whatever concerns the divine worship.[437]

Löw's commentary on the Instruction refers to "'community Masses,'" the celebration of which has "at times gone beyond what the general existing legislation would allow," and of "striking variations" in diocesan directories.[438] Lest there be any doubt about the Holy See's intentions, Antonelli goes on to say:

> The Instruction...is not meant as a floodgate for the Liturgical Movement. Rather, it is meant as a dike, to protect it, in order that the Movement, remaining within the river-bed of the great principles repeatedly inculcated by the Holy See, may truly carry the living waters of the Saviour to all the faithful through an ever more active and conscious participation in the liturgical life of the Church.[439]

The Instruction's purpose is, then, to apply this fundamental aim of the Liturgical Movement to the liturgical situation in 1958 which, apparently, included exaggerations of its aim, and some distortions of it. Furthermore, in the words of Crichton, it shows the determination of the Holy See "that the principles of liturgical worship shall reach down to the level of practice in ordinary parishes."[440]

O'Connell welcomed the Instruction as "a document of unusual interest and importance for the ordinary priest doing pastoral work, and one which will greatly rejoice and encourage those who are engaged in actively promoting the Liturgical Movement."[441] He continues:

---

436 "Commentary" in: *Worship* vol. XXXII p. 627.
437 Ibid., p. 628.
438 "The New Instruction" in: *Worship* vol. XXXIII p. 3.
439 "Commentary" in: *Worship* vol. XXXII p. 628.
440 "The New Instruction" in: *Liturgy* vol. XXVIII p. 2.
441 *Sacred Music and Liturgy,* p. 9.

> The Instruction, by its wise and far-reaching provisions endeavours to bring the Liturgy from the cathedral, monastery and convent into the parish Church.
>
> After more than a thousand years of passive attendance by the people at the Liturgy this will not be easy, and, obviously, the Church's desire for full active participation by the congregation in community worship can only be attained gradually, by carefully prepared stages, with much patience and perseverance...[442]

The Instruction itself opens with terminological definitions that clarify its later provisions. These are unremarkable in themselves except that their language demonstrates profound respect for objective liturgical Tradition together with openness to its enhancement by what is truly good from the modern age. For example, on modern sacred music the Instruction rules:

> "Modern sacred music" is the music composed in more recent times in accordance with the progress of musical technique, for several voices, with or without musical accompaniment. Since it is directly intended for liturgical use, it should exhale the fragrance of piety and the sense of religion, and when it does it may be used in the service of the Liturgy.[443]

The provisions of the Instruction are pastoral in the sense of facilitating the participation of the faithful in the traditional Liturgy. This is done, amongst other ways, by permitting a limited use of the vernacular, especially in the scriptural readings, by encouraging the "dialogue Mass," and by calling for the people to sing those responses and parts of the Mass which pertain to them, including where possible the daily proper chants. Modern technological developments (microphones, amplifying, broadcasting and recording equipment) are welcomed where they would enhance the celebration of the living Liturgy, and are proscribed where they would detract from it.[444] The Instruction thus provides for the pastoral participation of the people in, and for the development in the light of the circumstances of the modern world of, objective liturgical Tradition, without displacing its substance.

At the 1959 U.S.A. Liturgical Week, McManus observed that the Instruction:

---

442 Ibid., p. 14.

443 No. 7; ibid., p. 21.

444 Cf. J.B. O'Connell's résumé of the Instruction; ibid., pp. 99-108.

> Is not, for the most part, novel legislation; it is only the summing up and restatement of laws already binding and principles more basic than the laws themselves;[445]

and referred to "the happy balance between the 'substantial uniformity' which it imposes and the liberty it leaves to local usages," before lauding its fundamental principle, that the "very nature of the Mass requires that all who are present take part in it, each in the way proper to him."[446] He sees this reform as a reassertion of the proper state of liturgical affairs, and even wonders "how much the Liturgical Movement would have been needed, if the laws and traditions of the Roman rite had been faithfully observed over the centuries."[447] McManus' conception of liturgical reform here is one that has as its basic aim that of the Liturgical Movement: to enable the people to participate in the objective traditional Liturgy, purified by authentic reform. Substantial ritual reform is not on his agenda here.

This Instruction's significance as an example of the Liturgical Movement's attitude to reform, may be seen in O'Connell's acclamation of it:

> The Instruction...represents the flowering of a seed sown by a saint, St Pius X, with an inspired appreciation of the needs of the Church in the twentieth century. That seed first appeared above ground as a tender seedling when fifty years ago the Liturgical Movement was inaugurated in Belgium by Dom Lambert Beauduin OSB...who laid its foundations firmly on a sound theological basis (especially in his booklet *La Piété de L'Église*), and vigorously promoted its growth by the indoctrination of the clergy into the real meaning of the Liturgy, and spread the true doctrine by liturgical "weeks," the writing of articles and the preparation and distribution of suitable books...and leaflets. Over the years the seedling...has grown into a sturdy plant through the exertions of the hierarchy in many countries...and the devoted and untiring labours of a band of clergy and layfolk...Now those of them who are still alive—and happily Father Beauduin is one of them[448]—see the visible triumph of their work and bless God for the success of their efforts.
>
> Now their endeavour to promote the active participation of the people in the Church's worship...has received the official sanction of the

---

445 "The Law, the Liturgy, and Participation" in: The Liturgical Conference, *Participation in the Mass: National Liturgical Week (USA) 1959*, p. 44.

446 Ibid., p. 47.

447 Ibid., p. 45.

448 Beauduin died on 11 January 1960. In July 1959 his foundational rôle in the Movement was lauded in a letter from the Cardinal Secretary of State marking the golden jubilee of the Movement; cf. G. Diekmann OSB, "A Papal Letter" in: *Worship* vol. XXXIII pp. 650-653.

> Church, and under the direction of the Sacred Congregation of Rites, at the hands of liturgical and musical experts, the chief forms of active participation have been systematised and have been issued as part of the Church's code of liturgical law.
>
> The fruits of the labours of fifty years must now be thankfully garnered by a multitude of priests, religious and layfolk of good will throughout the Latin Church...[449]

It is also significant that O'Connell published these words in 1959 some months after Blessed John XXIII's announcement of the Second Vatican Council (on January 25th). At that time, O'Connell did not look to the Council for the fulfilment of the ideals of the Movement. He saw them as having been largely realised. Yet again, we see that the desire for substantial structural reform of the Liturgy is not at the heart of the aims of the Liturgical Movement.

Indeed, from O'Connell's words it would not be unreasonable to assert that the publication of the Instruction gave rise to a certain satisfaction that the Movement's aims had been largely achieved, at least in terms of official reform: what remained was to effect these reforms throughout the Church. Such was not merely O'Connell's sentiment. Antonelli, in his commentary published while Pius XII was still living, spoke of the effect envisaged by the Instruction's implementation:

> If this is accomplished, the true, sound Liturgical Movement will take on a new life, some less praiseworthy exaggerations will be eliminated, and all the faithful—this is the most important point—will be brought ever nearer to the fountains of grace which the Liturgy opens up to them, while the Liturgy itself will become for the Christian people, as it was for centuries, the great school of supernatural life and holiness.[450]

---

[449] *Sacred Music and Liturgy*, p. 109.

[450] "Commentary" in: *Worship* vol. XXXII p. 637.

Further Liturgical Congresses

Liturgical congresses continued at a national level throughout the second half of the 1950s. The summer schools of the English Society of Saint Gregory promoted liturgical ideals,[451] as did the North American Liturgical Weeks.

The 1957 Strasbourg Congress[452] organised by the French *Centre de Pastorale Liturgique* on the Liturgy and the Word of God[453] occasioned another of Louis Bouyer's critical examinations of the Movement's efforts. The kernel was what he called "the Mass in duplicate;"[454] the use of commentators who duplicate the action of the Sacred Liturgy in words, the repetition of readings in the vernacular during or after their authentic liturgical proclamation, etc. To illustrate his point, Bouyer tries "to imagine what a liturgist of the twenty-first century…might well say of us all some day." Bouyer continues:

> I imagine the young and rash Aristarchus saying something like this: "In the middle of the twentieth century some worthy men, filled with good intentions, who erroneously thought of themselves as eminent liturgists, had substituted for the old Mass with three priests of the preceding centuries a Mass of their own invention with two priests. The first priest said the rubrical Mass…of which almost nothing was audible, but which they tried to make a little more visible than in the past by means of those devices which were the favourite liturgical playthings of those days long ago: the altar *versus populum*, the "podium," etc.
>
> "While the Mass was going on, and approximately in synchronisation with it, another priest went on talking, talking, usually the more untiringly the less he had prepared what he was going to say. At certain moments he read, out of a missal designed for the faithful, a mish-mash of periphrastic translations which he garnished according to his own taste. To vary the figure, between these *membra disiecta* he spread out a flood of comments and exhortations on which floated in disorder all the conventional phrases then current: 'Mystical Body,'

---

451 Cf. "Notes and News" in: *Liturgy* vol. XXV pp. 139-142; "Notes and News" in: *Liturgy* vol. XXVII pp. 105-109; "The Summer School" in *Liturgy* vol. XXVIII pp. 60-61.

452 Cf. S. Schmitt, *Die internationalen liturgischen Studientreffen 1951-1960*, p. 241.

453 The proceedings, A.G. Martimort et al., *The Liturgy and the Word of God*, date it 1958. However the report "The Strasbourg Liturgical Congress" in: *Liturgy* vol. XXVII pp. 19-20, and Schmitt, date it 1957. As the description of the papers contained in this report conforms with the published proceedings, it would appear that the Congress was in 1957.

454 "The Word of God Lives in the Liturgy" in: A.G. Martimort, *The Liturgy and the Word of God*, p. 58.

> 'Catholic Action'...'helping the worker,' 'presence in the world,' 'the Christian family,' 'responsibility of the laity,' etc.
>
> "Since nobody can talk continuously, he occasionally took a breath, giving the faithful time for a fine unanimous *Et cum spiritu tuo.* Or else he had them sing a Gelineau psalm[455] (always one of the most popular two or three). When the first priest had finished his Mass and retired with his paraphernalia, the second priest was seized with the vague notion that there had not been enough praying. And so there was an *Our Father* and a *Hail Mary* for the Chinese babies, for missionaries, for our dear departed...And the show was over."[456]

This caricature, which contains criticisms that from the perspective of the twenty-first century may be said to be prophetic,[457] serves to underline Bouyer's call for liturgical authenticity as foundational in liturgical reform. He illustrates his point from liturgical history:

> Let us glance...at the old Roman Churches—St Clement or St Mary-in-Cosmedin. Here the subdeacon did not chant the Epistle at the foot of the altar, carefully turning his back on the people for fear that somebody might hear him; the deacon did not solemnly go off to bump his nose on the north wall of the sanctuary. Each climbed up into high tribunes where they were visible to everyone, right in the middle of the congregation so that all could see them and hear them.[458]

Another international study meeting took place between 8-13 October 1958 at the Benedictine Abbey of Montserrat.[459] Two of the sacraments of Christian Initiation, Baptism and Confirmation, were studied. The desire expressed at Montserrat by missionaries and other pastoral clergy for a revival of the catechumenate may be said to be at least partially responsible for its restoration in 1962—one of the final works of the Pian commission, considered below.[460]

From 1954, liturgical Weeks were held in Ireland annually.[461] A report on the 1957 Week observed:

---

455 Gelineau was at the congress.

456 "The Word of God Lives in the Liturgy" in: A.G. Martimort, *The Liturgy and the Word of God,* p. 58.

457 Including: the verbosity of commentators, defective vernacular translations (in official liturgical use), the repudiation of the fashion of the priest facing the people, etc.

458 "The Word of God Lives in the Liturgy" in: A.G. Martimort, *The Liturgy and the Word of God,* p. 60.

459 Cf. S. Schmitt, *Die internationalen liturgischen Studientreffen 1951-1960,* pp. 241-262.

460 A list of the papers presented may be found in *Ephemerides Liturgicæ* vol. LXXIII (1959) p. 158. *LMD* no. 58 (1959) publishes some of them.

461 Cf. P. Murray OSB, *Studies in Pastoral Liturgy;* V. Ryan OSB, *Studies in Pastoral Liturgy,* II; "Liturgical Congress, Glenstal Priory" in: *Liturgy* vol. XXV pp. 102-104;

> With the restored Easter Liturgy so warmly acclaimed in Ireland by both priests and people, with a greater awareness stirring in our seminaries and among the younger clergy generally about what the Liturgy really is, the idea—never more than a quarter-truth—of the Irish as "unliturgical" may now be decently consigned to oblivion. Not that a crop of enthusiasts is to be expected who will campaign for the vernacular, concelebration or the altar facing the people. There is not yet in Ireland any coherent group advocating the Liturgy, or any sign of the emergence of such a group.[462]

The Benedictine Priory of Glenstal pioneered the weeks. Prominent international speakers contributed. Jungmann's presentation of the rationale for pastoral liturgical reform in 1960 is of particular interest. Having advanced his view of the longstanding and widespread corruption and decadence of ecclesial life and of the Liturgy, the theological root of which, Jungmann asserts, is the disregard of the nature of the Church as the Mystical Body of Christ, he explains that what is needed is:

> First above all the *renewal of the consciousness of the faith.* It is a renewal of the old power, of the old ardour, as Christianity once possessed it, when without external help, it was victorious over a pagan world. *That* is the reason today—and of course it is nearing the eleventh hour—for the working for such a renewal, for a genuine regeneration out of the powers which lie hidden in the Church and in her past...*That* is the reason for the Liturgical Movement...[463]

Such renewal may indeed be said to be consonant with the origins of the Movement, and a legitimate development of them. Jungmann is on sound ground here. However, in matters of actual ritual reform, his antiquarianism (usually, but not here, explicitly peppered with pastoral expediency) leads him to tell the Irish:

> When we consider everything that has been given back to us through the reform of Pius XII, we could say that something of the spirit of the early Church breathes again. Our age is very similar to the first centuries of Christianity. Today, as then, the Church must face a pagan world. Today also, the faithful, the truly Christian, are a minority in

"Fourth Liturgical Congress, Glenstal, Ireland" in: *Liturgy* vol. XXVI pp. 91-92; J. McGarry, "The Liturgy in Ireland" in: *Worship* vol. XXXI pp. 409-411; J. McGarry, "The Irish Congress" in: *Worship* vol. XXXII pp. 496-499; T. Stack "Irish Liturgical Congress" in: *Worship* vol. XXXIV pp. 463-465.

462 J. McGarry, "The Liturgy in Ireland" in: *Worship* vol. XXXI p. 409.

463 "The History of Holy Week as the Heart of the Liturgical Year" in: P. Murray OSB, *Studies in Pastoral Liturgy,* p. 23.

> most countries. That is why we need the heroic spirit of those early centuries so badly.[464]

Again, such a stance ignores legitimate organic developments of the past and the need for reforms themselves to be organic.

The irony of Jungmann asserting the necessity of pastoral liturgical reform and of a return to the practices of the early Church on the basis of being "a minority in most countries" in, of all places, Ireland in 1960, ought not to go unnoticed. The statement prompts the question: is such reform necessary where these conditions do not prevail?

In 1958 a *Living Parish Week* was held in Sydney, Australia. Its proceedings demonstrate the further spread of the ideals of the Liturgical Movement, with its principal concern being the active participation of the faithful (including the clergy) in the traditional Liturgy, and its applicability to lives of Catholic action in the modern world. Ritual reform was not a primary concern.[465]

Indeed, one may observe from the literature of the period that outside the relatively small northern European circle of liturgical scholars, the work of the Liturgical Movement was largely that of promoting liturgical piety. Pressure for ritual reform seems to have originated within such scholarly circles, rather than emerging from the wider Church.

In 1959 an international study week on Mission and Liturgy took place in Nijmegen, Holland.[466] It met to consider:

> The particular missionary value of well-formed worship. The study meeting of missionaries at Assisi [1956] had confirmed once again...that those engaged in mission work have paid too little attention to the proper formation of Christian worship. They must, therefore, be made acutely aware of the missionary value of the Liturgical renewal and...how missionary worship can be a pastoral factor of primary importance even now without special permissions from Rome.[467]

The participants drew "inspiration from the modern Liturgical Movement," but:

> Had not the mind to dabble in novelties or to give vent to an unbridled zeal for reform. Their idea was not to draft petitions to Rome, or even to pass resolutions. They had come for a week of study,

---

464 Ibid., p. 24.

465 Cf. Living Parish Series, *Living Parish Week*.

466 Cf. S. Schmitt, *Die internationalen liturgischen Studientreffen 1951-1960*, pp. 267-295.

467 J. Hofinger SJ, *Liturgy and the Missions*, p. 2.

> to face courageously the liturgical problems of the missions and to search for solutions that had the support of Tradition and authority.[468]

At the same time, the meeting was aware that:

> The fundamental study and probing into the missionary situation would also bring individual wishes to light which still await the approval of ecclesiastical authority.[469]

The difficulty of the use of a "transplanted" Western Liturgy in non-western cultures was recognised, and the desire was expressed that positive elements of these cultures be allowed to inform liturgical development. Boniface Luykx OPraem even proposed a departure from the Western rite in favour of Eastern ones, which, he argued, may be more culturally akin to the peoples of missionary lands. He is careful to note that:

> This, however, does not mean that we must switch over all at once. But [the] particular rite...could function as framework and foundation (according to the local needs) for the incorporation of these respective cultures and their positive cultural values into the universal Church, so that this particular rite can *gradually* become the *liturgia franca* of these countries, as the Roman Liturgy is for the Western Countries.[470]

The meeting's conclusions demonstrate its overall moderation. They recommend the use of the vernacular in parts of the Mass and the celebration of the sacraments, and seek the freedom to develop the Liturgy by incorporating apposite local customs, as well as the relaxation of certain rubrical restrictions. Greater liturgical authenticity is sought. The restoration of prayers of the faithful and the catechumenate are advocated, as is the embellishment of the rite of marriage. A need is also expressed for the establishment of centres of liturgical formation.[471]

A desire to open the treasures of the Liturgy to the peoples of missionary lands hand in hand with a desire to see the Liturgy develop so that it might better nurture the faith pervades the papers.[472] As suggestions for ritual reforms emerge from this, the Nijmegen conference may be said to be a sound dialogue, in harmony with the organic development of the Liturgy, in which contemporary needs seek respectfully to persuade objective liturgical Tradition. As such, it may be

---

468 Ibid., pp. 6-7.
469 Ibid., pp. 2-3.
470 "Adaptation of the Liturgy in the Missions;" ibid., p. 88.
471 Cf. ibid., pp. 14-17.
472 Cf. ibid., pp. 291-292.

regarded as a development of the Liturgical Movement that, overall, is in harmony with its nature.[473]

In August 1960 Munich hosted the International Eucharistic Congress[474] which, the German bishops explained, was "by its very nature a liturgical congress."[475] Its "positive results" witness to the growth of the Liturgical Movement's aims:

> 1. A clear demonstration that the celebration of the Mass constitutes the highest and foremost form of eucharistic worship, rather than processions and devotional exercises;
> 2. A proof that active and intelligent participation of the faithful is possible even in the most solemn forms of the Mass...
> 3. A convincing example of that universal fraternal charity which must be the necessary fruit of Mass and Communion.[476]

An international liturgical study meeting took place at Trier in conjunction with the congress[477] on the topic "The Celebration of the Eucharist in East and West." The organiser, Wagner, recounts that the meeting was private, and that Antonelli represented the Roman Curia.[478] Concelebration was discussed, with Jungmann and Martimort disagreeing along the lines of Mont-César in 1954. Martimort held out "little hope" that "sacramental concelebration will be introduced" in the Latin rite.[479]

Alberigo and Komonchak's *History of Vatican II* observes that the Munich Congress "provided a unique occasion for many of the future participants in Vatican II to meet one another."[480] In respect of liturgical reform, our outline of the study meetings held from 1951 onward demonstrates that Munich was far from unique. Indeed, Munich and its predecessors can be said to have created and maintained a momentum which had an impact upon the Second Vatican Council's consideration of liturgical reform.

---

473 A comparison of Duschak's contribution "The Possibilities of Forms of the Mass in Mission Territories," ibid., pp. 128-144, which, whilst progressive, is not repugnant to liturgical Tradition, and his calls only four years later for "An Ecumenical Mass Liturgy" (in: *Worship* vol. XXXVII pp. 538-546), suggests that the moderation of the 1959 meeting was soon abandoned by some.

474 Cf. H.E. Winstone, "Munich 1960" in: *Liturgy* vol. XXIX pp. 87-88.

475 A. Cornides, "The German Scene" in: *Worship* vol. XXXV p. 257.

476 Ibid.

477 Cf. S. Schmitt, *Die internationalen liturgischen Studientreffen 1951-1960*, pp. 295-321.

478 Cf. *Mein Weg Zur Liturgiereform 1936-1986*, p. 41.

479 A. Cornides, "The German Scene" in: *Worship* vol. XXXV p. 258.

480 J.O. Beozzo, "The External Climate" in: vol. I p. 387.

Permission for the Use of the Vernacular

The one exception to the calls for reform emanating from scholars is the desire for *some* use of the vernacular in the Liturgy, which had long since been advocated by pioneers of the Liturgical Movement (Michel, Parsch, etc.). The Holy See had increasingly permitted its use from as early as 1920.[481]

In the 1950's such permissions were granted more frequently. We have noted the admission of vernacular scripture readings in the 1958 Instruction. This period also saw the publication of vernacular editions of the ritual. In 1950 Germany followed the French (who had a vernacular ritual in 1947) in gaining permission. As Balthasar Fischer reported to an Irish Liturgical Congress, some vernacular rituals not only translated the traditional texts of the ritual, they included "regional" and "newly composed" elements.[482] Thus they were developments of Tradition which allowed a local diversity without displacing the traditional rites. In this sense they may be said to be authentically pastoral.

The USA gained a similar permission in 1954, though a splendid edition of a bilingual ritual had been published between 1946 and 1952.[483] It was not until 1959 that permission for limited use of the vernacular was obtained by the bishops of England and Wales, and it was 1961 before an updated edition of the ritual was published.[484] That this does not include any new compositions, or regional usages, suggests a different mentality to that of the French or German bishops and their liturgical advisors: in England and Wales development and innovation appear not to have been a concern.

The Pian commission, however, took a different line when it considered the vernacular for the prophecies of the paschal vigil in November 1951, deciding against it, having heard the objection of Dom Albareda that such a reform could compromise the value of the Church having one language in her official worship, and could, by renouncing Latin in so solemn a rite, constitute a grave precedent.[485] By 1959 however, the commission, after a "serene and full discussion" (in Albareda's absence), decided to propose to the (new) pope that he concede to the whole Church permission for the vernacular reading of

---

481 Cf. supra, p. 121.

482 Cf. "Impressions of the German Ritual" in: P. Murray OSB, *Studies in Pastoral Liturgy*, pp. 47-61.

483 Cf. P. Weller, *The Roman Ritual*, vols. I-III.

484 Cf. *Excerpta e Rituali Romano Pro Diocesibus Angliæ et Cambriæ Edita*.

485 Cf. N. Giampietro OFM Cap., *Il Card. Ferdinando Antonelli e gli sviluppi della riforma liturgica dal 1948 al 1970*, no. [212].

the Passion of Palm Sunday and Good Friday and the four readings of the paschal vigil.[486] Blessed John XXIII gave no such concession.[487]

The admission of the vernacular in this period appears to follow the principle that, in parts of the Liturgy where the liturgical text is of its nature intended to be immediately intelligible, the vernacular may be used in order that the faithful may directly follow the meaning of the text and participate more fully in the Liturgy. It may be argued that this is simply an application of the principle of liturgical authenticity, particularly when one is speaking of passages of Sacred Scripture read for the instruction of the faithful, or of texts of the ritual that are directly related to the immediate circumstances of a given person or persons.

It must be said that proposals for the admission of the vernacular to the Liturgy did not seek the vernacularisation of the Liturgy. The writings and official documents of the period regard it is unquestionably appropriate to retain the customary use of the Latin language for the core of the administration of the sacraments, for the non-instructional parts of the Mass, and in the Church's rich heritage of chant. It may be asserted then, that with regard to the vernacular, the Liturgical Movement sought a moderate pastoral reform that would enhance liturgical participation and liturgical piety: a development of objective liturgical Tradition, certainly, but not a development that sought to displace its sacred language or its proper chant.

H.A. Reinhold, ever looking to the future, raised the question of the quality of vernacular translations. With others of the Liturgical Movement he prefers to speak not of "the Liturgy in the vernacular" but of "vernacular in the Liturgy." But he also somewhat prophetically warns:

> What I am personally afraid of…is a "commission" of professors who know all about their fields but do not speak the language of the people, or the saints, or the poets, or whose spirituality is and has been fed on an individualistic, subjective diet, who will smooth over, streamline, modernise, make more dogmatic, less shocking, more elegant, less uneven, what they find. And then we shall be stuck with it. And that would be worse than what we have now, because it would falsify the spirit of our Roman Liturgy…If…what the martyrs, the Fathers and Popes created will once have been watered down in its

---

[486] Cf. ibid., no. [1091].

[487] Though in 1959 this was conceded *ad experimentum* to Germany; cf. appendix "Examples of the Privileges Regarding Use of the Vernacular Granted by Rome in Recent Years;" in: J. Hofinger SJ, *Liturgy and the Missions,* pp. 293-295. Blessed John XXIII's 1962 Apostolic Constitution *Veterum sapientia* (C. Braga CM, *Documenta,* pp. 1169-1175) underlined the importance of Latin.

entirety to our bourgeois mentality and speech, the damage may prove grave—and permanent.[488]

Publications on Liturgical Reform

As the liturgical reforms of the 1950's progressed, they generated discussions that not only evaluated what had been achieved, but which considered what might be possible in the future. A review of some of this literature is illustrative.

The December 1956 edition of *Worship* published a poem by an Irish priest:

The strangest things are happening to the rubrics of the Mass!
Old men like me don't understand, we thought our days would pass
Without disturbance of the way we learnt to celebrate.
Now worship, like the world itself, is in a dreadful state.

Some time ago the priest was sure of what was his to say,
And also that the altar-boys would answer up his way:
Now anything can happen from a hold-up to a strike,
Or someone making comments through a nuisance-making mike.

The people used to keep their place, and did not interfere
Except perhaps to cough or sneeze or snore, but in the rear:
They wouldn't dream of singing out or butting in with noise,
Or talking up in Latin like the Clerk and altar-boys.

Young Curates now don't seem to mind if Mass is started late,
Provided that the people who are there "participate:"
And some would like motets, and psalms and hymns and chants,
Distracting to the celebrant and pious maiden aunts.

A plague upon those liturgists and all their fussy ways,
There's nothing solid in them, 'tis a passing whim or craze:
Old men like me have battled for our faith and fatherland
With nothing but the Scripture and the Sacraments in hand.

Of course we had the Liturgy, a makeshift to be sure,
And more or less a native growth, but still Tradition pure;
We said the Mass and let the people pray as best they could,
That was the way in Penal times, and surely it was good.

The world is moving on, no doubt, and times have changed a lot,
The Church of Christ must follow—if her net is in a knot
She'll never catch the fishes that are milling round the boat:
She needs a change of tackle, sweeter bait and lighter float.

So say professors and divines, who ought to know a lot:

---

488 *The Dynamics of Liturgy,* p. 114.

Perhaps old trowlers like myself should try to change our trot:
I'll read that journal "Worship" and some book on Liturgy,
And maybe when I understand 'twont seem bizarre to me.[489]

The poem demonstrates the existence of at least three issues at the time. Firstly, it is clear that this veteran of pre-Liturgical Movement ways, who recognises the growth of the traditional Liturgy over time, feels obliged, but is not utterly convinced, that he and the Liturgy must change with the times. Let us note that he sees the source of this obligation as the "professors and divines, who ought to know a lot." Secondly, it is significant that he should articulate the questionable assumption, that the Church, therefore her Liturgy, should "follow" the changed circumstances of the world. And thirdly, it is perhaps of even more significance that he should clearly state the conviction that a change of rite is necessary for pastoral reasons.

Whilst this is a poem, perhaps published tongue-in-cheek by *Worship*, it does demonstrate that these issues were apparent to pastoral clergy in the 1950's. It also illustrates their docility in the acceptance of liturgical reforms, in spite of their own pastoral instincts. One wonders what the same priest's assessment of the subsequent reforms would have been ten or twenty years later?

A more studied contribution came from Dom Bernhard Durst OSB in 1953.[490] Motivated by a desire to organise the parish Mass:

> So that there will be awakened in the hearts of the faithful those dispositions and acts which must inspire them so that what takes place at the Consecration is a sacrifice offered not only by the Head, but by the Mystical Body of Christ...that the faithful at Mass offer their personal gift of self in sacrifice, and unite it to the sacrifice of Christ, and also, that in a spiritual manner they lay hold of the infinite worth of that sacrifice offered by Christ, and offer it to God.[491]

He argues for a pastorally expedient reconstruction of the Liturgy, singular in its extent: he does not shrink from calling for a reform and a rearrangement of the Roman canon itself.[492]

Durst justifies his reconstructionism on a distinction he reads into *Mediator Dei*, between the external acts of worship and the interior disposition of worship that people offer almighty God. The Liturgy needs to tailor the former in order to facilitate the latter, regardless of the

---

[489] J. Fennelly "Nihil Innovatur—No Change" in: *Worship* vol. XXXI pp. 54-55.

[490] *Das Wesen der Eucharistiefeier und des Christlichen Priestertums*, Studia Anselmiana: Pontificium Institutum S. Anselmi, Rome 1953. His proposals for the reform of the Mass are given by J. Murphy: *The Mass and Liturgical Reform*, pp. 214-238.

[491] Murphy, ibid., p. 168.

[492] Cf. ibid., pp. 236-238.

changes themselves, he argues, radically subjectivising objective liturgical Tradition in the process.[493]

Thus, Durst severs the intimate connection between external rites and interior worship, as did the Protestant reformers, and denies the fundamental tenet of Catholic liturgical theology: that the Liturgy is sacramental in a manner analogous to the Incarnation, and that its outward forms (and therefore liturgical Tradition) are themselves singularly privileged vehicles of grace and take on an objectivity which cannot be arbitrarily manipulated without doing them violence and jeopardising their pastoral value.

Durst's ideas were not unanimously applauded. Reinhold criticises his work as something which "changes and transposes texts at will without regard either to Tradition or to the theology of the Fathers,"[494] and *Archiv Für Liturgiewissenschaft* published against the validity of his distinction.[495]

Yet the currency of these ideas in the early 1950s, their propagation by Murphy's book,[496] and their reiteration in 1960,[497] illustrates that the Liturgical Movement in the period of "pressure for reform" did include some advocates of reform whose proposals showed scant regard for the nature of Catholic Liturgy and for the organic development of objective liturgical Tradition.

In 1956 Ellard published *The Mass in Transition,* necessary due to the reforms subsequent to his earlier works.

In the light of the reform of the paschal vigil, Ellard highlights:

> Two...pregnant principles worth special commendation:
> a) care "that the people can better follow the rites"
> b) and that the celebrant does not repeat what the minor ministers do.[498]

"Imagine the gains in authenticity and simplicity," he reflects, "if the [latter] principle were applied straight through, and to solemn Mass and the much more elaborate episcopal functions."[499] Ellard also welcomes the permission for the use of the vernacular that accompanied the new renewal of baptismal promises, and reprints the *desiderata* from the 1951

---

[493] Cf. his "Liturgie-Enzyklica und Meßfeierreform" in: *Theologie und Glaube* vol. 46 pp. 276-291.
[494] *Bringing the Mass to the People,* pp. 26.
[495] Cf. 1958 pp. 470-472.
[496] Cf. pp. 258ff. below.
[497] Cf. Durst's *Die Eucharistiefeier als Opfer der Gläubigen* (Rottenburg, 1960); also: A. Cornides, "The German Scene" in: *Worship* vol. XXXV p. 262.
[498] *The Mass in Transition,* p. 27.
[499] Ibid., pp. 28-29.

Maria Laach and the 1953 Lugano conferences with approbation and without critical examination.[500]

The book's theological emphasis on the priesthood of all believers, and its enthusiasm for the reform of Holy Week, the permission for evening Mass and the reduction of the Eucharistic fast, the dialogue Mass, the faithful singing liturgical chant, an increase in the amount of Sacred Scripture read at Mass, the restoration of bidding prayers and of offertory processions, Mass facing the people, and new forms of ecclesiastical art and architecture, are typical of the period. In what is a singularly early ecumenical observation, Ellard comments:

> Now that Mass modifications are being rigorously studied by the scholars it becomes clear that reform inevitably entails making some external aspects of the Mass more closely resemble non-Catholic worship; such changes will be hailed by our non-Catholic brethren.[501]

We should be clear that this is not seen as a tendency that would prejudice the orthodoxy of the rite, but as an impetus which will assist "the incomplete Eucharistic beliefs of many non-Catholics" to grow "toward the fuller reality already possessed by Catholics."[502] Ellard goes on to welcome signs of a revival of liturgical piety amongst different Protestant groups, and goes so far as to speak of the possible benefits of "worship…shared in common,"[503] though this is the expression of a hope rather than a concrete proposal for reform.

Ellard envisages the organic development of the Liturgy. "It is clear," he says, "that, whenever changes are made, all the best from the past will be saved and modified, and the newly created fitted into it."[504] The book, save its ecumenism, is largely unremarkable, and is more a catalogue of the state of the Movement at the time than any new call for significant liturgical change.

In 1956 John Murphy published *The Mass and Liturgical Reform,* which reflects various contemporary stances. His preface contains a salutary warning against liturgical activism:

> *Intelligent* participation is equally important as *active* participation in the Liturgy. We cannot, in other words, be satisfied when the faithful are *doing* many things at Mass; we must be sure that they also understand and appreciate what they do. This is a question, then, of proper religious instruction, related to a solid liturgical life, and a question of the possibility of liturgical reform. But to stop short of *intelligent* participation will mean that we will ultimately miss our

---

500 Cf. ibid., pp. 28, 29-30, 33.

501 Ibid., p. 317.

502 Ibid.

503 Ibid., p. 317.

504 Ibid., p. 25.

> goal. "Activism," even if it be liturgical activism, is not a legitimate answer to the needs of the Church of today. There must be solidity and depth in what we do; there must be profound spirituality. This comes about not simply by doing, but by doing intelligently.[505]

Thus, Murphy identifies himself with the aims of the Movement espoused from Beauduin onward. Significantly, he speaks of the "possibility" of reform only as a concomitant of liturgical education or formation.

Murphy also speaks of liturgical reform meeting "the needs of the Church of today." It is clear that, in the first place, he understands the necessity of a reform of outlook rather than of rites. He also accepts the legitimacy of liturgical development, and argues that some development of the rite would serve in the desired restoration of liturgical piety to its rightful place in the life of the Church. Murphy's stated aim is that the Liturgy become "a heart-warming *experience* with the supernatural realities that will overflow into the life of the Christian."[506] To achieve this he outlines three principles that he regards as essentially interrelated; one theological, one historical and one pastoral:

> An adequate and clear notion of the doctrine of the *Mystical Body* and the "theological" notion of *Liturgy* as a theandric act of the Whole Christ; second, it must be possessed by a keen sense of *history*; and, last, it must take its rise from the *pastoral needs* of the hour.[507]

The desire to overcome the pietistic individualism so foreign to the essence of the Liturgy is clear, as is an openness to genuinely needed pastoral developments. These are to be made with a "keen sense" of history which, significantly, is but one contributing factor to liturgical development as envisaged by Murphy.

Murphy expands on the respective roles of these principles:

> The final decisions must follow the path indicated by...pastoral sense—decisions, of course, which proceed from an awareness of the doctrine of the Mystical Body and which take into consideration the message of liturgical history. But granted that these two other points had been considered sufficiently well, if there were no immediate pastoral concern indicating the need for change, the question of liturgical reform would certainly be otiose.[508]

By way of example, Murphy applauds the recent reform of the Holy Week rites, and enthusiastically recalls the injunctions of St Pius X that the people should participate in the Mass, particularly through

505 *The Mass and Liturgical Reform*, p. vii.

506 Ibid., p. 101.

507 Ibid., p. 108.

508 Ibid., pp. 115-116.

singing the chant. He argues that for the future, the admission of vernacular readings at Mass would be apposite. Such calls for liturgical authenticity and actual participation in the objective traditional Liturgy, prudently developed, are clearly in harmony with the principles of liturgical reform.

Yet, in discussing "problems of participation," Murphy goes further, and arrives at a questionable position. He fixes his attention on the 'typical' person attending Mass in his parish Church ("John Jones, who works in a steel factory"). Such a person, he maintains, has little inclination for singing chant and participating in similarly exclusive liturgical enthusiasms promoted by "certain better trained, or more culturally minded, individuals," which may, perhaps, be appropriate in such "exceptional situations" as prevail in monasteries, seminaries, convents or schools.[509] Murphy regards the Liturgical Movement as having arrived at a critical junction. He asserts:

> There are two alternatives: either do something to bring about an active sharing in the present liturgical practice, or—if that proves to be well nigh impossible—do something to the Liturgy so that such participation will be possible.[510]

He quotes Clifford Howell SJ:

> The present Mass-Liturgy, though venerable from long usage, though filled with treasures of doctrine and devotion and beauty and art which are the delight of cultured people, is not fully functional as the vehicle of community worship of the 'toiling masses.'[511]

What we have here is the emergence of a condescending egalitarian pastoral expediency, based on subjective assumptions, that advocates choosing what appears to be the quickest and easiest route to liturgical participation, regardless of objective liturgical Tradition. The desired end thus justifies the means adopted, even if this involves a substantial departure from Tradition. Furthermore, Murphy's strong ultramontane stance with regard to the prudential judgement of the pope in matters of liturgical reform[512] carries the danger of regarding any reform authorised by the pope as not only unquestionably legitimate, but as irreformable.

Apart from Murphy's ultramontanism, and his liturgical egalitarianism, the error of his stance lies in his assumption that there in fact exists an 'either/or' situation. This is a false premise of his own

---

[509] Cf. ibid., pp. 152-165.

[510] Ibid., p. 152.

[511] Quoted in: ibid., p. 158.

[512] "In these matters of discipline, the Holy Father will enjoy the constant guidance of the Holy Spirit promised to the Church by Christ;" ibid., p. 153.

construction, which makes too absolute a distinction between two intrinsically related elements of liturgical development. The organic development of the Liturgy can certainly encompass measures that facilitate greater liturgical participation, as the reforms of the 1950's demonstrate, without displacing the qualities of the "venerable" rite which Howell and Murphy are all too ready to cast aside. At the same time, the difficult effort of doing "something to bring about an active sharing in the present liturgical practice" (the work of the Liturgical Movement since its inception) cannot simply be abandoned because John Jones hasn't yet been formed, or doesn't show any interest in being formed, in liturgical piety. Liturgical Movement pioneers such as Fortescue, Hellriegel and Parsch demonstrated that "to bring about an active sharing in the present liturgical practice" is not in fact "well nigh impossible" in parishes. Hand in hand with organic development of the Liturgy, such efforts could not but bear fruit over time. Murphy's impatience is, therefore, somewhat dangerous in that it permits of the hasty construction of (un-traditional) liturgical forms without the laying of the necessary foundations of formation in liturgical piety—and then John Jones simply hasn't got a chance, however immediately such new constructions are designed to speak to him.

We must remember that Murphy is writing in 1956. His theological account of the nature of the Mass is utterly traditional and incorporates the insights of *Mystici Corporis* and *Mediator Dei*.[513] He acknowledges that "there is a certain 'law of organic growth' attached to the Liturgy. The new is not suddenly 'formed;' it must, rather, grow out of the old,"[514] and cites the Pian reforms as examples of such organic growth. Yet, in a remark that risks rendering his respect for the law of organic development mere lip service, he says, "ultimately, of course, [liturgical reform] amounts to taking very radical steps."[515]

With the aim of facilitating open discussion, Murphy outlines at length what the "radical steps" could include. There is no doubt in his mind that the Liturgy will eventually be celebrated totally in the vernacular. He draws extensively on the *desiderata* for the reform of the missal expressed at Lugano, Sainte-Odile and Maria Laach. He uncritically reflects the antiquarian and pastorally expedient desires of Jungmann, and proffers Durst's reconstructionism.[516]

Murphy's stance is, therefore, somewhat enigmatic, encompassing an awareness of the nature of liturgical participation as well as a thirst for doing whatever is required, or possibly what is desired by scholars, to bring about such participation. He has a realisation that

---

513 Cf. ibid., chapter 10 "Twofold Sacrifice," pp. 172-191.

514 Ibid., p. 203.

515 Ibid.

516 Cf. ibid., pp. 223-238 & supra, pp. 256ff.

development must be organic, but at the same time espouses an ultramontanism that unconsciously permits any duly authorised reform. There is no appreciation of the need for substantial continuity in the development of the rite. His is an orthodox, obedient, enthusiastic and well-read pastoral expediency with honourable intentions. Indeed, Murphy is a prime example of the presence of these components in the discussion and work of liturgical reform at the time. The question of precisely how they would relate, which if any would predominate, and whether they would indeed do no more than pay lip service to the law of organic development, remains.

The Abbot General of the Beuronese Benedictines, Dom Benedict Reetz, published an article in 1957[517] in which he asserted six principles of reform:

1. Account must be taken of the conditions of modern life...
2. The reduction of quantity in favour of quality...
3. More variety, especially in the readings.
4. A proper distribution of the various liturgical roles.
5. The abolition of ceremonies which have now no longer any practical significance...
6. The precedence of the ferial Mass and Office over the *Sanctorale*.[518]

The first is a principle of realism, and permission for evening Mass and the attenuation of the eucharistic fast is cited by way of example. The second principle can be seen as a call for some simplification, though this principle must be applied proportionately (pruning a tree is different to felling it). The third seeks the augmentation of liturgical Tradition (he also desired more prefaces), and the final three are call for liturgical authenticity,[519] though we must express a reservation at the advancement of "practical significance" as a measure of ceremonies' worth.

As Winstone observes, Reetz's principles are "all concerned with the perfection of the *form* of the Liturgy."[520] A desire for such perfection is in harmony with the fundamental aims of the Liturgical Movement, and is in no way detrimental to objective liturgical Tradition. However, it must be said that even such a noble desire is capable of damaging the Liturgy should disproportionate emphasis be placed on bringing it about.

In 1957 Andrew Greeley published an article in *Worship* entitled "What next?" After extolling the various reforms to date, he observed that:

---

517 Cf. *Heiliger Dienst* II (1957) pp. 18-29 & pp. 60-65; reported in: H.E. Winstone, "Pia Desideria: A Chapter in Liturgical Reform" in: *Liturgy* vol. XXVII pp. 99-101.
518 Winstone, ibid., p. 99.
519 Cf. ibid., pp. 99-101.
520 Ibid., p. 101.

> All about us there seems to be a spirit of openness in matters liturgical. More and more priests seem willing to experiment with the ideas of the Movement. Suggestions for liturgical reform are much less frequently condemned as wild-eyed fanaticism and are now listened to with sympathetic concern.
>
> Progress has been made, is being made, and seems destined to continue to be made in the foreseeable future.[521]

Greeley then incisively identifies a problem associated with these ongoing reforms. He identifies liturgical individualism as the obstacle to be overcome, and asserts:

> The more participation we have the better. But we must see participation in its proper perspective; if the goal of participation is intelligent and devout social worship then we must realise that in the present day participation must be seen as a part of a gigantic educational campaign which must reach the deepest recesses of the soul…The writer wishes to submit that this is a campaign which we have not even begun to plan.[522]

Greeley's thesis is that the pace of liturgical reform is overtaking the task of the formation of the faithful in liturgical piety: an edifice is being erected without sufficient foundation. This can be seen as the elucidation of a sociological principle of liturgical reform, which when related to the principle of organic development, appropriately seeks to ensure a harmony between reforms and the capacity of the Church to implement them. The same principle, however, if extricated from the scope provided by the principle of organic development, is capable of underpinning a reconstruction of liturgical practice and attitude though the imposition of ideological re-education programmes. But in 1957 this is not Greeley's intention. He speaks of "our campaign for the Sung Mass" and of the welcome increase in frequent communion,[523] demonstrating his identification with the Movement's traditional aims.

What both Greeley and Murphy identify is a disjunction between the necessary bedrock of formation in liturgical piety and the effecting of liturgical reforms. It is possible, then, to ask whether in the late 1950's those applying "pressure for reform" perhaps paid insufficient attention to the achievement of this formation before working to bring about ritual reform. Certainly, the sense of organic development is one of gradual

---

521 "What Next?" in: *Worship* vol. XXXI pp. 587-588.

522 Ibid., p. 590.

523 Cf. ibid., pp. 587, 591.

change amidst overall equilibrium, not one of "radical" or constant change.[524]

The fact that much basic liturgical formation remained to be done is underlined in Hellriegel's reflection on the ten years of the Liturgical Movement following the publication of *Mediator Dei* in the December 1957 edition of *Worship*.[525] Hellriegel rejoices in the "fruits from the healthy tree of *Mediator Dei*, the tree that sprang up from the power-laden seed of [St Pius X's] *Motu proprio* of November 22, 1903,"[526] but speaks of "that unfortunate number of people who have not as yet been touched by its spirit and pastoral directives,"[527] and is clear that:

> There are thousands of Catholics who are not even aware of the existence of either a *Motu proprio* or a *Mediator Dei*. There are hundreds of thousands who know of their existence, but have never "gotten around" to read them, much less meditate on them.[528]

While welcoming the reforms effected since *Mediator Dei*, any pressure for further reform is lacking from Hellriegel's reflection. His is a call to remember the fundamental nature of the Liturgical Movement—in the light of the phenomena identified by Murphy and Greeley, a timely one.

In 1948 the Archbishop of Paris, Cardinal Suhard, established a group of diocesan priests in the church of St Séverin in central Paris. In 1956 *Worship* acclaimed them:

> St Séverin has become synonymous with a Christian community courageously active: in worship and in work. Centre of the community is the altar and the group of diocesan priests…live a close community life: they sing part of the divine office together in church

---

524 The frustration felt by the laity who had not been formed in advance of reforms may be seen in Evelyn Waugh's Easter 1956 diary entry: "I went to Downside on the Wednesday of Holy Week and stayed until after the High Mass of Easter. There were no friends staying at the monastery this year so that the triduum was without distraction. It was indeed rather boring since the new Liturgy introduced for the first time this year leaves many hours unemployed...I found myself...resentful of the new Liturgy. On Thursday, instead of the morning Mass, mandatum, tenebræ and night vigil at the altar of repose, there was an afternoon Mass with the mandatum interpolated after the gospel and the altar of repose emptied at midnight. On Friday, instead of the Mass of the Presanctified, stations of the cross and tenebræ, an afternoon adoration of the cross and general communion. On Saturday nothing (except the conferences) all day until the Easter vigil at 10.30 in the same form we had suffered the last two years...In spite of all I found the triduum valuable;" cited in: S.M.P. Reid, *A Bitter Trial*, p. 26.

525 "1947 Mediator Dei 1957" in: *Worship* vol. XXXII pp. 2-7.

526 Ibid., p. 4.

527 Ibid., p. 7.

528 Ibid., pp. 2-3.

> morning, noon and night; they plan and pray together, discuss with parishioners—and then plunge into whatever newest experiment they have decided useful for the parish.[529]

In 1955 the community published *La Messe: Les chrétiens autour de l'autel,* sharing its liturgical and pastoral insights with the Church at large. Its import was underlined by the fact that it received a review in *L'Osservatore Romano,* which praised the community for their success in "assembling the Christians around the altar, and to make of the Mass an action that engages the entire community." *L'Osservatore Romano* noted that this was a "parish which does not fear to find itself in the *avant-garde,*" and added the caution that "provided the reader reminds himself to remain respectfully observant of the directives of the hierarchy, such a book will help in the diffusion of an experience rich in sacramental doctrine as well as in the psychology of both individuals and the masses."[530]

With so prominent a notice, it is not surprising that an English translation was published in 1958: *The Mass: Christians Around the Altar.* It explains the principles behind their *avant-garde* celebration of the Liturgy:

> The reforms which they have been led to make are designed to make the services more lively and rewarding, and these reforms take into account the authentic traditions of the Church and the needs of Christians of the twentieth century, as well as the particular people who frequent their sanctuary.[531]

Again we find the goal of liturgical participation, skewed towards pastoral expediency.

The book reveals that the congregation was encouraged to sing those parts of the chant proper to themselves including the entrance and communion antiphons. The Epistle and Gospel were read in the vernacular, the offertory procession was restored during which a vernacular hymn was sung and people's gifts incensed, people's intentions for prayers were read out at the offertory, parts, if not all, of the Roman canon were recited aloud, the kiss of peace was passed to the faithful and Holy Communion was administered to the faithful standing and responding *Amen* to the brief formula *Corpus Christi.*

The "Note to the English Edition" informs us that Suhard's successor, Cardinal Feltin, insisted that the liturgical practice of St Séverin conform to the *Directoire pour la pastorale de la Messe* published by the French hierarchy in 1956.[532] The preparatory prayers were to be said

---

529 "Liturgical Briefs" in: *Worship* vol. XXX pp. 159-160.

530 Ibid., p. 160.

531 Community of St Séverin, *The Mass: Christians Around the Altar*, p. 14.

532 For a discussion of this, Lercaro's, and two local French directories, cf. T. Maertens "La célébration de la messe à la lumiere des directoires recents" in:

at the altar, the Epistle and Gospel had to be chanted in Latin before being read in the vernacular, the proper chants of the Mass were not to be replaced with vernacular hymns, the Canon was to be said silently, and Holy Communion was to be received kneeling and administered with the traditional formula.[533]

St Séverin's innovations were far from radical, yet for their day they were certainly *avant-garde.* Their motivation was the promotion of active participation, and through it, of liturgical piety,[534] in order to bear pastoral fruit. The Community itself explicitly rejected the charge of liturgical antiquarianism:

> To believe that we draw closer to Jesus and his followers in so far as we get away from our present Liturgy and sacred signs, in order to bring back the Mass as a simple fraternal meal, is an illusion and an error.[535]

Indeed, whilst advocating purifying devotion to the Blessed Sacrament of sentimental excess, the book recognises the value of even such a comparatively late devotional practice: "To desire to return to the attitude of the early Church would not only be a mistake…but a loss."[536]

Yet the emphasis they place, time and time again, on the fact that, "the Mass is a *meal,*"[537]—which at one level is undoubtedly, but not exclusively, true—does permit of the tendency to diminish the conception of Liturgy as worship and to emphasise it more as a purely human event. The forms of the traditional Liturgy, and the limit to their adaptation upon which Cardinal Feltin insisted, were certainly sufficient to restrain this tendency at St Séverin in the 1950's. But we may ask whether due proportion could be ensured if the liturgical forms were themselves reconstructed in accordance with the strong emphasis placed

---

Paroisse et Liturgie vol. 39 pp. 159-179. The directories facilitate active participation by recommending minor ritual changes comparable to St Séverin's. Maertens argues: "Le baptisé a droit à la participation active au sacrifice du Christ…La tradition liturgique fixe les normes essentielles de cette participation en distinguant les éléments accessoires, en créant le chant, les répons, les attitudes. Les directoires ne font que remettre en valeur ces principes traditionnels. Les évêques ont conscience de leur responsibilité dans le domaine liturgique, ils veillent à l'application des normes traditionnelles et s'efforcent d'en promouvoir la pastoralisation;" p. 179.

533 Cf. *The Mass: Christians Around the Altar,* pp. 8-9.

534 Though the reception of Holy Communion whilst standing can hardly be said to have promoted liturgical piety.

535 *The Mass: Christians Around the Altar,* p. 104.

536 Ibid., p. 146.

537 Ibid., p. 18.

upon the Mass as a meal,[538] certainly underlined by the increasing fashion of celebration facing the people.[539]

In 1960 Ellard published "People Need a Simpler Mass,"[540] a short article which argues, partially from the motivation of expediting Sunday morning Mass schedules, for a pruning of the Order of Mass. His suggestions are familiar, and apply the steps previewed in the reform of the Holy Week rites. He advocates another scripture reading (with an extra collect), bidding prayers, an offertory procession and a shorter form for the administration of Holy Communion. Ellard goes further, proposing the abolition of the *confiteor* and the *orate fratres,* and the reconstruction of the offertory, because of their late origin. Clearly, these are in part inspired by archaeologism.

Interestingly, Ellard's interpretation of *Mediator Dei's* definition of the Sacred Liturgy[541] underpins a position that excludes the legitimacy of silent prayers at either the offertory or the Canon. This was certainly not the position of Pius XII or of earlier Liturgical Movement leaders.[542] Such insistence on hearing every liturgical word (perhaps a result of the promotion of the people's missal and the dialogue Mass) risks destroying the auditory nuances of the Roman rite.

1960 also saw the publication of Reinhold's *Bringing the Mass to the People,* which "sets out on a mighty mission" to restore the Mass "to comprehensibility to men."[543] It draws upon the aspirations of many in the Liturgical Movement to propose a reform of the *Ordo Missæ,*[544]

---

538 A supplement to *Fêtes et Saisons* no. 89 "La Messe," depicts the celebration of celebrating facing the people. The text, by P. Papillon, seeks to respond to the question, the raising of which is significant: "Si la messe est un repas, pourquoi se présente-t-elle comme une longue suite de gestes, de prières, de chants?" In 1959 a children's booklet was published in Belgium: *Ons Misboekje.* Compiled by B. Luykx OPraem, its text is theologically traditional, yet its illustrations, from the Abbey Church of Postel, depict the celebration of Mass facing the people as the norm. An offertory procession depicted in the Belgian edition (p. 21) was omitted from the 1961 English edition.

539 On recent visits to St Séverin the author has been unable to distinguish the quality of its parochial or liturgical life from that prevalent throughout Paris. The church has been structurally reordered since the time of Suhard's experimental community.

540 "People Need a Simpler Mass" in: *Worship* vol. XXXIV pp. 131-137.

541 Cf. supra, p. 127 & ibid., pp. 134-135.

542 Cf. P. Parsch on the value of the silent Canon: supra, p. 154.

543 Cf. G. Casey (review) in: *Worship* vol. XXXV p. 66.

544 Although the announcement of the Second Vatican Council preceded the publication of this book, it "was actually written in 1957" with revisions completed in "June 1959;" cf. p. 23.

prescinding entirely from the question of the use of the vernacular, which he articulated elsewhere.[545]

Frederick McManus provides a lengthy introduction. The Liturgical Movement, McManus says, "as a popular program…is chiefly concerned with teaching the faithful the meaning of the Sacred Liturgy as it exists today, defective as it may appear to the experts and to the Holy See."[546] He lauds the effect that the petitions of bishops, liturgical congresses, scholars and of private individuals, have had in assisting the Holy See to remedy such defects to date, and asserts that all of these will "help the Roman pontiff to shape the Sacred Liturgy"[547] in what he calls "the pontifical restoration of the Liturgy."[548] Once again Jungmann's corruption theory arises. The prospect of a remedy underlined by papal authority in response to the *desiderata* of liturgically enlightened pastors, individuals or groups also looms.

Although McManus quotes *Mediator Dei's* acknowledgement of the growth of the Liturgy, and speaks of "the gradual and fruitful progress of the Liturgy,"[549] he does not explicitly accord any weight to, or articulate, the principle of organic development. We may read his reference to "gradual" development as a measure of pastoral prudence rather than as an indication of a profound respect for the objective traditional Liturgy, which he regards as "defective." He advocates liturgical reform based on ultramontanism, pastoral expediency and a selective scholarly antiquarianism.

Reinhold introduces his own work by recounting a significant anecdote:

> It is reported that the late Pius XII...told a group of European liturgists, about the year 1952, before one of their study meetings, that the liturgists had tried with commendable success to bring the "people to the Mass" by several devices like the dialogue Mass in its various forms, but that they had reached an impasse. It was now time, he said, to "bring the Mass to the people by reform and adaptation," and before his time came to die he hoped to achieve so much in this field that the advance would have become irreversible and would have laid down clear principles for future work.[550]

The mention of "clear principles" is also significant. Reinhold regards two as fundamental: pastoral needs and historical scholarship. Though he explains:

---

545 Cf. supra p. 254.

546 *Bringing the Mass to the People,* p. 21.

547 Ibid., p. 20.

548 Ibid., p. 16.

549 Ibid., p. 22.

550 Ibid., p. 24.

> Proposals for reforms which are based on purely historical grounds, attempting to reconstruct the Mass in its "original" or "classical" form, must end up with some re-establishment of a synagogal prayer service and of a primitive meal form of the Eucharist; unless, of course, an arbitrary limit is set to this process of going back to origins—the time of Gregory, say, or of Charlemagne. An equally unsatisfactory reform would result from exclusively pastoral considerations not nourished and guided by Tradition; we would go aground in the same shallow waters of individualism in which so many other pious undertakings have been stranded.[551]

There is a sense of proportion here, which certainly does not preclude reform from being an organic development. Reinhold's warnings are salutary. However, in what he calls "the coming reconstruction of the Mass," there is also a sense of everything being negotiable.[552] "Reconstruction" implies a prior deconstruction. How can such not fail to give the respect due to objective liturgical Tradition?

The aim of this reform, and the aim of his book, Reinhold states, is "to restore and to bring out clearly the essential structure and line of action of the Mass."[553] He distinguishes, rightly, between what is "primary" and what is "secondary" in liturgical rites (the prayers at the foot of the altar are secondary in relation to the Canon). In considering what is appropriate in the reform of a rite such a distinction may prove helpful. However, if "secondary" is used pejoratively, and all such developments are to be jettisoned, one would indeed end up with an "unsatisfactory" reversion such as Reinhold proscribes above.

Reinhold's "guiding rules" include the following nine principles:

1. To preserve intact what Tradition has wrought, unless weighty considerations advise change.
2. To eliminate the excrescences that exist in the rite due to the accumulation of prayers over time (e.g. in the Offertory prayers and in Ash Wednesday's blessing of ashes).
3. To render the essential outline of the Mass clearer.
4. To make parish Liturgy as lucid and simple as possible for parishioners without oversimplifying its nature as a mystery and losing its dignity and beauty.
5. Archaic remnants or inexplicable rites (e.g. with the empty paten after the *Pater Noster*) should be eliminated to avoid confusion and to render the main points of emphasis clearer.
6. Proper liturgical participation should be restored with the laity exercising a variety of legitimate functions.

---

551 Ibid., p. 25.

552 Ibid., p. 29.

553 Ibid., p. 30.

7. The Mass of the Catechumens should be celebrated in a part of the Church distinct from the altar.
8. In parish churches (not in monasteries, cathedrals, etc.) the spirit of the Last Supper ought be restored. The core of sacramental worship should be freed of all unnecessary pomp.
9. The reforms found in the restored Holy Week and in the 1958 Instruction *Musicam Sacram* should be extended to the Mass.[554]

Reinhold warns of:

> A serious danger of overshooting the aim, once one embarks upon the exhilarating task of putting things in order. Room must be left for "solemnity," to avoid triteness, a romantically conceived "evangelical simplicity," formless individualism, or the victimising of the congregation by a tasteless and uninspired mystagogue. All that is noble and dignified, all that rises above ephemeral inspiration, must be preserved. The Roman Liturgy is magnanimous, solemn, sober, and warm: it should never lose these qualities, even when carried out in the smallest chapel.[555]

From this we can distil another principle: that the reformed rite as a whole, whatever decisions be taken about particular ritual elements, be, overall, in perceptible continuity with the traditional Liturgy.

In the first principle, we hear the voice of Capelle. In others the echo of the resolutions of the study weeks and of the various desires expressed throughout the 1950s. With the probable exception of the eighth, which is in part remarkably similar to the liturgical aims of the Protestant reformers and which raises questions about the theological nature of the Mass, none by itself is incompatible with an organic development of the objective traditional Liturgy. Indeed, if filtered by the tenth principle, deduced from Reinhold's warning above, one might hope for just that.

Nevertheless, Reinhold advocates reordering the sanctuary so that Mass might be celebrated facing the people,[556] which itself takes significant if not irreversible steps down the very path Reinhold warned against. This readiness to return to an earlier practice on the grounds that it is the more pure liturgical form betrays archaeologism, and indeed a defective understanding of liturgical Tradition. This defective understanding becomes explicit when, in sketching his reformed Mass, Reinhold asserts that "sound tradition" is "in most cases…that practice which is closest in time to the composition of the texts and the rites."[557] Such a stance, based on Jungmann's corruption theory, and echoing

---

[554] Cf. ibid., pp. 36-39.
[555] Ibid., p. 37.
[556] Cf. ibid., p. 44.
[557] Ibid., p. 63.

Diekmann's defective theology of Tradition, vanquishes the claim of later liturgical developments to any respect and, almost perversely, exalts antiquarianism in the very name of Tradition.

In Reinhold's proposed *Ordo Missæ*, we find a distinction between "Solemn Mass" with deacon, subdeacon, and other ministers, a "Chanted Mass" with a priest and some other ministers, a "Recited Mass" where there is no singing, and a "Devotional Mass;" private Mass with a priest and server only. He summarises his proposals in five schemas.[558]

They include many of the sensible and longstanding aspirations of the Movement: the restoration of congregational participation in the chant, the desire for bidding prayers and an offertory procession, etc. However, they also illustrate the willingness to undertake a wholesale reconstruction of the rite, as is particularly evident in schemas III and V, and in the sheer quantity of changes or rearrangements proposed. It is therefore difficult, if not impossible, to regard this as within the bounds of gradual, organic growth or development. Rather, it is a call for a wholesale reconstruction according to scholarly and pastoral *desiderata*.

In a postscript, Reinhold demonstrates the confidence felt by advocates of reform at the time:

> After finishing the manuscript of this small book, I described its plan and purpose to a friend of mine, a rabbi. He listened very attentively, and then said: "A very neat plan indeed—too neat for me. We Jews reformed our rites a hundred years ago; we cut off what was wild growth, as we saw it, and we introduced the 'colloquial'—which means more than a 'vernacular'—language. But we have learned that we have made a mistake: we lost our sacredness and the mystery of our rites. Now all is obvious and trite; the beauty is gone."
>
> Many people besides my rabbi friend may have the same fears; but are these in any way justified? I really do not think there is any resemblance between the two cases...The Mass has a basic plan, an essential structure which may unfold in various ways; the reform is being planned with a deep respect for Tradition, a vast store of historical data and, above all, the supervision of the Apostolic See.[559]

This confidence is blind to the essential distinction between the Liturgy unfolding in history and in response to various cultures and ages (in which the rôle of scholars and authority is predominantly passive), and the Liturgy being reconstructed according to an archaeological plan of scholarly currency, and being unfolded anew (for every generation?), by (wholly active) reformers. In the book's final paragraph this

---

558 Reproduced in Appendix II.

559 *Bringing the Mass the People*, p. 101.

confidence assumes a breathtaking, gnostic, ultramontane, historical arrogance:

> The reform now underway is superior to preceding ones both in knowledge and in motive. As to knowledge: the research of the last decades has put us in a position better than that enjoyed by our predecessors for understanding the essential structure of the Mass and the development of the various rites. As to motive: the purpose of the reform of Charlemagne and Alcuin was uniformity, discipline and the personal reform of the clergy; the purpose of that of Trent was simply to put an end to confusion. But Pius XII, following St Pius X, wanted to enable the spiritually underfed and thirsting masses to refresh themselves at the "primary and indispensable source of the true Christian spirit," and to make the Sacrament a matter of true prayer, to which a feeling of wonderment is only a preliminary step.[560]

To suggest, as Reinhold does here, that the Carolingian and Tridentine reforms did not, within the circumstances of their time, seek to and ensure that the Liturgy be "a matter of true prayer" in which the faithful could find the "primary and indispensable source of the true Christian spirit," both fails to accord those reforms a fair historical analysis, and makes the ultimate archaeological (and protestant) claim: that the Catholic Liturgy has been fundamentally defective for over a thousand years.[561]

The strength of this (Jungmannian) assumption among proponents of reform is clear. As with Reinhold, it often co-existed alongside language that acknowledged the importance of liturgical Tradition. However such a concept of Tradition was defective. When liturgical Tradition is thus subordinated to historical scholarship, it ceases to be a living, developing entity, and in fact becomes an archaeological quarry. Reform based on such an assumption cannot be regard as an organic development of objective liturgical Tradition.

Reinhold is somewhat enigmatic. Within a year of publishing this provocative book, another appeared recapitulating many of the fundamental desires of the Movement. Discussing the Holy Week

---

560 Ibid., p. 103.

561 A. Bugnini CM repeated this sentiment in 1969, speaking of "the millions and hundreds of millions of faithful who have at last achieved worship in spirit and truth;" *TRL* p. 283, note 16; "milioni e centinaia di milioni di fedeli che hanno ritrovato, finalmente, il culto in spirito e verità;" *LRL* p. 284, note 17. J.D. Crichton's 1999 work *As it Was* says "It seems to me that when people could celebrate the Liturgy in their own language they experienced a great liberation. They were able to worship God with mind and heart and voice and that is what worship is all about;" p. 7. See also L. Beauduin OSB's criticism of the use of the term "in spirit and in truth" at the beginning of the twentieth century: cf. *Liturgy the Life of the Church* (2002) p. 28.

reforms he declares: "the reform I have in mind is...one of attitudes: habits of thinking and acting, not of rubrics and texts."[562] In evaluating his calls for ritual reform (and those of others involved in the earlier promotion of the Movement), it is, perhaps, important to bear in mind that the more fundamental reform to which Reinhold here refers, is assumed in their thinking. The danger arises that should the reform of attitude be forgotten, ritual reform of whatever kind would lead to the erection of an edifice without the necessary foundations.

In 1961 Thierry Maertens published *Les Risques de Plafonnement du Mouvement Liturgique*. It is a response to the author's perception that the Movement is, at least in France, in danger of losing its vitality because of a widespread lack of openness to change by laity and clergy. Correcting this, he argues, is an urgent task in view of the forthcoming ecumenical council.[563]

He responds directly to slogans proffered countering the measures introduced by the French pastoral directories,[564] complaining of a lack of clear-sightedness and thought in matters of liturgical renewal. His desire for participation in the Liturgy, simplified according to the directories and theologically refocused on the central eucharistic mystery (i.e. shorn of religious sentimentality),[565] and his hope that reform will continue along similar lines to further accommodate 'modern Christians,' is expressed as an urgent pastoral challenge effecting the Church's catechetical, missionary and sociological activity.

Maertens is clear: "a simpler Liturgy will allow more profound prayer and more festive assemblies."[566] They key to this simplification is an antiquarian "return to the sources" and an "uncovering of the purity of the primitive lines of the Liturgy" which, given the importance he places on the Liturgy speaking to modern man, he curiously says is not by way of concession to "this nervous age."[567] The simplification is to be guided by pastoral "poles:"

> We believe, for our part, that following the integration of the Liturgical Movement into the pastoral arena, it is the theological vision

---

562 *The Dynamics of the Liturgy*, p. 53.

563 "Cette tâche est d'autant plus urgente qu'on peut espérer du prochain concile des modifications importantes auxquelles l'esprit de nos fidèles risque de n'être pas ouvert;" p. 12.

564 Cf. supra, p. 265.

565 Cf. *Les Risques de Plafonnement du Mouvement Liturgique*, pp. 39-40.

566 "une liturgie plus simple permettrait une prière plus profonde et une assemblée plus festive;" ibid., p. 66.

567 "Que la simplification ne soit pas une concession à notre époque nerveuse, mais une retour aux sources, une mise en valeur des fonctions essentielles par la suppression des fonctions accidentelles qui, comme le lierre, ont fait disparaître l'arbre, une redécouverte de la pureté des lignes primitives;" ibid.

of our apostolate which is more than adequately able to serve as the poles for the liturgical reform.[568]

Maertens advocates what we might term imperative pastoral expediency: all must be subjected to the end of rendering the Liturgy pastorally effective. Certainly, he is right to assert that liturgical piety and the liturgical apostolate are in no way optional,[569] and that in this there is a pastoral imperative. But he casts objective liturgical Tradition aside, exalting pastoral expediency to a disproportionate level and subjectifying objective liturgical Tradition.

The sense of urgency in his writing is telling. It demonstrates both an assumption that the forthcoming council will effect a liturgical reform, and the effort of at least one "pastoral liturgist" in 1961 to influence its direction. There is nothing covert in his efforts, giving rise to the question: to what extent would such pressure influence the Council Fathers in their consideration of liturgical reform?[570]

The Final Work of the Pian Commission

On January 25th 1959 Blessed John XXIII announced his intention to convoke an ecumenical council. After a consultation with the world's episcopate, preparatory commissions were established in June 1960: one was for the Liturgy.[571] The Pian commission's final meeting was in July 1960.[572] Clearly, there was an understanding that further liturgical reform would be considered at the Council.

Nevertheless, the fruits of the commission's work continued to appear. July 1960 saw perhaps its greatest: a new code of rubrics for the breviary and missal. McManus called this "a singular fruit" of the Liturgical Movement.[573] It applied the principle of liturgical authenticity and effected some simplification of the rite along the lines found in the

---

568 "Nous croyons, pour notre part, que c'est la vision théologale de notre pastorale, et ensuite l'insertion du mouvement liturgique dans la pastorale d'ensemble, qui peuvent le plus adéquatement servir des pôles à la réforme liturgique;" ibid., p. 59.

569 Cf. ibid., pp. 49-50.

570 The Archbishop of Westminster, Cardinal Heenan complained: "It is a pity that the Mass had to be altered but it seems that all the liturgists are agreed that the ceremonies must be simplified and made more like the primitive Mass;" letter 29 April 1967.

571 Cf. G. Alberigo & J. Komonchak, *History of Vatican II* vol. I pp. 206-211; G. Alberigo & A. Melloni, *Verso Il Concilio Vaticano II (1960-1962)*.

572 Cf. N. Giampietro OFM Cap., *Il Card. Ferdinando Antonelli e gli sviluppi della riforma liturgica dal 1948 al 1970*, nos. [1210-1220]. Only one person served on both commissions: Bugnini, secretary of both; cf. A. Bugnini CM, *LRL* pp. 903-905.

573 *Handbook for the New Rubrics*, p. 2.

earlier reform of Holy Week. Henceforth the priest was not to repeat texts spoken by other ministers, and the office was slightly abbreviated and simplified.[574] All in all, it was a pastoral reform in line with those of preceding years that respected objective liturgical Tradition and which enabled the Church "to enjoy the benefits of a much simpler and uniform set of rubrics."[575]

John XXIII's Apostolic Letter puts the reform in context regarding both the work of Pius XII and the forthcoming council:

> And we, after having under divine guidance, decreed that an Œcumenical Council should be convened, have given much thought as to what could be done about this initiative of our Predecessor. After long and mature consideration we have reached the conclusion that the basic principles for a general liturgical restoration [altiora principia, generalem liturgicam instaurationem[576] respicientia] should be referred to the Fathers of the forthcoming Œcumenical Council, but that the correction of the rubrics of the breviary and missal should not be postponed any longer.[577]

Richstatter observes that the *altiora principia* (fundamental principles) of which John XXIII speaks are those of the 1948 *Memoria* (and that it is these which "are to be the subject of the schema for the Liturgy presented to the Council Fathers").[578]

McManus, a consulter to the conciliar liturgical preparatory commission, was also clear that the new rubrics were one step in an ongoing process:

> There is every expectation that further restorations of the Sacred Liturgy will come, especially in the period following the Second Vatican Council...

---

574 For detailed summaries, cf. ibid., pp. 81-83, 101-105.

575 P.L. Murphy, *The New Rubrics,* p. vi.

576 The use of "instauratio" (restoration/renewal) as distinct from "reformatio" (a transformation/reshaping) itself speaks of the substantial continuity inherent in organic development, which is clearly what is envisaged by Blessed John XXIII. Vatican II's *Sacrosanctum Concilium* repeatedly speaks of a liturgical "instauratio." The content of this word is often lost in English, when liturgical "reform" is spoken of instead of liturgical "restoration" or "renewal."

577 J.B. O'Connell, *The Rubrics of the Roman Breviary and Missal,* p. 3.

578 *Liturgical Law,* p. 50. A letter to the author received on 4th March 1994 from Carlo Braga CM, member of the Pian commission from 1960, states: "I principi enunciati nella "Memoria," così come sono nella Memoria, sono passati al Vaticano II solo idealmente, ma diversamente formulati e più ampliati e con altro spirito." (The principles enunciated in the *Memoria,* passed as they are in the *Memoria* to Vatican II only theoretically, but formulated differently and further enlarged and with another spirit.)

> The reform of the missal's *Ritus Servandus* ("the rite to be observed in the celebration of Mass," rubrics untouched by the new codification), the use of the vernacular languages in Western liturgies, the improved selection of the lessons read at holy Mass and in the divine office, the adaptation of the baptismal rite to the modern catechumenate, the law and the rite of eucharistic concelebration, the structure of the canonical hours—these are a few of the many matters which may possibly be considered and decided—in general, one way or another—by the Fathers of the Council under the presidency of the Roman Pontiff.[579]

From John XXIII's letter and from McManus' examples (most of which we have seen proposed throughout the 1950s and none of which is, of itself, repugnant to the organic development of objective liturgical Tradition), it is clear that the Pope limited this reform to relatively minor rubrical details, and wished more major considerations to be presented to the episcopate gathered in ecumenical council. Nevertheless, the new code of rubrics represents another organic development of Tradition.[580]

A new typical edition of the breviary incorporating the new code of rubrics was published in 1961,[581] and a new edition of the missal in 1962.[582] Johnson and Ward's introduction to their recent edition of this missal states:

> The 1962 text represented the final stage of development in a thrust towards liturgical reform that had made itself felt from at least the dawn of the modern age, and which is indeed an inherent aspect of the Church's dynamic. The missal of 1570 was itself a fruit of that movement and within the stable and dignified juridical framework that it provided the liturgical rites had been reformed with quickening pace over the first half of the twentieth century. The 1962 edition summed up the gains that had been made by the eve of the Second Vatican Council...[583]

---

579 "Responses" in: *Worship* vol. XXXIV pp. 637, 638; also cf. *Handbook for the New Rubrics*, pp. 11ff.

580 Cf. C. Braga CM, *In Novum Codicem Rubricarum.*

581 Cf. *Breviarium Romanum*, Mame 1961.

582 Richstatter, *Liturgical Law*, p. 49, incorrectly ascribes this to 1961. New editions of the missal were published with the approbation of the Sacred Congregation of Rites (cf. *Missale Romanum*, Desclée 1961) before it approved the new *editio typica* on 23 June 1962: cf. C. Braga CM, *Documenta*, p. 1201. The Vatican *editio typica* (reproducded by C. Johnson OSB and A. Ward SM, *Missale Romanum Anno 1962 Promulgatum*) includes John XXIII's extraordinarily ultramontane insertion of St Joseph into the Roman Canon, promulgated only in *November* 1962: cf. C. Braga CM, *Documenta*, p. 1213.

583 *Missale Romanum Anno 1962 Promulgatum*, pp. v-vi. They continue: "and its existence facilitated the further steps which were to take developments to a fuller reform yet. While at the Council's behest further texts were to be added in order to reflect better the riches of the Church's Tradition and in response to the needs

The overall continuity of the new editions of the breviary and missal make them largely unremarkable, except that they indeed represent a "final stage of development" prior to the council. More significant reforms were promulgated in the 1961 new edition of the second part of the Roman pontifical (dealing with the main consecrations and blessings of places and objects), and with the new rite for baptism of adults in 1962.

Considered by the commission from 1958 onward,[584] a *Positio* published by the historical section of the Sacred Congregation of Rites in 1960[585] makes clear that the reform of the pontifical was occasioned by the need expressed by publishers to reprint it.[586] Bugnini and Braga were largely responsible for the work.[587] Martimort, Capelle, Jungmann, Jounel, and Bishops Rossi and Mistrorigo were consulted.[588]

The *Positio* enunciates "criteria and principles" for the work of "revision and simplification" it advocates. The first combines "the sense of Tradition and the concrete vision of the pastoral exigencies of today."[589] The second seeks to conserve and give full value to the essential elements of the rites by prudently stripping accretions to the primitive nucleus.[590] The third proposes freeing the rites from secondary elements and additions,[591] the fourth to restore various parts of the rite to

---

of the people, and while some existing texts were to be corrected to reflect more accurately the gains of textual scholarship, the lines and substance of the missal of 1970 remain unmistakably those of 1962. The missal of 1970 is the missal of 1962, reinvigorated, enriched, and endowed with new lustre, like a precious stone whose perennial beauty is enhanced by being ensconced in a new setting. Yet what was there in 1962 had already its own particular splendour." In the light of *The Ottaviani Intervention,* the writings of Klaus Gamber and Joseph Ratzinger (cit. supra), and of J. Ratzinger, *Milestones* pp. 122-124, A. Cekada, *The Problems with the Prayers of the Modern Mass,* L. Pristas, "Theological Principles that Guided the Redaction of the Roman Missal (1970)," in: *The Thomist* vol. 67 pp. 157-195, and of Michael Davies, this assertion of substantial continuity can only be said to be highly questionable.

584 Cf. N. Giampietro OFM Cap., *Il Card. Ferdinando Antonelli e gli sviluppi della riforma liturgica dal 1948 al 1970,* nos. [1046]ff.

585 *De Editione Typica Emendata Partis Secundæ Pontificalis Romani.*

586 "favorita dalla necessità di una ristampa da parte degli editori;" ibid., p. 5.

587 Cf. ibid., p. 25.

588 Cf. ibid., pp. 7-8.

589 "Il senso tradizionale e la visione concreta delle esigenze pastorali odierne;" ibid., p. 9.

590 "Conservare e valorizzare gli elementi essenziali, riconoscibili attraverso la prudente sfondatura delle accessioni successive al nucleo primitivo;" ibid.

591 "Alleggerire i riti dagli elementi secondari e additizi, specialmente da quelli causati da fatti occasionali o introdotti dall'uno o dall'altro autore, senza particolari motivi inerenti al rito stesso;" ibid.

their original functionality:[592] psalms once again being sung responsorially with the people, litanies accompanying processions, etc. The fifth proposes reducing the number of collects in the rites, and giving the celebrant the option of choosing between them.[593] The sixth advocates the cautious correction of the liturgical texts according to critical scholarly editions,[594] and the seventh to use the psalms of the new edition of the vulgate. The eighth proposes the elimination of repetitive gestures to underline the functionality and efficacy of the rites performed.[595]

These principles clearly move beyond those of the *Memoria* and those articulated by Capelle in 1951, particularly in the pastoral expediency, the archaeological deprecation of later developments, and the abbreviation which they espouse. Their promotion of liturgical authenticity and the underlying desire to promote liturgical participation, though, are wholesome.

We have maintained that organic development can include a proportionate measure of simplification and change. Similarly, it unquestionably encompasses a return to liturgical authenticity: obsolete rites are indeed that, and are justly omitted from new editions of liturgical books. Where the real purpose of an extant rite has been lost, its restoration enhances liturgical Tradition. However, "stripping accretions to the primitive [liturgical] nucleus" and discarding "secondary elements" do violence to developed liturgical Tradition.

The reform, promulgated in 1961,[596] effected a "sweeping simplification and abbreviation" of the rites, "according to the plan and principle of the Holy Week restoration, but in a much more radical fashion."[597] "By much rearrangement of prayers and ceremonial actions," it sought to achieve a "clear structure" in the rites.[598] Two new rites were added,[599] and some twenty-five obsolete rites were omitted.[600] It was,

---

592 "Restituzione di alcuni elementi alla loro nativa funzionalità;" ibid.

593 "Gli *Oremus* sono stati ridotti di numero;" ibid., p. 10.

594 "I testi sono stati revisionati in base alle edizioni critiche, che ormai abbiamo per tutti i libri liturgici e in modo così perfetto. Il lavoro è stato condotto con estrema delicatezza e cautela. Mai un testo è stato ritoccato, o cambiato, sia pure in una virgola, se la correzione non era più che giustificata;" ibid.

595 "Infine molti riti che venivano ripetuti più volte, non perchè si dubitasse della efficacia di un segno di croce o di una unzione, ma per obbedire a parallele cerimonie descritte nei testi biblici veterotestamentari, sono stati alleggeriti e semplificati, in vista della loro funzionalità ed efficacia immediata;" ibid.

596 Cf. C. Braga CM, *Documenta*, pp. 1140-1142.

597 F. McManus "The New Pontifical" in: *Worship* vol. XXXVI pp. 274, 272.

598 Ibid., p. 274.

599 The blessing of an *antimension*, originally from the Oriental Liturgy, and the *blessing* of a Church: the ritual had included a rite for this for use by a priest. Cf. ibid., p. 273.

600 Listed in: A. Ward SM & C. Johnson OSB, *Pontificale Romanum*, pp. xxvi-xxvii.

moreover, "a thoroughgoing revision of texts and rubrics and constitute[d] a truly new edition."[601]

Speaking specifically of the reform of the consecration of a church, Löw explained:

> However inherently beautiful [the former] ritual may have been, our modern, technical, and hurried generation came increasingly to feel that the ceremony of a dedication of a church was far too lengthy and overloaded. A reasonable simplification was desired, a clearer, more lucid structuring of the entire ceremony, and a better possibility for the faithful to take an understanding part in all of it. In brief, the conviction grew that the consecration of a church (and other similar, prolix consecrations, of altars, bells, etc.) was in need of a thoroughgoing revision and simplification...[602]

Ward and Johnson describe the reform as:

> The consolidation of the second part into a revised complex of rites centred on the dedication of a church. Some superfluous elements and positioning of material which obscured the lines of the rite were remedied, repetitions attenuated, texts restored according to critical editions, and dispositions given that would help facilitate the participation of the faithful.[603]

Aspects of this reform are in harmony with the law of organic development. Yet some underlying principles, if unchecked, are capable of ignoring it. The possible effects of accommodating "our modern, technical, and hurried generation" are grave. Much valuable liturgical material was certainly lost in the "sweeping simplification and abbreviation." Yet it can be accepted that some pruning was necessary. A clearer arrangement of a rite can render it more pure, and can facilitate liturgical piety. But a wholesale rearrangement can result in an entirely different construction, and sweeping abbreviation impoverishes the rite. Certainly, there was little innovation, and the reformed rites were neither novel nor complete reconstructions. However we cannot but deprecate the principles underlying this reform. It may be possible to judge the pontifical thus reformed as being in substantial, albeit lean, continuity with objective liturgical Tradition, but the principles operative in its reform are themselves radically subjective.

This reform was seen as a precedent. McManus was clear:

> The new pontifical is the second important section of the liturgical books restored as part of the project initiated by Pope Pius XII...the new volume indicates clearly the principles and pattern to be followed

---

601 F. McManus "The New Pontifical" in: *Worship* vol. XXXVI, p. 275.

602 "The New Rite of Consecration," p. 529.

603 *Pontificale Romanum,* p. xxv.

> in other instances—and above all in the restoration of the Roman missal itself.[604]

And that:

> Now it is evident that the liturgical books should be evaluated in each generation so that the participation of the people in sacred worship may be greater and their understanding the deeper.[605]

That the missal and other liturgical books should be revised had been advocated since 1948. However asserting that "each generation" should evaluate the liturgical books is tantamount to advocating the subjectifying of objective liturgical Tradition and the relativising of its content. That this should be called for in March 1962 by a member of the conciliar liturgical preparatory commission is a matter of concern.

The new rite of adult baptism, restoring the traditional catechumenate, promulgated in 1962 in response to requests from mainly missionary lands,[606] operates from different principles. The absence of any consideration of this reform from the commission's minutes,[607] which suggests that it is the work of at least some other personnel, may explain this difference.

McManus reported that "the new text is not a radical revision of the prayer texts for baptismal initiation." He envisaged a "thoroughgoing reconsideration and emendation" in the light of the *altiora principia* to be considered at the Council, rather, one which:

> Fills a serious *lacuna* in the life of the Church and is much more than a stopgap provision. It almost revolutionises the ordinary plan of catechetical instruction of converts, by involving all the members of the Church in the spiritual preparation of the catechumens and by involving the candidates for baptism in the prayer-life of the Church…
>
> With the seven distinct services spread over a period of weeks or even longer, the Liturgy of baptismal initiation is clear and impressive. Although few ritual or ceremonial changes and almost no textual changes have been introduced, even a slight familiarity with the old rite shows a sharp contrast…The former…appears, by comparison, to be confused, repetitious, and burdensome.[608]

Furthermore, it provided for the "more generous and widespread use" of

---

604 F. McManus "The New Pontifical" in: *Worship* vol. XXXVI p. 275.

605 Ibid., p. 280. This 1962 revision would itself be the subject of substantial revision within ten years.

606 Cf. K. Seasoltz OSB, *The New Liturgy*, pp. 462-466; C. Braga CM, *Documenta*, pp. 1180-1200. Again incorrectly dated 1961 by Richstatter, *Liturgical Law*, p. 49.

607 Cf. N. Giampietro OFM Cap., *Il Card. Ferdinando Antonelli e gli sviluppi della riforma liturgica dal 1948 al 1970*, pp. 278-388.

608 "The Restored Liturgical Catechumenate" in: *Worship* vol. XXXVI pp. 537, 538.

the vernacular, and recognised "the need for local adaptations and variations" and emphasised the people's participation in the rites.[609]

This was a pastorally motivated restoration to authentic liturgical practice, without substantially reforming the liturgical rites themselves, certainly in harmony with the ideals of the Liturgical Movement and with the principles articulated in the *Memoria* and by Capelle. Here, papal authority is appositely exercised and respects objective liturgical Tradition: indeed, it revivifies it.

McManus sees this reform as "a part of the Church's renewal promised by Pope John—and another starting point for the deliberations and discussions of the Fathers of the Council."[610] He asserts:

> There must be growth and addition and adaptation, lest the Roman rite, of unquestioned excellence in itself, deteriorate utterly though excessive rigidity.[611]

Such growth, addition and adaptation, when, as in this instance, grounded in the principles of liturgical authenticity and substantial continuity (which are themselves a necessary component of authentic pastoral reform), cannot but be organic. The holding up of this reform as a starting point for conciliar deliberation is promising. But the predominant principles contrast markedly with the preceding reform of the pontifical.

This was the final pre-conciliar reform. Its predecessor was the last work of the Pian commission. Some have found the continuation of the work of reform on the eve of the Council puzzling.[612] However, in the light of the only moderate calls for liturgical reform made in response to the antepreparatory consultation of the world-wide episcopate in 1959,[613] and in the light of the scope and importance of the liturgical books published up to 1962, it is fair to say that on the eve of the Council neither John XXIII, the dicasteries of the Holy See, the Pian commission, the world-wide episcopate, nor the publishers of liturgical books envisaged that a root and branch liturgical reform was imminent.

Certainly, these bodies anticipated the consideration of *altiora principia*. But one may assert that the continued efforts to implement the principles articulated in, and since, 1948 (albeit in some instances with some questionable augmentation), and the ongoing publication of reformed editions of the principal liturgical books up to the eve of the Council, demonstrate that continuity was widely envisaged. This is not to

---

609 Cf. ibid. pp. 537-545.

610 Ibid., p. 549.

611 Ibid., p. 548.

612 Cf. Richstatter, *Liturgical Law*, p. 49.

613 Cf. the preliminary results of the research of B. Harrison OS in: "A Reform of the Mass? Britain has Other Priorities;" in: *Apropos* no. 18, pp. 69-74.

say that further developments were not anticipated. Clearly they were. But it was inconceivable that there could be a radical or a substantial discontinuity with the preconciliar work of reform. Had such been envisaged, the late preconciliar reforms could only have been seen at the time to be futile: and they were not. There is no reason to believe that anyone held that liturgical Tradition would grind to a halt at this point in history. But there is every reason to believe that future developments were widely expected to be organic.

Bugnini, looking back over the work of the Pian Commision in 1963, praises their "hidden and diligent work, delicate and persevering, work filled with responsibility and with hopes for liturgical restoration," and states that the "slight abbreviation of one or the other rite was not really the concern of the men responsible for the restoration; it was an inevitable outcome of the task." Their reforms, he states, sought:

> To make the rites easier, to set the essential ones in relief, to facilitate prayer, to combat routine and unconscious repetition, to enable priestly piety to soar again in a genuine and joyful expanse of liturgical prayer.[614]

Yet, he asks, "is this all there is to restoration?" His answer is telling:

> Not by any stretch of the imagination. Every good rebuilder begins by removing the gross accretions, the more evident distortions; then with more delicacy and attention he sets out to revise particulars. The latter remains to be achieved for the Liturgy so that the fullness, dignity and harmony may shine forth once again.[615]

For Bugnini at the dawn of the Council then, as for Jungmann, organic development was not sufficient.

Conclusion

The Liturgical Movement achieved much between 1948 and the opening of the Second Vatican Council. Its goal of placing liturgical piety at the centre of the life of the Church, underlined by Pius XII in *Mediator Dei,* was adopted and widely promoted by numerous individuals and groups. As McManus wrote in 1961:

> The Liturgical Movement is many things, but above all it is an attempt to strengthen and to deepen the faith and piety of the Christian people.[616]

---

614 "Breviary Reform" in: *Worship* vol. XXXVII pp. 221-222.

615 Ibid., p. 222.

616 Preface to I. Dalmais OP, *Introduction to the Liturgy,* p. ix.

It was unthinkable, then, that the promotion of liturgical piety would not be at the heart of the forthcoming Council's consideration of the Sacred Liturgy.

The influence (or "pressure") of some, if not many, involved in the Liturgical Movement undoubtedly accelerated liturgical reform in this period. Whilst it is possible to question some of the prudential decisions taken, and whilst we find the emergence of some proposals for, and principles of, reform, that are capable (if allowed disproportionate influence) of harming objective liturgical Tradition, which is indeed a matter of grave historical concern, we may say that in this period, without detracting from the reservations expressed above in respect of particular reforms, on the whole the reforms enacted fall within the bounds of organic development of the Roman rite.[617] Indeed, in many the Movement's reasonable aspirations find realisation.

Yet a momentum, an expectation of, if not thirst for, further reform, builds up, pre-eminently among European liturgists and scholars, which could only intensify with the establishment of the preparatory liturgical commission for the forthcoming Council. There is a sense among some writers that almost everything is negotiable, resulting in at least an implicit devaluation of the objective nature of liturgical Tradition: something foreign to the Liturgical Movement in its origins.

Early in 1963 Guardini published the essay: "Some Dangers of the Liturgical Revival."[618] He identifies: rubricism, "the tendency to attribute to the Liturgy an importance which it does not possess" at the expense of an appreciation of its proper place, and that of other aspects of ecclesiastical endeavour, in the life of the Church;[619] activism, "regarding the Liturgy as something pointless and superfluous" which seeks to suppress it "in favour of spiritual methods and forms of worship apparently more up-to-date and effective," and which attempts to refashion it "with a view to achieving moral or other stimulating effects;"[620] liturgical dilettantism, "the threat of hasty, disjointed, and insufficiently experienced action" now that the Liturgy had become a contemporary issue;[621] conservatism, which keenly feels the dangers of rubricism, activism and liturgical dilettantism, but which falls into the

---

617 In an interview by the author on 23rd February 1996 in the Vatican, Alfons Maria Cardinal Stickler SDB, a *peritus* of the Conciliar Liturgical Commission, stated that the alterations under Pius XII were appropriate "reforms." However in regard to the alterations following the Second Vatican Council he asserted: "we shouldn't say a reform because it was not a reform; it was changing, a destruction also."

618 Cited in: A. Kirchgaessner, *Unto the Altar*, pp. 13-22.

619 Cf. ibid., pp. 13-14.

620 Cf. ibid., pp. 14-15.

621 Cf. ibid., pp. 16-17.

danger of "rejecting anything to which [one] is not accustomed;"[622] and finally the danger of an administrative short circuit, that, out of a desire for order amid "arbitrary action and lack of discipline," the hierarchy will stifle legitimate liturgical work.[623]

As the assessment of the author of the seminal 1918 work *The Spirit of the Liturgy,* this is a significant evaluation of the various factors in play at this pivotal moment in liturgical history. That, after forty-five years, years which witnessed the spread of the Liturgical Movement and of its influence upon piety and upon ritual reform, Guardini should find it necessary to speak of "dangers" is no blanket indictment of the Movement's aims, promoters or endeavours. It is, rather; sagacious counsel that the Liturgy cannot be "destroyed for the sake of immediate results," that it is "an irreplaceable tool for pastoral work," that "the fewer intentions associated with it, the more blessings the Liturgy brings." It is a call to respect the fact that the Liturgy:

> Is a steady light, constantly burning; a gentle flame, continually warming; a force silently at work, moulding and purifying. As such it needs the peace and freedom to develop, unhampered by aims and motives, and if these are provided, it can create a foundation which supports anything and an order which makes its influence felt everywhere.[624]

---

622 Cf. ibid., pp. 17-20.
623 Cf. ibid., pp. 20-22.
624 Ibid., pp. 15-16.

General Conclusion

OUR review of liturgical reform in history leads us to the conclusion that, while liturgical history bears witness to the development of many rites, and at times to their reform, it is clear that Catholic Liturgy is by no means a subjective expression of the faith that can be altered at will according to contemporary fashions or desires. Rather, Catholic Liturgy is a singularly privileged and an objective and constituent element of Christian Tradition.[1] The liturgical rites and formulas themselves share in this objectivity. Their faithful transmission ensures continuity and orthodoxy of belief and practice. Their development—which at times is both necessary and desirable—can only be legitimate by ensuring substantial continuity with received Tradition.[2] We may therefore agree with Johannes Wagner that:

> History has proved a thousand times that there is nothing more dangerous for a religion, nothing is more likely to result in discontent, incertitude, division and apostasy than interference with the Liturgy and consequently with religious sensibility.[3]

Our study of the Liturgical Movement has seen that its essence was the return of liturgical piety, of *participatio actuosa* in the traditional Liturgy, to its rightful centrality in order that it might bear fruit in Christian life. The Movement's "spirit," as Winstone reiterated in 1960, was primarily ordered to achieving:

> A conversion from within: the raising of a Catholic people who shall be truly one in Christ, holy in the Spirit of God—the soul of the Church—catholic in outlook and apostolic in zeal.[4]

The assumption underlying this aim was the achievement of a Christian renewal of culture. As the twentieth century progressed, modern man, Catholic or not, was increasingly becoming a private citizen in an ever more secular world. The Liturgical Movement was well aware of this obstacle. On the eve of the Council, Bouyer stated:

> Even apart from all positive religion, the dreams of modern man, his poetry, and a whole complex of compensatory attitudes tend to restore

---

1 Cf. *Catechism of the Catholic Church,* no. 1124.
2 Cf. further: T. Fisch, *Liturgy and Tradition.*
3 *Reformation aus Rom* (Munich, 1967), in: M. Davies, *Cranmer's Godly Order,* p. 119.
4 "The Spirit of the Liturgical Movement" p. 476.

> to him the mythic universe which the technological civilisation in which he lives threatens to suppress...
>
> If this is so, there is all the more reason that our adaptations of the Liturgy should not attempt to rationalise it, to empty it not only of its mystery but also of its expressions that are not the chords in the heart of modern man which respond to these external expressions in order to restore to them their maximum efficacy. At the same time we must do everything in our power to revive man's atrophied faculties. It will be necessary to restore to the essential liturgical symbols their living richness which has been sadly weakened by our own rationalism. But it will be equally necessary to strive to bring back to our contemporaries a religious culture that will be human to the extent that it is also biblical.[5]

The Liturgical Movement's aim underpinned the beginnings of the work of ritual reform, which commenced precisely in order to facilitate a revival of liturgical piety. From the middle of the twentieth century onward, scholars and interested parties met frequently to consider reform, and they contributed both insight into and pressure for reforms. These directly influenced the reforms enacted by the Holy See.

It is possible that even before the Second Vatican Council, the pace of, or thirst for, ritual reform overtook the necessary *a priori* work of formation in liturgical piety. The questions arise: Were sufficient foundations laid? Were reformers too hasty? Did they risk building on sand? Was the Liturgical Movement distracted from its essential aim? In 1964 Bouyer wrote:

> How many priests even now complain that the [1955] reform of Holy Week, especially the restoration of the Easter vigil, has had little or no practical effect? How could it have been otherwise if the Christian people have not been made aware of the true significance of those most sacred celebrations of the Church? And how could they be made aware so long as their clergy are so insensitive, and, therefore, so little influenced, either in their spiritual practice or in their teaching by the spirit of the Liturgy itself?[6]

"Much more than on any reform of the rites...the future of the whole Liturgical Movement and the renovation of the entire life of the Church will depend," Bouyer continued, "on the full and practical understanding" of the clergy of the Paschal mystery.[7] In 1960 Charles Davis recalled:

---

[5] *Rite and Man,* p. 220. For a recent discussion of this question cf. G.L. Müller, "Can Mankind Understand the Spirit of the Liturgy Anymore?" in: *Antiphon* vol. 7 no. 2 pp. 2-5.

[6] *The Liturgy Revived,* p. 27.

[7] Ibid.

> There was in some quarters a too hasty adaptation of the Liturgy to the apostolate. This was a mistake. Liturgy cannot be created; it must be received. It is a traditional datum, which we must accept and make our own.[8]

To some extent, then, we may say that reform moved too quickly prior to the Council. More time needed to be spent preparing the foundations before renovating the edifice. Nevertheless, the Liturgical Movement was clear that some development[9] of the Liturgy was not only desirable, but also necessary in order to achieve its aim.

Given its theological centrality, the development of the Catholic Liturgy cannot be arbitrary, nor can it be based on subjective factors. The development of the Liturgy in history, the writings of the Liturgical Movement, and of the work of reform carried out by the Holy See from 1948 onward, enable us to distinguish principles of liturgical reform.

Some principles, such as archaeologism or substantial innovation, are clearly proscribed in Catholic liturgical reform, as they risk subjectifying objective liturgical Tradition, and rendering the Liturgy of the Church the construct of each passing age or ideology. Nevertheless, elements of the Liturgical Movement, and some personnel involved in the Holy See's work of reform, were not immune to their influence or their seduction.

This danger of subjectifying the Liturgy was exacerbated in the light of the development of liturgical scholarship in the twentieth century: a certain modern self-assuredness is discernible, particularly in the propagation and widespread acceptance of Jungmann's "corruption theory" and its ensuing principle of simplification, requiring the wholesale removal of so-called "accretions," to which it gave rise. However, as the Franciscan liturgical historian van Dijk asked in 1956:

> Why should cutting down in the twentieth century be a "true liturgical revival" and "decadence" seven hundred years ago? Unless we possess the monopoly of truth?[10]

Another prominent principle is the "pastoral" one. We have distinguished two uses of the term "pastoral." One is akin to the subjective principles outlined above and is foreign to the nature of the Liturgical Movement and to objective liturgical Tradition. "Pastoral" in this sense, is opposed to liturgical Tradition, and betrays the nature of the

---

[8] *Liturgy and Doctrine*, p. 16.

[9] We may be well advised to speak more of "liturgical development" than of "liturgical reform," for in English at least "reform" connotes change from one thing to another. Continuity, not change, is the overriding emphasis in the history of the Roman rite.

[10] "Liturgical Movement Past and Present" in: *The Clergy Review* vol. XLI p. 528.

Liturgical Movement by proceeding with apparently expedient reforms without sufficient regard for the nature of the Liturgy. Vernacular*ism* is perhaps its clearest example.

The second use of "pastoral," however, seeks the Christian renewal of culture and the development of rites in that context in order that liturgical piety might flourish. It takes no short cuts. Nor does it exclude modification of the liturgical rites, though it does so only with reverence and with profound respect for received Tradition. Such authentically pastoral action is in harmony with the essential aims of the Liturgical Movement.

The principle of authority in the development of the Liturgy has been seen to be crucial, particularly given the increase of centralism and of ultramontane obedience in the Catholic Church. Yet, it is clear that authority cannot stand alone as a principle of liturgical reform. The father of the Liturgical Movement, Dom Beauduin, regarded the Church as the "watchful guardian of the canon of the Liturgy."[11] Dom Baudot observed of the history of the Roman breviary:

> It was a work which slowly took shape under the united influence of people and clergy, each century contributing something to its construction. The divine authority of the Pontiffs intervened only at a later stage, and then rather to control the process of development than arrest it.[12]

In 1957 Bouyer refuted the claim that "the supreme authority of the Church is not bound by anything and could freely give us an entirely new Liturgy, answering today's needs, without any further concern for the past," stating that: "There could be no question of the Church's fabricating a new Liturgy."[13]

In the wake of the Council's *Constitution on the Sacred Liturgy* Bouyer explained the "exclusive" authority of the College of Bishops and of its Head with regard to liturgical reform:

> Insistence on the exclusive right of the episcopal body, always in conjunction with the Roman See, does not mean that this right is an arbitrary power. It is not to be understood, as has been declared too often, that the Liturgy is something external, decorative, a mere matter of ceremonial, and hence authority can direct it without paying regard to any superior law or principle. To believe this would be to forget,

---

[11] *Liturgy Life of the Church* (2002), p. 47.

[12] *The Roman Breviary,* p. 2.

[13] "The Word of God Lives in the Liturgy" in: Martimort, *The Liturgy and the Word of God,* p. 65. Bouyer continues, in a somewhat antiquarian tone: "but rather of going back to a more pure realisation of the traditional Liturgy, a realisation which would allow it to be adapted to modern needs without losing anything of its original vitality and of its unchangeable foundation."

> first, that in the Liturgy we have a most sacred expression and realisation of the divine truth...[14]

These limits were recently articulated by Cardinal Joseph Ratzinger:

> The pope's authority is bound to the Tradition of faith, and that also applies to the Liturgy. It is not "manufactured" by the authorities. Even the pope can only be a humble servant of its lawful development and abiding integrity and identity...
>
> The authority of the pope is not unlimited; it is at the service of Sacred Tradition.[15]

And they are clearly taught by the *Catechism of the Catholic Church*:

> Even the supreme authority in the Church may not change the Liturgy arbitrarily, but only in the obedience of faith and with religious respect for the mystery of the Liturgy.[16]

Catholic liturgical reform cannot, therefore, be an archaeologism or a pastoral expediency. It may not be hurried.[17] Nor may it be a scholarly revision, nor even may it simply be that which is authorised, nay initiated, by the Pope or the College of Bishops, unless it respect the one fundamental principle of liturgical reform in which all Catholic liturgical reform finds its legitimacy.

That principle is the principle of organic development. Whilst clearly a metaphor, "organic development" is, nevertheless, the metaphor employed by key persons throughout the Liturgical Movement and indeed by the Second Vatican Council itself[18] when speaking of liturgical reform. This study has sought to examine both its content and its context.

---

[14] *The Revived Liturgy,* p. 53. Bouyer again expresses antiquarianism.

[15] J. Ratzinger, *The Spirit of the Liturgy,* p. 166; cf. also A. Nichols OP, "Revelation, Tradition and the Liturgy" in: M. Carson-Rowland, *Faith and Liturgy,* p. 166.

[16] No. 1125. French original: *"Même l'autorité suprême dans l'Église ne peut changer la liturgie à son gré, mais seulment dans l'obéissance de la foi et dans le respect religieux du mystère de la liturgie;" Catéchisme de L'Église Catholique,* p. 247; Definitive Latin text: "Ipsa auctoritas Ecclesiæ suprema non potest liturgiam ad placitum commutare suum, sed solummodo in obedientia fidei et in religiosa mysterii liturgiæ observantia;" *Catechismus Catholicæ Ecclesiæ,* p. 310.

[17] In an interview by the author on 22nd February 1996 in Rome, Paul Augustin Cardinal Mayer OSB, former Prefect of the Congregation for Divine Worship, expressed the opinion that following on the work of Liturgical Movement "the reform after the Council...came too abruptly." Cardinal Mayer also recalled a 1984 conversation with Wagner in the wake of the publication of the indult of 3 October 1984—allowing the use of the liturgical books in use in 1962—in which Wagner said that he saw the need for such an indult, and stated that "from the beginning" he was "convinced" that at least "thirty years of transition" would be necessary for the implementation of a general reform.

[18] Cf. *Sacrosanctum Concilium,* no. 23.

Organic development holds openness to growth (prompted by pastoral needs) and continuity with Tradition in due proportion. It listens to scholarly *desiderata* and considers anew the value of practices lost in the passage of time, drawing upon them to improve liturgical Tradition gradually, only if and when this is truly necessary. Ecclesiastical authority supervises this growth, at times making prudential judgements about what is appropriate in the light of the needs of different ages, but always taking care that liturgical Tradition is never impoverished, and that what is handed on is truly that precious heritage received from our fathers, perhaps judiciously pruned and carefully augmented (but not wholly reconstructed), according to the circumstances of the Church in each age, ensuring continuity of belief and of practice.

This principle provides "the criteria by which one can judge" the legitimacy of liturgical developments.[19] It permits the Liturgy to be compared:

> Not to a piece of technical equipment, something manufactured, but to a plant, something organic that grows and whose laws of growth determine the possibilities of further development.[20]
>
> ...a development, though, that takes place without haste or aggressive intervention, like the grain that grows "of itself" in the earth (cf. Mk 4:28).[21]

This is a plant unashamedly and firmly rooted in Tradition:

> A most ancient and venerable Tradition. Here, indeed, we are in touch with mystery, and abstract, quantitative thought must give way before it. We must keep, and continue with the greatest respect, a Tradition handed down from century to century, a Tradition full of meaning (as everybody must admit), a Tradition, finally, which just because of its mysterious inspiration by the Holy Ghost, escapes all human calculations.[22]

This principle ensures that in Catholic Liturgy:

> Only respect for the Liturgy's fundamental unspontaneity and pre-existing identity can give us what we hope for: the feast in which the great reality comes to us that we ourselves do not manufacture, but receive as gift.[23]

---

[19] Cf. R. Weakland OSB, "The right road for the Liturgy" in: *The Tablet* 2 February 2002 p. 11. An application of organic development to ecclesiastical (or perhaps better, "liturgical") architecture is made by M. Rose in: *Ugly As Sin*, pp. 23, 26.

[20] J. Ratzinger, *The Spirit of the Liturgy*, p. 165.

[21] Ibid., p. 169.

[22] H. Schmidt, "The Structure of the Mass and its Restoration, as reflected in the new Holy Week Ordo" in: P. Murray OSB, *Studies in Pastoral Liturgy*, pp. 36-37.

[23] J. Ratzinger, *The Spirit of the Liturgy*, p. 168.

This principle was a given for Beauduin, Michel, Parsch, Casel, Andrieu, Capelle,[24] Ellard,[25] and Löw.[26] None of these men lived to guide liturgical reform beyond the Council.

Received history asserts that the Liturgical Movement and the postconciliar reform may be identified, as the opening paragraph of the first chapter of Bugnini's memoirs exemplifies:

> The reform that the Second Vatican Council inaugurated is differentiated from all others in the history of the Liturgy by its pastoral emphasis. The participation and active involvement of the people of God in the liturgical celebration is the ultimate goal of the reform, just as it was the goal of the Liturgical Movement.[27]

Yet recent writers hesitate to concede the achievement of the aims of the Movement:

> Perhaps the Liturgical Movement needs to be refounded...What is clear is that the vision to which the liturgical pioneers gave their lives remains unread, unfulfilled.[28]

---

24 "a moderating influence at a time when some would have been too venturous;" "Dom Bernard Capelle" in: *Liturgy* vol. XXXI p. 106. *Worship's* obituary spoke of "his reservations, which were perhaps excessive at times, concerning certain types of initiative in the field of pastoral Liturgy;" A. Tegels OSB, "Abbot Capelle 1884-1961" in: *Worship* vol. XXXVI pp. 19-20. A.G. Martimort wrote in 1961: "Dans les réunions internationales de liturgistes, il gardait une prudente réserve à l'égard des voeux de réforme. Ce n'était pas de sa part pusillanimité ou conservatisme: il savait, le cas échéant, faire lui aussi des propositions de remisse en ordre des rites et manifestait alors de l'esprit de décision et beaucoup de sens pastoral. Mais il craignait, à juste titre, de voir la liturgie enserreé dans des systèmes artificiels et frustrée par des manipulations malhabiles du trésor de la prière des Pères;" *Mirabile laudis canticum,* p. 315.

25 Cf. W.J. Leonard SJ, *Liturgy for the People,* pp. v-viii. At the 1961 National Liturgical Week (USA) McManus said "Father Ellard and others with him stand for the liturgical teaching and accomplishment of these many years past...Father Ellard and his companions, who wrote and taught in the '20s and '30s, 40's and '50s were right; they did express the mind of holy Church, they did think with the holy Church of God in those days—as the blessed developments of liturgical understanding and liturgical restoration in these last days have shown;" "Liturgical Week 1961" in: Liturgical Conference, *Bible, Life and Worship,* p. 3.

26 Who had a moderating role in the preparation of the conciliar liturgical schema: cf. G. Alberigo & J. Komonchak, *History of Vatican II,* vol. I, p. 314.

27 *TRL,* p. 5; "Nella storia della liturgia la riforma del Concilio Vaticano II si distingue da tutte le altre per la sua caratteristica pastorale. La partecipazione e l'inserimento attivo del popolo di Dio nella celebrazione liturgica sono lo scopo ultimo della riforma, sono stati l'obiettivo del movimento liturgico;" *LRL* p. 21.

28 K. Pecklers SJ, *The Unread Vision,* p. 287. See also: R. Neuhaus, "What Happened to the Liturgical Movement?" in: *Antiphon* vol. VI no. 2 pp. 5-7.

The ideals of the Liturgical Movement in no way exclude authentic pastoral reform. But such reform will carefully prune, not hack, the organism that is the Liturgy, it will tend the "gentle flame" of which Guardini spoke,[29] not "quench it utterly."[30] For as Bouyer wrote in 1964:

> Tradition is not opposed to progress, but is the living principle of a development faithful to the seed, however altered may be the soil where it has to rise, flower and fructify...Tradition cannot be maintained either by unprecedented innovations or by artificial archaisms. All healthy progress, as well as all true reformations, can only be effected by an organic process. One can neither add wholly foreign elements to the Liturgy from the outside, nor make it regress to some idealised vision of the past. One can, and sometimes should, either prune or enrich the Liturgy, but he should always keep in touch with the living organism which has been transmitted to us by our forefathers, and he should always respect the laws of its structure and of its growth. No innovation, therefore, can be accepted simply for the purpose of doing something new, and no restoration can be the product of a yen for romantic escape into a dead past. The continuity, the homogeneity of Tradition in this case must be retained by authority as the *sine qua non* condition for the perpetuated life of a reality which is not merely immensely sacred but even the life of the mystical body.[31]

We conclude then, that this, the principle, or law, of the organic development of objective liturgical Tradition, is indeed the *sine qua non* of Catholic liturgical reform. The original Liturgical Movement knew and respected this law, and expected that future reform would be in accord with it. However some of the Movement's activists pressuring for reform before the Second Vatican Council moved beyond its bounds.

The task of a thorough assessment of whether this law was respected in the reforms enacted following the Second Vatican Council remains.[32] Such an assessment cannot but be based upon this law,

---

[29] Cf. supra, p. 284.

[30] Cf. supra, p. 133.

[31] *The Revived Liturgy,* p. 54.

[32] Bouyer's later comments are of significance: introducing *Eucharist* (1968) he wrote "On one hand it has been a very long time since we have seen such a lively and widespread desire in the Catholic Church to rediscover a 'eucharist' that is fully living and real. Yet, unfortunately, there has also never been a time when we have been so confidently presented with such fantastic theories that, once put into practice, would make us lose practically everything of authentic Tradition that we have still preserved. May this volume contribute its part toward promoting this renewal and discouraging an ignorant and pretentious anarchy that could mean its downfall;" p. xi. Later in 1968 he wrote: "We must speak plainly: there is practically no Liturgy worthy of the name today in the Catholic Church. Yesterday's Liturgy was hardly more than an embalmed cadaver. What

reflecting the truth that "liturgies are not made, they grow in the devotion of the centuries."[33]

people call Liturgy today is little more than this same cadaver decomposed …Perhaps in no other area is there a greater distance (and even formal opposition) between what the Council worked out and what we actually have. Under the pretext of 'adapting' the Liturgy, people have simply forgotten that it can only be the traditional expression of the Christian mystery in all its spring-like fullness. I have perhaps spent the greater part of my priestly life in attempting to explain it. But now I have the impression, and I am not alone, that those who took it upon themselves to apply (?) the Council's directives on this point have turned their backs deliberately on what Beauduin, Casel and Pius Parsch had set out to do, and to which I had tried vainly to add some small contribution of my own;" *The Decomposition of Catholicism*, p. 105.

33 O. Chadwick, *The Reformation*, p. 119.

Appendix I

Pope Pius XII – *Mediator Dei*[1]

from Part I

49. From time immemorial the ecclesiastical hierarchy has exercised this right in matters liturgical. It has organised and regulated divine worship, enriching it constantly with new splendour and beauty, to the glory of God and the spiritual profit of Christians. What is more, it has not been slow—keeping the substance of the Mass and sacraments carefully intact—to modify what it deemed not altogether fitting, and to add what appeared more likely to increase the honour paid to Jesus Christ and the august Trinity, and to instruct and stimulate the Christian people to greater advantage.[2]

50. The Sacred Liturgy does, in fact, include divine as well as human elements. The former, instituted as they have been by God, cannot be changed in any way by men. But the human components admit of various modifications, as the needs of the age, circumstance and the good of souls may require, and as the ecclesiastical hierarchy, under guidance of the Holy Spirit, may have authorised. This will explain the marvellous variety of Eastern and Western rites. Here is the reason for the gradual addition, through successive development, of particular religious customs and practices of piety only faintly discernible in earlier times. Hence likewise it happens from time to time that certain devotions long since forgotten are revived and practised anew. All these developments attest the abiding life of the immaculate Spouse of Jesus Christ through these many centuries. They are the sacred language she uses, as the ages run their course, to profess to her divine Spouse her own faith along with that of the nations committed to her charge, and her own unfailing love. They furnish proof, besides, of the wisdom of the teaching method she employs to arouse and nourish constantly the "Christian instinct."

---

[1] English translations differ in paragraph numeration; the Latin original contains none, but is divided into four parts. Here the numeration contained in the text on the Vatican web site and published in: A. Reid OSB, *A Pope and a Council on the Sacred Liturgy*, is followed.

[2] Cf. Constitution *Divini cultus*, December 20, 1928.

51. Several causes, really have been instrumental in the progress and development of the Sacred Liturgy during the long and glorious life of the Church.

52. Thus, for example, as Catholic doctrine on the Incarnate Word of God, the eucharistic sacrament and sacrifice, and Mary the Virgin Mother of God came to be determined with greater certitude and clarity, new ritual forms were introduced through which the acts of the liturgy proceeded to reproduce this brighter light issuing from the decrees of the teaching authority of the Church, and to reflect it, in a sense so that it might reach the minds and hearts of Christ's people more readily.

53. The subsequent advances in ecclesiastical discipline for the administering of the sacraments, that of penance for example; the institution and later suppression of the catechumenate; and again, the practice of eucharistic communion under a single species, adopted in the Latin Church; these developments were assuredly responsible in no little measure for the modification of the ancient ritual in the course of time, and for the gradual introduction of new rites considered more in accord with prevailing discipline in these matters.

54. Just as notable a contribution to this progressive transformation was made by devotional trends and practices not directly related to the Sacred Liturgy, which began to appear, by God's wonderful design, in later periods, and grew to be so popular. We may instance the spread and ever mounting ardour of devotion to the Blessed Eucharist, devotion to the most bitter passion of our Redeemer, devotion to the most Sacred Heart of Jesus, to the Virgin Mother of God and to her most chaste spouse.

55. Other manifestations of piety have also played their circumstantial part in this same liturgical development. Among them may be cited the public pilgrimages to the tombs of the martyrs prompted by motives of devotion, the special periods of fasting instituted for the same reason, and lastly, in this gracious city of Rome, the penitential recitation of the litanies during the "station" processions, in which even the Sovereign Pontiff frequently joined.

56. It is likewise easy to understand that the progress of the fine arts, those of architecture, painting and music above all, has exerted considerable influence on the choice and disposition of the various external features of the Sacred Liturgy.

57. The Church has further used her right of control over liturgical observance to protect the purity of divine worship against abuse from dangerous and imprudent innovations introduced by private individuals and particular churches. Thus it came about—during the 16th century,

when usages and customs of this sort had become increasingly prevalent and exaggerated, and when private initiative in matters liturgical threatened to compromise the integrity of faith and devotion, to the great advantage of heretics and further spread of their errors—that in the year 1588, Our predecessor Sixtus V of immortal memory established the Sacred Congregation of Rites, charged with the defence of the legitimate rites of the Church and with the prohibition of any spurious innovation.[3] This body fulfils even today the official function of supervision and legislation with regard to all matters touching the Sacred Liturgy.[4]

58. It follows from this that the Sovereign Pontiff alone enjoys the right to recognise and establish any practice touching the worship of God, to introduce and approve new rites, as also to modify those he judges to require modification.[5] Bishops, for their part, have the right and duty carefully to watch over the exact observance of the prescriptions of the sacred canons respecting divine worship.[6] Private individuals, therefore, even though they be clerics, may not be left to decide for themselves in these holy and venerable matters, involving as they do the religious life of Christian society along with the exercise of the priesthood of Jesus Christ and worship of God; concerned as they are with the honour due to the Blessed Trinity, the Word Incarnate and His august mother and the other saints, and with the salvation of souls as well. For the same reason no private person has any authority to regulate external practices of this kind, which are intimately bound up with Church discipline and with the order, unity and concord of the Mystical Body and frequently even with the integrity of Catholic faith itself.

59. The Church is without question a living organism, and as an organism, in respect of the Sacred Liturgy also, she grows, matures, develops, adapts and accommodates herself to temporal needs and circumstances, provided only that the integrity of her doctrine be safeguarded. This notwithstanding, the temerity and daring of those who introduce novel liturgical practices, or call for the revival of obsolete rites out of harmony with prevailing laws and rubrics, deserve severe reproof. It has pained Us grievously to note, Venerable Brethren, that such innovations are actually being introduced, not merely in minor details but in matters of major importance as well. We instance, in point of fact, those who make use of the vernacular in the celebration of the august eucharistic sacrifice; those who transfer certain feast-days—which have been appointed and established after mature deliberation—to other dates; those, finally, who delete from the prayerbooks approved for

---

[3] Constitution *Immensa*, January 22, 1588.

[4] [1917] Code of Canon Law, can. 253.

[5] Cf. ibid., can. 1257.

[6] Cf. ibid., can. 1261.

public use the sacred texts of the Old Testament, deeming them little suited and inopportune for modern times.

60. The use of the Latin language, customary in a considerable portion of the Church, is a manifest and beautiful sign of unity, as well as an effective antidote for any corruption of doctrinal truth. In spite of this, the use of the mother tongue in connection with several of the rites may be of much advantage to the people. But the Apostolic See alone is empowered to grant this permission. It is forbidden, therefore, to take any action whatever of this nature without having requested and obtained such consent, since the Sacred Liturgy, as We have said, is entirely subject to the discretion and approval of the Holy See.

61. The same reasoning holds in the case of some persons who are bent on the restoration of all the ancient rites and ceremonies indiscriminately. The liturgy of the early ages is most certainly worthy of all veneration. But ancient usage must not be esteemed more suitable and proper, either in its own right or in its significance for later times and new situations, on the simple ground that it carries the savour and aroma of antiquity. The more recent liturgical rites likewise deserve reverence and respect. They, too, owe their inspiration to the Holy Spirit, who assists the Church in every age even to the consummation of the world.[7] They are equally the resources used by the majestic Spouse of Jesus Christ to promote and procure the sanctity of man.

62. Assuredly it is a wise and most laudable thing to return in spirit and affection to the sources of the Sacred Liturgy. For research in this field of study, by tracing it back to its origins, contributes valuable assistance towards a more thorough and careful investigation of the significance of feast-days, and of the meaning of the texts and sacred ceremonies employed on their occasion. But it is neither wise nor laudable to reduce everything to antiquity by every possible device. Thus, to cite some instances, one would be straying from the straight path were he to wish the altar restored to its primitive table form; were he to want black excluded as a colour for the liturgical vestments; were he to forbid the use of sacred images and statues in Churches; were he to order the crucifix so designed that the divine Redeemer's body shows no trace of His cruel sufferings; and lastly were he to disdain and reject polyphonic music or singing in parts, even where it conforms to regulations issued by the Holy See.

63. Clearly no sincere Catholic can refuse to accept the formulation of Christian doctrine more recently elaborated and proclaimed as dogmas by the Church, under the inspiration and guidance of the Holy Spirit

---

[7] Cf. Matt. 28:20.

with abundant fruit for souls, because it pleases him to hark back to the old formulas. No more can any Catholic in his right senses repudiate existing legislation of the Church to revert to prescriptions based on the earliest sources of canon law. Just as obviously unwise and mistaken is the zeal of one who in matters liturgical would go back to the rites and usage of antiquity, discarding the new patterns introduced by disposition of divine Providence to meet the changes of circumstances and situation.

64. This way of acting bids fair to revive the exaggerated and senseless antiquarianism to which the illegal Council of Pistoia gave rise. It likewise attempts to reinstate a series of errors which were responsible for the calling of that meeting as well as for those resulting from it, with grievous harm to souls, and which the Church, the ever watchful guardian of the "deposit of faith" committed to her charge by her divine Founder, had every right and reason to condemn.[8] For perverse designs and ventures of this sort tend to paralyse and weaken that process of sanctification by which the Sacred Liturgy directs the sons of adoption to their Heavenly Father for their souls' salvation.

65. In every measure taken, then, let proper contact with the ecclesiastical hierarchy be maintained. Let no one arrogate to himself the right to make regulations and impose them on others at will. Only the Sovereign Pontiff, as the successor of Saint Peter, charged by the divine Redeemer with the feeding of His entire flock,[9] and with him, in obedience to the Apostolic See, the bishops "whom the Holy Ghost has placed . . . to rule the Church of God,"[10] have the right and the duty to govern the Christian people. Consequently, Venerable Brethren, whenever you assert your authority—even on occasion with wholesome severity—you are not merely acquitting yourselves of your duty; you are defending the very will of the Founder of the Church.

---

[8] Cf. Pius VI, Constitution *Auctorem fidei*, August 28, 1794, nn. 31-34, 39, 62, 66, 69-74.

[9] Cf. John 21:15-17.

[10] Acts 20:28.

Appendix II

H.A. Reinhold – *Bringing the Mass to the People*[1]

Schema I: The Entrance Rite[2]

Everything takes place in the sanctuary (in choro) unless otherwise indicated.

	Solemn Mass	*Chanted Mass*	*Recited Mass*	*Devotional Mass*
Pre-Mass: Iudica and Confiteor	Sacristy*	ditto*	ditto*	altar
1. Asperges (Vidi)	Performed by celebrant & ministers near gate of baptistery*			
2. Antiphon and Psalm of Introit procession (en route*)	schola and* congregation	ditto*	lector* and cong.	celebrant
3. Kyrie at altar steps* and sedilia*	choir and cong. alternate*	ditto*	cel. & cong. alternate*	celebrant & server
4. Gloria (at the bench*); (less frequently than now*)	cel. intones, choir & cong. alternate	ditto	cel. intones, lector* & cong. alternate	celebrant
5. Dominus vobiscum (at the bench*)	celebrant	ditto	ditto	celebrant (at the altar)
Et cum spiritu tuo	cong*	ditto*	ditto*	server
Oremus (pause*)	celebrant	ditto	ditto	ditto
Collect (one only)	celebrant	ditto	ditto	ditto
6. Amen	all*	ditto*	ditto*	server

* Features that are either new, in a new setting or derived from principles ruling OHSI.

[1] Cf. supra pp. 267ff. These tables are taken from pp. 48, 53, 60, 65, & 73. Pertinent explanations from the text are added by way of footnote.
[2] Reinhold suggests that the sacred ministers not wear chasuble, dalmatic and tunicle until the offertory, and that stoles only be worn, with the possibility of the celebrant wearing a cope; cf. p. 51.

Schema II: The Service of the Word

Everything takes place in the sanctuary (in choro) unless otherwise indicated.

	Solemn Mass	*Chanted Mass*	*Recited Mass*	*Devotional Mass*
7. Old Testament Lesson and*[3]/or Epistle (all sit) read at lectern facing people* No Deo gratias*	subdeacon (or lector*)	lector*	ditto*	celebrant
8. Gradual, Alleluia, Tract, Sequence	choir	ditto	chorus*	celebrant
9. Munda cor, etc. Silent blessing	deacon celebrant	celebrant ditto	ditto ditto	ditto ditto
10. Gospel responses Gospel at ambo/pulpit* No response at the end*	all* deacon only*	ditto* celebrant	ditto* ditto	server ditto
11. Homily	celebrant (or deacon*)	celebrant	ditto	ditto
12. Announcements	celebrant (or deacon*)	celebrant	ditto	omit
Bidding prayers*[4]	celebrant (or deacon) & cong.*	celebrant & cong.*	ditto*	celebrant & server*
Confession[5]	celebrant (or deacon) & cong.*	celebrant & cong.*	ditto*	celebrant & server*

* Features that are either new, in a new setting or derived from principles ruling OHSI.

[3] Reinhold argues for the inclusion of a third reading from Sacred Scripture, and for a three or four year cycle of readings; cf. pp. 52-3.
[4] Cf. pp. 55-58.
[5] A penitential rite in addition to the priest's private preparation.

Schema III: Offertory Rites and Prayers[6]

	Solemn Mass	*Chanted Mass*	*Recited Mass*	*Devotional Mass*
13. Credo	cel. intones; choir & cong. alternate	ditto	cel. intones; lector* & cong. alt.	celebrant
	cel. washes hands at credence table* omitting psalm*	ditto	ditto	cel. washes hands at altar - omit psalm*
	sacred ministers vest in chasuble, tunic, etc. at credence table[*]	cel. vests in chas., at cr. table[*]	ditto*	omit
14. Preparation of Gifts	cel. & deacon at credence table*	cel. at cr. table*	ditto*	cel. at altar
Suscipe, Sancte Pater	celebrant	celebrant	celebrant	celebrant
Deus qui humanæ	omit*	ditto*	ditto*	ditto*
Offerimus*	celebrant	celebrant	celebrant	celebrant
Veni Sanctificator	omit*	ditto*	ditto*	ditto*
In spiritu humilitatis	omit*	ditto*	ditto*	ditto*
Suscipe Sancta Trinitas	omit*	ditto*	ditto*	ditto*
15. Offertory Antiphon and Verses (begun as soon as Credo is finished*)	choir & cong*	ditto*	leader & cong*	omit
16. Offertory Processions*	sacred min. & lay reps.*	cel. & lay reps.*	ditto*	omit
17. Orate Fratres[7]	celebrant	ditto	ditto	ditto
Suscipiat	omit*	ditto*	ditto*	ditto*
18. Secret (aloud*)	celebrant	ditto	ditto	ditto
19. Amen*	all	ditto	ditto	server

* Indicates a change of rite, text or place, or an omission.

[6] "Schema III shears away the superabundance of late medieval accretions and brings out the essentials; the readying of both persons and elements in simple, self-explanatory form;" p. 59.

[7] "I propose that this either be suppressed, as it is not, even at present, part of the singing at Mass, and is really directed to the clergy, not to the people; or, since it has been raised in significance by the OHSI, that it be used to introduce the Secret, leaving out the Suscipiat;" p. 62.

Schema IV: The Anaphora or Canon[8]

The entire Canon is audible. Certain indicated prayers are sung or recited in a loud voice.[9]

		Remarks
Dominus vobiscum	celebrant	
Et cum spiritu tuo	all	and so forth, for the other versicles preceding the Preface
Preface	celebrant	sung or recited in a loud voice
Sanctus (complete*)	intoned by schola	concluded by all, in a loud voice, including celebrant and sacred ministers*
Te igitur	celebrant	only one sign of the cross*
Memento	celebrant	omit "pro quibus tibi offerimus"*
Communicantes	celebrant	omit "Andreæ" to "Damiani"*
Hanc igitur	celebrant	omit "Per Christum, etc."*
Quam oblationem	celebrant	sign of the cross at "benedictam," "Corpus," and "Sanguis" only*
Words of Institution	celebrant	omit double elevation,* or, if retained, ring bell only once,* at the actual elevations
Unde et	celebrant	omit signs of the cross*
Supra quæ	celebrant	
Supplices te	celebrant	omit "Per eundem Christum, etc."*
Memento etiam	celebrant	omit "Per eundem Christum, etc."; bow of head transferred*
Nobis quoque	celebrant	omit "Matthia" to "Anastasia"*
Per quem	celebrant	only one large sign of the cross*
Per ipsum	celebrant	sung aloud; all crosses are omitted; and the Blessed Sacrament is elevated high enough to be seen by all*
Amen	all	modo solemniore*

* Indicates a change from the present rite.

The reduction of words and in the number of signs of the cross and so forth will help in the avoidance of unseemly haste and misinterpretation and will eliminate certain later and unnecessary additions to the rite...

[8] "No one wants to replace the venerable present Canon, but it is suggested that it be freed from its accrescences;" p. 64.

[9] A "radical departure from the more recent tradition;" p. 63.

Schema V: The Communion Rite

The present schema first of all numbers the parts of the present Communion service, so that it might more easily illustrate the omissions and rearrangements in the restored service. Please note that the responses in the restored service are assigned to proper groups.

1. Pater Noster	celebrant	1. Pater Noster	cel. & cong.
2. Sed libera nos	choir/server		
2a. Amen	celebrant		
3. Libera nos quæsumus	cel (low voice)	3. Libera nos quæsumus	celebrant (aloud)
4. Rite with empty paten	celebrant		
5. Breaking host	celebrant		
6. Per omnia sæcula	celebrant	6. Per omnia sæcula	celebrant
7a. Pax Domini (etc.)	celebrant	6a. Amen	all
7b. Drop particle (Commixtio)	celebrant	11. Domine Iesu Christe qui dixisti	celebr. & deac.
8. Et cum spiritu tuo	choir	7a. Pax Domini (etc.)	celebrant
9. Hæc commixtio	celebrant	8. Et cum spiritu tuo	all
10. Agnus Dei	celebrant/choir	12. Kiss of peace	cel./deac/all(?)
11. Domine Jesu Christe qui dixisti	celebrant/deacon	10. Agnus Dei	choir & congregation
12. Kiss of Peace	celebrant & ministers	5. Breaking Host (during Agnus Dei)	celebrant
13. Domine Jesu Christe	celebrant	13. Domine Jesu Christe…voluntate	cel. (facultative)
14. Perceptio (etc.)	celebrant	14. Perceptio (etc.)	cel. (facultative)
14a. Domine, non sum	celebrant	14a. Domine, non sum	cel. (omit bells)
15. Confiteor	subdeacon/server		
16. Absolutions	celebrant		
17. Ecce, Agnus Dei	celebrant	17. Ecce, Agnus Dei	celebrant
17a. Domine, non sum	celebrant	17a. Domine, non sum	all
		20. Communion antiph. & psalms	choir & congregation
18. Corpus Domini Nostri	celebrant	18. Corpus Christi	cel. (or deacon)
		18a. Amen	communicant
19. Remaining rites and prayers	celebrant ministers/server	19. Remaining rites and prayers	cel., min./serv.
20. Communion antiph.	celebrant/choir		
21. Dominus vobiscum	celebrant	21. Dom. vobiscum	celebrant
22. Et cum spiritu tuo	choir/server	22. Et cum spir. tuo	all
23. Oremus (Postcommunion prayer)	celebrant	23. Oremus (Postcomm. prayer)	cel. (with pause after Oremus)
24. Amen	choir/server	24. Amen	all
25. Dominus vobiscum	celebrant	25. Dom. vobiscum	celebrant
25a. Et cum spiritu tuo	choir	25a. Et cum spir. tuo	all
26. Ite/Benedicamus	deacon/celebrant	26. Ite/Benedicamus	deac./celebrant
27. Deo gratias	choir/server	27. Deo gratias	all
28. Placeat	celebrant		
29. Blessing	celebrant	29. Blessing	celebrant
30. Response	server	30. Response	all
31. Last Gospel	celebrant		
32. Deo gratias	server	32a. Recessional	all

Bibliography

Published Documents of the Holy See

Acta et Documenta Sacrosancti Concilii Œcumenici Vaticani II vol. II Pars. VI, Typis Polyglottis Vaticanis, Vatican City 1973.

Benedictine Monks of Solesmes, Daughters of Saint Paul trans., *Papal Teachings: The Liturgy,* St Paul Editions, Boston 1962.

Braga, Carlo, CM, & Bugnini, Annibale, CM, *Documenta Ad Instaurationem Liturgicam Spectantia (1903-1963),* Centro Liturgico Vincenziano, Roma 2000.

Bugnini, Annibale, CM, *Documenta Pontificia Ad Instaurationem Liturgicam Spectantia (1903-1953),* Bibliotheca "Ephemerides Liturgicæ" Sectio Practica 6, Edizioni Liturgiche, Roma 1953.

Canones et Decreta Concilii Tridentini ex editione Romana a MDCCCXXXIV repetiti, Edidit Sacerdos Ioseph Perella, Naples 1859.

Catechism of the Catholic Church, Chapman, London 1994.

Catéchisme de L'Église Catholique, Mame/Plon, Paris 1992.

Catechismus Catholicæ Ecclesiæ, Libreria Editrice Vaticana, Vatican City 1997.

Decreta Authentica Sacrorum Congregationis Rituum, vols I-V, Typographia Polyglotta S. C. de Propaganda Fide, Rome 1898-1901.

Denzinger, H., & Schönmetzer, A., *Enchiridion Symbolorum Definitionum et Declarationum de Rebus Fidei et Morum,* Editio XXXVI emendata, Herder, Barcelona, Friburg & Rome 1976.

Dogmatic Canons and Decrees, Tan, Rockford 1977.

Index of Prohibited Books, Vatican Polyglot Press, Vatican City 1930.

Pius VI, "Auctorem Fidei," 28 August 1794, in: Denzinger, H. & Schönmetzer, A., *Enchiridion Symbolorum,* nos. 2600-2700.

Pius X, "Abhinc duos annos," 23 October 1913, in: *Acta Apostolicæ Sedis* vol. V (1913), pp. 449-451.

______ "Divino Afflatu," 1 November 1911, in: *Acta Apostolicæ Sedis* vol. III (1911), pp. 633-638.

______ "Inter plurimas," 22 November 1903, in: *Acta Sanctæ Sedis* vol. XXXVI (1903-1904), pp. 387-389.

______ "Tra le sollecitudini," 22 November 1903, in: *Acta Sanctæ Sedis* vol. XXXVI (1903-1904), pp. 329-331.

Pius XI "Inter multiplices," 8 December 1924 in: *Missale Bracarense* pp. vii-ix.

Pius XII, *Mediator Dei,* in: A. Reid OSB, *A Pope and A Council on the Sacred Liturgy,* St Michael's Abbey Press, Farnborough 2002.

Sacra Rituum Congregatio, Circular Letter, 15 May 1912, in: *Acta Apostolicæ Sedis* vol. IV (1912) p. 376.

Sacra Rituum Congregatio, Sectio Historica, no. 12, *De Pontificali Romano Iussu Sanctissimi Domini Nostri Pii Papæ XI Emendato: I De Confirmandis,* Typis Polyglottis Vaticanis 1930.

______________________________, no. 71, *Memoria sulla Riforma Liturgica,* Tipografia Poliglotta Vaticana 1948.

______________________________, no. 76, *Memoria sulla Riforma Liturgica: Supplemento II – Annotazioni alla "Memoria,"* Tipografia Poliglotta Vaticana 1950.

———, no. 79, *Memoria sulla Riforma Liturgica: Supplemento III – Materiale Storico, Agiografico, Liturgico per la Riforma del Calendario*, Typis Polyglottis Vaticanis 1951.

———, no. 90, *De Instauratione Liturgica Maioris Hebdomadæ: Positio,* Typis Polyglottis Vaticanis 1955.

———, no. 97, *Memoria sulla Riforma Liturgica: Supplemento IV – Consultazione dell'Episcopato Intorno alla Riforma del Breviario Romano (1956-1957) Risultati e Deduzioni,* Tipografia Poliglotta Vaticana 1957.

———, no. 102, *De Editione Typica Emendata Partis Secundæ Pontificalis Romani: Positio,* Typis Polyglottis Vaticanis 1960.

Schroeder, H. J. trans., *Canons and Decrees of the Council of Trent,* Tan, Illinois 1978.

Seasoltz, R. Kevin, *The New Liturgy: A Documentation 1903-1965*, Herder, New York 1966.

Liturgical Books – Official Editions

Breviarium Romanum, 2 vols. Mame, Rome & Paris 1961.

The Divine Office: The Liturgy of the Hours According to the Roman Rite, vol. III, Collins, Dwyer, Talbot, London, Glasgow, Sydney & Dublin 1974.

Excerpta e Rituali Romano Pro Diocesibus Angliæ et Cambriæ Edita, Burns & Oates, London 1961.

Missale Bracarense, Typis Polyglottis Vaticanis, Rome 1924.

Missale Romanum, Desclée, Rome, Tournai & Paris 1911.

Missale Romanum Ex Decreto Sacrosancti Concilii Tridentini Restitutum Summorum Pontificium Cura Recognitum, Desclée Rome, Tournai, Paris & New York, 1961.

Missale Romanum Ex Decreto Sacrosancti Concilii Tridentini Restitutum, Pii V. Pont. Max. iussu editum, Cum Privilegiis, Ioannem Variscum, Hæredes Bartholomei Faleti, & Socios, Venice 1571.

Missale Romanum Ex Decreto Sacrosancti Concilii Tridentini Restitutum, Pii V. Pont Max. iussu editum, Iacob Keruner, Paris 1572.

Missale Romanum Slavonico Idiomate Iussu S.D.N. Urbani Octavi Editum, Typis Sac. Congr. de Propaganda Fide, Rome 1631.

Ordo Sabbati Sancti Quando Vigilia Paschalis Instaurata Peragitur, Typis Polyglottis Vaticanis, Vatican City 1951.

Ordo Hebdomadæ Sanctæ Instauratus, Typis Polyglottis Vaticanis, Vatican City 1956.

Rimski Missal Slověnskim Jesikom Prěsv. G. N. Urbana Papi VIII Povelěnjem Izdan-Missale Romanum Slavonico Idiomate ex Decreto Sacrosancti Concilii Tridentini Restitutum S. Pii V Pontificis Maximi Iussu Editum A Pio X Reformatum et SSMI D. N. Pii X Auctoritate Vulgatum, Typis Polyglottis Vaticanis, Rome 1927.

Liturgical Books – People's Editions

A Collection of Prayers Containing the Mass in Latin and English, Turner, London 1688.

Benedictine Monks of Farnborough, eds., *The Layfolk's Ritual,* Burns & Oates, London 1917.

Benedictine Nuns of Stanbrook, *The Day Hours of the Church*, Burns & Oates, London 1916.

Benedictine Nuns of Stanbrook, Charles Francis Brown ed., *The Roman Breviary*, Parts I-IV, Burns & Oates, London 1936-1937.

Benedictines of the Solesmes Congregation, eds., *Mass and Vespers with Gregorian Chant for Sundays and Holy Days: Latin and English text*, Desclée & Co., Paris, Tournai, Rome & New York 1957.

Cabrol, F., OSB, *My Missal: A New Missal for the Sundays and Principal Feasts of the Year*, Mame & Herder, London 1926.

______________, *The Roman Missal in Latin and English according to the latest Roman Edition: Compiled For The Use Of All English Speaking Countries*, Mame, Tours 1921.

______________, & Baudot, J., OSB, *L'Office Liturgique de Chaque Jour: Missel, Vespéral, Rituel*, Mame, Tours 1926.

Easter Eve: A Manual for the Faithful Attending the New Service of the Paschal Vigil, Liturgical Apostolate: Abbey of St André, Bruges 1954.

The Holy Week Book Compiled by Authority from the Roman Missal and Breviary as Reformed by Pius X, with an Introduction by Adrian Fortescue, pointed edition, Burns Oates & Washbourne, London 1916.

Husenbath, F.C., trans., *The Missal For The Use of the Laity With The Masses For All Days Throughout the Year According to the Roman Missal*, 4th edition, Charles Dolman, London 1845.

Lefebvre, Gaspar, *Saint Andrew Daily Missal*, Abbey of St André, Bruges & E.M. Lohman, St Paul 1940.

Luykx, Boniface, OPraem, *My Little Mass Book* [no publisher's details given] 1961.

______________________, *Ons Misboekje*, Brepols, Turnhout 1959.

John, Marquess of Bute, K.T., trans., *The Roman Breviary Reformed by the Holy Oecumenical Council of Trent Published by Order of Pope St Pius V and Revised by Clement VIII and Urban VIII Together with the Offices Since Granted*, 2 vols. William Blackwood & Sons, Edinburgh & London 1879.

Le Grand Paroissien Complet Contenant L'Office Des Dimanches et Fêtes en Latin et Français Selon L'Usage de Paris, nouvelle edition, revue, corrigée, Delarue, Paris 1839.

The Missal Compiled by Lawful Authority from the Missale Romanum: A new Edition agreeable with the reforms of Pope Pius X revised and with a preface by Adrian Fortescue, second edition, fourth impression, Burns Oates & Washbourne, London 1920.

Montague, Gerard, *Ceremonies of Holy Week*, Browne and Nolan, Dublin 1958.

Nouvea Paroissien Romain Très-Complet A L'Usage Du Diocèse De Carcassonne Contenant en Français et en Latin Les Offices De Tous Les Dimanches et De Toutes Les Fêtes De L'Année Qui Peuvent Se Célebrer Le Dimanche, Mame, Tours 1874.

Officia Nova Hebdomadæ Sanctæ; Desclee & Co., Paris, Tournai, Rome, New York 1956.

The Roman Missal for the Use of the Laity, Keating, Brown & Keating, London 1815.

The Roman Pontifical for the Use of the Laity: Part II The Ordination Service, Thomas Richardson and Son, Dublin and Derby 1848.

Stedman, Joseph F., *My Military Missal*, Confraternity of the Precious Blood, Brooklyn 1942.

The Holy Week Book, Burns Oates and Washbourne, London 1913.

Vespers: or the Evening Office of the Church in Latin and English according to the Roman Breviary, ninth edition, Keating Brown & Keating, London 1812.

Weller, Philip T. (ed. & trans.) *The Roman Ritual: In Latin and English with Rubrics and Plainchant Notation*, 3 vols, Bruce, Milwaukee, 1946, 1950, 1952.

Published Books

Autour de la Question Liturgique avec le Cardinal Ratzinger: Actes des Journeés liturgiques de Fontgombault 22-24 Juillet 2001, Association Petrus A Stella, Fontgombault 2001.

Abercrombie, Nigel, *The Life and Work of Edmund Bishop*, Longmans, London 1959.

Aigrain, R., ed., *Liturgia: Encyclopédie Populaire des Connaissances Liturgiques*, Bloud et Gay, Paris 1943.

Alberigo, Giuseppe, & Komonchak, Joseph A., eds., *History of Vatican II: vol. I Announcing and Preparing Vatican Council II Towards a new Era in Catholicism*, Orbis, Maryknoll & Peeters, Leuven 1995.

_______________, & Melloni, Alberto, eds., *Verso il Concilio Vaticano II (1960-1962): Passagi e problemi della preparazione conciliare,* Marietti, Genova 1993.

Allott, Stephen, *Alcuin of York: his life and letters,* Ebor Press, York 1974.

Alting von Gesau, L.G.M., H.J.J. Vaughan, trans., *Liturgy in Development,* Sheed & Ward/Stagbooks, London & Melbourne 1965.

Athill, Emmanuel, *Teaching Liturgy in Schools,* Challoner, London 1958.

Aumann, Jordan, OP, *Christian Spirituality in the Catholic Tradition,* Sheed & Ward & Ignatius, London & San Francisco 1988.

Baldeschi, Joseph, J.D. Hilarius Dale, trans., *Ceremonial According to the Roman Rite,* 2nd edition, Catholic Publishing & Bookselling Company, London 1859.

Batiffol, Pierre, Atwell M.Y. Baylay, trans., *History of the Roman Breviary,* Longmans, Green & Co., London, New York & Bombay 1898.

___________, Atwell M.Y. Baylay, trans., *History of the Roman Breviary,* Longmans, Green & Co., London, New York & Bombay 1912.

Baudot, Jules, OSB, Anon., trans., *The Roman Breviary: Its Sources and History,* Catholic Truth Society, London 1910.

Baumstark, Anton, F.L. Cross, trans., *Comparative Liturgy,* Mowbray & Co., London 1958.

Beauduin, Lambert, OSB, *La Piété de L'Eglise: Principes et Faits,* Abbaye du Mont-César & Abbaye de Maredsous, Louvain 1914.

__________________, Virgil Michel OSB trans., *Liturgy the Life of the Church,* second edition, The Liturgical Press, Collegeville 1929.

____, *Liturgy the Life of the Church,* third edition, St Michael's Abbey Press, Farnborough, 2002.

Bede, *A History of the English Church and People,* Penguin, Harmondsworth Middx. 1983.

Benedictine Liturgical Conference, *National Liturgical Week (USA) 1940,* Newark 1941.

Benedictine Liturgical Conference, *National Liturgical Week (USA) 1941,* Newark 1942.

Benedictine Liturgical Conference, *National Liturgical Week (USA) 1942,* Ferdinand 1943.

Belloc, Hillaire, *Path to Rome,* Thomas Nelson, London [no date given—first published 1902].

Berger, David, Christopher Grosz trans., *Thomas Aquinas and the Liturgy*, Sapientia Press, Ypsilanti 2004.

Bianchini, Geminiano, ed., *Lettera al Papa: Libellus ad Leonem X,* Artioli, Modena 1995.

Bishop, Edmund, *Liturgica Historica: Papers on the Liturgy and Religious Life of the Western Church*, Oxford University Press, Oxford 1918.

Bolton, Charles A., *Church Reform of 18th Century Italy (The Synod of Pistoia, 1786),* Martinus Nijhoff, The Hague 1969.

Bonneterre, Didier, *The Liturgical Movement: From Guéranger to Beauduin to Bugnini or The Trojan Horse in the City of God*, Angelus Press, Kansas City 2002.

Bonniwell, William R., OP, *A History of the Dominican Liturgy,* Joseph F. Wagner Inc., New York City 1944.

____________________, *The Dominican Ceremonial for Mass and Benediction*, Comet Press, New York 1946.

Botte, Bernard, OSB, John Sullivan, trans., *From Silence to Participation: An Insider's View of Liturgical Renewal,* Pastoral Press, Washington DC 1988.

________________, *Le Mouvement Liturgique: Témoignage et souvenirs*, Desclée et Cie, Paris 1973.

Bouyer, Louis, Cong. Orat., Charles Underhill Quinn, trans., *Eucharist*, University of Notre Dame Press, Notre Dame & London, 1968.

____________________, *Life and Liturgy*, Sheed & Ward, London 1956.

____________________, M. Joseph Costello, trans., *Rite and Man: Natural Sacredness and Christian Liturgy*, University of Notre Dame Press, Notre Dame 1963.

____________________, Charles Underhill Quinn, trans., *The Decomposition of Catholicism*, Franciscan Herald Press, Chicago 1969.

____________________, *The Liturgy Revived: A Doctrinal Commentary of the Conciliar Constitution on the Liturgy*, Libra: Darton, Longman & Todd, London 1965.

____________________, Sister Mary Benoit, trans., *The Paschal Mystery: Meditations on the Last Three Days of Holy Week*, Allen & Unwin, London 1951.

Braga, Carolus, *In Novum Codicem Rubricarum*, Edizioni Liturgiche, Rome 1960.

Bracali, Atto, *Atti e Decreti Del Concilio Diocesano Di Pistoia Dell'Anno MDCCLXXXVI*, Pistoia 1788.

Britt, Matthew, OSB, *The Hymns of the Breviary and Missal*, Burns, Oates & Washbourne, London 1922.

Brovelli, Franco, *Ritorno alla liturgia: Saggi di studio sul movimento liturgico*, Centro Liturgico Vincenziano, Rome 1989.

Bugnini, Annibale, CM, *La riforma liturgica 1948-1975*, 2nd ed., Centro Liturgico Vincenziano, Rome 1997.

____________________, Matthew J. O'Connell trans., *The Reform of the Liturgy 1948-1975*, Liturgical Press, Collegeville 1990.

____________________, Leonard J. Doyle trans., *The Simplification of the Rubrics*, Doyle and Finnegan, Collegeville 1955.

____________________, & Bellocchio, I., *De Rubricis ad simpliciorem formam redigendis: Commentarium ad Decretum S.R.C. Diei 23 Martii 1955*, Edizioni Liturgiche, Rome 1955.

Burke, Mary Gabriel, OSF, *Liturgy at Holy Cross: In Church & School*, Pio Decimo Press, St Louis 1952.

Burton, Edwin & Myers, Edward, *The New Psalter And Its Use*, Longmans, Green & Co., London 1912.

Burton, Katherine, *The Great Mantle: The Life of Giuseppe Melchiore Sarto, Pope Pius X*, Clonmore & Reynolds, Dublin 1950.

Cabrol, Fernand, OSB, C.M. Antony, trans., *The Mass of the Western Rites*, Sands & Co., London 1934.

____________________, & Leclercq, Henri, eds., *Dictionnaire d'Archéologie Chrétienne et de Liturgie*, Tome Premier, Premiére Partie, Letouzey et Ané, Paris 1924 & Tome Neuvième, Deuxième Partie, Letouzey et Ané, Paris 1930.

____________________, *La Réforme du Bréviaire et du Calendrier*, Bloud et Cie, Paris 1912.

Caldecott, Stratford, ed., *Beyond the Prosaic: Renewing the Liturgical Movement*, T & T Clark, Edinburgh 1998.

Campbell, S., FSC, *From Breviary to Liturgy of the Hours: The Structural Reform of the Roman Office 1964-1971*, Liturgical Press, Collegeville 1995.

Cardinal Archbishop and Bishops of the Province of Westminster, *A Vindication of the Bull 'Apostolicæ Curæ,'* second edition, Longmans Green & Co., London 1898.

Caronti, Emmanuele, OSB, Virgil Michel OSB, trans., *The Spirit of the Liturgy*, The Liturgical Press, Collegeville 1926.

Carson-Rowland, Michael, ed., *Faith and Liturgy: The Proceedings of the Seventh International Colloquium of Historical, Canonical and Theological Studies on the Roman Catholic Liturgy*, CIEL UK, Orpington 2002.

Casel, Odo, OSB, Neunheuser, Burkhard, OSB, ed., *The Mystery of Christian Worship and Other Writings*, Newmann Press & Darton, Longman & Todd, Westminster, Maryland & London 1962.

Cekada, Anthony, ed. & trans., *The Ottaviani Intervention: A Short Critical Study of the New Order of Mass*, Tan, Rockford 1992.

______________, *The Problems with the Prayers of the Modern Mass*, Tan, Rockford 1991.

Centre International d'Etudes Liturgiques, *La Liturgie: Trésor de l'Eglise*, Paris 1995.

Centro Liturgico Vincenziano, *50 Anni alla Luce Del Movimento Liturgico: La "Mediator Dei" – Il Centro di Azione Liturgica*, Rome 1998.

Chadwick, Owen, *From Bossuet to Newman*, second edition, CUP, Cambridge 1987.

______________, *The Reformation*, Penguin, Harmondsworth Middx. 1981.

Chupungco, Anscar J. OSB, *Cultural Adaptation of the Liturgy*, Paulist Press, New York 1982.

______________________, *Handbook for Liturgical Studies: Volume I – Introduction to the Liturgy*, Liturgical Press, Collegeville 1997.

______________________, *Handbook for Liturgical Studies: Volume II – Fundamental Liturgy*, Liturgical Press, Collegeville 1998.

Community of St Séverin, Margaret Clark, trans., *The Mass: Christians Around the Altar*, Geoffrey Chapman, London 1958.

Connelly, Joseph, *Hymns of the Roman Liturgy*, Longman, Green & Co., London, New York & Toronto, 1957.

Cours et Conférences de la Semaine Liturgique de Maredsous 19-24 Août 1912, Abbaye de Maredsous, Maredsous 1913.

Cours et Conférences des Semaines Liturgiques: Tome III – Congrès Liturgique Malines du 4 au 7 Août 1924, Abbaye du Mont-César, Louvain 1925.

Cours et Conférences des Semaines Liturgiques: Tome IV – La Paroisse: Louvain du 10 au 13 Août 1925, Abbaye du Mont-César, Louvain 1926.

Cours et Conférences des Semaines Liturgiques: Tome V – La Sainte Messe: Huy 1926, Abbaye du Mont-César, Louvain 1927.

Cours et Conférences des Semaines Liturgiques: Tome VI – La Préparation de l'Eucharistie: Louvain du 1 au 4 Août 1927, Abbaye du Mont-César, Louvain & Desclée, Bruges & Paris 1928.

Cours et Conférences des Semaines Liturgiques: Tome VII – Le Canon de la Messe: Tournai du 25 au 29 Juillet 1928, Abbaye du Mont-César, Louvain & Desclée, Bruges & Paris 1929.

Cours et Conférences des Semaines Liturgiques: Tome VIII – Tables (1912-1928), Abbaye du Mont-César, Louvain 1937.

Crichton, J.D., *As it Was: Reminiscences and Prophecies*, Decani Books, Mildenhall 1999.

___________, *Lights In Darkness: Forerunners of the Liturgical Movement*, Columba, Blackrock 1996.

___________, Winstone, H.E., & Ainslie, J.R., eds, *English Catholic Worship: Liturgical Renewal in England Since 1900*, Chapman, London 1979.

___________, The Once and the Future Liturgy, Veritas, Dublin 1977.

Crouan, Denis, Marc Sebanc, trans., *The Liturgy Betrayed*, Ignatius, San Francisco 2000.

__________________________, *The Liturgy After Vatican II: Collapsing or Resurgent*, Ignatius, San Francisco 2001.

Cunliffe, Charles R.A. ed., *English in the Liturgy: A Symposium*, Burns & Oates, London 1956.

Dalmais, I.H., OP, Roger Capel, trans., *Introduction to the Liturgy*, Geoffrey Chapman, London 1961.

Davies, Michael, *An Open Lesson to a Bishop: On the Development of the Roman Rite*, Tan Rockford, Illinois, 1980.

______________, *Cranmer's Godly Order*, second edition, Roman Catholic Books, New York 1995.

______________, *Pope Paul's New Mass*, Angelus Press, Dickinson, 1980.

Davis, Charles, *Liturgy and Doctrine*, Sheed & Ward/Stagbooks, London & New York 1960.

Day, Thomas, *Why Catholics Can't Sing: The Culture of Catholicism and the Triumph of Bad Taste*, Crossroad, New York 1991.

Des Semaines Liturgiques: Louvain du 10 au 14 Août 1913, Abbaye du Mont-César, Louvain 1914.

Duffy, Eamon, *The Stripping of the Altars: Traditional Religion in England 1400-1580*, Yale, New Haven & London 1992.

____________, *The Voices of Morebath: Reformation and Rebellion in an English Village*, Yale, New Haven & London 2001.

Ellard, Gerald, SJ, *Master Alcuin, Liturgist*, Loyola University Press, Chicago 1956.

________________, *Men at Work at Worship: America Joins the Liturgical Movement*, Longmans, Green & Co., New York & Toronto 1940.

________________, *Now Evening Mass: Our Latest Gift*, Liturgical Press, Collegeville 1954.

________________, *The Dialog Mass*, Longmans, Green & Co., New York & Toronto 1942.

________________,*The Mass of the Future*, Bruce Publishing Company, Milwaukee 1948.

________________, *The Mass in Transition*, Bruce Publishing Company, Milwaukee 1956.

Fenwick, John & Spinks, Bryan, *Worship in Transition: The Twentieth Century Liturgical Movement*, T & T Clark, Edinburgh 1995.

Filthaut, Theodor, Ronald Wallis, trans., *Learning to Worship*, Burns & Oates, London 1965.

Finnegan, Seán, ed., *Ministerial and Common Priesthood in the Eucharistic Celebration: The Proceedings of the Fourth International Colloquium of Historical, Canonical and Theological Studies on the Roman Catholic Liturgy*, Saint Austin Press & CIEL UK, London & Kingston & Surbiton 1999.

Fisch, Thomas, ed., *Liturgy and Tradition: Theological Reflections of Alexander Schmemann*, St Vladimir's Seminary Press, New York 1990.

Flanagan, Kieran, *Sociology and Liturgy: Re-Presentations of the Holy*, London 1991.

Fortescue, Adrian, *The Ceremonies of the Roman Rite Described*, Burns & Oates, London 1917.

__________________, *The Mass: A Study of the Roman Liturgy*, Longmans, Green & Co., London 1913.

__________________, *Latin Hymns Sung at the Church of Saint Hugh Letchworth*, Astley College, Letchworth 1913.

Franklin, R.W. & Spaeth, Robert L., *Virgil Michel: American Catholic*, Liturgical Press, Collegeville 1988.

Gamber, Klaus, Klaus D. Grimm, trans., *The Reform of the Roman Liturgy: Its Problems and Background*, Una Voce Press & Foundation for Catholic Reform, San Juan Capistrano & New York, 1993.

______________, Henry Taylor, trans., *The Modern Rite: Collected Essays on the Reform of the Liturgy*, Saint Michael's Abbey Press, Farnborough 2002.

______________, Simone Wallon, trans., *La Réforme Liturgique en Question*, Editions Sainte Madeleine, Barroux 1992.

Giampietro, Nicola, OFM Cap., *Il Card. Ferdinando Antonelli e gli sviluppi della riforma liturgica dal 1948 al 1970*, Pontificio Ateneo San Anselmo, Rome 1998.

Guardini, Romano, Ada Lane, trans., *The Church and the Catholic* and *The Spirit of the Liturgy*, Sheed & Ward, New York 1935.

_______________, Ada Lane, trans., *The Spirit of the Liturgy,* Sheed & Ward, London 1930.

Guéranger, Prosper, OSB, *Institutions Liturgiques,* vols. I & II, Débecort & Fleuriot, Paris et Mans 1840 & 1841.

_______________, *Institutions Liturgiques,* second edition, vols. I-IV, Palmé, Paris et Bruxelles 1878, 1880, 1883 & 1885.

_______________, Laurence Shepherd, trans., *The Liturgical Year: Advent,* second edition, Duffy, Dublin 1870.

Haquin, André, *Dom Lambert Beauduin et le Renouveau Liturgique,* Duculot, Gembloux 1970.

Harper, John, *The Forms and Orders of Western Liturgy from the Tenth to the Eighteenth Century,* Clarendon Press, Oxford 1991.

Hen, Yitzhak, *The Royal Patronage of Liturgy in Frankish Gaul to the Death of Charles the Bald (877),* Henry Bradshaw Society, Boydell, London 2001.

Hetherington, Arthur J., *Notes On The New Rubrics And The New Use Of The New Psalter,* Burns & Oates, London 1912.

Hitchcock, James, *The Recovery of the Sacred,* Ignatius Press, San Francisco 1995.

Hofinger, Johannes, SJ, ed., *Liturgy and the Missions: The Nijmegen Papers,* Burns & Oates, London 1960.

Howell, Clifford, SJ, *Preparing for Easter,* Burns & Oates, London 1957.

Hughes, Kathleen, RSCJ, ed., *How Firm a Foundation: Voices of the Early Liturgical Movement,* Liturgy Training Publications, Chicago 1990.

Hull, Geoffrey, *The Banished Heart: Origins of Heteropraxis in the Catholic Church,* Spes Nova League, Sydney 1995.

Johnson, Cuthbert, OSB, *Prosper Guéranger (1805-1875): A Liturgical Theologian: An Introduction to his liturgical writings and work,* Studia Anselmiana 89, Pontificio Ateneo S. Anselmo, Rome 1984.

Joseph, Peter, ed., Sheehan Michael, *Apologetics and Catholic Doctrine,* St Austin Press, London 2001.

_______________, & Ward, Anthony, eds., *Missale Romanum Anno 1962 Promulgatum* Centro Liturgico Vincenziano, Rome 1994.

Jungmann, Joseph A., SJ, Francis A. Brunner, trans., *The Early Liturgy to the time of Gregory the Great,* Darton, Longmann & Todd, London 1960.

_______________, Clifford Howell SJ, trans., *Liturgical Renewal in Retrospect and Prospect,* Challoner Books, London 1965.

_______________, *Pastoral Liturgy,* Challoner Books, London 1962.

_______________, A. Peeler, trans., *The Place of Christ in Liturgical Prayer,* Geoffrey Chapman, London & Dublin, 1965.

_______________, Clifford Howell SJ, trans., *Public Worship: A Survey,* Liturgical Press, Collegeville 1957.

_______________, Francis A. Brunner, CSsR, trans., *The Mass of the Roman Rite: Its Origins and Development (Missarium Solemnia),* 2 vols, Four Courts Press, Dublin 1986.

_______________, Clifford Howell SJ, trans., *The Sacrifice of the Church: The Meaning of the Mass,* Challoner Books, London 1956.

Ker, Ian, *Newman on Being A Christian,* Harper Collins, London 1990.

King, Archdale A., *Liturgies of the Past,* Longmans, London 1959.

_______________, *Liturgies of the Primatial Sees,* Longmans, London 1957.

_______________, *Liturgies of the Religious Orders,* Longmans, London 1955.

_______________, *Liturgy of the Roman Church,* Longmans, London 1957.

Kirchgaessner, A., *Unto the Altar: The Practice of Catholic Worship*, Herder & Nelson, Freiburg, Edinburgh & London 1963.

Klauser, Theodor, John Halliburton, trans., *A Short History of the Western Liturgy*, second edition, Oxford University Press, Oxford 1979.

Kocik, Thomas M., *The Reform of the Reform? – A Liturgical Debate: Reform or Return*, Ignatius Press, San Francisco 2003.

Koenker, Ernest B., *The Liturgical Renaissance in the Roman Catholic Church*, University of Chicago Press, Chicago 1954.

Korolevsky, Cyril, Donald Attwater, trans., *Living Languages in Catholic Worship: An Historical Enquiry*, Longmans, Green & Co., London, New York & Toronto 1957.

Lang, Jovian P., OFM, *Dictionary of the Liturgy*, Catholic Book Publishing Company, New York 1989.

Lang, U.M., *Turning Towards the Lord: Orientation in Liturgical Prayer*, Ignatius Press, San Francisco 2004.

Legg, J. Wickham, *The Reformed Breviary of Cardinal Tommasi*, SPCK, London 1904.

Leonard, William J., SJ, ed., *Liturgy for the People: Essays in honor of Gerald Ellard SJ 1894-1963*, Bruce, Milwaukee 1963.

Lesourd, P. et al., *Giacomo Cardinal Lercaro* [Men Who Make the Council: 3], University of Notre Dame Press, Notre Dame 1964.

Lippe, Robert, ed., *Missale Romanum Mediolani 1474*, Henry Bradshaw Society, London 1899.

The Liturgical Conference Inc., *Christ's Sacrifice and Ours: National Liturgical Week (USA) 1947*, Boston 1948.

____________________________, *National Liturgical Week (USA) 1943*, Ferdinand 1944.

____________________________, *National Liturgical Week (USA) 1944*, Chicago 1945.

____________________________, *The New Man in Christ: National Liturgical Week (USA) 1948*, Conception 1949.

____________________________, *Sanctification of Sunday: National Liturgical Week (USA) 1949*, Conception 1949.

____________________________, *The Priesthood of Christ: National Liturgical Week (USA) 1951*, Conception 1952.

____________________________, *The Easter Vigil: National Liturgical Week (USA) 1952*, Elsberry, Mo. 1953.

____________________________, *St Pius X and Social Worship: National Liturgical Week (USA) 1953*, Elsberry, Mo. 1953.

____________________________, *People's Participation and Holy Week: National Liturgical Week (USA) 1956*, Elsberry, Mo. 1957.

____________________________,*Education and the Liturgy: National Liturgical Week (USA) 1957*, Elsberry, Mo. 1958.

____________________________,*The Church Year: National Liturgical Week (USA) 1958*, Elsberry, Mo. 1959.

____________________________, *Participation in the Mass: National Liturgical Week (USA) 1959*, Washington D.C. 1960.

____________________________, *Bible, Life and Worship: National Liturgical Week (USA) 1961*, Washington D.C. 1961.

____________________________, *The Challenge of the Council: Person, Parish, World: National Liturgical Week (USA) 1964*, Washington D.C. 1964.

The Liturgical Press, *The Assisi Papers: Proceedings of the First International Congress of Pastoral Liturgy; Assisi-Rome, September 18-22, 1956*, Collegeville 1957.

Living Parish Series, *Living Parish Week*, Pellegrini & Co., Sydney 1958.

McDougall, Alan G., *Pange Lingua: Breviary Hymns of Old Uses*, Burns & Oates, London 1916.

McManus, Frederick, *Handbook for the New Rubrics*, Geoffrey Chapman, London 1961.

________________, *The Rites of Holy Week*, Saint Anthony Guild Press, New Jersey 1957.

Maas-Ewerd, Theodor, *Die Krise der Liturgischen Bewegung in Deutschland und Österreich: Zu den Auseinandersetzugen um die "liturgische Frage" in der Jahren 1939 bis 1944*, Friedrich Pustet, Regensburg 1981.

Maertens, Thierry, *Les Risques de Plafonnement du Mouvement Liturgique*, L'Apostolat Liturgique, Bruges 1961.

Martimort, A.G. ed., Austin Flannery OP, and Vincent Ryan OSB, English edition editors, *The Church at Prayer: Introduction to the Liturgy*, Irish University Press, Shannon 1968.

______________, et al., *The Liturgy and the Word of God*, Liturgical Press, Collegeville 1959.

______________, *Mirabile laudis canticum: melangés liturgiques*, Centro Liturgico Vincenziano, Rome 1991.

Marx, Paul B., OSB, *Virgil Michel and the Liturgical Movement*, Liturgical Press, Collegeville 1957.

Melbourne Diocesan Commission for the Liturgy and Sacred Music, *Australian Liturgical Week*, Advocate Press, Melbourne 1955.

Michel, Virgil, OSB, *My Sacrifice and Yours*, Liturgical Press, Collegeville 1927.

________________, *The Liturgy of the Church According to the Roman Rite*, Macmillan, New York 1938.

Mullerleile, Ernest, *At the Cradle of Folk-Liturgy: The Story of the Life Work of Father Pius Parsch*, Pio Decimo Press, Saint Louis [no date given—c. 1951].

Murphy, John L., *The Mass and Liturgical Reform*, Bruce, Milwaukee 1956.

Murphy, P. L., *The Ceremonies of Holy Week: Guide to the Restored Order*, St Patrick's College, Manly 1956.

____________ , ed., *The New Rubrics of the Roman Breviary and Missal*, Catholic Press Newspaper Co., Surrey Hills, 1960.

Murray, Placid, OSB, ed., *Studies in Pastoral Liturgy*, The Furrow Trust, Maynooth 1961.

Nero, Antonio, ed., *Quaderni Della Fondazione Giuseppe Sarto*, Asolo 1990.

Newman, John Henry, *An Essay on the Development of Christian Doctrine*, Longmans, Green & Co., London 1909.

________________, *Parochial and Plain Sermons*, Longmans Green & Co, London 1898.

Nichols, Aidan, OP, *Christendom Awake: On Re-energising the Church in Culture*, T & T Clark, Edinburgh 1999.

________________, *Dominican Gallery: Portrait of a Culture*, Gracewing, Leominster 1997.

________________, *Looking at the Liturgy: A Critical View of its Contemporary Form*, Ignatius, San Francisco 1996.

O'Connell, J. B., *Sacred Music and Liturgy*, Burns & Oates, London 1959.

______________, *Simplifying the Rubrics of the Roman Breviary and Missal: A Translation, with Commentary, of the Decree "Cum Nostra,"* Burns & Oates, London 1955.

______________, *The Celebration of Mass: A Study of the Rubrics of the Roman Missal Vol. II The Rite of the Celebration of Low Mass*, second edition, Burns Oates & Washbourne, London 1949.

______________, *The Ceremonies of Holy Week: Solemn Rite and Simple Rite*, Burns & Oates, London 1957.

______________, *The Rubrics of the Roman Breviary and Missal*, Burns & Oates, London 1960.

Overath, Johannes., ed., *Sacred Music and Liturgy Reform After Vatican II*, Consociatio Internationalis Musicæ Sacræ, Rome 1969.

Parsch, Pius, H.E. Winstone, trans., *The Liturgy of the Mass*, 3rd ed., Herder, London & St Louis 1957.

__________, H.E. Winstone, trans., *Seasons of Grace*, Challoner Publications, London 1963.

Pecklers, Keith F., SJ, *The Liturgical Movement in the United States of America: 1926-1955*, Excerptum ex Dissertatione ad Doctoram Sacræ Liturgiæ assequendum in Pontificio Instituto Liturgico Pontificium Athenaeum S. Anselmi De Urbe Pontificium Institutum Liturgicum, Rome 1996.

__________, *The Unread Vision: The Liturgical Movement in the United States of America: 1926-1955*, Liturgical Press, Collegeville 1998.

__________, *Worship*, Continuum, London & New York 2003.

Pepler, Conrad, OP, *Lent: A Liturgical Commentary on the Lessons and Gospels*, Herder, London and St Louis 1946.

__________, *Sacramental Prayer*, Bloomsbury, London 1959.

Pickstock, Catherine, *After Writing: On the Liturgical Consummation of Philosophy*, Blackwell, Oxford 1998.

Pierce, Joanne M. & Downey, Michael, eds., *Source and Summit: Commemorating Josef A. Jungmann SJ*, Liturgical Press, Collegeville 1999.

Pommarès, Jean-Marie, OSB, *Trente et le Missel: L'évolution de la question de l'autorité compétente en matère de Missels*, Centro Liturgico Vincenziano, Rome 1997.

Priests of St Séverin (Paris) and St Joseph (Nice), Lancelot C. Sheppard, trans. & adapter, *What is the Liturgical Movement?* Faith and Fact Books 110, Burns & Oates, London 1964.

Quitslund, Sonya A., *Beauduin: A Prophet Vindicated*, Newman, New York, Paramus NJ & Toronto 1973.

Ratzinger, Joseph, Martha M. Matesich, trans., *A New Song for the Lord: Faith in Christ and Liturgy Today*, Crossroad, New York 1997.

__________, Erasmo Leiva-Merikakis trans., *Milestones: Memoirs 1927-1977*, Ignatius, San Francisco 1997.

__________, Graham Harrison, trans., *The Feast of Faith: Approaches to a Theology of the Liturgy*, Ignatius, San Francisco 1986.

__________, John Saward, trans., *The Spirit of the Liturgy*, Ignatius, San Francisco 2000.

Regnault, Lucien, ed., *Dom Paul Delatte: Lettres*, Éditions des Solesmes, Solesmes 1991.

Reinhold, H.A., *The Autobiography of Father Reinhold*, Herder & Herder, New York 1968.

__________, *Bringing the Mass to the People*, Burns & Oates, London 1960.

__________, *The Dynamics of Liturgy*, Macmillan, New York 1961.

Richards, Michael, *The Liturgy in England*, Geoffrey Chapman, London 1966.

Richstatter, Thomas, OFM, *Liturgical Law Today: New Style, New Spirit*, Franciscan Herald Press, Chicago 1977.

Reid, Alcuin, OSB, ed., *A Pope and a Council on the Sacred Liturgy: Pope Pius XII's 'Mediator Dei' and the Second Vatican Council's 'Sacrosanctum Concilium' with a comparative study 'A Tale of Two Documents' by Aidan Nichols OP*, St Michael's Abbey Press, Farnborough 2002.

__________, ed., *Looking Again at the Question of the Liturgy with Cardinal Ratzinger: Proceedings of the July 2001 Fontgombault Liturgical Conference*, St Michael's Abbey Press, Farnborough 2003.

Reid, Scott M.P. ed., *A Bitter Trial: Evelyn Waugh and John Carmel Cardinal Heenan on the Liturgical Changes*, second edition, The Saint Austin Press, London 2000.

Rose, Michael S., *Ugly as Sin: Why They Changed Our Churches from Sacred Places to Meeting Spaces – and How We Can Change Them Back Again*, Sophia Institute Press, New Hampshire 2001.

Rousseau, Oliver, OSB, Benedictines of Westminster Priory, trans., *The Progress of the Liturgy: An Historical Sketch From the Beginning of the Nineteenth Century to the Pontificate of Pius X*, Newman, Maryland 1951.

Rowland, Tracey, *Culture and the Thomist Tradition After Vatican II*, Routledge, London 2003.

Ryan, Vincent, OSB, ed., *Studies in Pastoral Liturgy*, vol. II, Gill, Dublin 1963.

Schmitt, Siegfried, *Die internationalen liturgischen Studientreffen 1951-1960: Zur Vorgeschichte der Liturgiekonstitution*, Paulinus-Verlag, Trier 1992.

Sheppard, Lancelot C., *The Mass in the West*, Faith and Fact Books 114, Burns & Oates, London 1962.

__________________, ed., *True Worship*, Helicon Press, Baltimore & Darton, Longman & Todd, London 1963.

Shipley Duckett, Eleanor, *Alcuin, Friend of Charlemagne*, Macmillan, New York 1951.

Shirilla, Gerald M., *The Principle of Active Participation of the Faithful in Sacrosanctum Concilium*, Pontificium Institutum Liturgicum, Rome 1990.

Schuster, Ildefonso, OSB, Arthur Levelis-Marke (trans.), *The Sacramentary: Historical and Liturgical Notes on the Roman Missal*, vol. I, Burns, Oates & Washbourne, London 1924.

Society of Saint Pius X, *The Problem of the Liturgical Reform*, Angelus Press, Kansas City 2001.

Sodi, Manlio & Triacca, Achille Maria, eds., *Breviarium Romanum Editio Princeps 1568*, Libreria Editrice Vaticana, Vatican City 1999.

____, *Missale Romanum Editio Princeps 1570*, Libreria Editrice Vaticana, Vatican City 1998.

Spurr, Barry, *The Word in the Desert: Anglican and Roman Catholic Reactions to Liturgical Reform*, Lutterworth, Cambridge 1995.

Steuart, Benedict, OSB, *The Development of Christian Worship*, Longmans Green & Co., London 1953.

Strawley, James Herbert, *The Liturgical Movement: Its Origin and Growth*, Alcuin Club Tracts XXVII, A.R. Mowbray, London 1954.

Taft, Robert, SJ, *The Liturgy of the Hours in East and West: The Origins of the Divine Office and its Meaning for Today*, Liturgical Press, Collegeville 1986.

Torevell, David, *Losing The Sacred: Ritual, Modernity and Liturgical Reform*, T & T Clark, Edinburgh 2000.

Tuzik, Robert L., ed., *How Firm a Foundation: Leaders of the Early Liturgical Movement*, Liturgy Training Publications, Chicago 1990.

Vance, John G., & Fortescue, J.W., *Adrian Fortescue: A Memoir*, Burns, Oates & Washbourne 1924.

Van Dijk, S.J.P., OFM, & Walker, J. Hazelden, *The Origins of the Modern Roman Liturgy: The Liturgy of the Papal Court and the Franciscan Order in the Thirteenth Century*, Newman Press, Westminster MD & Darton, Longman & Todd, London 1960.

Vogel, Cyrille, William G. Storey & Niels Krogh Ramussen OP, trans., *Medieval Liturgy: An Introduction to the Sources*, Pastoral Press, Washington 1986.

Von Matt, L., & Vian, N., Sebastian Bullough, trans., *St Pius X: A Pictorial Biography*, Longmans, London 1955.

Vorgrimler, Herbert, ed., *Commentary on the Documents of Vatican II*, vol. I, Burns & Oates, Herder & Herder, London & New York 1967.

Wagner, Johannes, *Mein Weg Zur Liturgiereform: 1936-1986 Erinnerungen*, Herder, Frieburg, Basel, Wien 1993.

Walsh, Michael, *An Illustrated History of the Popes: Saint Peter to John Paul II,* Marshall Cavendish, London 1980.

Ward, Anthony, SM, & Johnson, Cuthbert, OSB, eds., *Missalis Romani Editio Princeps: Mediolani anno 1474 prelis mandata,* Centro Liturgico Vincenziano, Rome 1996.

____________________, *Pontificale Romanum Editio Iuxta Typicam 1962,* Centro Liturgico Vincenziano, Rome 1999.

Wesseling, Theodore, OSB, *Liturgy and Life,* Longmans, Green & Co., London 1938.

White, James F., *Roman Catholic Worship: Trent to Today,* Paulist Press, New York 1995.

Willis, G.G., *A History of Roman Liturgy to the Death of Gregory the Great,* Henry Bradshaw Society, Boydell, London 1994.

Wiseman, Nicholas, *Essays on Various Subjects,* vol. I, Dolman, London 1853.

____________, *Four Lectures on the Offices and Ceremonies of Holy Week,* Washbourne, London 1838.

Articles and Published Letters

Anson, P.F., "Fads and Fashions" in: *Orate Fratres* vol. XVI no. 10 1941/2 pp. 454-457.

Antonelli, Fernando, OFM, "Commentary" [on the Instruction on Sacred Music and the Liturgy] in: *Worship* vol. XXXII no. 10 1957/8 pp. 626-637.

Attwater, Donald, "The Liturgical Movement in England" in: *Orate Fratres* vol. I no. 11 1926/7 pp. 343-345.

____________, "The Liturgical Revival in England" in: The Liturgical Conference Inc., *Sanctification of Sunday: National Liturgical Week (USA) 1949,* pp. 150-156.

____________, "Two Years Later—and a Query" in: *Orate Fratres* vol. IV no. 4 1929/30 pp. 151-55.

Avery, Benedict R., OSB, "The Vulgate Psalter: A New Revision" in: *Worship* vol. XXXVI no. 10 1961/2 pp. 626-636.

Beauduin, Lambert, OSB, "Le décret de 9 Février 1951 et les espoirs qu'il suscite" in: *La Maison-Dieu* no. 26 1951 pp. 100-111.

____________, "L'Encyclique *Mediator Dei*" in: *La Maison-Dieu* no. 13 1948 pp. 7-25.

____________, "Liminaire a Restauration de la Semaine Sainte" in: *La Maison-Dieu* no. 45 1956 pp. 5-8.

____________, "Normes pratiques pour les réformes liturgiques" in: *La Maison-Dieu* no. 1 1945 pp. 9-22.

Bernareggi, Adriano, "The Liturgical Movement in Italy" in: *Orate Fratres* vol. V no. 5 1930/1 pp. 229-235.

____________, "The Liturgical Movement in Italy II" in: *Orate Fratres* vol. V no. 6 1930/1 pp. 272-281.

____________, "The Liturgical Movement in Italy III" in: *Orate Fratres* vol. V no. 7 1930/1 pp. 327-331.

Bévenot, Laurence, "De Musicæ Sacræ Disciplina" in: *Liturgy* vol. XXV no. 3, July 1956 pp. 77-83.

Bishop, Edmund, "The Liturgical Reforms of Charlemagne: their meaning and value" in: *The Downside Review* vol. XXXVII no. 1 1919 pp. 1-16.

____________, "La Réforme Liturgique de Charlemagne" in: *Ephemerides Liturgicæ* Anno XLV 1931 pp. 186-207.

Bouyer, Louis, Cong. Orat., "Où en est le Mouvement Liturgique?" in: *La Maison-Dieu* no. 25 1951 pp. 34-46.

____________, "The Word of God Lives in the Liturgy" in: Martimort et al., *The Liturgy and the Word of God,* pp. 53-66.

Brogan, Cuthbert, OSB, "Chapters in the History of Saint Michael's Abbey" in: *Laudetur* August 2001, pp. 16-25.

____________________, "Chapters in the History of Saint Michael's Abbey" in: *Laudetur* December 2001, pp. 13-22.

Bugnini, Annibale, CM, "Breviary Reform" in: *Worship* vol. XXXVII no. 4 1962/3 pp. 221-226.

____________________, "Mass with Deacon" in: *Worship* vol. XXXII no. 8 1957/8 pp. 459-463.

____________________, "Per una Riforma Liturgica Generale" in: *Ephemerides Liturgicæ* vol. LXIII 1949 pp. 166-184.

____________________, "Why a Liturgy Reform?" in: *Worship* vol. XXIX no. 10 1954/5 pp. 562-569.

Burrett, A.S.E., "Breviary and Calendar Reform" in: *The Clergy Review* vol. XXXV no. 4 April 1951 pp. 225-231.

Busch, William, "About the Encyclical *Mediator Dei*" in: *Orate Fratres* vol. XXII no. 4 1947/8 pp. 153-156.

_____________,"On Liturgical Reforms" in: *Orate Fratres* vol. XI no. 8 1936/7 pp. 352-357.

_____________, "Travel notes on the Liturgical Movement," in: *Orate Fratres* vol. I no. 2 1926/7 pp. 50-55.

Cabrol, Fernand, OSB, "Alcuin" in: F. Cabrol & H. Leclercq, eds., *Dictionnaire d'Archéologie Chrétienne et de Liturgie* I–1, col. 1072-1092.

____________________, "Introduction" to *The Day Hours of the Church* pp. ix-xxxiii.

Capelle, Bernard, OSB, "Crise du Mouvement liturgique?" in: *Questions Liturgiques et Paroissiales* no. 32 1951 pp. 209-217.

____________________, "Fraction et Commixtion: Aménagements souhaitables des rites actuels" in: *La Maison-Dieu* no. 35 1953 pp. 79-94.

____________________, "The Holy See and the Liturgical Movement" in: *Orate Fratres* vol. XI no. 1 1936/7 pp. 1-8.

____________________, "The Holy See and the Liturgical Movement (2)" in: *Orate Fratres* vol. XI no. 2 1936/7 pp. 50-61.

Carboni, Romolo, "The Liturgical Movement" in: Melbourne Diocesan Commission for the Liturgy and Sacred Music, *Australian Liturgical Week,* pp. 5-13.

Carroll, Thomas J., "Liturgical Week: What is it?" in: The Liturgical Conference, *People's Participation and Holy Week: National Liturgical Week (USA) 1956* pp. 4-12.

Casey, George W., review of: Reinhold, *Bringing the Mass to the People* in: *Worship* vol. XXXV no. 1 1960/1 pp. 66-68.

Catella, Alceste, "Dalla Constituzione Conciliare *Sacrosanctum Concilium* all'Enciclica *Mediator Dei*" in: Centro Liturgico Vincenziano, *50 Anni alla Luce Del Movimento Liturgico* pp. 11-43.

Challis, J., "Holy Week in Australian Parishes" in: Living Parish Series, *Living Parish Week* pp. 83-100.

Chupungco, Anscar J., OSB, "History of the Roman Liturgy until the Fifteenth Century" in: Chupungco, *Handbook for Liturgical Studies* vol. I pp. 131-152.

Chute, D., "Obsolete or Obsolescent?" in: *Liturgy* vol. XVIII no. 3, July 1949 pp. 89-94.

Congar, Yves M.-J. OP, "True and False Reform in the Church" in: *Orate Fratres* vol. XXIII no. 6 1948/9 pp. 252-259.

Connelly, J., "The Restored Paschal Vigil" in: *Liturgy* vol. XX no. 3, July 1951 pp. 73-81.

Coppersmith, Anselm, "Liturgy and the Armed Forces," in: The Liturgical Conference, *National Liturgical Week (USA) 1943* pp. 141-153.

Cornides, Augustine, "The German Scene" *Worship* vol. XXXV no. IV 1960/61 pp. 256.

Cowell, Edith, "Adrian Fortescue," in: *Blackfriars* vol. IV no. 41 August 1923 pp. 1029-1034.

Coyne, John J., "The Traditional Position" in: Cunliffe, *English in the Liturgy* pp. 92-108.

Crehan, Joseph H., SJ, "Fashioning the Liturgy" in: *The Month* vol. CLXXXVI no. 3 Dec 1948 pp. 314-316.

Crichton, J.D., "An Historical Sketch of the Roman Liturgy," in: Sheppard, *True Worship* pp. 45-82.

____________, "More About the Lugano Congress" in: *Liturgy* vol. XXIII no. 3, July 1954 pp. 111-113.

____________, "Notes and News" *Liturgy* vol. XXIV no. 1, January 1955 pp. 23-27.

____________, "Pastoral Reflections on the Restored Liturgy of Holy Week" in: *Liturgy* vol. XXV no. 3, July 1956 pp. 92-101.

____________, "The Decree *Maxima Redemptionis Mysteria*" in: *Liturgy* vol. XXV no. 2, April 1956 pp. 45-52.

____________, "The New Instruction" in: *Liturgy* vol. XXVIII no. 1 January 1959 pp. 2-13.

____________, "The Recent Changes in the Missal and Breviary" in: *Liturgy* vol. XXIV no. 5, July 1955 pp. 73-76.

____________, "Review Article" *Liturgy* vol. 20 no. 6 August-September 1996, pp. 249-258, 263;

____________, "Rome and Liturgical Reform: The Lugano Congress, September 1953" in: *Liturgy* vol. XXIII no. 1, January 1954 pp. 32-36.

____________, "The New Encyclical on the Liturgy" in: *Liturgy* vol. XVII no. 2, April 1948 pp. 35-40.

Diekmann, Godfrey, OSB, "Assisi in Retrospect" in: *Worship* vol. XXXI no. 1 1956/7 pp. 48-52.

____________________, "A Papal Letter" in: *Worship* vol. XXXIII no. 10 1958/9 pp. 650-653.

____________________, "The Easter-Eve Celebration" in: *Orate Fratres* vol. XXV no. 6 1950/1 pp. 278-283.

____________________, "Liturgical Briefs," in: *Worship* vol. XXXI no. 10 1956/7 pp. 610 ff.

____________________, "Louvain and Versailles" in: *Worship* vol. XXVIII no. 12 1953/4 pp. 537-544.

____________________, "Movement in Germany" in: *Orate Fratres* vol. XXIII no. 10 1948/9 pp. 471-474.

Duschak, William J., "The Possibilities of Forms of the Mass in Mission Territories" in: Hofinger, *Liturgy and the Missions*, pp. 128-144.

_______________, "An Ecumenical Mass Liturgy" in: *Worship* vol. XXXVII no. 8 1962/63 pp. 538-546.

Duffy, Eamon, *"Rewriting the Liturgy: The Theological Implications of Translation,"* in: Caldecott, *Beyond the Prosaic: Renewing the Liturgical Movement* pp. 97-126.

Durst, Bernhard, OSB, "Liturgie-Enzyklica un Meßfeierreform" in: *Theologie und Glaube* vol. 46 1956 pp. 276-291.

Ehman, Benedict "The Inevitability of Evening Mass" in: The Liturgical Conference Inc., *St Pius X and Social Worship: National Liturgical Week (USA) 1953* pp. 184-191.

Ellard, Gerald, SJ, "'A Spiritual Citadel of the Rhineland' Maria Laach and the Liturgical Movement" in: *Orate Fratres* vol. III no. 12 1928/9 pp. 384-388.

________________, "At Mass with my Encyclical" in: *Orate Fratres* vol. XXII no. 6 1947/8 pp. 241-246.

________________, "Blossoms of the second spring: the Liturgical Movement in England," in: *Orate Fratres* vol. II no. 10 1927/8 pp. 310-314.

________________, "From a Pilgrim's Notebook: St André by Bruges" in: *Orate Fratres* vol. IV no. 7 1929/30 pp. 301-305.

________________, "Jungmann's Volume Two" in: *Worship* vol. XXX no. 3 1955/6 pp. 217-219.

________________, "Liturgy for the common man in Austria," in: *Orate Fratres* vol. III no. 1 1928/9, pp. 17-22.

________________, "People Need a Simpler Mass" in: *Worship* vol. XXXIV no. 3 1959/60 pp. 131-137.

________________, "Pius Tenth and the New Liturgy," in: *Orate Fratres* vol. I no. 8 1926/7, pp. 241-246.

________________, "Pope Pius XI on Corporate Worship" in: *Orate Fratres* vol. X nos. 11-12 1935/6 pp. 553-561.

________________, "'Tiptoe on a Misty Mountain Top:' Thoughts on the Dialog Mass" in: *Orate Fratres* vol. IV no. 9-10 1929/30 pp. 394-399.

Ellebracht, Mary Pierre, "Martin Hellriegel: Pastor," in: Tuzik, *How Firm a Foundation: Leaders of the Early Liturgical Movement* pp. 184-190.

Evans, Illtud, OP, "The International Conference at Mt. Ste. Odile" in: *Worship* vol. XXVII no. 3 1952/3 pp. 149-153.

Falque, Ferdinand C., "Liturgical Spirit in Reform," in: *Orate Fratres* vol. XI no. 5 1936/7, pp. 209-213.

Fennelly, John, "Nihil Innovatur—No Change" in: *Worship* vol. XXXI no. 1 1956/7 pp. 54-55.

Fischer, Balthasar, "Impressions of the German Ritual" in: Murray, *Studies in Pastoral Liturgy* pp. 47-61.

Fitzsimons, J., "The Future of the Liturgical Movement in England:" in: *Liturgy* vol. XV no. 1, January 1945 pp. 10-23.

Ford, John C., "Teaching Liturgy in the Seminary" in: *Orate Fratres* vol. XXI no. 7 1946/7 pp. 289-299.

Fortescue, Adrian, "Concerning Hymns," in: McDougall, *Pange Lingua: Breviary Hymns of Old Uses* pp. xi-xxxix.

Gasparri, Peter Cardinal, letter to Rt Rev. P. Antonio M. Marcet, OSB, March 15, 1915 [no. 4820] in: "Pope Benedict XV and the Liturgy" in: *Orate Fratres* vol. IX no. 7 1934/5 p. 325.

Geaney, Dennis J., "Guarded Enthusiasm" in: *Worship* vol. XXXIII 1958/9 no. 7 pp. 417-421.

Geffré, Claude, Barrie Mackay, trans., "Traditionalism without Lefebvre" in: *Concilium* 202 no. 2 1989 pp. xi-xvi.

Greeley, Andrew M., "What Next?" in: *Worship* vol. XXXI no.10 1956/7 pp. 587-591.

Gromier, Léon, "The 'Restored' Holy Week," 1960, www.geocities.com/Athens/Styx/3121/gromier.html.

Guardini, Romano, "Some Dangers of the Liturgical Revival" in: A. Kirchgaessner, *Unto the Altar* pp. 13-22.

Hallinan, Paul "The Church's Liturgy: Growth and Development" in: *The Challenge of the Council: Person, Parish, World: National Liturgical Week (USA) 1964* pp. 94-100.

Harrison, Brian W., OS, "A Reform of the Mass? Britain has Other Priorities;" *Apropos* no. 18, May 1996 pp. 69-74.

_______________, "The Postconciliar Eucharistic Liturgy: Planning a 'Reform of the Reform'" in: Kocik, *The Reform of the Reform?* pp. 151-193.

Heenan, John Carmel, Intervention at the Synod of Bishops, Rome, October 1967, in: Reid, Scott M.P., ed., *A Bitter Trial* pp. 70-72.

Hellriegel, Martin, "1947 Mediator Dei 1957" in: *Worship* vol. XXXII no. 1 1957/8 pp. 2-7.

_______________, "The New Papal Permission" in: *Orate Fratres* vol. XXV no. 5 1950/1 pp. 225-229.

_______________,"A Pastor's Description of Liturgical Participation in His Parish (Continued)," in: Benedictine Liturgical Conference, *National Liturgical Week (USA) 1941* pp. 82-90.

_______________, "A survey of the Liturgical Movement," in: *Orate Fratres* vol. III no. 11 1928/9, pp. 333-339.

_______________, "Merely Suggesting" in: *Orate Fratres* vol. XV no. 9 1940/1 pp. 390-397.

_______________, "The Parish and Divine Worship," in: Benedictine Liturgical Conference, *National Liturgical Week (USA) 1940* pp. 31-38.

Howell, Clifford, SJ, "The Parish in the Life of the Church" in: Living Parish Series, *Living Parish Week* pp. 7-29.

Jedin, Hubert, "Das Konzil von Trient und die Reform der Liturgischen Bücher," in: *Ephemerides Liturgicæ* vol. LIX 1945, pp. 5-38.

John Paul II, "New saint gives special witness to scholars and pastors," Homily at the Canonisation of Blessed Giuseppe Maria Tommasi, in: *L'Osservatore Romano: Weekly Edition in English* 20 October 1986, pp. 8-9.

Jungmann, Joseph A., SJ, Lalit Adolphus trans., "Constitution on the Sacred Liturgy" in: Vorgrimler, *Commentary on the Documents of Vatican II* vol. I pp. 1-87.

_______________, "The History of Holy Week as the Heart of the Liturgical Year" in: Murray, *Studies in Pastoral Liturgy* pp. 11-24.

_______________, "The Pastoral Idea in the History of the Liturgy," in: The Liturgical Press, *The Assisi Papers* pp. 18-31.

_______________, "Problems of the Missal" in: *Worship* vol. XXVIII no. 3 1953/4 pp. 153-157.

_______________, Hugh M. Riley trans., "Vespers and the Devotional Service" in: Leonard, *Liturgy for the People* pp. 168-178.

_______________, "Liturgy on the Eve of the Reformation" in: *Worship* vol. XXXIII no. 8 1958/9 pp. 505–515.

Kelly, John E., "The Encyclical, *Mediator Dei*" in: The Liturgical Conference, *The New Man in Christ: National Liturgical Week (USA) 1948* pp. 9-14.

Knowles, David, OSB, letter to the editor, *The Tablet* vol. 225 no. 6842, 24 July 1971, p. 724.

Kuehn, Regina, "Romano Guardini: The Teacher of Teachers," in: Tuzik, *How Firm a Foundation: Leaders of the Early Liturgical Movement* pp. 36-49.

Leclercq, Henri, "Liturgistes" in: F. Cabrol & H. Leclercq, eds., *Dictionnaire d'Archéologie Chrétienne et de Liturgie*, IX-2 col. 1730-1749.

Lercaro, Giacomo, John R. M. Nolan trans., "The Christian Church" in: *The Furrow* June 1957 pp. 341-349.

Liturgy Forum of the Centre for Faith and Culture of Westminster College, Oxford, "The Oxford Declaration on Liturgy", in: *Communio* vol. XXIII no. 3 Fall 1996 pp. 633-634.

Lord, Joseph, "Neu-Deutschland and German Catholic Youth" in: *Orate Fratres* vol. V no. 7 1930/1 pp. 303-308.

Löw, Joseph, CSsR, "Assisi 1956 and Holy Week 1957" in: *Worship* vol. XXXI no. 5 1956/7 pp. 236-247.

_________________, "Tabernacle and Altar: Commentary" in: *Worship* vol. XXXI no. 10 1956/7 pp. 572-580.

_________________, "The New Holy Week Liturgy: A Pastoral Opportunity" in: *Worship* vol. XXX no. 2 1955/6 pp. 94-113.

_________________, "The New Instruction" in: *Worship* vol. XXXIII no. 1 1958/9 pp. 2-13.

_________________, "The New Rite of Consecration" in: *Worship* vol. XXXV no. 8 1960/61 pp. 527-536.

_________________, "We Must Celebrate the Easter Night" in: *Worship* vol. XXVII no. 4 1952/3 pp. 161-171.

Luykx, Bonifaas, OPraem, "Adaptation of the Liturgy in the Missions" in: Hofinger, *Liturgy and the Missions* pp. 76-88.

Maertens, Thierry, "La célébration de la messe à la lumiere des directoires recents" *Paroisse et Liturgie* 39 1957 pp. 159-179.

Masure, Eugene, "About the New Psalter" in: *Liturgy* vol. XVII no. 1 January 1948 pp 8-13.

Martindale, C.C., SJ, "Liturgy Reform," in: *Orate Fratres* vol. XI no. 6 1936/7 pp. 241-245.

McDonnell, Killian, "Calvin's Concept of the Liturgy and the Future of the Roman Catholic Liturgy," in: *Concilium* vol. 2 no. 5 February 1969 pp. 43-48.

McGarry, J.G., "The Liturgy in Ireland" in: *Worship* vol. XXXI no. 7 1956/7 pp. 409-411.

____________, "The Irish Congress" *Worship* vol. XXXII no. 8 1957/8 pp. 496-499.

McMahon, Joseph H., letter: "The Green Wood Reproaches the Dry" in: *Orate Fratres* vol. IV no. 12 1929/30 pp. 527-8.

McManus, Frederick R., "Liturgical Week 1961" in: The Liturgical Conference Inc., *Bible, Life and Worship: National Liturgical Week (USA) 1961* pp. 1-6.

____________________ "Responses" in: *Worship* vol. XXXIV no. 10 1959/60 pp. 637-641.

____________________ "The Law, the Liturgy, and Participation" in: The Liturgical Conference Inc., *Participation in the Mass: National Liturgical Week (USA) 1959* pp. 43-51.

____________________ "The New Pontifical" in: *Worship* vol. XXXVI no. 4 1961/62 pp. 272-281.

____________________ "The Restored Liturgical Catechumenate" in: *Worship* XXXVI no. 8 1961/62 pp. 536-549.

Miranda y Gómez, Miguel Dario "*Function of Sacred Music and Actuosa Participatio*" in: Overath, J., ed., *Sacred Music and Liturgy Reform After Vatican II* pp. 111-116.

Mitchell, Nathan, "Reform the Reform?" in: *Worship* vol. LXXI no. 6 1997 pp. 555-563.

Müller, Gerhard Ludwig, "Can Mankind Understand the Spirit of the Liturgy Anymore?" in: *Antiphon* vol. 7 no. 2 2002 pp. 2-5.

_______________, "Rereading Reform" in: *Worship* vol. LXXI no. 5 1997 pp. 462-470.

Neuhaus, Richard John, "What Happened to the Liturgical Movement?" in: *Antiphon* vol. VI no. 2 2001 pp. 5-7.

Neunheuser, Burkhard, "Report on Germany" in: *Orate Fratres* vol. XXI no. 3 1946/7 pp. 114-122.

Nichols, Aidan, OP, "A Tale of Two Documents: *Sacrosanctum Concilium* and *Mediator Dei*" in: *Antiphon* vol. V no. 1 2000 pp. 23-31.

_________________, "Odo Casel Revisited" in: *Antiphon* vol. III no. 1 1998 pp. 12-20.

_________________, "Revelation, Tradition and the Liturgy," in: Carson-Rowland, *Faith and Liturgy* pp. 155-168.

O'Connell, J.B., "The International Liturgical Congress at Assisi," in: *The Clergy Review* vol. XLI no. 11 November 1956, pp. 641-649.

____________, "The Liturgical Movement in Great Britain and Ireland," in: Jungmann, *Liturgical Renewal in Retrospect and Prospect* pp. 38-45.

Papillon, P., "La Messe," supplement to *Fêtes et Saisons* no. 89 October 1954.

Parsch, Pius, "Liturgical Action in Austria" in: *Orate Fratres* vol. V no. 3 1930/1 pp. 126-130.

__________, "Liturgical Action in Austria (Cont.)" in: *Orate Fratres* vol. V no. 4 1930/1 pp. 176-182.

__________, "The Weekly Psalter of the Roman Breviary," in: *Orate Fratres* vol. XIII no. 6 1938/9 pp. 270-274.

Parsons, John P., "A Reform of the Reform? Part I" in: Kocik, *The Reform of the Reform?* pp. 211-256.

Pecklers, Keith F., SJ, "History of the Roman Liturgy from the Sixteenth until the Twentieth Centuries" in: Chupungco, *Handbook for Liturgical Studies* vol. I pp. 153-178.

Peiffer, Robert, "Joseph Jungmann: Laying a Foundation for Vatican II" in: Tuzik, *How Firm a Foundation: Leaders of the Early Liturgical Movement* pp. 58-62.

Pérès, Marcel, "The Choirmaster and His Liturgical Role" in: Finnegan, S., ed., *Ministerial and Common Priesthood in the Eucharistic Celebration* pp. 169-178.

Peterson, John B., "Pistoia, Synod of," in: Herbermann et al. eds., *The Catholic Encyclopaedia* vol. 12, The Encyclopaedia Press, New York, 1911, pp. 116-117.

Pickstock, Catherine, "Medieval Liturgy and Modern Reform" in: *Antiphon* vol. VI 2001 no. 1 pp. 19-25.

Pristas, Lauren, "Theological Principles that Guided the Redaction of the Roman Missal (1970)," in: *The Thomist* vol. 67 (2003) pp. 157-195.

Ratzinger, Joseph, "Assessment and Future Prospects" in: Reid, *Looking Again at the Question of the Liturgy with Cardinal Ratzinger: Proceedings of the July 2001 Fontgombault Liturgical Conference* pp. 145-153.

______________, "Klaus Gamber: L'intrépidité d'un vrai témoin" in: Gamber, *La Réforme Liturgique en Question,* pp 6-8.

Reinhold, H. A., "A Turning Point: Lugano" in: *Worship* vol. XXVII no. 12 1952/3 pp. 557-563.

____________, "Desiderata to be Prayed For" in: *Orate Fratres* vol. XX no. 5 1945/6 pp. 230-235.

____________, "Dom Odo Casel" in: *Orate Fratres* vol. XXII no. 8 1947/8 pp. 366-372.

____________, "Jubé d'Asnières" in: *Orate Fratres* vol. XXI no. 11 1946/7 pp. 513-517.

____________, "Missarium Sollemnia" in: *Orate Fratres* vol. XXIII no. 3 1948/9 pp. 122-127.

____________, "More or Less Liturgical" in: *Orate Fratres* vol. XIII no. 4 1938/9 pp. 152-155.

____________, "More or Less Liturgical (continued)" in: *Orate Fratres* vol. XIII no. 5 1938/9 pp. 213-218.

____________, "My Dream Mass" in: *Orate Fratres* vol. XIV no. 6 1939/40 pp. 265-270.

____________, "Past and Present" in: *Worship*, vol. XXVI 1951/2 no. 4 pp. 179-186.

____________ "The Renewed Good Friday Liturgy" in: *Worship* vol. XXXI no. 5 1956/7 pp. 254-265.

____________, "The Liturgical Movement to Date" in: The Liturgical Conference Inc., *Christ's Sacrifice and Ours* pp. 9-20.

____________, "The New Eucharistic Decrees" in: *Worship* vol. XXVII no. 4 1952/3 pp. 187-190.

_____________, "Towards the Breviary Reform" in: *Orate Fratres* vol. XXIII no. 2 1948/9 pp. 74-79.

Sablayrolles, M., "Le Chant Grégorien" in: Aigrain, R., *Liturgia* pp. 440-478.

Sarto, Giuseppe Card., Pastoral Letter "Musica Sacra" 1 May 1895, in: Nero, A., *Quaderni Della Fondazione Giuseppe Sarto* pp. 66-74.

Sartore, Domenico, CSJ, "Pastoral Liturgy" in: Chupungco, *Handbook for Liturgical Studies* vol. I pp. 65-95.

Shilson, Arno, Emily Rielley trans., "Liturgy as the Presence of the Mysteries of the Life of Jesus According to Odo Casel" in: *Communio* vol. XXIX no 1 Spring 2002 pp. 39-46.

Schmidt, Herman, "The Structure of the Mass and its Restoration, as reflected in the new Holy Week Ordo" in: Murray, *Studies in Pastoral Liturgy* 25-46.

Schoenbechler, Roger, "On Liturgical Reforms" in: *Orate Fratres* vol. X nos. 11-12 1935/5 pp. 562-5.

Sheppard, Lancelot C., "Progress in the Liturgy" in: *The Downside Review* vol. 80 no. 258 January 1962 pp. 41-54.

_________________ "Reform of the Liturgy: Another View" in: *Orate Fratres* vol. XII no. 12 1937/8 pp. 535-538.

Sorg, Rembert "The Language of the Roman Liturgy" in: The Liturgical Conference Inc., *National Liturgical Week (USA) 1944* pp. 131-144.

Sperry-White, Grant, "William Busch: Educator" in: Tuzik, *How Firm a Foundation* pp. 200-206.

Stack, Thomas "Irish Liturgical Congress" in: *Worship* vol. XXXIV no. 8 1959/60 pp. 463-465.

Steuart, Benedict, OSB, "The Meaning of Liturgical Worship" in: *Liturgy* vol. XV no. 3 July 1946 pp. 67-70.

Tanner, Paul, "Why omit the liturgical kisses?" in: *Orate Fratres* vol. VII no. 3 1932/3 pp. 130-132.

Tegels, Aelred, OSB, "Abbot Capelle 1884-1961" *Worship* vol. XXXVI no. 1 1961/62 pp. 17-20.

Thorold, A., "The Liturgical Movement and the Social Forces of Our Time" *Liturgy* vol. XVIII no. 3, July 1949 pp. 71-80.

Tucker, Dunstan, "The Council of Trent, Guéranger and Pius X," in: *Orate Fratres* vol. X nos. 11-12 1935/6 pp. 538-544.

Tuzik, Robert L., "H. A. Reinhold: A Timely Tract for the American Church" in: Tuzik, *How Firm a Foundation* pp. 174-183.

Van Dijk, S.J.P., OFM, "Liturgical Movement Past and Present" in: *The Clergy Review* vol. XLI no. 9 September 1956 pp. 526-534.

Waldstein, Wolfgang, "Le mouvement liturgique de Dom Guéranger à la veille du concile de Vatican II," in: Centre International d'Etudes Liturgiques, *La Liturgie: Trésor de l'Eglise* pp. 163-182.

Weakland, Rembert G., OSB, "Liturgical Renewal: Two Latin Rites?" in: *America* vol. 176 no. 20 7-14 June 1997 pp. 12-15.

_________________________, "The right road for the Liturgy" in: *The Tablet* 2 February 2002 pp. 10-13.

_________________________, "The Song of the Church" *Origins* vol. 23 no. 1 20 May 1993 pp. 12-16.

Wesseling, Theodore, OSB, "Liturgy and Liturgy Reform" in: *The Tablet* 28 January 1939 p. 126.

Winstone, H. E., "Munich 1960" in: *Liturgy* vol. XXIX no. 4 October 1960 pp. 87-88.

______________, "Pia Desideria: A Chapter in Liturgical Reform" in: *Liturgy* vol. XXVII no. 4 October 1958 pp. 97-101.

______________, "Sunday Mass in a German Parish Church" in: *Liturgy* vol. XXVII no. 1 January 1958 pp. 9-18.

______________, "The Spirit of the Liturgical Movement" in: *The Clergy Review* vol. XLV no. 8 August 1960 pp. 465-476.

No Named Author:

"Conclusions of the First Congress, Maria Laach, 1951" in: *Worship* vol. XXVIII no. 3 1953/4 pp. 157-159.

"Conclusions of the Second Congress, Ste. Odile, 1952" in: *Worship* vol. XXVIII no. 3 1953/4 pp. 160-161.

"Conclusions of the Third Congress, Lugano, 1953" in: *Worship* vol. XXVIII no. 3 1953/4 pp. 162-167.

"Dom Bernard Capelle" *Liturgy* vol. XXXI no. 4 October 1962 pp. 105-106.

"Editorial" in: *La Maison-Dieu* no. 26 1951 pp. 7-10.

"Fourth Liturgical Congress, Glenstal, Ireland" in: *Liturgy* vol. XXVI no. 3 July 1957 pp. 91-92.

"In Annum 1948 Præloquium" in: *Ephemerides Liturgicæ* vol. LXII 1948 pp. 3-4.

"Liturgical Briefs" in: *Orate Fratres* vol. XXII no. 2 1947/8 pp. 89-90.

"Liturgical Briefs" in: *Orate Fratres* vol. XXII no. 3 1947/8 pp. 138-139.

"Liturgical Briefs" in: *Orate Fratres* vol. XXII no. 5 1947/8 pp. 235-236.

"Liturgical Briefs" in: *Worship* vol. XXVI no. 4 1951/2 pp. 201-205.

"Liturgical Briefs" in: *Worship*, vol. XXVI no. 7 1951/2 pp. 373-375.

"Liturgical Briefs" in: *Worship* vol. XXIX no. 10 1954/5 pp. 605-611.

"Liturgical Briefs" in: *Worship* vol. XXX no. 2 1955/6 pp. 156-163.

"Liturgical Briefs" in: *Worship* vol. XXX no. 2 1955/6 pp. 221-225.

"Liturgical Congress, Glenstal Priory" in: *Liturgy* vol. XXV no. 3, July 1956 pp. 102-104.

"The Lugano Conference" in: *Worship* vol. XXVIII no. 1 1953/4 pp. 28-29.

"Mediator Dei" in: *The Tablet* 6 December 1947, pp. 359-360.

"Notes and News" in: *Liturgy* vol. XXV no. 1, January 1956 pp. 38-41.

"Notes and News" in: *Liturgy* vol. XXV no. 4, October 1956 pp. 139-142.

"Notes and News" in: *Liturgy* vol. XXVII no. 4, October 1958 pp. 105-109

"Pope Pius XI and the Liturgical Movement" in: *Orate Fratres* vol. X no. 8 1935/6 pp. 377-37.

"The Apostolate—A sower and his reaping," in: *Orate Fratres* vol. III no. 8 1928/9 pp. 250-252.

"The Divine Office in France," in: *The Tablet* 14 June 1947 pp. 303-304.

"The Liturgical Movement as Approved by Pius XI" in: *Orate Fratres* vol. XVIII no. 7 1943/4 pp. 324-328.

"The Strasbourg Liturgical Congress" in: *Liturgy* vol. XXVII no. 1, January 1958 pp. 19-20.

"The Summer School" in: *Liturgy* vol. XXVIII nos. 3 & 4, October 1959 pp. 60-61.

"Two Papal Documents on the Liturgy" in: *Orate Fratres* vol. IX no. 4 1934/5 pp. 167-170.

Unpublished Material

Archives of the Diocese of Brentwood, England, Reports from Parishes on the 1951 Easter Vigil.

Archives of the Diocese of Brentwood, England, *Brentwood Diocesan Report on the New Holy Week Liturgy,* 7 pp. 16 July 1956.

Archives of the Diocese of Brentwood, England, Reports from Parishes on Holy Week 1956.

Archives of the Diocese of Brentwood, England, document "Item no. 5: Liturgical Conference at Assisi: Report," 1956.

Bliven, Edmond, typewritten letter to Ferdinando Antonelli OFM, 23 January 1956 Fondo Antonelli, Archive of the Congregation of the Causes of the Saints, Vatican City.

Braga, Carlo, CM, typewritten letter to the author, [no date: received 4 March 1994].

Carinci, Alfonso, Papers on the proposed reform of the Roman Breviary, 1945, Fondo Antonelli, Box 2: Commissione Riforma Liturgica Pio XII 1948-1960 Carte Varia, Archive of the Congregation of the Causes of the Saints, Vatican City.

Chadwick, Anthony, typescript: "The Tridentine Mass and Liturgical Reform: A Study of the History of the Codification of the Roman Mass Liturgy by Saint Pius V and the Principles of its Development in the Tradition of the Church" [no date: c. 1993].

Commissione per la Riforma Liturgica, typewritten document "Progetto per la semplificazione delle rubriche" 24 guigno 1953, 2pp., Fondo Antonelli, Archive of the Congregation of the Causes of the Saints, Vatican City.

Conti, Mario, typewritten letter to the author, 28 July 2000.

Diekmann, Godfrey, OSB, typewritten letter to Father Ferdinand Antonelli OFM, 5 July 1955, Fondo Antonelli, Archive of the Congregation of the Causes of the Saints, Vatican City.

Fortescue, Adrian, manuscript letter to Mrs May Crickmer, 2 December 1909, The Private Collection of Mr John Cruse.

________________, typewritten letter to Stanley Morison, 26 April 1920, Cambridge University Library, Morison Papers, I, 16-18; used by kind permission of the Syndics of Cambridge University Library.

Hitchcock, James, typewritten letter to the author, 15 November 1997.

Heenan, John Carmel, typewritten letter 29 April 1967, Archive of the Archbishop of Westminster HE 1/142.

Jungmann, Joseph A., SJ, typewritten letter to Ferdinand Antonelli, OFM, 30 March 1952, Fondo Antonelli, Archive of the Congregation of the Causes of the Saints, Vatican City.

King, Archdale A., manuscript letter to (? Possibly the Prior of Farnborough Abbey), 26 July 1970, Farnborough Abbey Library.

Manifesto of the Catholic Laity Concerning the Catholic Liturgy Pentecost 1943, Printed document from the Archive of the Archbishop of Westminster.

McManus, Frederick R., typewritten letter to the author, 24 April 1994.

Parsons, John P., Paper "The History of the Synod of Pistoia" read to the John XXIII Fellowship Conference, Sydney, December 1982.

Pecklers, K.F., SJ, *The Liturgical Movement in the United States of America: 1926-1955,* Dissertatio ad Doctoratum in Sacra Liturgia, Pontificium Athenaeum Sancti Anselmi De Urbe—Pontificium Institutum Liturgicum, Rome 1995.

Sacred Congregation of Divine Worship and the Discipline of the Sacraments, typewritten letter, Msgr Carmelo Nicolosi, Secretary, 18 March 1997, Prot. 550/97/L. & typewritten letter of Archbishop G. M. Agnelo, Under Secretary, 18 March 1997, Prot. 550/97/L.

Index

A

B

C

D

E

F

G

H

I

J

K

O

P

Q

R

S

T

U

V

The Benedictine Abbey
of Saint Michael at Farnborough
was founded from the French
Abbey of Solesmes in 1895. The monks live
a traditional life of prayer, work and study
in accordance with the ancient
Rule of Saint Benedict.
At the heart of their life is the praise of God
expressed through the solemn
celebration of the Sacred Liturgy,
and supported through their work,
of which this publication is an example.